THE DEADLY BROTHERHOOD

THE DEADLY BROTHERHOOD

THE AMERICAN COMBAT SOLDIER IN WORLD WAR II

JOHN C. MCMANUS

PRESIDIO

Published by Presidio Press
505 B San Marin Drive, Suite 300
Novato, CA 94945-1340

ISBN 0-89141-655-2

All photos courtesy the World War II Veterans Project, University of Tennessee.

Printed in the United States of America

CONTENTS

The rifleman fights without the promise of either reward or relief. Behind every river there's another hill—and behind that hill, another river. After weeks or months in the line only a wound can offer him the comfort of safety, shelter and a bed. Those who are left to fight, fight on, evading death, but knowing each day of evasion they have exhausted one more chance of survival. Sooner or later, unless victory comes, this chase must end on the litter or in the grave.

—Omar Bradley

ACKNOWLEDGMENTS

Without the time and effort of many dedicated people, this book would not have been written. The staff at the Special Collections Library at the University of Tennessee, especially Bill Eigelesbach and Nick Wyman, were always patient and accommodating. Thanks to them I was able to glean a remarkable archive of World War II primary sources, which have been compiled over the last two decades by the university's Center for the Study of War and Society. The same was true for Richard Sommers, Pam Cheney, and Dave Keough at the U.S. Army Military History Institute at Carlisle Barracks, Pennsylvania. They and the rest of the staff in the archives branch never failed to point me in the right direction in my research. In addition, they worked tirelessly to assure that I received all the assistance and resources I needed. The staff at the Western Historical Manuscript Collection in Columbia, Missouri, also provided valuable help in navigating their extensive archive of World War II letters.

The History Department at the University of Tennessee and the Center for the Study of War and Society provided much needed financial assistance for my research. The center's World War II Veteran's Project constituted the bedrock upon which this book was built. Credit goes to Dr. Russell Buhite who gave unselfishly of his time and provided me with valuable insights and. He has strengthened this work immeasurably. Thanks go to my mentor and dear friend Dr. Charles Johnson. He generously lent me his considerable guidance and expertise. His efforts in creating the World War II Veterans Project provided the necessary sources that made it possible to write this book. His knowledge and ideas about Americans in World War II have earned him a well deserved reputation of excellence in his field of study. He has provided wisdom, mentorship, insight, and, most importantly, friendship. He is the best teacher I have ever had. Without him, the following pages would not exist.

I would be remiss if I did not convey a word of thanks to the combat soldiers themselves. Rarely does the historian get to interact so intimately with his or her historical subjects. Throughout my work, the veterans whom I have interviewed or with whom I have corresponded have never failed to be accommodating and helpful no matter how foolish my questions might have seemed to them. Their courage and sacrifice were the original inspiration for this book.

The last word of thanks goes to my family. My wife Nancy has never failed to lend me her time and interest. It would be difficult to convey to her how much inspiration I draw from her love and from her belief in me. The greatest debt of gratitude belongs to my parents, Mike and Mary Jane McManus. Without their love and support this book would never have come to fruition. To them I am eternally grateful.

INTRODUCTION

Somewhere in the Ardennes Forest in a snowy, muddy hole with a small pool of slushy water at the bottom, an American soldier paused and collected his thoughts for a moment. Then he hoisted his weapon, left the dubious comfort and safety of his hole, and advanced toward his enemy while enduring machine-gun, small-arms, mortar, and artillery fire. He moved forward as he had dozens of times before and would dozens of times again if he wasn't killed or wounded. The reality for him was this: he had little or no hope of rotation out of his surroundings or transfer to a unit in safer circumstances. Combat was his world and he could hope to escape it only through death, wounding, capture, mental breakdown, desertion, or—if he even dared imagine—the end of the war. To make matters worse, the law of averages stated with certainty that sooner or later he would become a casualty. It was not a matter of if, but when. Yet, in spite of his nightmarish existence, he continued, with dogged frequency and regularity, to fight and fight well, grimly moving forward to attack his enemy.

This drama was repeated millions of times, not just in the Ardennes Forest in the winter of 1944–45 but in other parts the world. In fact, at the same moment that the Ardennes GI moved forward, chances were very good that another GI was prowling through the mountainous, rocky terrain of Italy and yet another was doing the same thing in a steamy, forbidding jungle somewhere in the Pacific. What did they have in common? They carried out the same dirty, monotonous, dangerous job day after day and did it successfully. Yet not only did they do it in radically different circumstances against different enemies, but often they themselves came from completely different regional or ethnic backgrounds.

Ultimately the most basic question is why they did it. Why did these World War II American combat soldiers endure what should have been unendurable? What made them perform effectively and co-hesively and draw on reserves of courage that they probably thought they did not possess? The answer is surprisingly simple. To a great extent they fought for one another; to an even greater extent they fought because of one another. The bond among American combat soldiers was so tight that it can be accurately termed a "brotherhood." The GI leaving his foxhole in the Ardennes did it primarily because the next soldier was doing it too. He might not have even liked the soldier next to him, but he would do almost anything to help him. The same was true for his counterpart in Italy and in the Pacific. This bond was the single most important sustaining and motivating force for the American combat soldier in World War II. Although some individual units were more cohesive than others, the brotherhood was not unique to any one unit, sector, or theater. Rather it was per-vasive among the troops who fought the war.

It is with those few who actually did the fighting—those at the so-called "Sharp End," as historian John Ellis has termed it—that this book is exclusively concerned. Surprisingly little has been written on the American ground combat soldier in World War II. Of course there is no shortage of books on Americans in World War II, and of-ten they include some discussion on the combat soldier. Good ex-amples of this are Lee Kennett's *G.I.: The American Soldier in World War II;* two books by Stephen Ambrose, *D-Day June 6th, 1944: The Cli-mactic Battle of World War II* and *Band of Brothers;* and Geoffrey Per-ret's *There's a War to Be Won: The United States Army in World War II.* Roger Fosdick's *A Call to Arms: The American Enlisted Soldier in World War II* and Francis Steckel's *Morale and Men: A Study of the American Soldier in World War II* are both excellent doctoral dissertations on the American soldier in general; combat soldiers are dealt with only as a part of the whole and, although combat is discussed, it is not the main focus. John Ellis, in his outstanding work *On the Front Lines: The Experience of War Through the Eyes of the Allied Soldiers in World War II,* focuses primarily on British combat soldiers.

In dealing with the attributes of the American combat soldier, it will also be necessary to take into account the important works of Trevor Dupuy *(A Genius for War: The German Army, 1807–1945)* and Russell Weigley *(The American Way of War: A History of United States Mil-itary Strategy and Policy).*

Richard Holmes in *Acts of War: The Behavior of Men in Battle,* William D. Henderson in *Cohesion: The Human Element in Combat,* and, of course, John Keegan in his classic *The Face of Battle* have done an excellent job of studying the realities of modern combat and its effect on those who fight. But their studies are necessarily general. They do not seek to focus on the combatants of one specific nation in one specific war.

By contrast, this book will concentrate exclusively on one group of combatants—Americans in World War II. Part One, entitled "The World of the Combat Soldier," seeks to answer the overarching question "What was it actually like?" Chapter 1 explains who did the fighting. Chapter 2 discusses the combat soldier's equipment and food and how he felt about them. Chapters 3 and 4 describe the conditions in which the American combat soldier fought. Chapter 5 concentrates on how he actually fought. Chapter 6 explains what it was like to become a casualty.

Part Two, entitled "The Soul of the Combat Soldier," answers another overarching question, "What was the combat soldier actually like?" Chapters 7 and 8 address his attitudes toward his Japanese and German enemies. Chapter 9 covers an element of the military experience that has constituted a near obsession with military historians—leadership. Far too much military history has been written exclusively from the perspective of those at the very top. Now it is the dogfaces' turn to talk. How did the dogface feel about his officers, and what constituted good and bad leadership in his eyes? Chapter 10 is something of a catchall, relating many commonly held attitudes and motivators of the combat soldiers and touching on the costly effects of total war. Chapter 11 addresses and refutes some commonly held myths about replacements in the U.S. Army without attempting in any way to defend the army's replacement system. Finally, Chapter 12 demonstrates unequivocally the crucial importance and pervasiveness of the brotherhood. It is the single most important theme of this book. Hopefully the reader will recognize elements of it in every chapter.

The sources used to prepare this work are overwhelmingly primary. Contemporary letters, diaries, and surveys were a gold mine of information. Generated later, but no less important, were the postwar memoirs, questionnaire responses, veterans' association publications, and oral histories of veterans. Some historians have expressed concern that, over time, memories of the veterans have faded, especially in oral histories. They caution that perhaps the veterans do not remember their experiences as they really were but rather as they wished they would have been. Certainly this view merits consideration and argues for caution. However, it is undeniable that most veterans express the same attitudes, feelings, and descriptions as they did in their wartime letters or diaries. And although memories do fade, the detail and alacrity with which World War II veterans recall their combat service is often startling. Often their memories have dulled regarding the mundane; but, for most of them, World War II was the defining moment of their lives. These men were part of something monumental, although they may not have been fully aware of it at the time. More importantly, they were young, and the fondness for memories of youth rarely diminishes.

The veterans were senior citizens by the mid-1990s. Although earlier in life they may have been reluctant to talk about their experiences, they now realize that if they do not tell their story, no one else will. With retirement or a decline in health, they have had more time to reflect on the past. For some, such as ex-paratrooper Howard Ruppel, writing his war memoir was an emotional but necessary experience. "As I wrote, checked, revised and corrected," he said, "I relived those harrowing moments, experiencing the agony once more and shed tears thinking what may have been." So why did he do it? "If I had not written this, I would have taken it all with me . . . and no one would ever know about . . . how I changed from a boy to a man."

Richard Roush, of the 84th Infantry Division, was motivated to write his experiences in a veterans' association newsletter because of a desire to communicate the truth. "Out of all the men that were there and the ones that survived there are probably a million stories that will never be told due to the fact that they were so bad, so horrible that nobody would believe them anyway."

The words of the soldiers, the historical actors themselves, will echo throughout this book. The historian in the 1990s dealing with mid-twentieth-century history has an advantage that scholars of earlier centuries do not. He or she can directly interact with those being studied. For this rare moment in history it is possible for a World

War II scholar to talk directly to "GI Joe." The author has gladly taken advantage of that privilege.

This is not another stolid examination of military doctrine, strategy, or generalship. This work is, more than anything, about flesh-and-blood people and the realities of their lives within the cataclysmic events of the recent past. One soldier writing home in July 1945 put it succinctly: "Confusion is still the god of war. Nobody, least of all the line soldier, understands war. Battles are more decisive to rear echelon generals than to the men whose blood is spilled winning them." Even if the line soldiers had understood the larger questions, they certainly could not have exerted any degree of control over them.

Without doubt, it is important for historians to study every aspect of America's involvement in World War II, including the war of the generals and policymakers. But the story of the ordinary man who carried out the policies and did the fighting has not been adequately related or understood. Accordingly, interested readers are left with a somewhat antiseptic and romanticized view of the war. This is often manifested in casualty descriptions. The terms *light* and *only* are often used, as in "The hill was taken with light casualties, as the unit lost only four killed and three wounded." To those seven individuals affected and their families, the cost of taking that hill was heavy indeed.

The main point is this: it is important to remember that the combat soldiers were not faceless robots but rather someone's son, brother, father, nephew, uncle, or friend. James Simms, in his memoir of his experiences in the 101st Airborne Division, wrote of his fellow paratroopers, "They were not cold statistics in a history book. They were warm human beings who were terribly afraid but who were anchored by their bravery and commitment."

Walter Slatoff, of the 78th Infantry Division, perhaps communicated it best in a passage he wrote to his son:

> My Son: War is a more terrible thing than all the words of man can say; more terrible than a man's mind can comprehend. It is the corpse of a friend, one moment ago a living human being with thoughts, hopes and a future just exactly like yourself—now nothing. It is the groans and the pain of the

wounded, and the expressions on their faces. It is the sound of new soldiers crying before battle; the louder sound of their silence afterwards. It is the filth and itching and hunger; the endless body discomfort; feeling like an animal; the fatigue so deep that to die would be good. It is the evil, snickering knowledge that sooner or later the law of averages will catch up with each soldier, and the horrible hope that it will take the form of a wound, not maiming or death. Remember what we are talking about. Not words, not soldiers, but human beings just exactly like yourself.

Slatoff's comrades, whether they were trudging through the Ardennes, Italy, or the Pacific, would certainly have agreed wholeheartedly with him and probably would have realized that they could not have said it any better.

PART ONE
THE WORLD OF THE COMBAT SOLDIER

CHAPTER 1
THE COMBAT SOLDIER:
WHO WAS HE?

What defined a combat soldier in the U.S. Army in World War II? Certainly, at one time or another, many soldiers from service arms found themselves in life-threatening situations. What distinguished the combat soldier from the others was that the combat soldier's job *necessarily* involved life-threatening situations.

This was not true of most service troops or, indeed, of most troops who were nominally assigned to combat divisions, even field artillery. Artillerymen by no means enjoyed a safe job, and the army thought of their branch as a combat arm. However, except for forward observers, who were often up front with the infantry, the vast majority of artillerymen were usually a mile or more behind the lines. This distance was reflected in casualties. One study found that infantry soldiers suffered an average of 92 percent of a typical division's battle casualties, as opposed to 4 percent for the artillery.

Thus, for the purposes of this study, a combat soldier shall mean armor, combat engineers, and, of course, infantry. Included under armor are tank destroyers and cavalry. Included under combat engineers are demolition experts, who often saw heavy combat in the Pacific. The infantry includes paratroopers, special forces, and rangers. Troops from these outfits did the vast majority of the fighting on the ground in World War II and took the lion's share of the casualties. They were a clear minority; even at the end of the war, only 25 percent of the army was assigned to ground combat divisions. Probably the majority of that 25 percent would not be classified in this study as combat soldiers. This is because much of the manpower of an American combat division was composed of field artillery, headquarters, military police, medical, quartermaster, and other service personnel. Historian Lee Kennett estimated that 50 percent of division personnel were primarily involved in noncombat logistics. The other 50 percent, at the most about 8,000 to 9,000 men per division, fought, bled, and died and along the way determined the outcome of the war. They represented a distinct minority among the millions of soldiers in the U.S. Army in World War II.

Needless to say, the designation "combat troop" also covers marines. In fact, owing to the Marine Corps ethos of "every marine a rifleman," the average marine was far more likely to have participated in combat than the average army soldier. Most World War II marines were infantrymen or combat engineers; as such, their accounts will form a bulwark of this book.

Frank Nisi, of the 3d Infantry Division, explained this well in a letter to his father:

> I would venture to say that only a very small percentage really know what war is all about. By that I mean that of the millions . . . only the Infantry and certain attachments, such as tanks or TDs [tank destroyers], were ever close enough to hear a shot fired in anger. Then that could be broken down still further to exclude the Reg't. Hq. Service Company etc. It gets down to the man with the rifle who has to live in the ground . . . or any place he possibly can, then go without sleep for several days and get up and fight, hike, run, creep, or crawl 25 miles or so. During this time the echelons in rear of him move up in vehicles, get their night's sleep and wait for him to advance again.

A 7th Infantry Division soldier named Roland Lea took great pride in being part of this minority. "The front lines soldier fought the battles, occupied the land, suffered and won the war. I'm proud that I was one of them." Brendan Phibbs, of the 12th Armored Division, worried that, after the war, "parasites from the quartermaster battalions would wave flags and scream about patriotism and nobody in the world would know or care that they, the tiny 10 percent, had pulled the whole war machine forward."

If the war was fought by a minority, then it is important to understand how the army organized its combat units at their smallest and most basic levels. Armored divisions, for example, were not primarily made up of tanks. A typical American armored division in the European theater was composed of three tank battalions in addition to three battalions of armored infantry (who functioned as ordinary infantry but rode in half-tracks), three battalions of armored artillery (equipped with self-propelled artillery), an armored cavalry reconnaissance battalion, a tank destroyer battalion, and an armored engineers battalion. Tank battalions, like infantry battalions, were broken down into companies of approximately sixteen tanks, four to a platoon. A tank company was often commanded by a captain and platoons by lieutenants. However, it was not at all uncommon for sergeants to command tank platoons. The majority of enlisted tankers held a rank above private first class much like bomber crewmen in the army air force. Also, it was common for various tank battalions within the same division to be equipped with different tanks, especially early in the war. Most U.S. tanks were crewed by five men.

Regarding armored infantry, 8th Armored Division soldier James McDonald explained it best: "Armored infantry units were organized a little different than the standard infantry battalion. We had a headquarters squad, two rifle squads, a machine [gun] squad and a mortar squad in each platoon. We had a lot of firepower."

As vitally important as armored formations were, regular infantry was the bulwark of the U.S. Army in World War II. Of the approximately ninety-one divisions that saw combat, sixty-eight were infantry divisions. Another four were airborne and one was a cavalry division. The airborne and cavalry units were equipped and functioned as infantry. The vast majority of combat soldiers, then, were infantrymen. Whether on the offensive or, much more rarely, the defensive, the infantry was the main component around which the army's ground combat forces were built. More often than not, the other branches found themselves in support of the infantry in combat. Thus, in spite of all the newfound technology and mobility in the U.S. Army of 1941–45, the infantry can be aptly described not just as the "queen of battle" but more appropriately the "king of battle." This was particularly true in the Pacific, where at times the terrain and conditions made armor useless.

Radford Carroll, who served as a rifleman in the 99th Infantry Division, personified these facts:

> The Infantry walks, except when it runs, and lives in the open as best it can. Battles and wars are not won unless the infantry is standing on the land that once belonged to the enemy. The infantry fighting is not remote from the foe; the enemy is visible and the bodies and blood of enemy and friend alike show the results of the fighting. The infantry lives under the hardest conditions and suffers the most danger of any of the branches of the military. It is the pits, a place to stay out of— and there I was.

In World War I, the U.S. Army was structured in a so-called quadrangular fashion, which basically meant that it was composed of four infantry regiments. The World War II American infantry division was triangular, as Carroll explains:

> A division was commanded by a general officer and contained about 15,000 people. A division was subdivided into regiments, usually 3 regiments to a division. A regiment was divided into battalions, usually 3 battalions to a regiment. A regiment was commanded by a colonel. A battalion was divided into companies, usually about 6 companies to a battalion. A battalion was commanded by a major. A company was divided into platoons, usually 4 platoons to a company. The company commanding officer was a captain. A platoon was divided into squads, usually 4 squads to a platoon. The platoon was commanded by a lieutenant. Each squad was composed of a sergeant, a corporal and 10 privates.

David Williams, a member of the same division as Carroll, related in greater detail the exact composition of the small units that actually did the fighting:

At full strength, an infantry company was composed of about 190 to 200 enlisted men and 6 officers, but due to casualties a line infantry company [one facing the enemy] was rarely at full strength. With the addition of . . . ten replacements, L Company had 173 enlisted men and 5 officers. Like all infantry companies, L Company had three rifle platoons, each consisting of three twelve-man squads, and a fourth platoon, called the weapons platoon, consisting of three mortar squads and two machine-gun squads. In addition to those in the platoons, there were clerks, cooks, medics, runners [messengers], and men in various other positions.

Howard Ruppel's unit, the 517th Parachute Infantry Regiment, was organized in much the same fashion. "The 517th Combat Team was a miniature army by itself. The team included rifle platoons, machine guns and mortar squads . . . field engineers, medical service . . . all clothing, arms and ammunition."

Combat engineers were nearly identical to infantry outfits in organization. The only exception is that there were few specialists—that is, machine gunners—as opposed to riflemen. The engineers were employed as a team to accomplish whatever mission needed to be done, whether that meant clearing mines, setting up barbed wire, building bridges under fire, or destroying pillboxes.

Unlike their sons in Vietnam who were sent home after a one-year tour of duty, or their comrades in the air force who rotated out of combat after a certain number of missions, these combat soldiers had little or no hope of rotation out of combat. They were in the war for the duration. Some units, such as Lloyd Pye's 1057th Provisional Infantry Battalion (Merrill's Marauders) in Burma, "had a rotation system within the battalion, to make heavy action and death as fair as possible." However, even in that system, troops were not permanently excused from combat.

The army did make a halfhearted effort at relieving individual veteran soldiers from combat, but 24th Infantry Division veteran Leonard Kjelstrom describes that as a "farce." Radford Carroll summed up the feelings of the individual combat soldier on this subject:

In the Army Air Force, after 25 [later 50] missions were completed the airman was sent back to the States. We really envied the Air Force that goal. An infantryman had no such arrangement. Instead the infantryman went into battle knowing that the odds were stacked against his survival. There were no promises of either reward or relief. Only a wound could offer the comfort of safety, shelter and a bed.

In the wake of the first peacetime draft in the nation's history in 1940, the army found itself in the welcome but uncomfortable position of having to evaluate hundreds of thousands of new men, most of whom had little or no military experience. For this purpose, the army devised a test, called the Army General Classification Test, or AGCT, which was given to all new recruits. They had forty minutes to complete it. The test consisted of 150 multiple-choice questions of three basic types: lock counting, synonym matching, and arithmetic. The tests were machine graded, then everyone was placed into one of five categories according to raw scores. Class I had a score of more than 130, class II between 110 and 129, class III 90 to 109, class IV 70 to 89, and class V 69 or less. Ordinarily the men tried their best on the AGCT, because of the general understanding that doing well might give them a better army job. For example, to qualify for officer candidate school a soldier needed a score of at least 110. It was also common knowledge that scoring high on the test would increase the chance of assignment to the army air force, a desirable branch of the service for most recruits.

The consensus among army leadership as well as those who have studied the effects of the AGCT was that it was a good measuring stick for general as well as technical aptitude. However, some felt that it had shortcomings: first, the speed factor in taking the test was not minimized when results were tabulated; second, scoring methods favored persons who were inclined to guess; and third, the test placed great emphasis upon spatial thinking and quantitative reasoning (math skills).

The top two classes of men were thought to be suitable for any army job. The average group (class III) was slated for any nontechnical job. Class IV covered a fairly wide group, from the barely functional to the slightly below average; this group was thought to be best for service or labor functions, often in the "zone of the interior," as the continental United States was called. Class V was thought to be made up of men who were mentally deficient, possibly even retarded in some way. In the first year or so of the war, combat units had the largest share of class IV and V men. This was to change.

The AGCT seems to have been a fairly good barometer of level and quality of schooling and also depth of experience. As such, it was somewhat biased against those without the benefits of extensive education, travel, or experience. Accordingly, it was slanted in favor of older white men in their late twenties to early thirties who may have had some college education or varied work experience. More importantly, it reflected to a significant degree the army's initial emphasis on technology at the expense of the infantry soldier.

As a group, blacks tended not to score well on the AGCT. More often than not, they did not have the benefits of education or experience. This led to a vicious cycle. The low scores that most blacks achieved seemed to confirm in the minds of the army's leadership their own assumptions of black inferiority. Many of the top brass felt that blacks were not fit for combat duty, so they were often shunted into labor and service jobs in the quartermaster or the noncombat engineer corps. Thus, blacks were by and large excluded from combat service in World War II. Along the way, the army lost an invaluable pool of talent and manpower. As the war dragged on, however, the views of the brass changed somewhat, and by 1944 a small minority of black troops began to see combat, albeit only in segregated units, such as the 92d and 93d Infantry Divisions, or the independent 761st Tank Battalion. It was only in the final months of the war in Europe that the army began experimenting with integration, albeit in a limited way. A platoon of black soldiers would sometimes fight alongside a platoon of white soldiers. Although the troops generally got along well, it was not the true integration that the army would later have in Korea, Vietnam, and the Gulf War. Generally, blacks fought as well as other American combat soldiers, and their voices are heard throughout this study in proportion to their numbers.

Regardless of whether a soldier was white or black, the AGCT was a major factor in how he was assigned his army job. In the first year of the war, the ground combat arms did not receive the intellectual quality of manpower that they would eventually need and receive to fight the war successfully. Between March and August 1942, the armored force received 28 percent of its replacements from class I or II, 33 percent from class III, and 39 percent from classes IV and V. The infantry received even more men from classes IV and V: about 27 percent of its replacements came from the top two classifications; 29 percent came from the average group; and a whopping 44 percent came from the bottom two classes.

How were the other branches that were classified as combat by the army faring during this first year of the war? It is difficult to assess the combat engineers because there are no separate numbers for combat and noncombat. This is significant because a large number of noncombat engineers were in black labor battalions. The combat engineers were all white, as were other frontline outfits. The cavalry received 26 percent of its men from classes I and II and 43 percent from classes IV and V. The field artillery got 24 percent from I and II and 46 percent from IV and V. The pattern was unquestionably the same in all combat branches: once the war started, combat branches got short shrift in the number of high-scoring men filling their ranks.

The main reason for this lies in the makeup of another combat branch of a special type—the army air force. Because the United States did not have an independent air force during World War II, the army had to create one. This was done, to a certain extent, at the expense of its ground forces. Men with greater technical and mechanical aptitude, as reflected in their AGCT scores, were sent to the air force. Forty-four percent of the army air force's replacements had tested in the top two AGCT classes in 1942. Another 35 percent were from the average group, and only 20 percent tested in classes IV and V. Men with high test scores were often only too happy to oblige the army. The prospect of holding an officer's rank and flying a plane instead of slogging along on foot, as well as the romanticism of pilot lore left over from World War I, tended to make the air force a far more attractive alternative than serving in the infantry. Nevertheless, in spite of their romantic notions, most men who joined the air force ended up as enlisted, nonflying personnel.

Clearly, more men considered by the army to be of higher quality ended up in the air arm in the first year of the war. The army had little choice in this. The air force, because it was so expensive to build and maintain, had been neglected in the isolationist, parsimonious atmosphere of the interwar years. Army leaders correctly believed in the significance of airpower, and they knew that, initially at least, the air force would have to do the bulk of the fighting.

Other factors complicated the expansion of the ground combat arms. Those men who had an education, a technical aptitude, or some other such marketable skill might be more likely to join the navy because, by its very nature, it utilized such qualifications more effectively than did the army. Many men who were patriotic, outraged by Pearl Harbor, and eager to fight the enemy on the ground with a rifle were attracted by the marines. The army was left with the rest—draftees who more often than not, and for understandable reasons, were hoping to avoid ground combat.

By the summer of 1943, though, it became clear to the army hierarchy that it would need hundreds of thousands or perhaps millions of motivated, trained, and intelligent ground combat troops if it hoped to win the coming campaigns in Europe and the Pacific. The air force was doing a fine job, but it was obvious to all but the most obtuse and stubborn advocates of strategic bombing that the war would eventually be decided on the ground. Although the air force continued to receive many of the best recruits, slowly but surely the ground forces were fleshed out with larger numbers of men from classes I, II, and III. A mass army geared for total war was built, and army ground forces began to receive the greatest quantity of new men. This meant simply that by early 1944, when Chief of Staff George C. Marshall ordered that prime eighteen to twenty year olds now be sent to the infantry, a new recruit had an excellent chance of ending up in a ground combat outfit regardless of his AGCT score.

Perhaps the most dramatic example of this new reality was the liquidation of the Army Specialized Training Program. The ASTP, as it was called, was created at the behest of Secretary of War Henry L. Stimson. It grew out of the notion that the cream of western youth had been slaughtered in the trenches in World War I. The hope was to keep bright young men (an AGCT score of 115 or higher) out of combat while training them for technical or specialist army jobs. After initial training, they were sent to college at government expense and given an accelerated curriculum. Marshall's directive doomed the program and ensured that 150,000 of America's best and brightest, who were in their late teens or early twenties, would end up in ground combat outfits.

The result of this policy was a dramatic upgrade in the quality of combat units and some very angry whiz kids. Irwin Shapiro, an ex-ASTPer who served in the 8th Armored Division, summed up his feelings and those of his comrades: "I think we resented it because it would have been a soft deal for us. We could have stayed out of combat. We could have stayed out of danger. We could have gotten our college careers going and that sounded very promising." Henri Atkins, who ended up in the 99th Infantry Division after the program was disbanded, conceded that "the ASTP was an elitist concept. It was supposed to put the smartest young men into college instead of . . . the infantry. Elitist or not, I was all for the program, which would place me in a major university for a three-year crash college program. I was eager to begin my studies. I was not at all eager to be shot at."

Whatever their reluctance, however, the bright youngsters turned out to be excellent soldiers.

Besides the ASTP program, the air cadet program, home of 71,000 additional bright young men who hoped to be pilots one day, was discontinued. A large proportion of these men also ended up in combat units. In addition, the growing Allied domination of the skies freed tens of thousands of antiaircraft troops for frontline duty.

It would be a mistake, then, to assume from the 1942 figures that the American combat soldier in World War II was generally from a disadvantaged or lower-class background. This may have been true briefly in late 1942, but certainly by the time the bulk of the ground fighting was done—1944 and beyond—it was no longer the case. The men who fought the war on the ground were white, came from backgrounds of modest income and education, and were of average or above average intelligence. In short they can be referred to as "middle class." Even the officers, who were usually better educated or wealthier than their men, did not hail from an aristocratic or ruling class in a European sense. Instead they received their commissions because of higher intellectual aptitude (as reflected in test scores), better education, or previous military training.

The term *middle class* does not necessarily mean a quantified demographic group so much as a shared perception. A 1940 *Fortune* magazine survey on class found that 79 percent of those who were asked which class they felt they belonged to (upper, middle, or lower) chose middle. Even those who, in terms of yearly income, would be classified as upper or lower class (74 percent and 70 percent, respectively) overwhelmingly described themselves as middle class.

In the U.S. Army in World War II, it was ordinary middle-class Americans who did the ground fighting. The wealthy and powerful often gravitated to the air force and navy. The "disadvantaged" (blacks) were barred from combat. The combat soldier did not come preponderantly from any one region or ethnic background. Curtis Whiteway's comments on his 99th Infantry Division comrades illuminates this fact: "In our entire Bn. [Battalion], 50% were Yanks . . . and 50% Rebels. One bed a Yank—next bed a Reb. Friction dissolved as we moved for combat."

Garland Godby, a rifle company commander in the 80th Infantry Division, put it this way in describing his men: "It's a shame to waste the cream of a people because that's who does the fighting . . . young, reasonably intelligent people who lead the country to a better future and you go out and kill them."

Thus, the American combat soldier in World War II must be seen for what he actually was, an everyman of average or above average intelligence, the son of a carpenter, construction worker, lawyer, farmer, minister, factory worker, small businessman, and engineer, among many other occupations. Probably the most important point to remember about their backgrounds is that they were, first and foremost, citizen-soldiers. Most were just "ordinary Americans," but they confronted the best that the forces of Fascist totalitarianism could throw against them, and they emerged victorious at nearly every turn.

CHAPTER 2
FOOD, EQUIPMENT, AND WEAPONS

It has been said that the American soldier in World War II was the best-fed, best-equipped soldier in history up to that time. The United States reportedly poured its vast wealth and resources into lavishing its soldiers with amenities that soldiers from other nations did not enjoy.

In a general sense, this impression is basically true; but, as with many generalities, there are exceptions. In terms of his overall menu, the GI was undoubtedly more fortunate than his foreign counterparts. But this does not mean that he was always well fed. Nor does it mean that he particularly enjoyed the food. By the same token, although he may have been issued large quantities of diverse equipment, this does not necessarily mean that the equipment performed well or that he had a high opinion of it. American ground combat weapons, for example, were in some ways inadequate, and the U.S. combat soldier often found himself outgunned. It was left to the user to improvise. Ultimately the combat soldier used or consumed whatever seemed to get the job done. If a can of rations was no good, he would not eat it. If his gas mask or some other piece of personal equipment was deemed to be useless, he threw it away. If his firearm did not perform adequately, he found one that did.

He was fed in one of two ways: by a field kitchen or by prepackaged rations supplemented by a certain amount of scrounging. The preferred option, of course, was the field kitchen. It was run by the company mess sergeant, many of whom were notorious for their insensitivity to the line troops. The mess sergeant had a squad of approximately twelve cooks under his command.

In spite of the callousness of some mess sergeants, combat soldiers generally felt that the mess troops did the best they could to get decent food to the front. One soldier wrote home: "Our cooks really keep working to bring up as much hot chow to us as possible. Except during an actual attack situation, they usually manage to bring us up something hot twice a day. Within reason, they do everything they can to make things easier on us. Believe me, we really appreciate it."

Bert Morphis, of the 1st Infantry Division, agreed. "Our cooks were great about bringing hot food right up to the front lines when it was possible at all. However, most of the time . . . it was just not possible. I remember one two-week period when every morning and evening they brought each of us one Spam sandwich and a cup of coffee. By the time it got to the front it was all cold."

Ninety-ninth Infantry Division veteran Henri Atkins described vividly how difficult it was to eat normally at the front, even when the field kitchens brought up chow:

> Headquarters would try to get a hot lunch to us every day. A jeep would load up with large containers of food and coffee. Half of the men at a time would go quickly to the area about 200 yards from our forward lines. Each man carried his rifle slung over his shoulder and spare clips in his pocket. He would carry his mess kit in one hand and a large canteen cup in the other hand. Arms full of food and our cup of coffee, we would hurry back so the others could go back for their food and drink. As often as not the "dirty Huns" would shell us at that precise moment. Half of the hot coffee would spill out and snow would cover our food.

The experiences of Charles Miller, of the 75th Infantry Division, were almost reminiscent of sensory deprivation:

> Some time after dark the kitchen truck came up and our canteen cups were collected and returned to us full of food. This provided a rather unique dining experience since in the dark I was not sure of some of what I was eating although I knew it

was familiar. I am sure that there was a canned peach half for "dessert" since it was thoughtfully placed on top of the milange [sic]. Interest was added by the German artillery which was shelling the woods behind us and shell fragments were buzzing through the trees like angry bees.

Lawrence Nickell, of the 5th Infantry Division, outlined how his unit's kitchen operated:

> If conditions were favorable, no enemy in close proximity etc., the kitchen would set up and cook a hot meal for us. They tried to send up hot foods in insulated Marmac containers if we were in a stable position, but the kitchen could not be close enough for us to go form a chow line. Carrying parties would go back and carry up food and coffee in Jerry cans . . . but the coffee was almost always cold and heavily flavored with chlorine.

Ferdinand Huber, of the 99th Infantry Division, underscored the salient point that the food, even when it did manage to reach the front, was not always appetizing. "In the middle of the night the cooks would come up with large thermos containers, so we would have a hot meal—mostly breakfast victuals such as rubbery eggs, cold pancakes, or the army's version of French toast—stale GI bread partially soaked with eggs and sugar."

David Williams, who joined the 99th Division after the Battle of the Bulge, learned to improvise. "We didn't carry our mess kits with us. The cooks brought those items when a hot meal was brought up. Since we weren't carrying mess kits, we didn't have a utensil with which to eat the canned items in the K rations. I took a dessert fork from a set of silverware and stuck it in the strap on the side of one of my combat boots."

Even though combat soldiers usually lived a life of privation, sometimes everything would fall into place perfectly. Earl Reitan, of the 3rd Infantry Division, had fond memories of a meal in Italy. "Just as we were getting famished a truck came up with fresh-baked bread, Spam, and cans of water. I long remembered that meal along an Italian road as one of the most enjoyable I ever ate."

John Roche wrote of a similar special meal that he and his 88th Infantry Division brethren enjoyed:

> In the evening, Co. K's mess sergeant showed up with delicious "kosher specials." I went through the line twice, four specials the first time, and two the second. The Co. K mess sergeant was damned if he was going to scour the countryside for his company, so we obliged him as much as we could with the consumption of specials, sauerkraut, and fried potatoes (items unknown in our own mess), then called upon the locals to turn out again in sufficient numbers to finish the lot.

One can surmise from this passage that Roche held a dim view of his mess sergeant, as did many combat soldiers. Roche's feelings are even more apparent in his description of the same mess sergeant preparing too much food and having to haul it all away: "The mess sergeant came up in the evening with hot chow. When he realized he had prepared three times too much food, for the first time he seemed sorry for us riflemen, who had to bear the burdens of fatigue, shock, injury and premature death."

Not all mess sergeants were disliked, though. Some, such as Frank Miller's in the 36th Infantry Division, who demonstrated sensitivity and courage, were held in high esteem by the frontline troops they served:

> At Company C, our food was prepared by a gentleman known as "Big Sarge." He and his crew deserved a medal for their work. Someone told me that Big Sarge liked to play poker and would use his winnings to buy fresh vegetables for us. My fondest recollection of Big Sarge was the day I saw him up to his elbows in flour, making jelly rolls.

Harry Arnold, of the 99th Infantry Division, described in an even more positive fashion the job his company mess sergeant did:

> Mess Sgts are noted for vile tempers, since they get so little sleep, but Sam was always mild mannered and friendly. Before

daylight, in the bitter cold, and after [dark] in the evenings, he loaded food-filled urns on his jeep and made the hazardous dash down to the company line position. German artillery always made his trips memorable ones, but he never gave in to his fears. E Company often got warm food when the other companies were eating cold rations. It was one thing for us to be in foxholes with some insulation from the cold and screaming shells, but quite another to be in a moving, open jeep plowing through the worst the Germans and the weather could offer. That Sam survived a few such trips stirs the imagination, and that he survived the war is miraculous. I salute Sam . . . that compassionate, gentle man who cared so much. . . . He was a rarity.

As often as not, the combat situation precluded the mess troops from bringing up any sort of meal. In that case, the soldiers depended on rations. There were three basic types of rations eaten by the American combat soldier in World War II: C rations, K rations, and 10 in 1 rations.

William Meissner, of the 71st Infantry Division, explained what made up a C ration:

C rations were two cans, smaller than a normal soup can. One held crackers, soluble coffee or tea, lemonade, bouillon, sugar, toilet paper, candy and four cigarettes. The other can held food to be warmed. Beef stew, chicken and noodles, Spam and potatoes, corned beef hash, etc. We would warm these foods in the daylight using our gasoline-fired stoves, which we carried, one stove per squad.

John Lane, of the 4th Marine Division, related the more common way of cooking C rations. "We would break open packs of the plastic explosive C-2, compress the doughy stuff into thin wafers and set them on fire. It burned with intense, smokeless heat."

Some types of C rations were more desirable than others. Paul Swenson's outfit in the 70th Infantry Division devised an equitable way of distributing the rations:

A case of C rations had 6 different menus in it, including frankfurters and beans, spaghetti and meatballs and macaroni and cheese. If we opened a case with the labels up, most of the desirable cans disappeared in a flash. Instead, we opened the cases so only the bottoms of the cans showed; then it was more like a lottery.

Some men did not like C rations at all. Carlie Berryhill, of the 6th Infantry Division, was more understated than some of his comrades: "Most of our rations overseas were C rations and I didn't care too much for them." Berryhill's division, which fought at New Guinea, was poorly supplied, as were many combat units in the Pacific early in the war. This is reflected in Frank Caudillo's description of 6th Division rations: "On New Guinea our C rations were of WWI variety with worms, and very bad cans, not suitable for foot soldiers, too bulky." Salvatore Lamagna, of the 43d Infantry Division, said, "C rations were terrible"; Francis Stone, of the same unit, described them as "bitter, monotonous." Tanker Tom Wood, a member of the 1st Armored Division, described them as "atrocious." Evan Voss, who served with the 36th Division in Italy, wrote that C rations often made him nauseous. "You'd eat a can of that cold greasy hash and an hour later you'd have stomach pains. . . . You thought, the food will get us before the Germans." Rifle company commander Charles Henne, of the 37th Infantry Division, made this assessment: "We hated them until we ran out and started to starve. Then the corned beef hash, weiner and beans, beef stew with a biscuit, and condiment cans became winners. The problem was getting enough of them."

As a blurb from an 84th Infantry Division newspaper indicates, C rations improved toward the end of the war. "After continual griping over the monotony of army C rations, medics in the battalion aid station finally received a case that stopped all complaints. It was a new-type case containing cans of chicken and noodles, chicken and vegetables, frankfurters and beans, spaghetti and meatballs and other new varieties."

The hungrier one was, the better a C ration could taste. Harry Martin's story illustrates this point. His 106th Infantry Division, which bore much of the brunt of the German Ardennes offensive during the first days of the Battle of the Bulge, was cut off from the unit and wandered about aimlessly in search of other Americans. The men had no food, water, or sleep. Martin was so tired that he separated from the others and slept in a barn, even though German patrols were everywhere. The next morning he awoke, still lost and hungry but uncaptured:

> It was a little frightening to realize I was behind enemy lines, but I was determined to get back to my company. As I was crossing the snow-covered road, I saw a C ration biscuit wrapped in cellophane. It looked like it had been run over by a dozen tanks but I picked it up anyway. I found a small packet of powdered lemonade in my pocket. I took out my canteen cup, filled it with ice water, and mixed [in] the lemonade powder. I opened the crushed biscuit, taking just a nibble with small sips of lemonade. I savored each little nibble and sip. I was no longer cold or tired, and the war was completely out of my mind. I got more pleasure out of the little biscuit than any meal I have ever had. When I finished, I got up . . . and said out loud, "Well, let's go find the war and the 106th Division." It was Christmas Eve, just before dark, when I got back to the American lines.

C rations, then, were what you made of them. They could be monotonous, greasy, or even tasteless, but they probably were better than what the enemy was eating.

K rations were far more common, if for no other reasons than they weighed less and were easier to carry. C ration cans were often considered too bulky, especially in the Pacific where the hot conditions led dogfaces to carry even less cargo than their counterparts in Europe.

Lathrop Mitchell, a medic in the 92d Infantry Division in Italy, described K rations in his diary: "These K rations come in a waxed box like a small cigar box. The food consists of a can of cheese or Spam, crackers, meat loaf in a can, instant coffee, candy, cigarettes, gum and toilet paper. The German rations are often tins of sardines and bread in a can and sausages in a can."

In a written memoir, 99th Infantry Division veteran Denis Huston gave a detailed description of K rations:

The K rations proved to be a convenient if not too appetizing food package. They came in three models marked B, L, or D (Breakfast, Lunch, Dinner). The boxes were about 7 to 8 inches long, 4 inches wide, and a little under 2 inches thick. The outer box of this cardboard contained another snug-fitting, wax-sealed inner box which held the rations. The wax-sealed box served two purposes—waterproofing and enough combustible material when torn into small pieces to heat a canteen of water for coffee. The B box included a small packet of Nescafe, enough for one canteen of coffee, a can of ground-up ham and eggs, a candy bar, a package of toilet paper, four cigarettes, matches, sugar, and a package of hardtack. The L box, the most unpopular of the three, contained a can of rubbery cheese, a packet of lemonade powder, sugar, four cigarettes, crackers, and candy Necco wafers, which contributed to the blandness of the diet. The D box included a can of hash or some other mixture of foodstuff not always readily identifiable by sight, smell or taste, a candy bar, four cigarettes, sugar, Nescafe, and crackers or hardtack. The cigarettes and candy bars were of a variety nobody had ever heard of before or since the war. It was only during the last month of the war that name brands began to appear in K rations, and a dried, pre-sweetened cereal with powdered milk needing a little water before eating was included in the B package.

Even though K rations were cold, combat soldiers often improvised to provide some sort of warmth to their food. Max Kocour, of the 90th Infantry Division, wrote:

> The American GI soon found that a hot meal of sorts could be attained by heating the flat can in the burning paraffin-coated container while holding a canteen cup of water with coffee powder etc. over the flame. It was not great, but what the hell. In the Bulge . . . our K rations were usually frozen, not quite as tasty unless we could burn . . . the container and heat things up.

Harry Arnold noted: "By burning the containers enough heat was provided to heat the contents reasonably. Raw replacements were prone to apply too much heat too quickly without first puncturing a vent in the can, resulting in deformed and exploding cans."

Radford Carroll noted the advantages and disadvantages of K rations:

There were two advantages to K rations. First we were almost independent of the kitchen . . . and second the amount of dysentery was drastically reduced. If you don't think that's important, imagine trying to do hard and dangerous work while afflicted with cramps that in normal times would put you in bed. The bad part was that rations quickly became very monotonous. Also, because they were concentrated, if we ate K rations continuously our stomachs became so small that we could not eat much normal food when it was delivered.

In the Pacific, men had the advantage of selecting their own K rations before an invasion. As one soldier in the 27th Infantry Division said, "We found it was a good idea to try out the K rations before the landing to see just what agreed with us. What we didn't like, we discarded, and we still had more than enough to eat."

In the Pacific, combat often lasted only a few days or weeks, and the heat encouraged less food consumption. Troops in Europe—in a cooler climate, spending more continuous time at the front; surrounded by farms and towns—had far more inclination to eat.

No matter where a man was located, he may not have enjoyed his K rations much. Murphy Simoneaux, of the 81st Infantry Division, stated unequivocally that "the K ration in combat was terrible." First Armored Division tanker Philip Jewett was not much more impressed than Simoneaux: "K rations you'd eat when you got hungry enough—like starving."

Screamin' Eagle James Simms wrote of an incident in which he did not find his K-ration meal very appetizing:

I broke open my K ration and when I opened the can it contained cold greasy potted meat. I listened to . . . tanks firing out there. I looked at the bloody eyeball hanging on that boy's [a wounded comrade's] cheek. I looked at the greasy mess in that can. I backed my ears and dug in. When a lump of that mess would get about even with my Adam's apple . . . I would find myself silently saying, "Stay down, you greasy son of a bitch!"

Most men, however, felt that K rations were the best that could be done under the conditions. Boyd Miller, a platoon leader in the 29th Infantry Division, remembered a quiet moment in Normandy in which he enjoyed a K-ration lunch. "It was quiet . . . and we dined on our K rations. I had grown especially fond of the chocolate bars. Even the cheese didn't taste bad. And it was surprising how soothing the coffee brewed from powder tasted when the air was chilly."

Paratrooper Edward Laughlin, of the 82d Airborne Division, enjoyed one particular part of the K ration: "Most GIs did not like the fruit bar that was part of many of these rations. They would curse and throw it away since it did not compare with the more desired bar of chocolate. I kind of liked the fruit bar—a gooey mass . . . made up of all kinds of fruits, including prunes."

K rations were generally higher quality than C rations. Only at the end of the war, when C rations became more diversified, did they measure up to the K rations. Harry Arnold put the soldiers' preference bluntly: "Usually the K variety was favored over the C, but both were rather unappetizing after weeks of much of the same."

For most combat troops, stomaching the 10 in 1 ration was not a problem. The majority of men had a positive view of this somewhat uncommon combat food. Radford Carroll described it well:

There was an even bulkier ration called a 10 in 1, which was supposed to be one meal for 10 men, or 10 meals for one man. One man could not use it unless he only opened one can for each meal. The 10 in 1 was packed in a cardboard box and required a fire to use it. Thus the 10 in 1 was useless for combat troops in the field. That didn't prevent us from getting them one time. The rations were divided among the men, who went back to their holes to eat them—as I recall I got a can of green beans.

Lawrence Nickell's infantry outfit also found the 10 in 1s too difficult to carry. "Unfortunately it was bulky and not suited for infantry to carry, and we rarely had it but regarded it as a . . . treat when we did. When we rode tanks we could carry the 10 in 1 on the tanks, and tank personnel often gave us some of their 10 in 1 ration."

Colin McLaurin, a rifle company commander in the 29th Infantry Division, remembered a rare instance in Normandy in which his unit received 10 in 1 rations. He found himself apportioning the coveted food much the same way Paul Swenson's 70th Division distributed C rations:

> We received the rations in several wooden boxes which had been constructed for overseas shipment, so it was difficult to open them. The second difficulty was "breaking them down," as we say in the Army. The food was packed in cans, boxes and bags. The problem was dividing the rations so that everyone received an equal share of everything, and this division had to be accomplished in the dark. This aspect may not sound so important to a well fed and underexercised civilian, but I knew that the men would howl if somebody else had something that they did not have or if the shares were not equal. The task was eventually accomplished though, and in due course I received my share.

Because the 10 in 1 ration was usually reserved for tankers simply because they had the room to carry it, this produced some degree of envy among the foot-slogging infantry, as Howard Gaertner, of the 78th Infantry Division, wrote. "We . . . envied the tankers' far superior 10 in 1 rations."

"I thought 10 in 1 rations . . . were great," wrote Donald MacLeod, of the 45th Infantry Division. On the other side of the world in the Pacific, 24th Infantry Division soldier William Wheeler agreed: "Ten in one rations were good."

The 10 in 1 can be seen, then, as a somewhat rare treat for the majority of combat soldiers, because most of that select group was in the infantry. Also, tank crews found themselves eating C and K rations often, particularly in the breakout and dash across France in the summer of 1944 when they were ahead of their supply lines. So 10 in 1s were not exactly standard fare even for tankers. Like C and K rations, 10 in 1s consisted of reasonably high-quality food and contained large portions. The chances are good, however, that if most combat soldiers had been forced to eat them every day, they would have grown tired of them.

There was one more ration that was issued to the troops in substantial quantities. It was called a D bar or D ration, which was designed primarily for emergency use when men could get to no other food. Lawerence Nickell described it as:

> . . . a very hard chocolate bar wrapped in a waxed cardboard box. It was very difficult to eat, hard as a rock and rather bitter, but apparently three or four contained enough calories to sustain one for a day's caloric needs. It was also thought to be very constipating, probably mainly due to the fact that it provided no fiber. I usually tried to shave part of it in a canteen cup of boiling water, making a sort of chocolate drink, or I would shave it into small fragments, to prevent tooth fracture.

Apparently the D bar was successful for what it was intended to do, as a story by American Division veteran Ray Poynter suggests. "On a long patrol in Bougainville we got cut off from our main unit ten miles out and were there for six days. We only had three days' rations and these emergency D bars. They served their purpose. We lived on them [until we got] back to our unit."

However effective the D bar may have been, Paul Swenson pointed out that it had drawbacks. "It was powerful stuff, and I had a hard time eating one bar without getting a little nauseated."

Jack Thacker, of the 30th Infantry Division, found himself struggling with the D bar's hardness:

> Like the present-day M & M, it will not melt in the hand. I wonder if it even melts in the stomach. It is extremely hard and cannot be broken in two by simply bending it between one's hands. So I attempted to solve the problem by placing the bar on my leg, putting the point of my trench knife in the middle

of the bar, and pounding on the handle of the knife. I found, much to my sorrow, that the knife would eventually penetrate the candy bar and a portion of my leg.

Charles Henne said the D bar left "a funny taste in your mouth." Donald Dencker, of the 96th Infantry Division in the Pacific, bluntly referred to it as "a dog turd."

Water was also important to a combat soldier, especially in the Pacific, where blazing heat often threatened to dehydrate the body. One 27th Infantry Division soldier said he always made sure to carry plenty of water:

> You should keep from drinking it as long as possible. While the supply was plentiful in most cases, there was one time when we were in a position where water just could not be brought in. We had to drink some out of our machine gun and from coconuts. The climate is hot, and you sweat like the devil, so two canteens should always be carried.

Colin McLaurin pointed out that "drinking water is a very important commodity to an infantryman in combat, and it is a serious matter to be without it for any length of time." One veteran 36th Infantry Division soldier in Italy told *Yank* correspondent Burtt Evans that "water discipline has never been stressed enough. When our whole battalion was cut off for three days at Mount Maggiore, the new men almost died of thirst. We caught some water in C-ration cans and helmets."

Most of the time, drinking water came from one's surroundings. As such, men had to make sure that it was clean enough to drink. "Of course," Harry Arnold wrote, "we used the Halizone tablets provided . . . for disinfecting drinking water—two tablets per canteen of water and a wait of half an hour rendered the water potable."

Cigarettes were no less important to many combat soldiers. For the most part, American combat troops had plenty to smoke. Lawrence Nickell said that his unit was "issued a carton of cigarettes a week and there were 12 cigarettes in a day's K rations as well." Harry Arnold said it was the same in his outfit:

Since individual rations usually contained a small packet of four cigarettes, and since some of the men were not smokers, smokers, by trade or gift, managed. Many considered quitting the habit for health reasons, but reconsidered when contemplating other hazards of our line of work. Entertaining such thoughts would bring a sigh or wry grin. Giving up the habit was a foolish dream, the benefits being so uncertain.

Thomas Rosell, of the 34th Infantry Division in Italy, remembered the Red Cross giving out cigarettes. "I think they tried to issue a pack of cigarettes a day to the soldiers that wanted them."

In addition to his rations, the American combat soldier had one other major source of food—the land. Most men were all too eager to find something different to eat, particularly something fresh. Some called it looting. Others thought of it as foraging. But the average soldier thought of anything edible in his surroundings as fair game and the rightful spoils of war.

William Meissner explained the process by which American combat troops would appropriate food:

As we went through the countryside, we would occasionally come upon a farm which was still occupied. We would stop and "liberate" some eggs, fresh meat, vegetables and canned goods. These, when we could get them, gave us welcome changes in our food supply. Almost always, we would leave our unwanted C or Ks in exchange for our liberated produce. We laughed when the farmers thanked us profusely for these despised rations.

The farmers whom 3d Infantry Division rifle platoon leader Joseph Martin dealt with in Sicily and Italy were not quite as pleased with the exchange system. "We outran our rations most of the time. We ate almonds, green olives off the trees and watermelons . . . out of the fields, much to the farmers' disgust."

Riland West and his 87th Infantry Division comrades in Germany wanted extra food but were still on the alert for double-crossing German civilians. "If we went into a house and asked them for some food

. . . they'd go out of their way to give us something but then we were afraid . . . they might poison us. So most of the time we'd try to catch a chicken or anything we could eat."

Sometimes combat troops ate strange diets by necessity, as was the case for Raymond Jones and the rest of the 1st Marine Division on Guadalcanal. "We had to eat jap food, smoke jap cigarettes. If they hadn't had large warehouses there, we would have had one hell of a time."

In the early days of the war, the doomed American troops on the Philippines had to eat anything they could get. "We'd eat the same things the Filipinos did," Clarence Daniels remembered. "They had rice and soup and some kind of Spam. Some of them ate monkeys." Jim Horton, of the 57th Infantry Regiment, recalled his rations on Bataan as "rice twice a day. Once in a while we might have some carabao meat. A canteen cup full of rice was about it."

During the Battle of the Bulge, Harry Martin and his buddies had little food and even less time to eat it:

> The men grabbed a chicken and cut its head off with a bayonet. While the chicken was being plucked, we started a small fire. Just as the chicken was put over the fire, the word came that the Germans were closing in once again. We ran down the road, passing the raw chicken around, with each man ripping off a piece. We were so hungry that we ate the raw chicken like wild animals.

Most of the time, however, conditions were not that desperate for American combat soldiers. Sometimes they even ate like kings. Earl Reitan's tale of a captured German warehouse is a good example:

> The warehouse was full of German food and supplies, and it was good to have something different to eat for a change. The most important find was metal boxes, about the size of a cigarette case, which opened on the sides to make a little stove. For fuel you used white pellets which burned with a clear blue flame. This was ideal for heating water or C rations. I loaded up on as many of the pellets as I could carry, and for the rest of my time in Alsace I had hot food.

James Graff, of the 35th Infantry Division, benefited from a lucky find. "We found a half of beef hanging in a tree. We ate it and then killed another and left it for the next outfit." Harry Arnold's platoon also got lucky one time. "A couple of cows were lying a few yards from our OP holes. Some of the men cut some steaks from one of the cows, and Doc put them on the range. We waited in anticipation, licking our chops like hungry wolves."

American soldiers could be resourceful when it came to food. Dewey Mann, of the 36th Infantry Division, wrote of an incident that happened in France:

> A cow was killed by rifle fire from some of our men, who mistook it to be the enemy attacking at night. Thinking it unwise to see such good beef go to waste, our cooks proceeded to butcher. However, this butcher action attracted enemy fire. To overcome this, a rope was attached to the cow, and it was dragged by a jeep to a safer place, and the work was done unmolested. The meat was then approved by the Regimental Surgeon and served to the men.

Robert Seabrook, of the 6th Cavalry Regiment, explained a unique way of fishing that he and his buddies devised:

> Getting tired of canned rations, we decided to have a big fish fry. We had one-pound blocks of TNT starch, which is what we would use to blow up a bridge or a roadblock. You could take a hammer and pound one of the blocks of powder and it would not explode. It took a percussion cap to set it off. We found that by setting the block off near the top of the water, we got more fish. With two or three explosions we secured enough fish to feed our troop of two hundred men.

Sometimes combat men augmented their own portions by heisting food from other units. Harry Arnold recounted one such instance:

> We observed How. [Howitzer] Company men picking up K rations from a stack of them. We sauntered over to the stack of

wooden crates as if we owned the lot, and hoisted a crate each to our shoulders. No one noticed as we walked confidently away with our loot. We learned later that a search was under way for stolen rations.

Units also did favors for one another, as Frank Caudillo relates. "Once on Luzon a paratrooper unit reinforced us and after taking our objective they ordered a drop of one pork chop sandwich for each of us."

Herman Steenstra, a combat officer in the 32d Infantry Division, commented on how the food improved as the war wore on: "In the beginning rations were poor, one handful of rice per day. Rations improved as time went on, nourishing and plentiful." The only problem was that most American combat soldiers initially had unrealistic expectations, because they had generally eaten well in civilian life. J. R. McIlroy, of the 99th Infantry Division, expressed this fact the best when he wrote: "D bars, K rations, and C rations might sustain you for a while, but what we wanted was a good old American hamburger or our mother's home cooking."

Sooner or later most combat soldiers learned that, in the context of a total war, their country was doing the best it possibly could to feed them. Eventually most of them came to realize, as 75th Infantry Division soldier William Eberhart did: "Of course rations were usually routine, but we always had food and water to maintain our fighting strength."

If the American combat soldier was fortunate in the quality of his food, was he also fortunate in the quality of his equipment? The answer is mixed. Some of his equipment was excellent. Some was useless or even destructive. As with his food, what the American combat soldier could not productively use, he threw away.

In the category of failures, perhaps the most notorious was the combat boot. Made of leather in most cases, it proved remarkably inadequate in both the European theater of operations (ETO) and in the Pacific. In the ETO it failed to protect the troops' feet against wet and cold conditions. In the Pacific it rotted after a short time. As Edward Laughlin makes clear, not only were standard combat boots, or "shoes," subpar, so were the more highly regarded "jump boots" for paratroopers:

I had an initial issue of GI shoes, ankle high, and when worn in the field it was with leggings from WWI. . . . These later fell into disuse when the combat boot was issued—a raw leather boot that defied polish that extended to mid-calf with the upper part being secured by two straps and buckles. The paratrooper boot, all leather with the slanted rubber heel, was really more of a "show" boot—but worn in all kinds of weather and in combat would not repel heat, cold or water.

Eugene Schermerhorn, of the 65th Infantry Division, said he "would have been pleased with better shoes and feet protection, as I and thousands of others froze our feet in France and Belgium in the winter of '44." Donald Vanhooser, of the same division, put it even more succinctly: "Combat boots were not too adequate in winter conditions . . . instrumental in a lot of trench foot." This condition, explained Robert Seabrook, "is caused from long days of wet feet with no dry socks and no dry boots."

Even tankers, who had the chance to ride inside vehicles rather than slosh through snow and water like their infantry counterparts, experienced major problems with foot gear. Cecil Roberts, of the 1st Armored Division, described his boots as "pitiful . . . for cold weather." David Harrison, a tank commander in France with the 2d Armored Division, had an equally low regard for his boots: "The combat boot was terrible. They gave us dubbin to waterproof the boot. The dubbin went through the boot and infected the feet. [One] soldier had immersion feet and toes amputated."

Many other American combat men suffered a similar fate. Some lost their feet altogether. Tank commander Charles Harbold, in the 4th Armored Division, said: "Footwear was very poor for the severe winter weather. Trench foot was common in the infantry units." Walter Richardson, of the 3d Armored Division, went so far as to call his boots "the worst abomination ever issued to soldiers."

Far too late, overshoes called "shoepacs" were issued to soldiers in the ETO. However, as *Yank* correspondent Pete Kelley reported, often the very soldiers who needed them most received them last. "The men want boots badly, and say they need them more than the Blue Star Commandos, as supply and rear area troops are called."

Even the shoepacs, though, were not always the answer to the foot problems. James McKnight, an armor infantryman in the 11th Armored Division, wrote: "The bootpacks froze our feet. In January and February we would sweat . . . when we walked, then freeze our feet when we sat."

While he and his fellow Screamin' Eagles held out at Bastogne against some of the best the Germans could throw at them, James Simms found that shoepacs were barely adequate:

> I think they dropped us galoshes in air supply. Our feet were just about gone by then, since our boots and feet were wet the first few days and then when the snow came the awful cold nearly finished the job. I found myself wiggling my toes all the time trying to keep my feet from going completely numb and trying to prevent trench foot. The galoshes helped keep our feet drier and a little warmer but they were heavy, clumsy things to have to slip and slide around in.

In the Pacific the problem was not trench foot but simply the fact that the combat boots could not stand up to the harsh terrain and conditions. Herchel McFadden, of the Americal Division, said: "In the South Pacific we could have used better jungle boots." John Drugan, an infantryman in the 41st Infantry Division, said that the boots "were too big and heavy and caused boils on my ankles."

The Pacific climate, along with the poor footgear, caused a special kind of foot problem. "The boots were canvas and rubber," wrote Salvatore Lamagna. "Your feet would sweat and with the wet boots you'd develop jungle rot." Jungle rot was a fungus that attacked the skin, causing it to die and flake off in layers. In its most advanced stages, it could eat away so much of a man's foot that amputation was required.

Another poor piece of equipment was the overcoat, designed to keep infantrymen warm during the cold European winters. For the actual troops on the line, it did not work out that way. "We wouldn't wear our raincoats because we silhouetted like Germans," wrote Lester Clear, of the 97th Infantry Division. That was one major reason why the overcoats were not worn. The Germans had an overcoat (apparently much warmer and better designed) that looked similar, particularly in the dark. Most American combat soldiers felt that the enemy was dangerous enough without getting accidentally shot by your own side.

The other reason that most troops did not wear the overcoats was that, as J. R. McIlroy pointed out, they were not very warm. "Only the replacements had overcoats. No experienced combat soldier would wear one, as they were heavy and would freeze when wet."

Edward Laughlin described his overcoat:

> Always too tight a fit in the chest and in the shoulders and . . . made of heavy wool. [We] learned that in the cold air, wind would stream up the cut in the rear of the coat, come right up to your neck and even swirl around in your steel helmet! A terrible garment—thick, unwieldy, unpackable, unwearable.

Perhaps the most useless item was the gas mask—useless not necessarily because it was a bad piece of equipment but because poison gas was never used in World War II. Newman Phillips, of the 32d Infantry Division, referred to gas masks as "the most useless things I ever saw." Robert LaChausee, of the 38th Infantry Division, said they were worse than useless; they were cumbersome. "The field protective mask was a bulky pain in the neck. All of us threw them away at the first opportunity."

Harry Arnold described the almost comical process by which he and his buddies divested themselves of the useless masks. "We would ditch them and quartermasters would come along and pick them up and reissue them, only to find them again a few miles farther along." With ingenuity typical of the American combat soldier, Tom Wood and his comrades finally found a use for the mask—"to carry cognac."

One item of equipment that worked beautifully was the M1 helmet. By most accounts it performed exceedingly well, and soldiers found many uses for it. Lawrence Nickell outlined what made up the basic American field helmet of World War II:

> The helmet . . . was in two parts, the liner which was made of plastic and had internal straps adjustable to our head size,

and the external steel helmet which was an all-purpose affair. We wore it for protection, used it as a washbasin, drank from it, could boil water or cook in it . . . and, if pinned down in a foxhole, used it as a urinal. The chin strap on the liner was worn fastened around the back of our heads, which kept it on while we ran and was more comfortable than the helmet chin strap.

Ferdinand Huber, of the 99th Infantry Division, also liked his helmet:

The helmet was not really of any benefit, as it could not stop anything but a well spent piece of shrapnel. It mostly acted as a refuge, as one felt naked without it. It was also a convenient bucket for bathing and cooking. The steel part was bare inside and was intended to fit over a helmet liner of fiberglass which contained leather and canvas bands.

Charles Henne pointed out that the M1 helmet was a vast improvement over the old World War I tin hats. "If you ever wore the old helmet you would appreciate how much we loved the new one. It was utilitarian. It was more than head protection; it was a treasured tool."

The clothing, mainly fatigues and OD (olive drab) uniforms, received mixed reviews. American combat clothing was generally made of substantial, quality material, but it could not be all things to all people. No uniform could possibly be right for every circumstance. This is evident from a statement made by Thomas Rosell when discussing his uniforms: "In Europe we wore wool trousers and wool shirts. The disadvantage of that uniform was that, being wool, if it got wet . . . it seemed like it'd never dry out." But wool could also be an advantage, as Charles Murphy and the rest of the 1st Infantry Division found out when they invaded North Africa. "We were issued the OD wool uniform and it was gas impregnated, stiff as a board and we couldn't figure out what in the hell we were doing going south with wool OD uniforms, but it sure came in handy."

In spite of all the clothing that 87th Infantry Division soldier John McAuliffe had on during the Battle of the Bulge, he still was not warm. "That winter I wore long woolen underwear and two sets of olive drabs and a sweater and field jacket with a scarf . . . with two pairs of woolen socks under my combat boots and galoshes. I had no feeling in my toes for two months." Tanker Lawrence Butler, of the 1st Armored Division in Italy, had a high opinion of his uniform. "[Tankers'] clothing was good. Combat jacket and pants were good but the parka made you more comfortable."

Yank correspondent Pete Kelley described how most combat soldiers dressed for their dirty jobs:

> Most of the infantrymen wore impregnite hoods from their impregnated clothing to keep snow from dropping down their necks. Others found a GI towel makes an excellent muffler or even a set of earmuffs when wrapped around the head under the helmet. Still another improvisation was the use of sleeping bags as combat suits. Some of the men cut leg holes in them and drew the bags up tight like a pair of combat jumpers. During the day, the bags made warm uniforms; at night, they served their original purpose as sleeping bags.

In the Pacific, the men found that their jungle fatigues were often too hot. Leonard Stein, of the 24th Infantry Division, certainly thought so. "Camoflauge uniforms were uncomfortable for use in the Pacific theater, not permitting body heat to escape and irritating the skin." Robert LaChausee thought that the clothing should have been lighter: "Our fatigues were a little heavy. It took a long time to dry when you got wet." On the other hand, Daniel Chomiw, of the 77th Infantry Division, thought that his fatigues were "the best money could buy."

Probably the fairest assessment of the clothing and personal equipment of the American combat soldier in World War II came from 32d Infantry Division veteran Robert Teeples: "I don't believe there is any clothing or equipment adequate for jungle fighting."

The weapons used by the American combat soldier were, like his food and equipment, a mixed bag. Some performed much better than anyone had a right to expect. Others were dismal failures. Although American weapons were usually well made and reasonably reliable, they were generally inferior to what the enemy, particularly the Germans, possessed. Too often the American combat soldier found himself outgunned. If it had not been for his artillery, air, and, at times, naval support, along with his own initiative and remarkable resiliency, the combat soldier may have found himself on the losing side of the battle.

Tanks are a good example. The main battle tank of the U.S. Army in World War II was the M4 Sherman. Speedy and blessed with excellent maneuverability, the Sherman was light (approximately 32 tons) and had only 75 millimeters of armor plating. Its armament included a 75mm gun (later in the war, most models had a short or long 76mm), one .50-caliber machine gun, and two .30-caliber machine guns. The tank was powered by a 353-horsepower engine. The tanks' 20-foot frame housed a five-man crew.

By almost all accounts the Sherman was not a match in one-on-one combat with the German Mark V or VI, although it usually did well enough against the Mark IV. Lawrence Butler summed up the Sherman's shortcomings:

> The 75mm on the . . . M4 medium tank was very poor in comparison to the German 77mm and 88mm that could fire accurately at 5,000 yards. We could start firing at 2,500 yards. We won the war by losing more tanks and cluttering up the battlefield. I think the M4 medium tank had enough armor plate but was too high profile. The engine operated on gasoline, had poor power and [the tank] was a death trap. At one time I was on fire thirteen times in one day.

The Sherman was so flammable that its crews nicknamed it "Ronson," after a popular cigarette lighter.

One of Butler's 1st Armored Division comrades, Raymond Janus, said of his tank's armament: "They did not stop or penetrate a German Mark VI tank, but we did have . . . excellent gunners that stopped them." In other words, American tankers used ingenuity to make up for their lack of effective gunnery. Henry Brown, of the 2d Armored Division in France, said: "AP [armor piercing] shells would bounce off Panther and Tiger tanks." Glen Alford, of the 3d Armored Division, pointed out another problem with the Sherman's guns: "Our 75s and 76s had a nasty habit of getting their retractors stuck—some pretty hairy times. I think that's when I started getting white hair."

The upside to the Sherman was that it was technically sound and reliable. First Armored Division tanker Eugene Thibideau underscored this point: "They were very reliable. Once in a while a tank would throw a track but not if they were used properly."

Thus, as outgunned and outarmored as U.S. tankers were in World War II, they knew that their equipment would hold up well under the strain of combat. This was not always true of German tanks, which sacrificed durability and mechanical reliability for heavier armament and armor. Because American tanks held up better, tankers could simply keep more of them operational and put more into combat. This meant that, even if their tanks were generally inferior, American tankers usually outnumbered their enemy.

Toward the end of the war, some new tank models that had been designed to mimic the formidable German tanks were introduced. One of these was the M26 Pershing, which, at 41 tons, was far heavier than the Sherman. It also had a five-man crew, but it was armed with a 90mm gun and its armor was 102 millimeters thick. The machine guns were identical to those on the Sherman, but the tank's engine was more powerful, at 500 horsepower.

Certainly the Pershings were generally more effective than the Shermans. Garland Godby remembered using them for fire support for his rifle company. "In Luxembourg I got a section . . . with our 90 millimeter on it and you could sit there and pick off trucks and things ninety yards away." Even so, the new 90mm tanks did not stand up to the heaviest the Germans could put into the field. Harry Arnold recounted a conversation he had with a Pershing commander. "It was an impressive looking vehicle, and far better than the old Sherman it replaced. At the first opportunity I asked a Pershing commander how the Pershing stood up against the Tiger. The answer was, 'When we come up on a Tiger, we turn around and run like hell!'"

If most American tanks were inferior to their German counterparts, how did American mortars hold up in combat? For the most part, they were effective. There were two basic American mortars used in combat in World War II—the light 60mm mortar and the 81mm mortar. Mortarman Lawrence Nickell explained the anatomy and workings of the 60mm:

> It consisted of a short nonrifled tube which had a fixed firing pin in the base. The mortar was fired by dropping the shell after removing a safety pin which prevented detonation if not removed into the tube. The shell had a firing charge, consisting of a shotgun shell on its base and four separate charges of a green leadlike explosive which were attached to the guiding vanes on its base. It struck the firing pin, detonating the explosive charges, propelling the shell in a high arching trajectory to its target. The "business end" of the shell consisted of an explosive charge detonating when the shell struck and scattering shrapnel. The complete shell weighed about three pounds. The firing range of the mortar was 2,000 yards and was varied by adjusting the angle of elevation by an elevating screw on a two-legged support, called a bipod, attached to the tube. Usually several "zeroing-in" rounds were fired until one of the guns was on target, then all three guns fired three rounds or more "for effect."

Colbert Renfroe, of the 11th Airborne Division in the Pacific, said that he had a high regard for the 60mm. "We grew to love it and understand it." Charles Henne, however, thought it was not suited for the jungle fighting in which his unit was involved. "The 60mm mortar was too light for bush fighting." Robert Manning, of the 81st Infantry Division, found that "the 60mm mortar shell did not explode 30 percent of the time."

In general, though, the 60mm mortar did exactly as it was intended to do. It provided effective direct fire support from a distance of only about 200 yards behind the forward positions without completely weighing down its crews (the 60mm weighed 43 pounds).

The 81mm was more than three times as heavy as the 60mm. It weighed 136 pounds, had a range of 2,500 yards, and fired a 10-pound projectile. Its firing mechanism worked the same way as that of the 60mm.

The 81mm was too heavy for its crew to break down and carry but could be conveniently mounted on a number of different carriages. Rex Whitehead, of the 99th Infantry Division, described how the mortar was carried when a crew could not find transportation for it. "The 81s break into three parts, each weighing about 51 pounds, and consist of a bipod, tube, and base plate. There is only one way to carry the parts and that is on your shoulder and it soon hurts."

Charles Henne wrote that the 81mm was "great in the bush with the HE [high explosive] heavy and delayed fuse setting that could get down through the big canopy." There were drawbacks, though, as 45th Infantry Division veteran Donald MacLeod explained: "Sometimes an 81mm shell would not fire, which meant that it had to be taken out of the firing tube—a little scary but we were all young."

The Germans had a terrific weapon called the *panzerfaust,* which was used by infantry to destroy tanks. The American answer to that was the M1 bazooka. Five feet long and weighing 18 pounds, it fired a rocket 2.36 inches in diameter and could be carried fairly easily by one man and employed by two. It probably was not as good a weapon as the German *panzerfaust,* but, unlike the *panzerfaust,* it could be reused.

Gene Curry, who often handled bazookas, wrote that it could:

> . . . blow a hole right through a tank's thick metal. It would start the ammo on fire inside the tank. The only thing wrong with this job was that the Germans, like us, had infantry troops to protect their tanks from guys like me. The tank has to be fairly close in order to knock it out. Once you've fired a round and given your position away, their infantry are on you like a swarm of bees. You might as well put your head between your legs and kiss your butt good-bye.

Firing a bazooka, then, was a dangerous job even though it could accomplish the task of destroying a tank. Donald Greener, an armored infantryman with the 1st Armored Division, did not enjoy having to fire his bazooka:

> One had to wear an eye and face shield and gloves and had to have someone as a loader. When detonated fire flew out of

both ends. I wasn't sure I could hit a tank with one. In later years I talked to people who swore by them. You only got one chance, and I didn't think I could hit my target given those odds.

Another weapon that was effective but also exceedingly danger-ous was the flamethrower. American combat troops often used flamethrowers in the Pacific to root out the stubborn Japanese, but they were also commonly employed in Europe against pillboxes and bunkers. Carrying a flamethrower was an extremely unpopular job. Japanese American Yukio Kawamoto, who served with the 37th In-fantry Division, referred to the weapon as "barbarous." Naturally any sane enemy who saw that he was about to be burned to cinders would try to kill the man carrying the flamethrower. "Snipers really looked for them," recalled Charlie Burchett, of the 1st Marine Division. If a flamethrower man was hit, he had almost no chance of survival. Indeed, he would probably meet a fiery death.

Edward Laughlin, who once got roped into flamethrower duty, re-called the rudiments of the weapon and his stint as a flamethrower man:

> The flamethrower consisted of two metal tanks with a web harness that was worn on the back. One tank had highly volatile fuel in it and the other had a jellylike substance—like napalm. The two tanks had hoses on each that came together over the shoulder into some metal tubes about 30 inches long, less than 1/2 inch in diameter and extended into a nozzle. When the trigger was pulled, and it had to be held with both hands, the "stuff" shot out and was ignited. The fluid ignited the napalm which, when it hit something, would cling to the object and burn. It required someone to turn on the valves on the top of the tanks to release the fluids, as the person carrying this ap-paratus could not reach them.

Laughlin recounted how he unluckily got drafted into carrying the flamethrower:

The lieutenant said, "Sergeant, put someone on that flamethrower." I sensed we were all trying to shrink up in our uniforms, as none of us wanted that job. Then he said, "Laughlin, you do it." I had to endure a number of ribald comments, some pity, and some cynical requests for my girlfriend's address. I was very disgruntled about being selected—why me I'll never know—and I considered refusing to do it and then decided against that. [After the mission] I gave loud notice that I wasn't going to have another turn and I was not called upon again to carry that flamethrower.

Another infantry weapon that was designed for use in close proximity to the enemy was the hand grenade. In general, U.S. forces used fragmentation grenades, which simply meant that when they exploded, they would propel shrapnel within the affected area. The most commonly used was the Mark III A2, which was ideal for attack situations. American grenades generally performed well as long as the user was combat experienced. As one 36th Infantry Division veteran put it, "The most valuable thing I learned in training was how to lob a grenade. You can't get any distance if you throw them like baseballs. It takes experience to knock out a pillbox at twenty-five yards from a prone position."

Michael Stubinski, of the 36th Infantry Division, had an opportunity to compare German and American grenades. "I captured a German Potato Masher, my first, and threw it. It went off, just a concussion grenade, not like ours, which we carried on our belts. Ours contained shrapnel and tears a body to pieces, whereas the Potato Masher shook the hell out of you."

Some American grenades were designed to be fitted onto rifles. The rifle could then propel them, acting as a sort of impromptu grenade launcher. This was an effective weapon in urban combat. Radford Carroll explained this process:

The grenades were launched from a special fitting on a standard M1 rifle. To operate a rifle grenade, you clipped the special fitting on the end of the barrel—this prevented the rifle from operating in a semiautomatic mode. The rifle was loaded with a blank cartridge, the grenade was slipped over the fitting, the safety pin was pulled from the grenade, the rifle was aimed so the grenade could be lobbed about 75 yards.

The grenade, then, was one area in which the American combat soldier held an advantage over his German and Japanese antagonists.

One category in which American weapons were badly outclassed was in machine guns. The Japanese Nambu and the German MG-34 and MG-42 were clearly superior to the American mainline light machine gun, the Browning M1919 A6, commonly referred to as the "30 cal." Derived from a World War I weapon, the 30 cal. had circular cooling holes in a jacket around the barrel and featured a belt feed for ammunition. It had a pistol grip and a carrying handle and could be mounted on a bipod. At 31 pounds it was also heavy and awkward; it fired, at best, only about 500 rounds per minute. Another problem, as 78th Infantry Division veteran Thomas Yochim pointed out, was that the "barrel pitted very rapidly and, unlike its German counterpart, had to be completely stripped to replace it." German machine guns could be fitted with a new barrel in a matter of seconds, whereas many minutes were required to do the same job on the American gun. James McKnight, of the 11th Armored Division, had this very problem. "I was a machine gunner on a .30 light. It did not fire because the barrel was too tight; you had to screw it all the way in, then half turn out. I'm sure they got around to improving it after the war." Many men—Colin McLaurin for one—remembered with a shudder the contrast in sounds between the weak American machine gun and the feared German one: "A [German] machine gun opened up and its rate of fire was so great that it sounded like a piece of cloth tearing. This was a sharp contrast to ours, which was more of a chatter." Thomas Rosell had similar recollections: "I can remember the difference in machine guns, the very fast, high . . . cyclic rate of the German MG-34 or MG-42. Then the U.S. . . . tat-tat-tat-tat."

In the area of submachine guns, American soldiers were not as badly outclassed. The Japanese had no submachine gun in widespread use. The German MP-40, or "burp gun," was probably better than both of its American counterparts, but the gap was not as wide as it was between the light machine guns of the two nations.

American combat soldiers were armed with two different types of submachine gun. The first was the Thompson, or "tommy gun," which fired .45-caliber ammunition. It was a little heavy at 11 pounds, and it was generally loaded with 20-round magazines. Basically, you either liked the Thompson or you hated it. Charlie Burchett, who was involved in much close-in combat, swore by his. "I traded . . . for a Thompson submachine gun. We were in . . . caves and . . . I was covering my buddies. The stopping power of the .45 is great." As 1st Armored Division combat soldier Robert Peck put it, "The tommy gun was real good close up." Ivan Shepherd, in the same unit, concurred: "I was armed with a Thompson submachinegun. It . . . had a lot of firepower at short range." The problem was that much of the combat in World War II did not take place at close range. If you were any more than thirty yards or so away from the enemy, the Thompson was ineffective.

Another problem with the Thompson was that it was difficult to maintain. Twenty-fourth Infantry Division combat soldier William Wheeler reported that it "failed if the least bit dirty." Ralph Schmidt, of the 32d Infantry Division, felt that it was "no good in the field; the driving rod spring was too light [and it] jammed with one grain of sand in the chamber."

The experiences of Richard Talley, of the 36th Infantry Division, were probably typical of those using the Thompson. "It only let me down once. The gun jammed on me when I stepped from behind a wall and tried to open fire on the Jerries, but it served me well after that. The failure was due to a weak clip. It was a real good gun for close firing."

The M3, or so-called "grease gun" because of its resemblance to the same, was an average weapon that achieved mixed results. Radford Carroll analyzed the one he was issued:

The M3 was made of stamped sheet metal with a metal extendable stock, a very cheaply made device. It had its merits but also . . . some serious defects. The two major defects were that the springs were not correctly tempered. Unless the bolt springs were stretched every so often, the gun would not function. The magazine was designed to hold 30 bullets, but if 30 bullets were loaded the magazine springs would not have enough force to lift the bullets, so I had to load only 20. Even then I had to empty the magazine every so often and stretch the springs again. Also, the .45 cal. ammunition was heavy and had a slow muzzle velocity. The bullets hit with a big impact, but they had a short range and were not very penetrating.

Garland Godby did not like the grease gun at all. "It had such a slow cyclic rate. It was too mechanical." Horace Leach, who fought with Merrill's Marauders in Burma, credited a malfunctioning grease gun with saving him from taking a life. "At about 20 feet I aimed and pulled the trigger; nothing happened. The old grease gun was jammed with sand. I . . . realized that a defective gun probably saved me from taking a direct life in combat."

Like the Thompson, the grease gun could also be difficult to maintain. "My M3 jammed very easily," wrote Walter Powell, of the 6th Armored Division, "as the tiniest piece of sand would jam the cylinders. We heard they cost the government about eight bucks apiece."

It almost bears asking at this point if there were any unqualified successes in the American arsenal in World War II. Happily, the answer to that question is yes. The rifles used by American combat soldiers were superior in almost every way to those of the enemy. The first American ground combat troops in World War II fought with the old bolt-action Springfield rifle left over from World War I. Although this was not a bad weapon, highly accurate at long distances with excellent sights and very dependable, it was soon phased out as the primary infantry rifle. By and large, U.S. combat troops used one of three main rifles—the M1 carbine; the Browning automatic rifle, or BAR; and the M1 Garand.

At only five pounds, the M1 carbine was extremely light and was designed for officers, mortarmen, antitank gunners, and other non-rifleman infantry soldiers. It had a 15-round magazine and fired light .30-caliber ammunition, which sacrificed much of its killing power. The men dubbed it the "pea shooter."

Richard Lovett, of the Americal Division, was one of several who did not like the carbine for that reason. "It didn't have stopping power. Enemy soldiers were shot many times but kept on coming."

Armored infantryman Herb Miller, of the 8th Amored Division, pointed out the M1's strong points. "I was very happy with the carbine. We did some tricks with that carbine at short range. It's fast; it's easy to use in a hurry. For churches and houses and things like that, it was good."

It was also durable, as 96th Infantry Division combat soldier Melvin Coobs found out. "I carried a carbine for a while. During one period on Okinawa I got it muddy and wet and couldn't clean it for two weeks and it still fired okay."

The BAR, on the other hand, was heavy and deadly. It dated back to World War I, so it was not exactly state of the art, but it provided something that American small units were sadly lacking—mobile firepower. Because American infantry did not have an effective light machine gun at their disposal, the BAR was the next best thing, and it worked splendidly. It took a twenty-round clip, which it fired with lightning speed, and it came equipped with a bipod, which was of dubious usefulness. *Yank* correspondent Burtt Evans heard one combat veteran in the Italian theater ask three other vets which weapon they would want if they could have only one. The answer was unanimous—the BAR. However, one of the vets did not like the bipod. "We've never yet had a chance to set it up. And it's heavy and catches on things on patrols."

As William Allen, of the 4th Marine Division, recalled, the BAR had such awesome firepower that it was difficult to keep supplied with ammunition. "The BAR had to have a couple of ammunition carriers. They couldn't carry all the ammunition they could fire. It was kind of like a machine gun . . . the way it fired." Garland Godby described how his unit employed the BAR. "You used it in . . . what you'd call marching fire, put it in a sling, and don't fire it from the shoulder."

One problem with the BAR was that the firing chamber had to be kept clean, which was sometimes difficult to do in combat conditions. Jack Hartzog, of the 78th Infantry Division, complained that "it

wouldn't fire if it got the least bit dirty." Paratrooper Richard Durkee, of the 508th Parachute Infantry Regiment, echoed this complaint. "Any dirt entering the receiver would cause a stoppage."

The men devised some rather unusual ways of cleaning out the
chamber, as 36th Infantry Division rifleman Pete Opengari remembered. "We had a BAR that wouldn't fire. It had sand or dirt in the
chamber. One of our men said to me, 'Give me that gun, quick.' I
handed it to him and he took a leak right into the chamber. That
gun . . . did its duty that night."

There were, of course, more orthodox ways to get the BAR back
into service, as men from the 83d Infantry Division demonstrated
when they found the chambers frozen. Said one man, "We thawed
them out by cupping our hands over the chamber or holding a heat
ration near it until it let loose."

One weapon in the U.S. arsenal was even better than the BAR. The
M1 Garand, so named for its inventor, John Garand, weighed only
about eight pounds and was probably the best infantry rifle of World
War II. Most combat soldiers loved it. Radford Carroll explained how
it worked:

> It was loaded with eight bullets in a metal clip by pressing
> the clip into the open magazine with the thumb while holding
> the rifle bolt back with the edge of the palm. The clip was
> pushed down until it locked in place, then the thumb was with-
> drawn and the bolt released. A powerful spring slammed the
> bolt forward and jammed the cartridge into the rifle cham-
> ber—ready to shoot. If the thumb wasn't withdrawn in time, it
> got a nasty pinch from the bolt, [called] M1 thumb. The rifle
> would fire as fast as the trigger could be pulled for eight shots.
> After the eighth shot the bolt locked in the open position, the
> empty metal clip automatically ejected and the rifle could be
> loaded with another full clip. It was the best in the world at that
> time.

Gene Curry pinpointed one of the advantages that the M1 gave
American combat soldiers over the enemy. "The German rifleman
had to load each round in his rifle one round at a time, as he only

had what is known as a bolt action." Sidney Richess, an officer in the 40th Infantry Division, said that the M1's semiautomatic feature saved his life. "During an encounter with an enemy force in a busy gully, an enemy rifleman fired at me at close range but missed. Knowing he was working his bolt and hidden from view . . . my runner . . . fired and wasted the guy." Ellis Blake, of the 33d Infantry Division, felt simply that "the M1 rifle was the best in use by an army during World War II." Robert Russell, of the 87th Infantry Division, vouched for the durability of his M1. "It would fire in the water, sand or dirt or anything. It didn't ever jam up."

Of course not everyone loved it. Thomas Yochim thought it was "too heavy and prone to misfire unless the gas port was kept clean." Charles Brennan, of the 32d Infantry Division, said it was "too heavy and bulky for jungle fighting." But John Margreiter, an armored infantryman in the 7th Armored Division, pinpointed the probable source of any kind of trouble with the M1. "Mine jammed during a firefight in the Ruhr pocket because I had not cleaned the chamber during four or five days of heavy fighting."

Newman Phillips identified not only the biggest flaw in the M1 but in all U.S. small arms when compared with enemy weapons in World War II. "The greatest fault was the lack of smokeless powder." This lack gave away U.S. positions; often American combat troops found themselves facing German soldiers who had the advantage, and hence the concealment, derived from smokeless powder. Thus, even within U.S. strengths there were weaknesses.

Shooting it out with the enemy was not the only concern of American combat soldiers. Even combat soldiers spent only a minority of their time actually fighting. Much of their time and effort was spent coping with weather, diseases, and appalling surroundings. In addition, there was plenty of time to deal with indigenous civilians, take in the awful sights and smells of the battlefield, and scrounge for alcohol and souvenirs.

The most intrusive condition of the combat soldier's world was the weather. This was especially true for the infantry, who generally fought, ate, slept, and moved in the outdoors no matter what the weather. In Europe, weather conditions were often intolerable. In their letters, diaries, and memoirs, dogfaces rarely talked about good weather. Only inclement conditions made an impression on them, as this excerpt from a letter by 9th Infantry Division soldier Don Mackerer indicates: "The weather over here is nothing short of atrocious: rain, snow, cold and more snow."

Perhaps it is only human nature to emphasize the worst. Thus, it is important to remember that, although most weather references speak of awful conditions, most days for U.S. soldiers in Europe were not typified by poor weather. For every one or two days of bitter cold, there were probably four or five days with mild temperatures. However, because most bad weather came in streaks, especially in wintertime, a soldier could go an entire month exposed to subfreezing temperatures, or he could find himself enduring rain for a solid week. As was true of many aspects of the combat soldier's existence, weather usually was a matter of blind chance.

That blind chance was dictated by the weather tendencies of the particular region in which the combat soldier found himself. For example, in Normandy the summer climate was forgiving. From June to August, when the Normandy campaign was fought, average temperatures ranged from about fifty-three degrees to about sixty-eight degrees, and the rainfall totaled two to three inches per month. Southern France, where American soldiers fought in August and September 1944, was somewhat warmer. Average temperatures for those two months ranged from sixty-one degrees to around eighty-three degrees. There was less than an inch of rain in August and close to three inches in September. Eastern France in the wintertime was a far less accommodating place; temperatures usually ranged from the low thirties to the low forties, and precipitation (usually snow) often topped two inches per month. The severity of the winter of 1944 in eastern France has been well chronicled.

Not surprisingly, southern Italy and North Africa were often comfortable. In Tunisia, where much of the North Africa campaign was fought, temperatures between November and March ranged from the low fifties to the seventies, although the nights could be cold. In April and May, average temperatures ranged, respectively, from fifty-four and sixty-one degrees to seventy-four and seventy-nine degrees. Precipitation was less than half an inch per month. American troops fought in Sicily in the heat of the summer when high temperatures ranged from eighty-two to eighty-seven degrees. With low humidity, though, the climate was generally bearable. The same went for southern Italy, where American soldiers fighting in the fall of 1943 experienced average low temperatures in the fifties and high temperatures in the seventies to low eighties.

What surprised many combat soldiers as they moved north up the Italian boot was the sheer volume of cold, rainy weather. Even though temperatures usually did not drop below freezing, central and northern Italy often received between three and five inches of precipitation per month during the winter. That made for miserable, muddy days for men on the front lines.

Weather in western Germany, where most of the final battles of the war in Europe were fought, was often cold and raw. January and February average temperatures ranged, respectively, from twenty-nine and thirty-one degrees to only thirty-seven and forty-two degrees. Things warmed up slightly in March and April, with low temperatures in the midthirties and high temperatures in the high forties. Precipitation usually averaged one and a half inches per month.

Sometimes the cold weather in Europe meant rain or snow. Other times it meant dry, subzero temperatures. Rain was a fairly common occurrence; 80th Infantry Division rifle company commander Garland Godby loathed it more than snow. "What gets you is that icy drizzle. You just can't get warm unless you go inside. You can't eat properly. You've got a mess kit in your hand and you see bacon with frost." Ken Weaver also hated the rain. He wrote to his mother: "In a war rain doesn't make things clean and green. It makes mud and slop and cold wet clothes. The toilet paper in your pocket disintegrates from being soaked." Sydney Kessler, of the 87th Infantry Division, described the rain: "[It] pinged and ticked off helmets, speckled the face and bare neck with cold. It came on steadily, and a transparent sheathing of ice began to loosen and fall from trees. Wet to the skin, the body shivered without pause; lips trembled; and now the ache of hunger."

Harry Arnold, of the 99th Infantry Division, related what a typical rainy night was like:

> A night of misery was had by all. Men sprawled on the wet ground in the pelting rain, wrapped in raincoats, blankets, shelter halves, ponchos—all presoaked. We felt our way in the rain to the chow line, accepted and ate whatever was put in our kits, and wondered . . . what it was. In the rain the food could not be identified by texture or taste.

On another occasion Arnold and his buddies were called upon to move out in the rain:

> Just as we got . . . to sleep we were ordered to pack up and be ready to go. We packed our equipment and stood in the rain waiting for the order to move out. Finally, already soaked, and still with no order to move out, I climbed back in the hole and went to sleep in four inches of water, using my helmet to keep my head out of the water.

Unfortunately, such instances were all too common. Sometimes the real problem was not so much the rain but the wet aftermath, as Ferdinand Huber, of the 99th Infantry Division, discovered:

> The water was so cold and no one did anything for what seemed forever. You were relatively comfortable in the water as long as you did not move. Movement would only stir the water so that the warm water next to your body was replaced with cold. I had been in the water so long that when I was helped out, I had a tremendous cramp in my thighs . . . and was in a state of complete . . . panic.

Snow and cold were much greater sources of misery for the dog-face than rain. During the extremely frigid winter of 1944–45, American soldiers endured dangerously cold conditions, the likes of which had previously been seen in World War II only on the Eastern Front. The weather during the Battle of the Bulge and the Colmar Pocket tested the very limits of a GI's character.

"I often wonder how in the world we pulled through just the weather itself," Jason Byrd, of the 1st Infantry Division, remarked. This is not an idle musing. The intense cold left a lifelong impression on most combat veterans. Brice Jordan, a glider infantry soldier with the 17th Airborne Division, wrote to his wife about the cold: "I wonder sometimes how I kept from freezing. It was a job trying to keep warm. I always dreaded to see night come, because then we couldn't have a fire." Victor Wade, of the 3d Infantry Division, remembered a freezing night in Italy: "I made the mistake of removing my boots. The next morning my feet were swollen and I had great difficulty getting my boots back on. I don't think I have ever been so cold in all my life as I was on that particular night."

Bert Morphis, of the 1st Infantry Division, wrote:

> I think everyone's most vivid memories are of the numbing cold. Mine certainly are! The cold was enough of an adversary without the Germans. Just staying alive took all of one's ingenuity. I remember being on outpost right in front of the German lines where the choice seemed to be between moving and being shot, or lying perfectly still and freezing to death. Some-

how we survived. The evergreen trees were so thick you could hardly walk between them, and they were all totally covered with snow. If you happened to bump one too hard you found yourself totally buried in snow. Sometimes it snowed so hard that one would almost smother. You had to cover your mouth just to breathe.

Howard Ruppel, of the 517th Parachute Infantry Regiment, described what it was like to walk in such dense snow: "Simple walking becomes a concentrated effort, each step planned . . . feeling for firm footing as one goes along. Plodding over relatively flat terrain is the easy part, then come the gulleys, slippery slopes and ravines."

Henri Atkins, of the 99th Infantry Division, remembered taking extreme measures to get warm:

We made heaters from C ration cans. We would open the can, eat the contents and peel back the lid and fill it with pine needles. We would add a little gasoline and press down the lid to leave a small opening. Then we would light it and huddle around the "stove," which at least warmed our hands and faces. After a few of these "heaters" blew up, Headquarters forbade their use.

Ed Stewart and his 84th Infantry Division buddies devised their own way of attempting to keep warm:

One of the things you do, you lie down on your side and bring your knees up. And you'd be paired with another guy who is facing you so your knees would go into his stomach and your head around his head. You have two people in the womb position taking advantage of that position to preserve body heat and life.

J. R. McIlroy and his 99th Infantry Division buddies used the same method to keep warm. "No matter how dirty or smelly our foxhole buddy was, we snuggled. The body heat probably kept us from freezing." It is easy to see how, under such conditions, men could become as close as brothers.

Radford Carroll, who was in the same unit as Henri Atkins, wrote that the cold sometimes caused strange things to happen. "Snow sifted into my clothing and then melted from my body heat. The water was drawn by capillary action through all the layers of clothing. I could feel the water sloshing in my boots, and I was wet to the skin, yet the outer layer of clothing was icy and dry." Some soldiers found that it was so cold that the water in their canteens froze. To solve the problem, they took to stashing them under their blanket while they slept.

Harry Arnold made the point that the snow and cold were sometimes a mixed blessing:

> If the deep snow was a curse, there also were benefits. Snow has a good dampening effect on blast and fragments, absorbing both like a friendly sponge. It was possible to avoid injury from a shell strike one yard away by lying prone in deep snow. Melted snow provided water when none else was available. The same cold that killed unattended wounded by freezing, and froze weapons, noses, ears, hands and feet, could also mercifully slow blood loss and reduce perception of pain for the wounded.

Perhaps the most poignant and compelling description of what it was actually like to endure inhuman cold came from paratrooper James Simms. He and the rest of the 101st Airborne Division were surrounded at Bastogne and forced to take up positions outside the town. Much of the time, the temperatures were well below zero. By most accounts, it was cold enough to drive a man insane:

> About the most unbearable thing we had to contend with was the cold. Twenty-four hours a day you'd wiggle your toes to try to keep circulation in your feet. We had the unhappy experience of feeling nothing but extreme misery down to pure torture. The nights were the worst, and when it was your turn for guard, that was the worst of all. When you would get up out of the miserable cold hole to stand up in the . . . cold, then that was when suffering began. After you've been up about five min-

utes you start thinking, Well, I've been up about five minutes, only one hour and fifty-five minutes left to go. You try not to dwell on it but your mind comes right back to it. After fifteen or twenty minutes you began to lose your judgment of time and by now you are so cold you wonder how you are going to stand it for another hour and a half. Finally after thinking of everything you can think of to take your mind off the cold, you conclude that an hour has passed. Now, all there is to look forward to is another hour more miserable than the first.

The cold and wet conditions made for major foot problems for American soldiers. Although poor-quality footgear was a major factor in the epidemic of trench foot, or "frozen feet," among American soldiers, even the best footgear could not have stood up to the conditions that soldiers sometimes faced. Standing in knee-deep snow or sloshing through cold water for weeks on end eventually have an extremely deleterious effect on a man's feet. One combat engineer platoon leader wrote home that after just a week on the line, his unit had suffered "only two battle casualties . . . but fourteen trench foot casualties."

The problem was that extreme cold or wet conditions would slowly cut off circulation, causing a soldier's feet to die a slow death unless he could get them dry and warm, a virtual impossibility on the front lines. Bart Hagerman, of the 17th Airborne Division, described men with frozen feet: "Their feet were just as black as coal . . . maybe a gun-steel blue if you want to put it that way. And in the first stages, they swell quite a bit, but then after that, when they start turning blue and everything, they get almost flat. It kind of turns your stomach. It was a bad sight."

Jim Foster remembered what happened to the worst cases: "If you didn't get circulation back in X number of days . . . then there was a good possibility that gangrene was setting in. If you went another three or four days . . . they amputated feet." Kenny Dallas, of the 26th Infantry Division, got trench foot while fighting in the bitter Alsace campaign in late 1944. "Trench foot is NOT athlete's foot. Trench foot is like frozen feet—your feet swell up and sometimes gangrene sets in. I almost had it in my left foot. I came near losing it."

Edward Laughlin, of the 82d Airborne Division, also had a bad case of trench foot:

> My feet had been continually wet and cold all day long . . . and my boots froze each night. My big toe on each foot turned a very deep purple—almost black—and the examining doctor told me that he might have to amputate them. Great thick chunks of skin kept falling and peeling off them. Many soldiers had to have toes . . . amputated.

The problems were just as acute in the surprisingly uncomfortable Italian winters. Dan Ray, of the 36th Infantry Division, wrote:

> My feet were frozen and I could not even feel them. They carried me back to an aid station and medics thawed my feet out by putting them in a tub of ice water and gradually warming the water up. They massaged them all the time while this was going on, and even though I lost the skin off the bottom of my feet and they would bleed a lot when I would do too much walking, I finally got them toughened up after five or six years.

Evan Voss, also of the 36th Division, suffered permanent damage in the bitter fighting at Mount Cairo. "Many of our men came off that mountain with feet that were black with trench foot. Some were so bad, their feet busted their boots open. I, for one, had no feeling in my toes for a year. Even today, I have no nails on my toes."

Dysentery could also be a problem for combat troops. Often they had to drink any water or eat any food they could find. Add to that the fact that they were constantly moving and pushing themselves to extreme levels of fatigue, and it is easy to see how dysentery became a problem.

Robert Seabrook, of the 6th Cavalry Regiment, explained how he got his case of the "GIs." "We had been warned not to drink any French water that came out of the hydrants unless it had been purified first. Forgetting this, I drank water from the hydrant in the house we were staying in. I found out the hard way why we were not to drink the water, because I had diarrhea for a week."

Henri Atkins described the misery of dysentery:

All of us had at least one bout. Picture the sufferer when a bout strikes in the middle of the night. The soldier has to climb out of his sleeping bag, then out of his foxhole in the bitter cold. He then must walk into no man's land, hoping that none of our guards shoot him first and ask questions later. Then down go his pants. Now he is really freezing. Finally he creeps back into his sleeping bag and settles into a fitful sleep only to repeat the process an hour later.

Bob Conroy, of the 75th Infantry Division, remembered a particularly bad case of dysentery:

A Boston guy, McCarthy, was suffering from both dysentery and upset stomach and he was throwing up—he was working both ends and he got awfully weak. And on one [artillery] attack . . . he passed out right in the middle of the attack. His guys took him over to a haystack, pulled it apart, put him in it, packed him down to keep him from freezing, finished off the attack and came back and got him later on.

Most cases of dysentery were not that severe. The only option was to wait it out and hope it would eventually go away.

One disease that reared its ugly head was malaria. Although the disease is generally associated with the Pacific theater, it did occur among troops in Italy, particularly Sicily, during the summer. Charles Murphy, who commanded an engineer company in the 1st Infantry Division, contracted a case.

We ran out of Atabrine [a malaria-fighting drug] and we were having trouble getting supplies and half my company came down with malaria. I got malaria. I have no idea how I left Sicily. I was yellow as a Chinese. I don't remember anything else until I woke up in . . . Algiers, in the hospital. I was there about two months, I guess. I got down to 123 pounds and my normal weight at that time was 185, so you can see I was a walking skeleton. Eyes yellow. Fingernails purple. Have you ever seen anybody with malaria? It ain't pretty.

Lice, body-clinging vermin that have plagued soldiers for time immemorial, did not seem to be a major problem in Europe. Even so, James Graff, of the 35th Infantry Division, remembered a comrade who was afflicted with the pests:

> Pitcock complained of a crawling sensation around his body. He took off his shirt and then his long underwear top and it literally crawled across the table. It was full of body lice. Soon we were all making a similar inspection . . . but so far I was escaping this pest so despised by soldiers of all wars.

Seasickness was a common malady for all those who came ashore in the European theater invasions. Francis Lambert, who came ashore at Normandy on D day with the 4th Infantry Division, remembered his awful experiences:

> Then misery took over. Everyone got sick. The vomit bags filled. It was impossible to empty them overboard into tricky winds. The chemically impregnated fatigues chafed our necks and wrists. Grunts and groans preempted conversation. Our officers tried to boost morale, but gave up. Each bore the misery in his own way.

Perhaps the best description of the cumulative effects of winter conditions and all its common maladies on the combat soldier comes from Bob Wandesforde, also of the 4th Division:

> I hadn't washed or shaved for weeks. Everything I wore or carried was mud brown. I had trench foot, my hands and face were black, my fingertips and lips were split and raw. While moving up one night I had walked in my sleep and fallen in a cement drainage ditch leaving dried blood and scabs on my face. I had eaten almost nothing but K rations and C rations in my filthy black canteen cup . . . and had slept in bombed-out

houses or in the snow for over a month. But I didn't look any worse than the rest of my outfit and I considered myself lucky to be alive.

Mud, always available in rich, glutinous quantities in France and Italy, tested the patience and resolve of many American combat men. Wrote Kenny Dallas, "Mud was in everything—in your food, in your rifle, in your clothing and in your thoughts and hopes." Gene Tippins, of the 80th Infantry Division, agreed. "You ate in mud, slept in mud, dug foxholes filled with mud, and sometimes you died in the mud." Even tanker Eugene Thibideau, of the 1st Armored Division in Italy, had trouble with mud: "Our feet were constantly wet from mud up to our ankles."

Lawrence Nickell, a mortarman with the 5th Infantry Division, remembered how difficult mud made it to carry the mortars:

> The going, with the heavy loads we were bearing, was slow and tiresome as our feet sank ankle deep in the mud and the thick tenacious mud stuck to our feet, adding extra pounds to the burden we already carried. A company of tanks was supporting the battalion; a tank would occasionally bog down and others would have to pull it out.

The extreme darkness of the combat zone could also be a nuisance. Harry Arnold remembered one occasion when his outfit attempted to move during the night:

> On through the dark we stumbled and cursed, alternately running to catch up, or standing still waiting for the column to move on ahead—the classic accordian effect that is imposed on a column whose lead elements are uncertain and having to pick their way. In the slippery dark we were constantly falling down. Those who fell on their backs flailed about like overturned beetles, their packs and equipment resisting all attempts to be turned upright.

Justin Gray described a night mission with the 3d Ranger Battalion in Italy:

It was pitch black. We moved in two columns, one on each side of the road, the men about twenty yards apart. You couldn't really see the man in front of you. But you could feel him out. You knew that there were units bivouacked on either side of the road, but there was no sign of life—just a desolate stretch of road ending in darkness.

Dark nights held other dangers, as 71st Infantry Division veteran William Meissner recalled:

On the war front there were no lights at all. None. The only possible source of light might be from an occasionally burning building. Men who smoked, and there were a lot of them with the free cigarettes included in the rations, learned to light their smokes under their jackets . . . so that even the flame from the match could not be seen. They learned to cup their hands around the glowing tip of the smoke. It had been discovered that even the glow from a cigarette could bring in enemy fire.

One unusual surrounding that would have a great effect on the dogfaces was the hedgerows in Normandy. It is well known that the ancient hedgerows greatly hindered the progress of Allied troops in the Battle of Normandy. What is more, they caused innumerable casualties. Lawrence Nickell described a hedgerow:

They were stone walls erected hundreds of years ago as the rocky fields of Normandy were cleared for cultivation. Over the years they had become overgrown with vines, trees had grown up on them and they were often three feet or more in thickness and six feet or more high. The Germans dug deep, standing-depth foxholes behind the hedgerows and punched holes in the base of the hedgerow to permit a good field of fire for the machine guns they relied on so heavily.

Charles Murphy's men found the hedgerows to be formidable:

You have a hillock of earth pushed together that may be four to six feet tall, and a hedge going up the sides and on top of it.

Very narrow roads between. We were kept busy knocking holes in these hedgerows, and the Germans would just move one hedgerow back. Then you had to make another attack.

Colin McLaurin, of the 29th Infantry Division, remembered that "most of the hedgrows had small trees, bushes, briars and vines growing out of them, and frequently we had to hack, kick, push and squirm our way through." Hedgerows were unquestionably a boon to German defenders and a death trap for American soldiers. The average GI despised them.

Sometimes, though, nature was in the eye of the beholder. In the middle of snow and bitter cold, 106th Infantry Division rifleman Jack Brugh actually took time out to notice the aesthetic beauty of his surroundings:

> I vividly recall the beauty of the [Ardennes] forest, especially where no trucks or equipment had plowed it up. As I looked out over the fir trees, it reminded me of a Christmas card scene with icicles two feet long and snow-covered trees. The snow was about eight inches deep, and it was cloudy and foggy with snow continuing very lightly.

Most combat soldiers did not take time out to notice their surroundings. One soldier wrote that "under combat conditions we are not in the least concerned with the blending of the trees, the sky, the brooks, and gently rolling hills into a little patch of Beauty." All combat soldiers would probably have agreed with Howard Ruppel's assertion:

> Fresh snow-covered pine forests and meadows unblemished by man or beast may be a picturesque scene to look at, but not to live in, especially when there is no escape and you are compelled to live in the stuff day and night suffering from cold wet feet from wet boots and no dry place to sit, squat, kneel or prop the firearm.

Dealing with the harshness of nature was bad enough, but combat soldiers in Europe also had to deal with an ingenious and tenacious enemy. Digging foxholes often meant the difference between life and death in a combat zone. Huddling in a hole underground offered a soldier at least some measure of protection against the flying steel that sought to kill and maim him.

Foxholes were usually anything but deluxe, as Evan Voss explained. "Our two-man holes were slit-trenches and . . . the holes were so small, when we got a couple hours to sleep, we had to fold our bodies together to lie down."

Digging the holes was hard work, and soldiers were often exhausted even before they set out to dig. Zane Schlemmer, of the 82d Airborne Division, remembered one such instance on Christmas Day 1944:

> Weary and worn, alternately sweating and freezing, we continued to dig and camouflauge our holes and set up our weapons . . . before the attack would surely come. Snow began to fall, masking our lines, and in our canteens the water froze solid. Each of us, when finished, sought the shelter of our foxholes for the warmth and protection afforded.

Radford Carroll related an incident in which he and his buddies dug for pure self-preservation under a brutal artillery barrage:

> Everyone began to dig a sheltering hole in the ground wherever they were. The digging was done while lying flat on the ground and hacking and scraping with anything available. First a hole big enough for the head, then enlarge and deepen for the shoulders. There was nothing like the power of those exploding shells to encourage digging energy. When the shelling slacked off . . . everyone still alive was in a gravelike hole.

At times excessive cold made it nearly impossible to dig holes, as Bert Morphis recalled:

> It was bitterly cold and the ground was covered with two to three feet of snow. The ground was frozen so deeply and so hard it was almost impossible to penetrate. So we carried quar-

ter pound blocks of TNT with detonators to loosen the frozen crust. With a pickax we would dig a small hole to accommodate the TNT, set it off and then proceed to dig our foxhole. Our practice was to dig a hole just deep enough to work in, cut logs to provide cover, cover the logs with dirt, then crawl inside and finish digging the hole to size. Frequently we would no sooner finish a shelter than we would move and leave it. I don't recall ever being so tired!

Of course some holes were better than others. Franklin Bland, of the 277th Combat Engineers, wrote to his family about the hole that he and his buddies inhabited:

Our foxhole holds four men—it is a large hole dug in the ground and covered over with boards, dirt and snow. The floor of it is covered very thick with straw and we have a small stove from a German home in one end of it. At the other end we have a trench to stand watch in and we have plenty of blankets to hang over the opening to keep the cold and snow out. When we get inside and get a good fire going you would be surprised how warm it is.

Far more often for men constantly on the move, the holes were as William Maher described them in a letter to his parents: "These damn holes are infested with rats and vermin of every kind."

Foxholes could not protect men from one of the most frightening weapons of modern war—mines. The Germans made extensive use of mines, primarily as a defensive weapon against American soldiers. *Yank* correspondent Mack Morriss saw evidence of this in the Huertgen Forest. "In one break there was a . . . mine every eight paces for three miles; in another over 500 mines in the narrow break. One stretch of road held 300 . . . mines, each one with a pull device, in addition to the normal pressure detonator." Part of what made a mine so frightening was that it could strike anytime and anywhere. You only had to step on one, and in an instant you were killed or maimed for life.

One of the primary tasks of the combat engineers was to find and clear mines. Any typical infantryman would not have wanted to exchange places with his combat engineer buddy when it came time for mine-clearing detail. Jason Byrd explained the process: "The nerve racking part is when you're taking them up because you take a bayonet and you're probing the ground and you finally find one, you try to find the edge of it, dig around it, and . . . you take all the dirt off." Once a soldier did that, he could then disarm the mine. However, as Byrd explained, a man still had to be careful of another peril. "Sometimes the Germans would lay a mine and booby-trap it too and if you pulled the mine out . . . maybe the mine next to it was hooked onto this one and then you'd set that one off."

J. D. Jones, an engineer officer with the 3d Infantry Division, explained the process that he and his men went through in North Africa and Italy:

> I worked with cleaning up mine fields. That would make you sweat a little bit down the back, I tell you. We'd find a handle on [the mine], and then put up a stick, run a piece of rope with a bent nail and put that hook up around the handle, get off a ways, and pull it. And of course it would blow.

A soldier did not necessarily have to be in the engineers to get drafted into mine detail, as rifleman James Graff found out. The mines he disarmed were "wooden boxes the size of a shoe box. All parts were made of wood and plastic. Mine detectors were not much good. You could only find [the mines] by probing with a trench knife, bayonet or pitchfork." Graff was probably describing the German schuh mine, which was primarily designed not to kill a man but instead blow off his foot.

Another feared German mine was the so-called "Bouncing Betty," which was also encased in wood to avoid metal-activated U.S. mine detectors. Jason Byrd encountered these awful weapons: "It had three prongs. You step on any one of those prongs, this little thing would go up in the air and it had about six hundred beebees. You had to run and fall because . . . it'd tear you to pieces." Byrd neglected to add that the Bouncing Betty was specifically designed not to explode until it was waist high so that it could destroy a man's reproductive organs.

The Germans were also skilled at setting booby traps, another classic form of defensive warfare. During the cold Vosges campaign in France, Victor Wade and his comrades holed up in a farmhouse, with tragic results:

> All of a sudden there was a tremendous explosion, and I was blown from the bed up to the ceiling. We ran into the kitchen and found the room totally destroyed. Three men in that room were killed outright. We then heard screaming from the attached barn area. We ran there and started digging . . . for survivors. We found Lieutenant Orluck, who was wounded. He said he was blinded by the explosion. The explosion was caused when one of the men in the squad picked up this black wooden box and brought it into the kitchen and tried to open it. It contained 20 lbs. of TNT. That day we lost six men, and my lieutenant was . . . blinded because one man was curious about that wooden box.

Henri Atkins underscored the need to watch for anything unusual. "The Germans were extremely tricky at making disguised booby traps. Things that looked appealing were, in fact, deadly. Open a box and you were likely to have a hand blown off or a face full of steel shards." Jason Byrd claimed that the Germans would even booby-trap their own dead. Accordingly, caution was the watchword. "Anything that had any value to it, we were told not to touch it until you examined it real good and not pull at it."

Booby traps were particularly common in Italy during the German retreat in the summer of 1944 as German forces attempted to slow the Allied advance. Michael Stubinski, of the 36th Infantry Division, remembered the tense atmosphere that the booby traps caused for soldiers and civilians alike. "Enter a house, turn on the [light] switch and the whole room would blow up. Walk in the door and you set off an explosion. Whole families were killed. People begged us to check their houses out. We did but the damage was already done." The Germans must have realized that many or most victims of their booby traps would be unsuspecting civilians, and it is legitimate to wonder whether they booby-trapped for purely military reasons or perhaps for vengeance against Italians with Allied sympathies.

One aspect of the combat soldier's existence that has been given little or no attention by historians is the issue of bodily functions. When a soldier went into combat, the natural needs and functions of his body did not cease. Just as he needed to eat, he also needed to dispose of bodily waste.

On the front lines this could be a tricky and dangerous process. Milton Landry, of the 36th Infantry Division, was wounded while relieving himself. His recounting of the incident describes how many soldiers took care of bodily functions:

> I felt mother nature informing me that I needed to take immediate steps to relieve myself. Even on the battlefield these things happen. You don't read much about it in books, but it does happen. First I borrowed an entrenching shovel from one of the men, then looked for a secluded nook where I could have some privacy. I soon found what I thought was the perfect place behind a . . . wall. To get into proper position I first dug a nice hole with my shovel, took off my combat jacket, unstrapped my combat trousers, then lowered my long handle drawers to half mast and the same for my undershorts. After all this I was really ready and I immediately assumed the proper position and did what comes naturally. I then retrieved the GI issue toilet paper from inside my helmet and completed the task. Just as I stood up . . . over the wall came an assault grenade compliments of a German soldier who saw or heard me. The grenade exploded as it hit my arm.

Radford Carroll handled the delicate task in the following manner:

> Just after dark I would pop out of the foxhole and take a few steps, dig a hole in the snow and start removing layers of clothing. Since the snow was about ankle deep, a squat not only brought my bare rear level with the snow, but if any wind was

blowing the snow drifted into the dropped drawers. It was especially annoying if the Germans decided to shell again just at that time. When a shell comes down, you lay down, no matter when or what. Then things did get chilly because snow got scooped up in my underwear. I could do all this faster than you would think. Urine was much more easily disposed of. I kept a cardboard tube [that the bazooka rockets were shipped in] that could be used as a urinal. It was simply emptied whenever there was a lull in the shelling.

Evan Voss recalled that, in the mountains of Italy, "when nature called, we did it in our helmets and sat it outside the hole until dark." At Anzio it was usually dangerous for a soldier to get out of his hole at any time of the day. Thus, urinating or defecating could be deadly. "We learned to tend to that matter without getting out of the hole," J. D. Jones said. He and his men would defecate in empty K ration boxes and then "toss that thing out of the hole and when it gets dark you cover it up. It smells a little bad, but it beats getting shot."

Donald MacDonald and his 45th Infantry Division also fought at Anzio. He related the routine of tending to bodily functions. "If caught short by nature in daylight, squat over an empty K ration box, keep your head down and proceed, throw not-so-empty K ration box as far as you can."

American soldiers were fortunate in that their combat rations were specifically designed to minimize bodily excretions. Also, they were amply supplied with toilet paper. Max Kocour, of the 90th Infantry Division, recognized these facts in his war memoir. "God bless the USA paper industry. We never ran out; also K rations kept such body excretions to a bare minimum. The Germans did not seem to have much . . . paper . . . and would sometimes clean themselves with the tail flap of their underwear."

In his everyday existence, the American combat soldier in Europe often dealt with civilians, the majority of whom were from friendly countries that he was attempting to liberate. Frontline troops rubbed shoulders with French, Italians, Belgians, Dutch, Luxembourgers, and Germans in large numbers. In the most general sense, American combat soldiers were well behaved and enjoyed friendly relations with civilians, even Germans. This does not mean, however, that their relations with civilians were without any tension. In North Africa it was not uncommon for Arabs to spy for the side that paid them the most. Steven Sally and his 1st Infantry Division comrades caught one such group of Arabs. "We lined them up and tied them all up one evening. We made them dig their graves. We lined them up and shot them."

In Alsace-Lorraine, an area with mixed German-French loyalties, Lawrence Nickell's outfit caught a civilian who was actively helping the Germans. "We were baffled by relatively accurate fire falling in an area not observable by the enemy. A few nights later a civilian was detected signaling the Germans with a flashlight and . . . summarily executed." Clearly, when it came to self-preservation, American soldiers were willing to deal harshly with civilians. Incidents such as these, though, were rare.

Most unsavory relations were of a more minor nature. In France there were some bad feelings stemming from Allied bombing but not nearly as much as there could have been. After all, Allied air forces killed thousands of French civilians and destroyed the country's railroads and bridges. The average Frenchman understood, though, that the bombing had been necessary for his liberation.

On an everyday basis, tension often came from cultural differences, such as one that 12th Armored Division veteran Gene Curry observed in France: "One day I saw two men and a woman talking next to a pile of . . . manure. All at once one of the men turned around and relieved himself. I later found out that was common in France." This French habit, viewed as quirky by Americans, was something that most GIs could not understand. It has even been suggested that American soldiers felt more in common with their German enemy than their French allies.

Don Mackerer explained the phenomenon:

At that time, France was a lot less sophisticated than it is now so far as plumbing and niceties and the standard of living. When we . . . went through France, their farmlands and rural areas were pretty crude in many respects but when we went into

Germany the standard of living was noticeably higher. The plumbing was better. They had better radios. They had furniture. And the American soldier could relate to the German way of living much better than he could the French. I remember some of the soldiers . . . saying, "What are we fighting these guys for? They're more like us than the Frogs." They looked upon the French . . . as being kind of backward and sloppy.

Although that attitude did exist among some combat troops, it has been greatly overblown in the postwar era, when Franco-American relations have often been tense and the French have been arbitrarily (and unfairly) labeled in popular American culture as rude. Most problems surfaced with French people who associated with Germans or those who were pro-German. Jason Byrd recalled GIs beating French women:

> We knew they'd been fraternizing with the Germans or married to the Germans. I never did but some of the guys would walk up and just backhand them because we'd capture some of the Germans . . . and these French girls would grab them and say "don't take them." They were afraid we were going to take them off and shoot them.

Harley Reynolds, also a member of the 1st Infantry Division, wrote that he and his buddies found some collaborators who, on D day, committed suicide rather than submit to American control. "They were in formal dress. He in long tails, she in a black gown and the girl in a white gown. The midsection of all three had been blown away. They had simply stood embracing themselves about a German potato masher [grenade]."

As often as not, what small amount of combat soldier acrimony that existed was stirred up by German civilians. Edgar Wilson, an artillery forward observer in the 80th Infantry Division, related an instance in which a German civilian scolded him for shelling her property:

> She said she was a cousin of the King of England and that there was no earthly reason for us to damage the roof and the

stained glass windows on her castle; furthermore that there were no German troops in the Castle and had been none. Nevertheless we found plenty of evidence that the Castle had been their headquarters: uniforms, weapons, ammunition, fresh rations. So I thought, the King be damned! Our mission was accomplished.

Gene Curry and his buddies once took a stove from a German home, much to the consternation of the German woman who lived there. He summed up the attitude of most combat soldiers. "That's war! If it weren't for people like her, I could have been in Seattle having a ball."

Lawrence Nickell and his comrades were not terribly concerned with German sensibilities:

> I suspect there are a number of German civilians who remember us with some degree of hostility. Whenever we could we billeted in homes and it must have been a shock for a German housewife to find her spotless featherbeds and comforters soiled beyond belief when we left.

Charles Murphy explained the process by which Americans would take over a town:

> The way we did it is I had complete command of the town. I would just talk to the burgomeister and tell him what I wanted, and there would be an officer or enlisted man to see that it got done. Once we were in Germany we didn't hesitate to kick people out of towns. In Aachen we just kicked them out of their apartments and put my men in decent living conditions.

Radford Carroll asserted that black troops especially frightened German civilians:

> When we entered a town some of the civilians began to relax at once, since outside the uniform we could have been

hometown boys. But when the negro platoon came in there were gasps of panic, the women started to cry, the men turned white, and the children ran. The negro troops got a big kick out of that. In contrast to the rest of us they kept their bayonets on their rifles to enhance the fright power.

Most of the time, relations with civilians were pleasant, no matter what the country. Max Kocour summed up well the way most Americans were treated in Normandy. "Here we were, tearing up their country—and they loved us. Marvelous people." William Meissner wrote that "the French liked and respected us as liberators who had driven out their hated 'bosch' after 4 or more years of occupation." John Worthman, a medic in the 4th Infantry Division, remembered the joyous entry into Paris. "The people cheered and laughed and cried and wanted to embrace us, give us a drink, feed us newly ripe tomatoes . . . and just try to believe that we were really there and the Germans gone. I kissed babies, children, young women, old women, and women in between."

Fraternization with French women was not uncommon, as 4th Infantry Division veteran Alton Pearson recalled. "If these girls had been German soldiers, we would all have been dead because there was one or two in practically every pup tent. You could hear them laughing all night long." Robert Garcia, of the 29th Infantry Division, struck up a warm friendship with a French couple. "There was a platter of eggs, potatoes and sausage waiting for me. All the time the French couple were bustling about as if they were entertaining nobility." Eventually he had to leave. "But not before thanking the French people profusely and leaving them a good supply of cigarettes, with much embracing and handshaking."

The friendly feelings also extended into Belgium. Roger Garland, of the 9th Infantry Division, wrote to his wife that "the townspeople strewed the streets with flowers, served us wine with waffles, cake and plenty of fruit. Every fellow in my company received a large piece of cherry pie." Harry Arnold wrote that "the Belgians were . . . demonstrative, cheering, waving, and giving the victory sign, and presenting us with bread, fruit, wine. Their obvious appreciation of our presence did much for our mood."

Americans were welcomed so enthusiastically because they generally treated people well. During the Battle of the Bulge, 76th Infantry Division medic Walter Mietus came across a Belgian woman whose baby was suffering from malnutrition. "She showed me the baby. It had sores on its face. In the lining of my field jacket I was carrying an orange, which I had been saving for about three weeks. I gave it to the lady. I never knew an orange could be so greatly appreciated."

Jeffie Duty, of the 106th Infantry Division, saw an old man who had no shoes in the midst of the freezing winter:

> This old fellow was walking around. The sole of his foot was on the ground and it was cold. I had an extra pair of combat boots in my duffle bag. I went back across the road to this old fellow and handed him these boots so he could have something on his feet. As I think about it, I can get emotional. The old fellow just stood there with tears running . . . down his cheeks.

During the bitter fighting at Aachen, Mack Morriss found infantrymen who were softhearted and helped German civilians evacuate their homes. "Some old lady 80 years old will remember that she left her kerchief, and of course she'll want to go back and get it. Or some little girl about six will have run off without her coat and her mother will want to go back to the house and get it. . . ." One finds it difficult to imagine SS troops being concerned with the needs of a helpless old woman or a coatless little girl.

In Italy, Americans were generally held in high esteem, which made relations with Italians good overall. Everywhere they went, combat soldiers were greeted as liberators. Rome was especially jubilant in the way it greeted American soldiers. Warren Taney, of the 36th Infantry Division, recorded in his diary that "people were glad to see us. They lined the streets for miles, waving and cheering us. They were kissing each other, some were throwing flowers at us. We were all amazed at the beautiful buildings and girls."

R. K. Doughty, also a T-patcher, wrote: "It would be difficult to describe the utter joy of the populace as they surged along on all sides of us thrusting wine and flowers into the hands of dog-tired troops."

Dan Ray recalled that, as his unit traveled through the city, "girls swarmed all over the vehicles, hugging, kissing and giving us drinks of all description. They had flowers for the occasion." Earl Reitan and his 3d Infantry Division buddies would see starving Italian children and give them food from their mess line.

Lathrop Mitchell, a medic in the 92d Infantry Division, admired the partisans whom his unit encountered:

> They are a rough, young-looking bunch of men, in a ragtag of various uniforms, German, Italian, American, and British. They are friendly to us, but wary. Odd that most of the underground in the German-occupied countries were Communists. The only ones with much discipline and guts. They help us through mine fields and are our Allies.

The combination of the general ruthlessness of the Germans and the general benevolence of the Americans made for good relations between Americans and European civilians. Whereas the Germans had come as conquerors, the Americans came as liberators. Thus, it is not in the least bit surprising that the average GI got along well with civilians.

Civilians were one of the more pleasant aspects of a combat soldier's life. The most unpleasant was the combat zone itself. The battlefield was a horror-filled cauldron of evil sights and smells. It was insane, arbitrary, violent, and crude. For most American combat soldiers, it was a radical departure from everything they had previously known. Mel Cotton, a medic in the 91st Infantry Division in Italy, wrote that "nothing could ever be more cruel than to ask any outsider or uninitiated human being to view an active battlefield."

Lawrence Nickell remembered well the sobering moment that he and his green comrades saw their first dead Americans:

> We were in high spirits until we saw the dead American soldiers and smelled the unique stench of decaying human flesh. Perhaps the most surprising thing was the fact that so many of the dead had turned black in the process of decay; not just the livor mortis of blood seeking a dependent position after death, which is purple discoloration, but a definite black color. Laugh-

ing and lighthearted joking came to a screeching halt. At that point we realized that war was something besides rationing, headlines and brass bands.

Gene Tippins saw dead Americans being trucked to the rear while his unit moved toward the front. "Sad to say it but the bodies would be lying one on top of another, face down, and as many as the trucks would hold. Always the stench of death would follow down the road after a load of bodies went by."

After coming ashore in Normandy six days after D day, Jack Thacker's 30th Infantry Division was initially put to work burying dead bodies. He recalled:

Bodies of both Americans and Germans were scattered over the landscape as far as the eye could see. We were required to wear gas masks due to the sickening sharp, sweet smell of decaying flesh. I thought at first it would become easier with each body picked up, but it didn't. As my partner and I picked up a body, it felt like a rubber bag half full of water. I seldom could let myself look at a face. It was a brutal revelation.

Cleaning up the battlefield was one thing; participating in the battle another. Bob Kay, of the 4th Infantry Division, never forgot the sounds of the combat zone:

I am sure that the earliest and most impressionable sounds of war were the distant "thump and rumble" of artillery and the not to be forgotten distinctive "rrrrip" of German machine pistols. And it did not take long for every man to seek cover as the deadly sound and high whine of a German 88 passed over or air-burst ahead in a puff of gray-white smoke.

Ed Laughlin remembered finding dead bodies during the Battle of the Bulge:

As the snow melted during the day, many . . . dead . . . GIs and Germans were exposed, scattered among the wrecked tanks, half-tracks, jeeps, abandoned artillery, and there was even a dead GI evidently blown off his bulldozer which had plowed up a land mine. When it warmed up during the day his body had that terrible sweet-sickening smell of rotting flesh. Life was cheap, short, brutal.

William Warde, of the 42d Infantry Division, saw the carnage that U.S. artillery and airpower could cause:

> For most of a day, heavy American artillery fire and fighter-bombers pounded an area ahead of us. The next day we passed through a German artillery column that had been caught on the road. Dead and wounded German soldiers littered the road. Many burned bodies on trucks only had stumps remaining with bones protruding from [what] once had been arms and legs.

Medic George Boocks came ashore late on D day with the 5th Engineer Special Brigade and was greeted by grisly sights:

> The dead, some twisted in oddly grotesque positions, still lay as they had fallen. Fire-blackened remains of tanks, and battered hulls of landing craft were ugly reminders of the battle . . . continuing to rage over the crest of the hill. Among the regular issued equipment lay small personal items, having little meaning . . . other than [to] the men to whom they had belonged; a picture of a loved one, a battered pipe, a broken harmonica. Pathetic reminders of happier days.

Another medic, John Worthman, treated wounded amid the carnage. "The dead and dying . . . behind all the hedgerows were an appalling sight. So was the aroma. The smells became worse, the sights of mutilation and death more terrible, but strangely, we began to live with them and accept them." John Meier wrote to his parents of the sights he witnessed. "I have seen the chaos and destruction in all the principal cities where blood has washed the stones of every street. There is hardly a place that has not felt the onslaught and . . . rolling terror of war." Michael Stubinski noticed that "a dead

German would always look white in the face; an American looked tan. Dead Italian women would be blown up twice their size, the same as dead German horses with their legs standing straight up and lying on their backs."

Bert Morphis recalled the effect the cold had on dead bodies. "Most were frozen in such grotesque positions, it was difficult to keep them on a stretcher. They had frozen stiff in the exact positions in which they had died." Sometimes the only way to move them was to break their limbs with a two-by-four board.

Radford Carroll made a grisly mistake one day while searching around a knocked-out U.S. tank. "I knew better than to look inside, but there was some debris around the tank including a combat boot. I kicked the boot aside, only to discover that there was a foot still inside it. I didn't kick any more boots after that."

Perhaps the most disturbing sight was one that Jason Byrd witnessed. He saw an infant trying to nurse on the breast of its dead mother sprawled in the street. "Now that touches you. There's nothing you can do. You just walk by hard-hearted. That still comes back to my mind quite a bit."

The battlefield was by no means the sanitized, organized, rational place often portrayed in movies or described in history books. The front line was not a "field of honor" on which generals executed flanking maneuvers and troops cheered their way to victory. The brutal reality was that the battlefield was a dirty, cruel, ruthless world filled with horror and tragedy. No one who was part of it could ever forget it.

Americans were notorious souvenir hunters. The twisted world of combat offered men unique opportunities for first dibs on everything from weapons to belt buckles. Robert Russell, of the 84th Infantry Division, remembered seeing veteran soldiers looting a dead German for souvenirs. "First thing somebody done . . . was to kick him over with their foot and look and see if he had any rings on. And somebody . . . cut his finger off and got the ring. It surprised me. I wouldn't have thought about doing things like that." Vic Ciffichiello, of the 8th Armored Division, recalled a macabre incident in which he and some other men found a dead British soldier. "On a rafter was a hand. That was all that was left of that soldier. And I can remember someone within the group wanting to take it as a souvenir. How gruesome can you get? To this day, I can see that hand."

Combat soldiers often shared dark humor when it came to possession of souvenirs. Frank Miller, of the 36th Infantry Division, wrote that his captain snatched a camera off a dead German officer. Miller wanted the camera badly and let his commanding officer know about it. "[My captain] finally said, 'Tell you what. When I get killed or wounded, you can have it.' The only trouble with that idea was, when he got killed, I wasn't looking for a camera. I was trying to save my hide." The men in James Simms's outfit kidded one enthusiastic looter. "They said he could shoot a German and loot him before he hit the ground."

Things were not always that stark, though. Don Loth, of the 12th Armored Division, claimed: "Our division helped redistribute possessions of both the Frenchmen and the Germans. Cars, guitars, accordians, saxophones and jewelry were appropriated, moved on to the next city and discarded." William Meissner's outfit once found an enormous cellar stashed with treasures from fine wine to gourmet food.

Combat soldiers, particularly infantrymen, found it difficult to hang on to souvenirs. There were two main reasons for this. The first was that, because the combat troops were in close contact with German soldiers, most of the men did not want to be captured with any German equipment. Gene Curry explained: "I didn't have a lot of German souvenirs, as you didn't want to be captured by the enemy with any of their stuff on you. They might think the same as we did, that you had shot or killed one of their buddies to get it." The other and more overarching reason was that most combat soldiers could not carry the extra weight of a souvenir. It simply was not worth it to lug a camera or a pair of binoculars everywhere you went.

Harry Arnold summed up the souvenir phenomenon by recounting his and a buddy's attempt to round up some souvenirs and send them home:

> Emerson and I braved falling snow and shells to collect German helmets, daggers, rifles and such. After lugging the extra weight for days and tagging each item as directed, not one item

reached my home. All was swallowed up by the heroic minions to our rear. A sad fact: A man with a house full of war souvenirs is not an infantryman—he can lug only so much. Noncombat personnel are the most successful collectors of war trophies other than death, dismemberment, and injury.

Another war trophy that was no less sought after but far more usable to combat troops was alcohol. In Europe alcohol was fairly accessible. A dogface did not have to look too hard to find wine or liquor. Henri Atkins asserted that "with so many towns and villages being liberated after the invasion, the GIs also 'liberated' the wine cellars. The 'natives '. . . passed bottles of wine and other spirits on to the troops." Joseph Martin, of the 3d Infantry Division, recalled that "we would find things like a carload of brandy. It was so sweet and it was so good." A man did not have to worry about lugging wine bottles around the front lines. He and his buddies could drink a bottle's contents on the spot.

Alcohol could also be an escape from the realities of combat, as 36th Infantry Division veteran Del Kendall claimed. One of the men in his outfit traded for some alcohol:

> Quickly canteen cups rattled out as each man mixed his own drink. A little syrup, a little alky and some water. The men drank in hearty gulps. The men drank and kidded each other, their faces now flushed and more alive, that foxhole pallor, gone for now at least, a reprieve from that killing ground, called San Pietro.

There were unwelcome consequences, though, as Harvey Reves, in the same division as Kendall, found out when he accepted wine from an Italian couple:

> It tasted good at the time and after a few swigs things were looking very rosy; my pack and the little I was carrying became weightless. I was feeling good. This was a great war! But that soon wore off and later we stopped for a break and I started to eat a can of pork loaf from my K rations. Oooh, that was all it

took. I think I vomited up everything I had ever eaten in my life. Boy, what a lesson.

William Warde's experience with alcohol paralleled that of Reves:

I soon found that my physical system was not prepared for the champagne we drank like water. To make matters worse, we encountered a firefight in the next valley with me having the worst stomach cramps in my life. Would you believe that I had to drop my pants or explode while we were receiving fire from all around us. Thanks to our medic, I was able to dry out by spending the night in a captured German vehicle.

At times alcohol use could have tragic consequences. Ed Laughlin wrote that one day he came across two soldiers in his outfit, nicknamed Mutt and Jeff, who appeared to be very drunk:

They offered me a drink—they were mixing it in their canteen cups. I took one gulp and that was enough for me! I choked and coughed and Mutt and Jeff were hysterical at my reaction and discomfort. I told them they better not drink any more of that stuff . . . and went off and left them. About 8 P.M. there was a lot of moaning and crying out . . . from where Mutt and Jeff had their bedrolls. The moans turned into screams and someone ran to get the medics. By the time the medics got there, Mutt and Jeff were having convulsions, tearing at their stomachs . . . trying to vomit, blood was trickling out of their mouths. It was determined at the hospital that they were drinking wood alcohol, no one knew where they were getting it, and Mutt and Jeff died horrible deaths shortly after midnight.

Wood alcohol immediately attacks the brain and destroys the nervous system, slowly strangling its victim to death. Incidents such as Laughlin's could not be said to be rare in Europe in World War II. Soldiers did tragically die from alcohol poisoning. But far more commonly, American combat troops used alcohol to blow off accumulated steam. Wine, beer, and liquor were tension relievers—particularly during a lull in the action—nothing more, nothing less. The majority of combat soldiers probably had experiences like those of Reves and Warde and quickly realized that they could not drink excessively in combat. Most would have agreed with Garland Godby's observation that "drinking's just not part of the scene up there [on the front lines]. You need all the judgment you can get."

Although conditions in Europe could at times be pleasant, as when a combat soldier socialized with friendly civilians, drank wine, or found an iron cross, they usually were difficult. American soldiers endured harsh weather, diseases, vermin, and awful battlefield conditions until they reached the nadir of extreme fatigue. George Polakiewicz, who fought with the 34th Infantry Division in Italy, said he was completely exhausted:

> After crossing the Rapido River and climbing the mountains of Monte Cassino, to be welcomed by an enemy counterattack, freezing weather, unable to dig in as the ground was hard as cement, sleeping on the ground and enduring wet weather plus screaming mimis [German rocket launchers], mortar and artillery fire.

Perhaps Lawrence Nickell summed up best the conditions in Europe and the way the American combat soldier dealt with them when he wrote:

> Carrying a pack board of mortar or machine gun ammunition up a steep, muddy hill on a rainy night when you can't see three feet in front of you, falling and sliding back two feet for every three feet in a forward direction quickly rids one of the notion of the glory of war.

Like their counterparts in Europe, combat troops in the Pacific also spent a substantial amount of time and effort coping with conditions that were alien to most Americans. Hot, humid climates character-ized most areas of the Pacific in which American troops fought. Thus, while many footsloggers braved bitter cold winter tempera-tures in the European theater, most combat men in the Pacific ex-perienced the opposite problem—intense heat. Diseases were also common in the Pacific, especially malaria and jungle rot. During their combat duty, most men existed in wet, steamy jungles or on barren islands. Frequently they found themselves beleaguered by rain and insects.

Pacific battles were often fought in what marines would refer to as the "boondocks," a term meaning the middle of nowhere. This meant that American combat soldiers in that theater sometimes found themselves with no familiar surroundings or amenities such as towns, churches, and plumbing. Even so, many of the Pacific war's biggest battles were fought in developed, inhabited areas such as the Philippines, Guam, Saipan, and Okinawa. Thus, substantial numbers of American combat troops interacted with indigenous civilians.

Combat GIs in the Pacific dealt with the disposal of bodily waste in the same fashion as their comrades in Europe. As in Europe, booby traps could also be a menace. The sights and smells of the bat-tlefield that Pacific troops encountered were, of course, affected by the climate, but the degree of death and destruction was not sub-stantially different from what ETO veterans saw. Looting was also a favorite pastime among American combat men in the Pacific, al-though they probably had less to choose from than those in Europe.

Like their buddies in the ETO, they too found that it was the rear-echelon men who usually got the best souvenirs and alcohol.

Throughout the Pacific battle areas, the average temperatures were far higher than those of European combat sites. Most American soldiers were not used to the kind of heat, humidity, and precipitation they experienced. On New Guinea, the year-round average temperatures were often remarkably consistent—between seventy-five and eighty-eight degrees—although it was by no means unusual for temperatures to soar well into the nineties. Humidity was usually at least 70 percent, and the rainfall routinely totaled over ten inches per month.

Temperatures in the Burma-India theater ranged year-round into the eighties and nineties. The humidity was more than 80 percent in most areas of the theater. The Mariana Islands, where American troops fought in the summer of 1944, had average low and high June and July temperatures between seventy-seven and eighty-eight degrees, respectively. The rainfall averaged between six and nine inches for the summer months, and the humidity was slightly over 70 percent.

American troops fought in the Philippines in 1941–42 and then again in 1944–45. In that part of the world, it was rare for temperatures to go below seventy degrees, and the high temperatures year-round were usually in the high eighties to low nineties. During the exceedingly rainy summer months, soldiers could expect to endure up to seventeen inches of rain per month. It all added up to a steamy, hot, uncomfortable existence for the average combat man.

Like European cold, Pacific heat had its extremes. William Hoelzel, of the Americal Division, wrote that "the jungle was well over a hundred degrees." That kind of intense heat was not uncommon for U.S. combat troops in the Pacific.

George Wyatt, of the 1st Marine Division, attempted to describe the heat that he and his fellow marines endured on Guadalcanal: "I could compare the heat on Guadalcanal to being in a hothouse. Steamy, and extremely hot, it was difficult to breathe and you can't imagine just how badly a human body can sweat. Often a light [rain] shower would only worsen the already steamy conditions." Wyatt's 1st Marine buddy Don Zobel also remembered how stifling the heat could be. "The heat would not let up, night and day we would sweat and keep close track of our salt tablets. This was not a cure . . . but it was all we had."

E. B. Sledge, who joined the 1st Marines at Peleliu, saw an odd incident that illustrated just how hot temperatures often became. "The sun bore down on us like a giant heat lamp. I saw a misplaced phosphorus grenade explode on the coral from the sun's intense heat."

On Saipan in the Mariana Islands, 27th Infantry Division combat soldier John O'Brien found that the heat was so bad, he and his buddies were almost crazed with thirst:

> We stopped at a cistern to get a drink. There were three rats floating in the cistern. We were supposed to take Halizone tablets and put them in our canteens after filling them up and wait half an hour. We didn't do that exactly according to the U.S. Army manual. We dipped our canteen cups into the water and drank till we were full. Then we took our Halizone tablets with the last drink.

Americal veteran Harry Wiens described the heat he experienced:

> With not a breath of air stirring, eventually a low grade headache would prevail, and you would lift your helmet to attempt to cool your brow—and the metal was hot enough, you felt, to fry an egg. But no cool air moved or entered under it. Then you lowered it again upon your head, for without the steel pot you felt utterly undressed . . . and you must endure the headache. Luckily, the helmet liner was a reasonably effective insulator.

As bad as the heat was, Wiens preferred it to cold weather, as did many other Pacific theater of operations (PTO) veterans. Said Wiens: "One of the great plusses of our 'corner of the war' was that you were never cold. If soaked at night there would be some discomfort, but never really shivering cold. I often thought of how I would have hated to fight a war in . . . wintertime."

Even the rain that often fell on Pacific battlefields did not always help relieve men from their inferno-like existence. In fact, as Don

Zobel remembered, it sometimes only made conditions even steamier: "You would get steamy and your back would sting like a thousand needles were piercing it. You could stand in the rain and take a bath most any time but you could never get dry so the steam would begin again, bringing with it the invisible needles." George Wyatt saw only one positive aspect of the rain that he experienced at Guadalcanal: "It temporarily grounds all the bothersome mosquitoes." The problem with the rain was that it often came down in torrents instead of in cool, steady showers. Wyatt remembered that sometimes it rained ten to twelve inches a day on Guadalcanal. Robert Jackson, a platoon leader in the 96th Infantry Division, claimed that, in the Philippines, a tropical storm immobilized his unit. Harry Swan's 11th Airborne Division had a similar experience at Leyte. "It was miserable, raining, no shelter, no rations and no resupply at all. We were paratroopers and we accepted it." E. B. Sledge recalled that on Okinawa, "the rains became so heavy that at times we could barely see our buddies in the neighboring foxhole. We had to bail out our . . . foxholes during and after each downpour or they filled with water."

The torrential rains often created a sticky, slippery world in which everything and everyone got wet. Robert Jackson wrote:

> We were constantly wet. It was extremely difficult just putting one sloppy, muddy boot before another. More than one man had to be helped out of an unseen bog. One of my machine gunners arose from his slit trench and shook himself like a dog: his fatigues were as wet and stuck to him as if he'd jumped into a swimming pool.

Of course, such humid, sticky, wet conditions were what caused jungles to thrive. Early in the war Americans fought in jungle terrain at Bougainville, Guadalcanal, and New Guinea. Most were unprepared for the perils of the jungle. Richard Lovett, an Americal Division veteran who fought at Bougainville, recalled the main danger of the jungle. "You couldn't see the enemy because of dense jungle. It was very nerve-wracking."

Edward Sears, also in the Americal, wrote:

Patrolling in the jungle is a very dangerous job. The jungle was very thick with vegetation. You had to stay on the main trails or . . . would lose contact with each other. Over five feet you lost visual contact with your buddy. When you think of the jungle you think of rain, rain and more rain. I don't think we ever dried out. The jungle always smelled of rotten vegetation.

Lewis Goodman, who served with the 1st Marine Division, wrote in a letter that the jungle itself at Bougainville was a big enough obstacle, not to mention the Japanese. "We had lost nearly half of our company and hadn't even seen a Jap. The jungle was so thick they [the Japs] just kept getting a few of our men each day. How I ever stood up under all that I'll never know. Rain, heat, mud, flies and mosquitoes and still we pushed on into the jungle."

With the jungle came insects and animals of every variety. Mosquitoes and flies were the most common insects. The former were notorious as disease carriers but, more commonly, were an annoyance. Predictably, the men hated them. Justin Gray even hated the sound they made: "The mosquitoes were out in force. I poured a bottle of Skat [mosquito repellant] over myself but it didn't seem to do much good. I didn't mind the bites so much, but the constant buzzing around my ears upset me."

As bad as mosquitoes were, flies presented different problems, most of which centered on the fact that they were both disgusting and numerous. Marine Byron Peterson wrote to his hometown paper that "the flies grow big here. They thrive on rotten bodies, both Jap and American, it makes no difference to them." Charlie Burchett, of the 1st Marine Division, said that it was sometimes difficult to eat on Okinawa because of all the flies. "You'd have to take your spoon in one hand and with the other hand wave it and you'd have to do that all the way to your mouth because . . . at least two flies maybe more would hit your spoon between your mess plate and your mouth. And these were big green flies . . . off the dead Japs."

The main reason there were so many flies was because of all the death and destruction of the battlefield. E. B. Sledge described the flies:

In this garbage-filled environment the flies, always numerous in the tropics anyway, underwent a population explosion. This species was not the unimposing common housefly. This creature has a plump, metallic, greenish blue body, and its wings often make a humming sound during flight. With human corpses, human excrement, and rotting rations scattered across Peleliu's ridges, those nasty insects were so large, so glutted, and so lazy that some could scarcely fly. They could not be waved away or frightened off a can of rations or a chocolate bar. Frequently they tumbled off the side of my canteen cup into my coffee. We actually had to shake the food to dislodge the flies, and even then they sometimes refused to move. I usually had to balance my can of stew on my knee, spooning it up with my right hand while I picked the sluggish creatures off the stew with my left. It was revolting, to say the least, to watch big fat blowflies leave a corpse and swarm into our C rations.

In these sorts of conditions, leeches, which sometimes carried diseases, could also be a problem. Robert Jackson saw some of his men crawl through a stinking swamp to safety:

As the men came in they were all shaken by . . . the numbers of leeches that had attached themselves to noses, eyelids, and every soft spot available. My platoon sergeant . . . and I lit cigarettes and touched the leeches to force them to release themselves. It is still nightmarish to me!

Land crabs were also a nuisance. Crawling noisily, they were often mistaken for Japanese soldiers. Harry Wiens recalled one such instance:

I heard the damndest commotion. It sounded like a platoon of Japs not even attempting to move silently. And then I saw the culprit. It was a land crab, and his course would cross in front of my hole. I couldn't resist the temptation, and drew a careful bead. I fired one shot and completely obliterated that poor, noisy crab. Then someone else, who must have heard that clatter, but likely did not see the crab, fired, then another round, and soon a machine gun fired a burst. Then the whole line flared up in a magnificent eruption of firing, and I thought, what a hell of a war you stirred up by this single round placed upon an innocent land crab.

As in Europe, mud could also be a major problem in the Pacific war. George Wyatt wrote of the sticky, clinging mud that he and his fellow marines battled around Henderson Field on Guadalcanal:

> Mud was another obstacle we had to deal with. Due to a large rainfall amount . . . at times the field was so muddy our equipment would become stuck and the oozing brown mud would suck greedily at our shoes. The mud, the intense heat, and the malaria-carrying mosquito population made for backbreaking work.

The mud on Okinawa was reminiscent of the western front trenches in World War I. This was particularly true in the final stages of the campaign when American troops slowly slugged it out with the Japanese in a deadly war of attrition. E. B. Sledge was there:

> The mud was knee deep in some places, probably deeper in others if one dared venture there. For several feet around every corpse, maggots crawled about in the muck and then were washed away by the runoff of the rain. There wasn't a tree or bush left. All was open country. Shells had torn up the turf so completely that ground cover was nonexistent. The scene was nothing but mud; shell fire; flooded craters with their silent, pathetic, rotting occupants . . . utter desolation.

In the wild, overgrown areas of Guadalcanal, George Wyatt became familiar with kunai grass, a peculiar vegetation that grows unchecked in the Tropics:

> Kunai grass grows taller than a man's head, and the coarse, thick, saw-toothed-edged shoots cut off any cooling breezes.

The grass would easily slice the skin, sometimes causing what was termed "elephantitis," or severe swelling. We traded off positions as trailbreaker, swathing the tough grass down with a machete in a path wide enough to walk through.

A generation later, the sons of many World War II veterans would also experience kunai grass in Vietnam.

Many Pacific battlegrounds were small islands or atolls. This meant that the average combat soldier in the Pacific, at some time or another, probably dealt with sand. Usually the sand that made up the beaches of the South and Central Pacific were not a major problem for combat men. However, this was not the case on the island of Iwo Jima. The "sand" at Iwo was really nothing more than volcanic ash that had originated from Mount Suribachi, a peak that dominated the entire island. It caused major difficulties for the marines who came ashore in the first waves, because they could not dig in adequately to avoid murderous Japanese shell fire. Ira Hayes, of the 5th Marine Division, came ashore at Iwo just half an hour after the first wave. "The sand on the beach was black volcanic ash, and was a menace to our running, and to our weapons. My pack got mighty heavy." Hayes made it to the top of Suribachi and was one of the flag raisers in the most famous military picture in American history. Bill Reed, who covered the Battle of Iwo Jima for *Yank* magazine, attested to the fact that not only was the island's unique sand deadly to the marines, it was also pervasive. "The sand got into their eyes and caked around their eyelashes. It became mixed in their hair like gritty dandruff. It invaded small cans of K ration ham and eggs as soon as they were opened. It crept over the tops of the men's leggings and worked to the bottom of their shoes."

The untamed environment of the Pacific was a fertile breeding ground for diseases, the foremost of which was malaria. Carried by mosquitoes, malaria was sometimes a major problem. In the early stages of the Pacific war, the 32d and 41st Infantry Divisions lost vital manpower to the disease. In fact, it was estimated that by December 1942, 20 percent of the men in every line company of the 32d Division were down with malaria. By the end of the Buna campaign in January 1943, about 53 percent of the troops had a fever, the number one cause of which was malaria. It was found that there were more than 5,000 cases of the disease in the division (out of a total strength of nearly 11,000).

The marines on Guadalcanal were similarly afflicted. By October 1942, the pivotal moment of the campaign, 1,900 men of the 1st Marine Division had to be hospitalized for malarial fever. Of the 8,580 cases of disease experienced at Guadalcanal, the number one disease was malaria.

Lewis Brown, a paratrooper with the 503d Parachute Infantry Regiment on New Guinea, asserted that malaria was widespread. "I guess malaria . . . was the biggest thing. About everybody had that." Although preventive measures improved during the war, the medics were not able to completely subdue the disease. Raymond Jones, of the 1st Marine Division, contracted a case on Guadalcanal and described its effects in a letter to his family. "I had malaria on the Island and I guess that was the closest I came to 'cashing in my chips.' I had a 106 degree temperature for 2 days. I didn't eat for 6 days. I lost 28 pounds but I am now gaining it back."

Not all cases were as bad as Jones's. In fact, if a man took Atabrine, a preventive drug, he could avoid malaria altogether, as Harry Wiens and many of his buddies did:

> Malaria, which had thinned Marine ranks considerably, had not been quite that great a problem in the 1-6-4 [164th Infantry Regiment]. There were cases; but generally that yellow, bitter dye . . . Atabrine, had kept it considerably in check. I believe our Atabrine discipline and anti-malarial measures were more effective than in some other units, like not rolling up our sleeves and thereby minimizing exposure of our arms to mosquito bites, and that sort of thing. Our skins were distinctly yellow. However, this coloring of the skin was only temporary, and would disappear a few months after discontinuing the drug.

Jungle rot could also cause problems. The hot, humid climes of the Pacific were ideal for the fungus that causes jungle rot. If a man could not keep his feet dry, he was especially vulnerable; as in Europe, dry feet were nearly impossible. "They would look like prunes because they had been wet so long," Americal Division veteran

Herchel McFadden said of his feet. Edward Sears recalled how pervasive and tenacious jungle rot could be: "We all contracted what we
called jungle rot. It was like ringworm. That stuff was hard to get rid
of." Antonio Renna, of the 81st Infantry Division, remembered that
at Angaur he and his comrades were "living in the same clothes in
heat and rain for forty-five days before we got some foot powder and
a change of socks. Boy, did that feel good." But even foot powder
was not very effective in combating the fungus that caused jungle rot,
as Robert Jackson discovered:

> Our feet were a mess because we dared not take off our
> boots: we might not get them on again. Most of us had devel-
> oped fungus . . . but were unable to take the correct precau-
> tions of changing socks. I took off my boots . . . and was
> shocked at the huge ringworm type lesions all over my feet and
> up my legs. The carefully husbanded foot powder was about as
> useful as an invocation to the gods.

Whayland Greene, a rifleman with the 32d Infantry Division, had
a case of jungle rot that was much worse than Jackson's:

> My feet were hurting so bad that I could not run fast when
> they [the Japanese] were shooting at me. I had jungle rot on
> them real bad. The medic looked at them and said I should
> have been in the hospital several days ago so he sent me back.
> I got to the hospital and my boots were almost rotted off. The
> doctor had to cut my socks off because my socks had grown to
> the skin on my feet and blood came off with the rotten socks.

Demonstrating a bit of ingenuity, Harry Wiens devised a way to
avoid jungle rot. "Keeping feet healthy had been a . . . problem. I
found that walking in the surf and letting saltwater penetrate my
boots was most helpful in curing any incipient fungus infection."
Needless to say, though, this practice was not widespread for the simple reason that most combat troops did not have constant access to
the sea.

The process of disposing of bodily waste in the Pacific was the same as in Europe—namely, make sure you do what had to be done but stay out of danger. Leonard Lazarick, of the 96th Infantry Division, described the process. "If under fire we took care of our bladder & bowels in our foxholes. We would bury our fecal matter when possible." Justin Gray observed the manner in which his foxhole buddy answered the call of nature. "Wyatt, not daring to leave the hole, urinated into an empty tin that used to hold a bottle of plasma and threw the water over the wall."

Harry Wiens also used his foxhole as a commode:

> Anything that moved outside of a hole was automatically presumed to be Japanese, so the only solution was to dig a small excavation for excrement in [the bottom of your foxhole], then cover it with earth, and live with it till morning. Come daylight, there was added some additional depth to your position as you excavated the soiled earth.

As U.S. forces closed in on Japan, they began to assault populated areas on Saipan, Guam, the Philippines, and Okinawa. This gave American combat troops a chance to see Asian civilians; as was his counterpart in Europe, the American combat GI was generally well behaved.

On Guam and the Philippines, former U.S. colonies, American troops were welcomed with open arms. But on Saipan and Okinawa, the story was different. Substantial Japanese populations had settled on those two large islands. Like many Japanese soldiers, these civilians were convinced that it would be dishonorable to fall into the hands of the enemy. What is more, many of them believed that American troops would rape and murder them ruthlessly. This led to one of the great tragedies of the war—the mass suicides of Japanese noncombatants.

Charles Stewart, of the 27th Infantry Division, witnessed the aftermath of one such suicide spree on Saipan. "It was a bad feeling seeing dead men, women and children everywhere you looked. . . . It was harder on some men than others." Charles Lindsay, a combat engineer officer in the 4th Marine Division, saw the remnants of a similar suicide, and it left an indelible impression on him. "What we found I'll never forget. Lying on the beach hidden from view of the shore were eight people, men and women, stark naked, with no heads and one hand blown off. They had committed suicide with a hand grenade held up against the head."

Glenn Searles, of the 77th Infantry Division, did not simply witness the aftermath of such scenes; he was an active participant. His unit came to a cave on Okinawa and found it packed with civilians:

> They must have thought we were going to rape and murder them because they started killing their children and themselves with knives and swords. A Japanese-American showed up and persuaded them to stop the killing. I won't forget the look on a young mother's face when she realized that her dead babe-in-arms had died unnecessarily.

Later in the day, Searles's unit came to a village. Again, the civilians began to kill themselves:

> We heard grenade explosions and lots of screaming and wailing. When we got there we witnessed some of the worst sights possible. There must have been over a hundred adults and children from the village killing each other and themselves. They had seen us coming and, having been told we would murder and rape, started committing suicide. We yelled at them to stop but it did no good. Old men were cutting the throats of small children and young girls. We began shooting those adults who had knives, but had to fall back as dozens of grenades started exploding. Those left alive were aided as best our Medics could, but most were too far gone to be saved.

Things were not always so grim, though, when dealing with the Japanese. Charles Lindsay recalled an incident on Okinawa in which his men gaped at a group of attractive Japanese women:

> As they passed the stunned Marines you could hear a pin drop in the sand. One Marine got enough courage to proposition the maidens in a not too gentle way. He was thinking, of

course that they couldn't understand him. The lead girl went straight to him and asked in perfect English for a drink of water. The flustered Marine said, "Yes, Ma'am" and handed her his canteen amid the laughter of his buddies.

The vast majority of Filipinos were thrilled to see Americans return to their soil in 1944. Japanese occupation had been brutal. Accordingly, American combat soldiers were treated during the campaign like visiting royalty. Combat correspondent Dick Hanley was with a group of GIs from the 37th Infantry Division as they fought their way through Manila:

> Out of nowhere Filipino men, women and children descended on the tired Yanks. They held armfuls of dark colored bottles and gave them out along the files of soldiers, greeting each GI with the now familiar "Victoree," their stock expression of grateful welcome to all American soldiers in the Philippine Islands. The bottles were ice-cold. The Filipinos were giving them cold beer. Friendly Filipinos ran up and warned us of Jap snipers hidden among the gravestones. As we got into the city more civilians began to appear. They ran out of their houses and their apartments handing out coconut candy, chewing gum, cigars . . . and anything else . . . they could give us. Pretty girls ran up and threw their arms around the sweaty . . . Yanks and kissed them.

One soldier came upon a Filipino who was offering coffee amid sniper fire:

> "Coffee, sir?" he asked the infantryman. The GI growled angrily at the friendly civilian. "You can get hurt out here, Joe," he said. The Filipino answered: "I know. We Filipinos are so happy to see you. We have waited so long for you to come. We would gladly die for you now that you are here." The battle-weary infantry veteran fixed the safety of his M1, took the cup and gulped down its lukewarm contents.

Combat GIs in the Pacific were no different from those in Europe in that they generally treated people well. Glenn Searles recalled giving food to hungry Filipinos:

> There were civilians everywhere and they were all hungry. We were forbidden to feed them, but the officers turned a blind eye to our going back for seconds, then sort of moseying back into the bushes where families would be waiting with tin cans for handouts. Nothing tugs at the heartstrings like seeing a hungry child with pleading eyes holding up a can for food. After we had been there awhile, the rules were relaxed so that after the troops had been fed, the locals could bring their cans and get helpings of what was left.

One struggles to imagine Japanese soldiers going out of their way to feed Filipino civilians. American combat men generally had a soft heart where civilians were concerned and, consequently, their relations with them were reasonably pleasant.

Perhaps this softness was an attempt to escape from the brutal, disgusting nature of the battlefield. Pacific battlegrounds were probably even more gruesome and nasty than European battlegrounds, mainly because of the heat, which exacerbated the decomposition of bodies. Charlie Burchett recounted seeing ditches full of dead civilians who had been unluckily caught in the cross fire of combat on Okinawa. "They were stacked on top of each other as far as I could see on this road. The bodies would expand with gasses and blow up like balloons and then they would break and . . . the odor, you couldn't believe the odor." Glenn Searles witnessed another such tragic scene on Okinawa. "I saw one young mother who had been shot through the heart by a single bullet. The slug passed through her and drilled the infant on her back, in the head."

The most enduring impression on combat men was the sight and smell of dead soldiers, mainly enemy soldiers. On the front lines a man did not disappear once he was killed. Nor was there anything tidy about his death. Because of the especially violent and "take-no-prisoners" nature of the war in the Pacific, it was difficult for American graves registration teams to remove dead bodies. What is more, the banzai charge tactics that the Japanese often employed almost guaranteed a dirty battlefield. The Japanese were willing to leave their dead behind. The result was a steamy, stench-filled world replete with every sort of putrifying odor that the human brain could possibly process. E. B. Sledge underscored this point:

It is difficult to convey to anyone who has not experienced it, the ghastly horror of having your sense of smell saturated constantly with the putrid odor of rotting human flesh day after day, night after night. In the tropics the dead became bloated and gave off a terrific stench within a few hours after death. Added to the awful stench of the dead of both sides was the repulsive odor of human excrement everywhere. Added to this was the odor of thousands of rotting, discarded Japanese and American rations. At every breath, one inhaled hot, humid air heavy with countless repulsive odors. I felt as though my lungs would never be cleansed of all those foul vapors.

It was the same for Harry Wiens:

The air was always putrid. It smelled of dead and rotting flesh, and I doubt if anyone ever filled his lungs completely with a deep, full breath of air. You only allowed enough air to enter your lungs to stay alive. Worst part was, we knew that some of those decaying bodies were from our own battalion.

John Lane, of the 4th Marine Division, fought for three weeks on Iwo Jima. What he saw never left his mind:

You did not smell the dead; you tasted them far up the nose and back in the throat. Burned, decaying meat. I tasted it for twenty days, and I can taste it now. You'd come across little piles of dead marines, waiting to be collected. Six or seven guys piled up, turning greenish-gray, then black. Dead Japanese, some hit by flamethrowers. Eyes boiled out, lips burned away, white teeth grinning; uniforms burned away and sometimes the first layer of skin too, so the muscles would show as in an anatomical sketch. Penis sticking up like a black candle stub. The napalm boiled the blood, causing an erection, some said.

Horace Leach, of Merrill's Mauraders, saw a macabre sight in Burma. "A Japanese soldier was sitting cross-legged under a tree holding a bowl of food between his legs. It was a restful position, with one exception, the absence of his head, which was lying nearby." Combat correspondent Merle Miller, who was with the 7th Infantry Division during the Battle of Kwajalein, wrote of the nightmarish scenes he witnessed. "The sight and smell of dead Japs are everywhere on this island. Puddles of water are deep red with their blood. The beaches are lined with their bodies or parts of their bodies— shoes with feet, nothing else . . . scattered arms and legs, far from the bodies to which they belong."

Such scenes were common in the world of Glenn Searles and his buddies:

> A Jap laying on his back tended to have a swollen abdomen which, in turn, would occasionally pull the knees up. Just to make sure they were all dead we occasionally put a round through their guts. This turned on a thin whistle as the gas escaped. Our rations, our water, and even us all soon smelled of putrification.

On Leyte, Edward Sears, a hardened combat veteran, found the smells overpowering. "The stench of bodies . . . was terrible. It made me so sick that I threw up half the night. The next morning I had one terrible headache."

The constant witnessing of such inhuman, degrading sights took its inevitable toll on combat men. Some became hardened to the sight of dead bodies, especially enemy dead. Because of this attitude and perhaps also because of their hatred for the Japanese, some troops took to looting enemy bodies for gold tooth fillings. Harry Wiens recalled one man who looted hundreds of Japanese bodies, yanking out their fillings with a pair of pliers. "This seems so gruesome today but was almost a matter-of-fact sort of happening then.

I personally didn't like it and never participated. But in this brutal . . . conflict we were in, it really . . . didn't seem so out of place."

E. B. Sledge explained how men went about collecting the teeth:

The way you extracted gold teeth was by putting the tip of
the [knife] blade on the tooth of the dead Japanese—I've seen
guys do it to wounded ones—and hit the hilt of the knife to
knock the tooth loose. How could American boys do this? If
you're reduced to savagery by a situation, anything's possible.

On another occasion, Sledge witnessed one of his buddies playing a bizarre game with the body of a Japanese soldier who had had
the top of his skull blown off:

This Jap gunner didn't fall over for some reason. He was just
sitting upright. His eyes were wide open. It had rained all night
and the rain had collected inside of his skull. I noticed this
buddy of mine flippin' chunks of coral into the skull about
three feet away. Every time he'd get one in there, it'd splash. It
was just so unreal. This was just a mild-mannered kid who was
now a twentieth-century savage.

Sometimes combat men did not have to deal with such inhuman
scenes. For a short time on Guadalcanal, this was the case for George
Wyatt and his fellow marines:

We benefitted from the voracious appetites of the crocodiles.
After a battle when dead Japs lay strewn about the banks of the
rivers and streams, the beasts made their way to the carcasses,
devouring the fallen soldiers, leaving for us no smell of rotting
decaying flesh and no debris for the hordes of flies to mass
upon.

When it came to looting, combat troops in the Pacific were no different from those in Europe. Almost all looting centered on the
search for two things, alcohol and souvenirs. In Europe a GI could
usually find local wine, beer, or liquor to sample. This was not usu-

ally the case in the Pacific, even in the inhabited areas. Thus, it was usually incumbent on the soldiers to make their own alcohol.

The most common form of homemade alcohol was referred to as "jungle juice." Horace Fader, of the 32d Infantry Division, said that much of his off-duty time on Aitape was spent "making illicit jungle juice." Charlie Burchett, a nondrinker, nevertheless had many opportunities to observe his fellow marines make jungle juice. "They would steal a gallon can of fruit cocktail. They'd put coconut juice and raisins and potato peels and set that stuff out somewhere and it'd ferment in a week or so." Robert Jackson claimed that he and his men looked forward to jungle juice or any other kind of alcohol as an escape after harrowing combat patrols. "It was great with canned grapefruit juice but we had to ration it because 95 percent alcohol can be deadly. It was a stupendous reviver after small patrol actions: we didn't obey the rule that enlisted men couldn't drink 'hard liquor.'"

Even though indigenous alcohol was not common, there were instances when American combat troops found some to drink, as at Manila when the 37th Infantry Division liberated a brewery and the men had the unheard-of treat of cold beer. Dick Hanley was there. "The men could see the neon signs of the Balintawak brewery. There in the refrigerating plant soldier after soldier filled his helmet with the amber beverage and came out into the light of day refreshed."

Like their brethren in Europe, the Pacific theater combat men hunted for souvenirs. Invariably the hunt centered on some sought-after piece of Japanese equipment. John Lane recalled the process:

> Everybody wanted a Japanese sword. The nearest I got to having one was carrying Private Peck's sword. He was . . . "point man" sometimes on patrol, and didn't want to be encumbered. If he got hit, I was to get the sword. He didn't, and I didn't. I was a bit too squeamish to rob the dead outright, but I did pick up one of the usual Japanese flags. I found it near a corpse.

Most men were not especially squeamish about robbing dead Japanese. Instead they were cautious. The Japanese were even more notorious than the Germans for booby-trapping their dead. Deane Marks, who fought with the 11th Airborne Division in the Battle of Manila, summed up the whole souvenir-hunting phenomenon in the Pacific:

> On one occasion, a dead Jap was turned over to be searched. His foot or arm was trip wired to a twenty-foot torpedo, which exploded and took out a couple of guys. From that point on, we didn't trust anything, that is, if you wanted to live. Most souvenirs were picked up long after the fighting part of the army moved on. One reason was the booby traps. The other was no way of carrying anything extra. Most of those fancy swords, pistols, field glasses, etc. you see were all sopped up by the rear echelon service troops.

Conditions in the Pacific were uniquely harsh and forbidding. The alien atmosphere of oppressive heat, steamy jungles, tiny islands, and monsoonlike rains were enough to test even the most veteran combat soldiers. Occasionally there were pleasant diversions such as friendly Filipino civilians or homemade jungle juice. But, as often as not, the Pacific was an extremely difficult place in which to fight a war that was already remarkable in its ferocity. The horrible sights and smells of the battlefield were made even worse by the consistently hot temperatures. In spite of all this, though, American combat soldiers endured and learned to live with the harsh conditions.

Myths can be both instructive and dangerous. They are instructive in the sense that most of them grow out of a kernel of truth, but they become exceedingly dangerous when taken as the whole truth. Such is the case with historian S. L. A. Marshall and his so-called "ratio of fire" theory. In his book *Men Against Fire,* Marshall asserted that only 15 to 25 percent of American soldiers ever fired their weapons in combat in World War II. He cited as his evidence afteraction interviews with "hundreds" of different rifle companies but did not elaborate any further. Because of Marshall's insider status in the army and his bullying, authoritarian manner with anyone who challenged him, his ratio of fire theory was taken as gospel by both the army hierarchy and future military historians. It did not matter that Marshall could produce no statistics or specific footnoted citations to support his claim. "Slam" Marshall had said it and thus it had to be true, reasoned many military thinkers.

The bold truth, which has come to light only in recent years, is that Marshall's claim was and is absurd and is based on no factual evidence of any kind. Marshall's first major challenger was Harold Leinbaugh, who was a rifle company commander in the 84th Infantry Division. Drawing on his own combat experiences, Leinbaugh could remember no such reluctance to fire on the part of his men. In talking with other veterans while he wrote his book *The Men of Company K: The Autobiography of a World War II Rifle Company,* Leinbaugh found few, if any, who recalled not shooting their weapons. Leinbaugh took Marshall's ratio of fire theory as a personal affront to the American combat soldier, and he set out to debunk the myth. He met Dr. Roger Spiller, the deputy director of the U.S. Army Combat Studies Institute, and discussed *Men Against Fire* with him. Spiller thoroughly investigated Marshall's contentions and published his findings in the Royal United Services Institute journal in an article entitled "S. L. A. Marshall and the Ratio of Fire."

An admirer of Marshall, Spiller nevertheless concluded that the ratio of fire theory could not have been true. He found that Marshall at various times claimed to have interviewed between four hundred and six hundred rifle companies and claimed that it took three days to interview them."By the most generous calculation," Spiller wrote, "Marshall would have finished approximately 400 interviews sometime in October or November 1946." Needless to say, that is well after the war was over, which meant that it would have been impossible to conduct on-the-spot afteraction interviews. Perhaps the most damning fact that Spiller uncovered, though, was from Marshall's assistant Dr. John Westover, who sat in on the interviews that Marshall did conduct and who worked closely with him.Westover maintained that Marshall never, under any circumstances, asked a soldier if he had fired his weapon in combat. Nor did he ever discuss the issue in their many private conversations. In addition, Spiller found that none of Marshall's correspondence or field notebooks included any notations about combat troops failing to fire. In fact, one of his notebooks included just the opposite—afteraction interviews in which almost all the soldiers told of firing their weapons.

In exploring Marshall's character, Spiller and later Leinbaugh also found a great deal of evidence to suggest that Marshall misrepresented his World War I service record as well as his combat experiences. In addition, Gen. James Gavin, the legendary paratrooper fighting general and a man who knew quite a bit about infantry combat, told Spiller that he met Marshall in 1944 and that he seemed to lack knowledge and understanding of the infantry. Gavin's men apparently shared his view. They resented Marshall as a "rear echelon" type who did not know what he was talking about, and they resolved to tell him nothing. This seems odd when weighed against Marshall's longtime reputation as an expert on combat.

The sad but inescapable truth is that Marshall, in all probability, made up the whole ratio of fire myth. It is true that American soldiers were quick to take cover (they were usually attacking and thus vulnerable), and it is probably true that there were some soldiers who never fired their weapons. Marshall, always contemptuous of methodology and evidentiary citations, probably took a few anecdotes he had heard and extrapolated them to all American combat soldiers. In so doing, he created one of the most enduring myths to come out of World War II and did a great disservice to the American combat soldier. The latter was probably not his intention. Marshall was an early advocate of "bottom up" military history. He maintained that studying the men at the front was where the real story of military history could be found. His intense interest in the fighting troops probably lent more credence to his ideas than they deserved.

In conducting the research for this book, the author found so many accounts (both contemporary and after the fact) of men firing their weapons that it would be impossible to chronicle them in twenty volumes. When discussing combat, some of these veterans were aware of the ratio of fire theory, but most were not. Most of the men who were asked about the ratio of fire said that it certainly was not true in their unit. So did Dick Peters, an armored infantryman in the 8th Armored Division:

> They say there was a percentage of GIs in World War II that never fired their weapons. I don't know how accurate that statistic is, but in my unit, at the platoon level and before that at the squad level, I can't conceive . . . of too many fellows who never had occasion to fire at the enemy.

In propagating his myth, Marshall missed an important point—that it is comforting for infantrymen in combat to shoot. Indeed, one of the characteristics of green troops was that they tended to be trigger happy. Robert Knauss, a rifleman with the 37th Infantry Division, wrote of being "scared at first until I started to shoot back." In fact, for most men the first time they fired at the enemy was a seminal moment. Edward Laughlin, a paratrooper in the 82d Airborne Division, underscored this point:

> I strongly suspect that infantry soldiers entering combat always remember the first time that they fired their weapons in combat. Perhaps with all of the training, it is done on an im-

mediate reflex action. My recollection was on the first combat patrol . . . as a team member attacking a partially disabled German "Tiger" tank.

Shooting at the enemy made a man part of the "team," or "brotherhood." There were, of course, many times when soldiers did not want to shoot, such as at night when they did not want to give away a position or on reconnaissance patrols. But, in the main, no combat soldier in his right mind would have deliberately sought to go through the entire war without ever firing his weapon, not only because he would have been excluded from the brotherhood but also because it would have been detrimental to his own survival. One of Leinbaugh's NCOs summed it up best when discussing Marshall. "Did the SOB think we *clubbed* the Germans to death?"

Perhaps because of the force of Marshall's reputation, many military historians have all too often neglected to ask themselves such common-sense questions. They have simply accepted Marshall's myth at face value without any scholarly probing or inquiry. Accordingly, the common perception of the American combat soldier has been that not only was he reluctant to fire but he also lacked initiative. This cliché seemed to paint the picture that American combat men spent most of their time cowering in their foxholes clutching their brand-new rifles, waiting for the war outside to go away, or for someone else to do what needed to be done. Nothing could be further from the truth, and it is unfortunate that Marshall's myth has contributed to this perception. Excellent historians such as Russell Weigley, Trevor DuPuy, and Martin van Creveld have all questioned the quality of the American combat solider. In the case of the latter two, their discussion of the American combat soldier was only in relation to his German counterpart. They found the GI lacking in comparison. Weigley, a traditional "top-down" military historian, even used Marshall's ratio of fire ideas to buttress an assertion that American combat soldiers lacked aggression and initiative. The exposure of Marshall's ratio of fire theory as a myth means that one of the major criticisms of American combat soldiers voiced by these historians has been built on a house of cards.

The actual truth about the American combat soldier ought to be built instead upon two fundamental and interrelated realities. The first is that the American soldier was of good quality and generally fought well. The second, which came about directly as a result of the first, is that the American soldier won nearly all the time. This is not to suggest that the GI was some sort of supersoldier blessed with the fighting heart of a lion. It is merely to say that the American combat soldier did his job and did it well. The material superiority enjoyed by the United States would have been useless if the combat soldier had not been willing again and again to put his life on the line in order to achieve victory. The outcome of the war was not a foregone conclusion. It took courageous men to prosecute it successfully. The combat soldier utilized the strengths of his nation in order to accomplish his dirty task. If that meant calling for available artillery or air support to accomplish a mission instead of charging head-on at a pillbox, he would have been foolish not to.

Harry Arnold, a rifleman in the 99th Infantry Division, expressed this "do what it takes" concept well; in so doing, he located the origin of much of the criticism of the American combat soldier:

> One German criticism of American infantry . . . concerned an alleged penchant for going to ground or cover when fired upon. I plead guilty of such on numerous occasions, and with much pride. We weren't there to oblige the Germans by presenting ourselves as clay pigeons for their sport. We were there to overcome—and we did.

Marvin Reickman, of the 24th Infantry Division, pointed out another reality that has too long been overlooked. "Although we were amateurs we were able to beat the professionals who had been at it for many years. We were good at what we did."

Naturally there is a certain amount of self-promotion and pride in the self-assessments of these veterans. They are proud of what they did. That should not detract from the fact that they did a fine job as fighting soldiers fifty years ago. The proof is in the results and not necessarily the words. Newman Phillips, of the 32d Infantry Division, said that the war taught him that "if we have to, American soldiers will fight as good as any soldiers in the world." Perhaps Donald Trachta, of the 97th Infantry Division, summed it up best: "I think the American will to fight was the key to victory."

Trachta's statement is precisely correct. The combat soldiers were willing to risk their lives day after day with no promise of any relief. They might not have liked it and they may have done everything in their power to ensure survival, including taking cover and calling for help, but their willingness to fight was surely the key to victory.

In a letter to his family, Melvin Bush described how he and his comrades reacted when ordered to attack strong German positions in Normandy. "When the order came to move ahead we moved as one. Without hesitating or faltering, all went ahead." That statement would be familiar to most combat troops, because it is what they did constantly, no questions asked, with the quiet and low-key heroism that won the war. To falter or hesitate would mean letting down your buddies, something unthinkable to most combat men. Robert Jackson, a rifle platoon leader in the 96th Infantry Division, expressed it this way when assessing the performance of his men: "Looking back, I see what a well-trained unit we were. There was little panic and jobs were done to the best of our abilities under terrible circumstances. This was not the stuff of awards, but competent soldierly activity under the great stress of fear. I am proud of them for that." No greater or more truthful epitaph or description could be written for the fighting quality of the American combat soldier in World War II.

The combat soldier accordingly went about his job in the same dependable, quietly effective manner. In the experiences of most men, there often seemed to be a pervasive sense of teamwork. Edward Laughlin's description of how he and his buddies captured a farmhouse reflects this sense:

> After I fired two clips through the windows and into the structure, Tommy ran up and lobbed a couple of frag grenades through the window. Shaky then ran up with his Thompson submachine gun and put about twenty rounds through the doorway. Tommy then vaulted through the window; Shaky with his tommy gun firing from his hip went through the doorway and I followed as I was reloading my weapon. There were two German soldiers laying there dead in one of the rooms.

This maneuver reflected the main American tactic known as fire and movement. It dictated that some troops would shoot at the enemy to immobilize him while others closed with the enemy to destroy him. Laughlin described the way it was done: "Our technique was to work over the top . . . or around behind the position, creeping up close enough to throw either a fragmentation or concussion grenade into their position and then quickly close in firing our rifles and submachine guns." In the strictest sense, that is what was meant by the phrase "closing with the enemy."

Fire and movement obviously required soldiers to fire their weapons so they could cover their buddies. It necessitated and led to trust between soldiers and was a major reason for the brotherhood between them. This tactic of envelopment was one of the main tenets emphasized in the doctrine of the U.S. Army and the training of its soldiers. Fire and movement was a departure from the head-on charge concepts of the past; generally it was successful for American combat soldiers.

Of course there were as many different wars as there were men in combat. Infantry, armor, and engineers all existed to accomplish different tasks. Thus, the way they fought was not always the same, both in Europe and the Pacific. Henri Atkins was a lead scout, or point man, in the 99th Infantry Division. He described explicitly how he led his unit in combat:

> A point man needs a willingness to die. He is nothing more . . . than a decoy. When he is shot, the enemy position is revealed. Don't confuse this willingness with "bravery." A point man is just doing his job, what he has trained to do. Usually, a scout is way out ahead of the attacking forces, ready to signal back enemy contact. He has a chance of survival, but not much of one. The tough question is, why did I volunteer as company first scout . . . when I knew how dangerous the position could be? I didn't get paid more. It was the most dangerous position in a rifle company. I was important to my company. They needed me. I could do the job. I could be counted on. Is that an answer? I don't know, but it's as good an answer as any.

Lawrence Nickell, an infantryman in the 5th Infantry Division, recalled the American method of attack. "Normally the riflemen would hit the dirt and then advance by short rushes before going to ground again, the men on the ground giving covering fire as others advanced in leapfrog manner."

John Worthman, who served in the 4th Infantry Division, recalled how he and his comrades breached the Siegfried line in Germany:

First heavy small arms fire at all embrasures while flame throwers and pole charge men moved up. The flame throwers then heated an embrasure and the pole charge men moved in and deposited their high explosive on the heated embrasure. If it went well, the metal and cement yielded and the bunker was breached.

Harold Wells, an infantry officer in the 45th Infantry Division in Italy and France, outlined how he and his men went about fighting:

If we were trying to attack, I always felt exposed, especially if we were trying to locate the enemy position. We had patrols out in front and on our flanks. Once contact was made, it seemed like a relief just knowing where they were. In a defensive situation we were not necessarily under constant fire.

Riland West, a forward observer with the 87th Infantry Division, described an advance:

We advanced on foot most of the time but we had three tank destroyers attached to us and they would let us ride . . . till we hit resistance. Then the tanks would disperse out and start firing for us. Then the artillery was called in. We repelled the enemy where we could advance, then usually we'd jump back on the tanks again.

Max Kocour, a forward observer in the 90th Infantry Division, wrote that in Normandy they did not always adhere to the army manuals. They did what worked:

We were . . . trained to use encoded coordinates and thrust point terms over our walkie-talkies to identify locations in order to avoid the consequences of German monitoring. The problem was, it took too long to code and encode with accuracy. So, we developed a "check point" method (not in the manuals) which was simply identifying and marking, the night before, certain terrain features that could then be referred to in the clear. In other words, on our maps we would identify XY road junction as check point #1, the roadside shrine as check point #2 and so on.

The 92d Infantry Division, made up mostly of black troops, spent part of the war holding static positions in Italy. Edgar Piggot remembered what that was like. "We'd have a briefing about what our mission would be, that is, combat patrol, scouting patrol or observation. We might patrol gaps in our lines for enemy intrusion, contact enemy troops, estimate their strength, plot their positions or call for artillery and mortars."

For tankers, combat often meant movement and fire support. Bartlett Allen, a tank commander in the 1st Armored Division, wrote that "you normally strike rapidly with the infantry and are drawn back to cover. There were times when we supported the infantry for several days in succession."

Clarence Hitchcock, also a tank crewman in the 1st Armored, described a typical day in combat: "We would take up positions and fire at targets. Sometimes we had to pull back and get more ammunition and fuel. We would learn sometimes of some of our tanks that had been hit and our friends killed. Then we'd go back and fight some more." John Jones, another 1st Armored tanker, made the point that it was unusual for tanks to be at the forward positions. "Tanks were rarely stationed on the front line except when called on to attack or counterattack. They're normally stationed a cannon shot to the rear." Hartson Sexton, a recon platoon leader in the 1st Armored, described a typical day: "We would usually move out at first light and keep moving until we could see the enemy and report back to the task force commander so he would know what to expect."

It was much the same process for tankers in other divisions. Charles Hogg, of the 6th Armored Division, remembered their attack methods:

> The armored point usually consisted of five light tanks, five medium tanks, a platoon of armored infantry, two little 5mm

"priests," a squad of engineers and a forward observer in a light tank. We kept moving until contact was made and then engaged the enemy. If the enemy proved to be too strong, we kept them engaged until reinforcements arrived.

Engineers spent much of their time in front of the forward American positions. Combat correspondent Mack Morriss watched 4th Infantry Division engineers clear booby traps and minefields in the Huertgen Forest:

Men threw ropes around the logs of a roadblock and yanked them to explode the mines and booby traps, and then shoved the trees aside, clearing the way. Engineers on their hands and knees probed the earth with . . . wire to find and uncover metallic schuh mines and box mines. The wire, or a bayonet, was shoved into the ground at an angle in the hope that it would touch the mines on their sides rather than on the tops, for these mines detonated at a two- to three-pound pressure.

Raymond Buch, of the 11th Armored Division, recalled how harrowing the job could be:

We went about our jobs fearful every minute that mines, booby traps and . . . artillery barrages would kill some of us. We were ordered to clear mines ahead of advancing tanks.We'd be subjected to mortar and rifle fire. We had to call in artillery to clear out the Germans.

For Robert Gravlin, a combat engineer in the 6th Armored Division, the process was not much different."We would follow behind a Sherman tank or half-track. As the lead tank would get hit or hit a mine, we combat engineers would move forward with our mine detectors and in most cases we'd come under machine gun and/or artillery fire."

Jason Byrd, a member of the 1st Infantry Division and a combat engineer, recalled how a gung-ho buddy influenced him to take extreme chances:

He wasn't afraid of nothing. There'd be a pillbox. He'd take us up to where you could almost punch a guy in the nose. Flares would come up and . . . there we'd lay just out in the open . . . waiting for the machine gun to tear us all to pieces. We'd find the machine gun. Sometimes we'd destroy it. Sometimes we'd go back and get a mortar outfit to destroy it. If it was . . . just an outpost, two or three Germans, he or one of us would throw a hand grenade in and blow it up.

On the front lines there was no room for sentimentality or softness if a man hoped to survive. Mindful of this, GIs went about their business with a controlled brutality. As famous cartoonist Bill Mauldin wrote, there was nothing honorable or sporting about the way combat soldiers went about fighting Germans:

You don't fight a kraut by Marquis of Queensberry rules. You shoot him in the back, you blow him apart with mines, you kill or maim him the quickest and most effective way you can with the least danger to yourself. He does the same to you. He tricks you and cheats you, and if you don't beat him at his own game you don't live to appreciate your own nobleness.

This fight-to-the-death mentality was even worse in the Pacific, where the ferocity of the fighting was sometimes mind-boggling. George Wyatt, of the 1st Marine Division, was frank about how he and his fellow leathernecks approached combat:

Hollywood movies do not actually portray the realities of war, as in many cases the enemy was shot from behind or stabbed from behind or blown up from behind easier than front-on. This is not a step-by-step hip-swinging, gun-throwing, honor-bound situation. Actually, you were out to save your own neck in the safest, easiest possible way.

The forbidding terrain of most Pacific battlegrounds made it difficult for troops to feel secure. Glenn Searles, of the 77th Infantry Division, described a ritual that was often repeated. "A perimeter is the way combat troops in the field bivouac in a circle. There are no 'front lines,' so the troops dig foxholes around the CP [command post] for protection from all sides."

Frank Caudillo, who fought in the Philippines with the 6th Infantry Division, recalled how his unit fought. "Advance through snipers, mortars, artillery all day. Dig in before dark, prepare a perimeter for the [Japanese] attack at night. Fight most of the night with no sleep." Emil Lindenbusch, who served in the same outfit as Caudillo, remembered often being on the move. "We started out at daylight in the morning, patrol in front, usually a squad of riflemen, then came the light machine guns and mortar section. We'd keep going till the patrol drew fire, the mortar section would set up, mortars fired shells into the enemy position."

Leonard Kjelstrom's 24th Infantry Division fought mostly on New Guinea and the Philippines. "Mainly it was outpost duty and patrols. Days we would hunt out snipers, nighttime we would sleep with a machete in one hand and a bayonet or knife in the other. One person would always . . . have their ears attuned to the slightest noise."

Bryan Baldwin, of the 25th Infantry Division, recalled the way in which his unit fought the Japanese in the Philippines:

> We were on the move a lot, rarely spent more than two or three days in one spot. Constant recon and combat patrols was the norm, patrol and move and take a hill. It was extremely tiring and the nights were no better. Either we were hitting them or they banzaied our lines. Exhaustion was the norm.

Common on every battlefront was the sense that combat soldiers were usually extremely tired. Combat against the tenacious Japanese required the kind of vigilance that led to exhaustion. One 27th Infantry Division soldier interviewed on Makin said that such vigilance was a must: "Never take anyone's word for it that any area is clear of Japs. Don't pass by any holes. Watch the trees, too. They're the favorite sniper hangout. Always look out for Number 1." His buddy added: "No one will call you a coward for trying to have buddies cover you every time you advance. And it's no disgrace to crawl . . . zigzag and take cover behind trees or anything else you see."

The 32d Infantry Division found itself in some of the earliest ground combat in the Pacific war at New Guinea. Newman Phillips was there. "We would move in a column. When the scouts encountered the enemy, then we would assault the position, sometimes fighting all day or only minutes. We never moved at night, fighting only defensive actions after dark."

Robert LaChausee had remarkably similar experiences in the 38th Infantry Division. "We generally moved until contact, or if no contact until 3 or 4 P.M. We would dig in, set up trip wires and booby traps."

This search and destroy type of warfare, which would be familiar to a later generation in Vietnam, was the method by which much of the Pacific war was fought.

As a "recon" trooper in the Americal Division, William McLaughlin was often hunting out the Japanese far away from friendly troops. "We would be trucked out to the lines, walk to the infantry trenches and off on the west or Numa Numa trail. Either we would meet with Japs and fight them or we'd reconnoiter and return unless we stayed out, sometimes for seven or eight days in front of the lines."

Melvin Coobs, who was at Okinawa with the 96th Infantry Division, fought much the same way that troops in Europe did:

> Most of the time we were on the attack. Sometimes our advances could be measured in feet or yards and every night was filled with the tension of watching for infiltrators. We went from hill to hill and ridge to ridge, always the exposed attacker trying to root out the concealed defender. If there was anything typical about the days, it was the continual need to protect yourself from enemy fire.

Combat engineers worked closely with the infantry in the Pacific, often fighting as infantry themselves. Sometimes, though, the situation called for more traditional engineering tasks, as Charles Brennan, of the 32d Infantry Division, recalled. "We were an engineer unit committed to keeping the infantry moving. If the infantry needed a bridge we built it. They would give us protective fire."

The Pacific war was largely an infantryman's war. Even so, tanks were sometimes used in the bigger battles. Although no armored divisions were sent to the Pacific, there were small, independent tank outfits that were sometimes attached to infantry units there. Richard Forse, a tanker, was a member of one such small armored formation; he found himself working with infantrymen of the 77th Infantry Division in the Philippines:

> Sometimes we'd go forward in skirmish lines, sometimes in column depending on the terrain. We would be committed depending on whether we were close by or if they needed more tanks. We usually fired machine guns . . . and then if we had a good field of fire we'd use the 75mm gun. We'd continue the advance until late afternoon . . . before we'd stop for the day. We'd all dig in a battalion defensive perimeter.

The American combat soldier had a clear advantage over his enemies in the realm of fire support. American small-unit weapons may have been lacking, but there was usually no shortage of support weapons such as tanks, artillery, aircraft, and naval guns. Carlie Berryhill, of the 6th Infantry Division, felt that "the fire support that we received from artillery, air and naval was . . . very effective. We could not have done without that support." Another 6th Division soldier, Robert Klenk, had a similar opinion. "Our support was good and effective. I was impressed by the P-51 and P-38 air strikes that we got."

In recalling the fire support that his 24th Infantry Division received, Leonard Stein wrote that "our artillery support was generally effective. Army air support was too dangerous to use. They stayed at high altitude. We only trusted the 24th Marine Aviation [Group]."

Bryan Baldwin, of the 25th Infantry Division, felt that "tanks were useless in the jungle and only drew fire. Artillery and air was there when you needed them. Air saved our butts several times."

Edwin Hanson, of the 37th Infantry Division, saw tanks at use in jungle terrain in the Philippines:

> All of a sudden, as I was watching the tank, I noticed what appeared to be rain falling and dancing off the tank turret. The sky was clear, but here was this sparkling stuff showering on top of the tank. That wasn't rain—it was Nambu fire coming from

Knob Hill. The tank shifted into reverse and slowly backed toward . . . safety.

Apparently the jungle was so stifling that machine guns could drive away tanks.

Lyle McCann, who fought with the 81st Infantry Division, did not remember any outside support. "Our fighting was mostly close quarters. We got our own support from mortars. Machine guns, tanks and artillery fire [came] from Cannon Company."

Donald Dencker, of the 96th Infantry Division, assessed his unit's support in the following manner: "Air support was not that effective against extremely well dug-in Japs on Okinawa. Tanks . . . usually drew counterartillery or antitank fire. Flamethrowing tanks were great, blasted, roasted them out."

Combat correspondent Bill Reed observed firsthand the vital role that support fire played at Iwo Jima for the marines. "The supporting air and naval fire did much. Hour after hour of surface and air bombardment couldn't fail to wipe out many emplacements, imprison many Japs in their caves and slowly eat away the mountain fortress itself."

Airpower was only as effective as the pilots and their aircraft. It was the only form of support that William Hoelzel and his Americal Division buddies received in their exotic battlegrounds. "Our only fire support in the jungle was airpower, mostly machine-gun fire from planes, no bombs."

A few American troops were lucky to get any air cover at all. Cecil Forinash was a lieutenant in the Philippine Division. He and his men fought desperately for their lives at Bataan in early 1942. "We didn't have any airpower. [The Japanese] had the only airplanes flying. They bombed the living hell out of us. We kept getting these messages from MacArthur that hundreds of planes . . . were on their way. I think that had an adverse effect." The vast majority of American combat soldiers were lucky enough to avoid that sort of situation.

Most men felt that the navy did a good job of lending fire support. Roy Yates, of the 7th Infantry Division, definitely thought so. "We had good supporting fire. I had my own destroyer to fire ahead of me at Kwajalein Atoll."

Raymond Jones, of the 1st Marine Division, told his parents that at Guadalcanal, when the situation was the most critical, the navy saved his unit:

> The most serious time was Oct. 12–15 but thanks to our great Navy we made it. That is the outfit that saved us—the greatest Navy in the world and do not let anyone tell you different for we saw them work. Boy, I mean those guys are good. If it wasn't for those guys I wouldn't be here now.

In Europe, American fire support was probably even more effective than in the Pacific, thanks to the more open European terrain. This was particularly true in the realm of air support, which was vital to the success of American armies. Alton Pearson, of the 4th Infantry Division, saw the massive Allied bombing that preceded the breakout at Saint-Lô in Normandy. "While we were in our position behind hedgerows, I could hear the roars of bombers. They came in one squadron at a time, each one dropping bombs where the other ended and so on. The ground was shaking . . . so bad that it would knock out your breath if you lay on the ground."

Harry Gunlock, of the 36th Infantry Division, recalled saving a downed pilot who had moments before helped to fend off a German attack:

> As he floated to the ground, his comrade in the other plane circled him. We ran to him, waved at his buddy, who could tell that friendly troops were at hand. The pilot landed in a rocky place and his legs were hurt. As we got to him, he was fearful that we were Germans. He was much relieved to see who we were.

Robert Russell, of the 84th Infantry Division, recalled an air strike that his unit got when it was stalled by machine guns and mortars in France:

> They called in four P-47s. They came in a formation. One of them would peel off and dive . . . shooting rockets. Well, they (the Germans) were shooting antiaircraft at him and machine

guns. As he turned they were shooting at him. While they were shooting at him, this other one came in. About three passes like that and they silenced that thing. We never heard another shot. Then we were able to move on.

Gene Curry, of the 12th Armored Division, also saw fighter-bombers at work. "Sometimes our tanks or artillery couldn't put a German weapon out of business. The air force would send in a P-47 fighter plane. They would dive right at their target through all the bullets being fired at them."

Edward Laughlin also liked the fighters:

Our favorites were the P-47 and the P-51 Mustang. Sometimes we could see them at very low altitudes working over the German troops in small towns out in front of us—like flies buzzing around honey—particularly when they could shoot up church steeples because the Germans had a practice of using these steeples . . . to conceal their artillery observers.

Not all combat troops were so enamored with the air force. Close air support is often dangerous, because if everything is not done correctly, friendly troops can get hit. This was the gist of 88th Infantry Division John Roche's criticism of the air force:

Absolutely useless and, indeed, a menace was air support. The only good plane in the skies of Italy was the Piper cub, used for reconnaissance and artillery observation. The German Stukas were better than our fighter-bombers: they bombed and strafed the enemy, not friendly forces.

Although tanks were held in reasonably high esteem, the most common complaints were that they tended to draw fire and that they were sometimes tentative, as 35th Infantry Division rifleman James Graff found out:

I . . . managed to see some krauts in the vicinity of an underpass directly to our front. As the mortar crews could not bring their weapons to bear on them, I went downstairs to ask the assistance of the tank crew. They informed me that an officer would have to order them to fire, but I suspected they were afraid of exposing their position or didn't want to have to clean their gun.

More commonly, though, tankers were willing to do everything they could to help the infantry. The problem was that their tanks often could not survive against German armor. Lawrence Nickell saw a tank company get torn to pieces in a matter of minutes:

> The 7th Armored sent in a company of tanks, sixteen in all, to try to assist in the attack, but all but one of them were knocked out in less than half an hour from dug-in 88mm guns and Tiger tanks. The field was littered with burning tanks, their ammunition exploding and the tank personnel bailing out, some on fire. Bad way to die.

Bud Berkelbach, of the 63d Infantry Division, wrote of an incident in which tanks were very effective. He and his unit were pinned down somewhere in France under murderous fire for an entire day. Just as it seemed they would all die, some tanks appeared:

> All of a sudden I heard tanks coming behind us—I couldn't look or I'd get shot—so all I did was pray. I looked up to see two of our medium tanks move into position. They swung their guns around and opened up. For about fifteen minutes they fired their shells and also both their 50 and 30 cal machine guns at the German positions. During this time we got what men there were left and we carried the wounded to two medic jeeps that came up with the tanks. They kept firing . . . to give us cover till we got the wounded out. The tanks started to pull back. We jumped on the sides and then they took off.

The most common form of support for frontline troops in Europe was artillery. American artillery often saved the day. It could be both effective and overwhelming. Charles Murphy, an engineer officer in the 1st Infantry Division, got to know his supporting artillery well. "We got to working so closely I often operated as a forward observer. When I saw a lucrative target, I'd say "put me one out." They'd throw . . . smoke out and I'd say, 'okay, you're 200 yards to the right and 50 under.' Next round would be right on. Then they would fire for effect."

Harry Arnold recalled an instance in combat in which artillery was very effective:

> From the trail behind us an Artillery . . . forward observer and radioman crawled up. Consulting his map he called coordinates to the gunners. The first 105mm shell tore overhead and slammed into the woods beyond, too far. He adjusted the range, and now the battery guns joined in. The fire mission ceased abruptly and there was silence. Our lesson was important: try to force the enemy to show himself before engaging in small arms action with him, lean on your support weapons.

Nicholas Bozic, a forward observer with the 36th Infantry Division, recorded in his diary how effective his fire was on German positions near Monte Cassino:

> I began to fire at the antitank gun and silence it with about fifteen rounds. Then I started on the machine guns. The wind was in my favor. Watching the machine guns, I picked up some German infantry going in position, so I opened fire on them. I decided to use high explosives with delayed fuses to start an avalanche with all the high cliffs. Then I started with phosphorus again to burn them out.

Thomas Yochim said that he and his 78th Infantry Division buddies benefited from a close relationship with a forward observer. "High praise for the artillery. We soon learned to befriend their forward observers who, in turn, took good care of our needs." Mel Cotton, a medic in the 91st Infantry Division, underscored how important for morale good artillery support could be. "It is always encouraging to a combat rifleman to witness the visible support his artillery gave him in . . . critical situations. Nothing is more morale building to a forward soldier under fire than to recognize firsthand the real teamwork of those who supported him."

Jesse Brewer, a black combat soldier in the 92d Infantry Division, thought that artillery was good but indicated that his unit could not often get it. "Artillery fire was . . . rationed, not available most of the time." Spencer Moore, a black officer who was also in the 92d, echoed Brewer's observation. "Artillery was terrific, always rationed amounts of fire when you could get it."

The majority of American combat troops in Europe did not have occasion to receive fire support from naval gunfire. But for those involved in invasions, working with the navy was a fact of life. On D day, Charles Murphy got vital support from a destroyer offshore. "A destroyer came in. He couldn't have been 200 yards off the beach. He pumped four rounds right in that brazier (of a pillbox). Boy, that was the end. Then things started moving fast. I loved the Navy from then on."

As Donald Greener, an armored infantryman in the 1st Armored Division, recalled, naval support was a matter of life and death at Anzio. "The ships in the harbor gave us supporting fire many times to keep Jerry from driving us off the beachead." The 45th Infantry Division was another division bottled up at Anzio. John Piazza was there. "The naval gunfire offshore . . . saved the day during a huge German offensive." Harold Wells, also in the 45th, said that at Anzio his unit was forced to call on every gun that could shoot. "We could not do without them. They were effective. We used our armor, artillery, air force and naval gunfire at one time or another. At Anzio we used them all at once. It was awesome."

The same was true for most combat soldiers in the course of the war. At one time or another some form of support fire probably helped save their lives and propel them to victory. Although they showed they could still fight well when they were without fire support, as at the Battle of the Bulge, generally fire support was a major advantage that American combat troops enjoyed.

One common aspect of the combat soldier's existence on the front lines was patrols. Henri Atkins, a frequent member of patrols, explained the process:

> We . . . went on patrols which were of two types. The combat patrol was sent out to kill Germans and return with pris-

oners for interrogation. This type of patrol was dangerous. We did not volunteer to go on these patrols because they were deadly; we had to be ordered to go. The other type was the reconnaissance patrol, or recon patrol. It was sent to scout out the enemy position but to avoid contact with the enemy. This type was less dangerous.

Harry Arnold had no love for patrol work:

> I disliked patrolling, though my training had been in I & R [Intelligence and Reconnaissance], and despite the fact that casualties during patrol work were . . . surprisingly light. A tripped foot, a broken twig, a dislodged stone, a frog in your throat that must be cleared—all seem to invite the ears of hundreds of enemy perched behind black-snouted MGs with full belts.

The Pacific war often featured its own special type of patrols, as Don Zobel, of the 1st Marine Division, recalled. "Jungle patrol is more often than not hand to hand combat. There is not enough time for rifles; besides the sound of the shots would carry too far, alerting other enemies that could be nearby. Bayonets and knives became old and trusted friends."

David Arvizu, of the 36th Infantry Division, had a harrowing experience on one recon patrol in the Vosges Mountains in France:

> The mission of the patrol was to find out if there were any small isolated enemy units in the area to our right front. I could see a group of at least eight enemy soldiers. Suddenly the BAR man called out to me, "Look out, Zu!" I glanced over my left shoulder and there stood a German soldier on the footpath wearing a large poncho. He leveled his rifle at me and pulled the trigger, but the weapon did not fire!

Arvizu and his men were able to escape to safety. Arvizu was lucky that he did not have to dodge bullets, thanks to the jammed rifle of the German soldier.

Other men who were not as lucky found themselves dodging bullets. They reported that there is a misconception about the sound of bullets. Most accounts describe bullets as whizzing by men or ricocheting and whining. James Simms, of the 101st Airborne Division, asserted that "high-powered bullets break the sound barrier, so that they make an explosive popping sound as they go by. You can tell their distance by the loudness of the pop." Sidney Richess concurred: "I don't know where some of these writers get the idea that bullets whine, buzz, whiz, or whistle as they pass. Anyone who had worked the range pits or been fired at knows that a round will 'snap' as . . . it goes by, breaking the sound barrier." Joseph Kiss, of the 2d Infantry Division, also concurred. "When bullets come close to your head, they split the air so fast that air coming back together pops like a hard clap of hands (really pops; only ricochets will buzz or whine or whir. So much for movie phoniness)."

When it came to the actual fighting, no two men had the same experience. The intensity, danger, and pacing of combat varied greatly from theater to theater and even from small unit to small unit. Harley Reynolds, of the 1st Infantry Division, never forgot the bravery of a bangalore torpedo man who attempted to blow up German obstacles on D day at Omaha Beach:

> He pulled the string to the fuselighter and pushed himself backward. The first didn't light. After a few seconds the man calmly crawled forward, exposing himself again. He removed the bad lighter, replaced it with another, and started to repeat his first moves. He turned his head in my direction . . . when he flinched . . . and closed his eyes looking into mine. Death was so fast for him. His eyes seemed to have a question or pleading look in them.

Alton Pearson attempted to save a wounded man under machine-gun fire:

> I was really suffering, seeing that brave boy dying out there. I told Charlie [his buddy] I wouldn't want my brother left out there and I would go get him if someone would help me carry him. Charlie said, "I'll go with you." I said, "God be with us."

We stood up on the hedgerow, and all firing stopped until we got him back.

Glenn Searles had many violent experiences fighting the Japanese, but one on Okinawa stood out:

Every time a flare would fizzle out, here they would come, inching along with only a grenade or two for weapons. One Jap made it right up to our hole so quietly I didn't know he was anywhere near. With a reflex action, I poked my BAR in his ear and pulled the trigger. His head opened like a cantaloupe and we were splattered with brains.

One night during the Battle of the Bulge, Edward Laughlin woke up and noticed that a German patrol was in his midst:

I heard the crunch of boots on the snow, slow and deliberate steps in an attempt to reduce the sound. By this time, the Germans had to see the bundles in the snow and knew they were passing thru sleeping GIs. I caught a quick look at a silhouette against the snow, not five feet away, a menacing figure in a slight crouch and the outline of a short-barreled weapon, undoubtedly their automatic Schmeiser pistol. He could have killed us all before we could have made any return fire! The patrol kept moving on through . . . us.

On another occasion, Laughlin's unit ran directly into a German tank:

The tank wasn't much more than 50–60 yards away when some explosive hit it in the side and knocked one track off. I saw a trooper run up behind the tank and toss a high explosive grenade on top of the engine. It exploded, the back end of the tank broke into smoke and flames, and the German crew opened the turret hatch and started scrambling frantically— only to be met by a hail of American rifle and machine gun fire.

William McLaughlin was on a recon patrol when he ran into Japanese soldiers. A firefight broke out. "I took a group of five soldiers and crossed the road to check on . . . a sniper. I found one crawling away and shot him. At that moment another stood up barely ten feet away and cut down on me. One of my men . . . saw him. He fired from the hip and distracted the Jap's aim."

David Snoke, of the 1st Infantry Division, came ashore with the first wave on Omaha Beach:

> I was first in line to get off our boat. I glanced behind in time to see the Lieutenant get hit in the head with an 88. That was when I first started to get scared. He was only 5 ft. behind me. Not even a minute after that, I saw Cpl. Armstrong get hit in the head and shoulder by machine gun fire. I dropped all of my equipment and laid down on the beach and fired 2 clips of ammo at some Jerries I saw running around beyond the beach.

Harold Hoffen, a member of the 2d Infantry Division, came face to face with a German Panther tank. He had only a bazooka as protection:

> Our first shot from the bazooka glanced off the area between the tracks, the most vulnerable area. The Panther then spun around and came rumbling directly for . . . me. On it came, firing. We completely circled the building, with the Panther in hot pursuit again, when I spied a stone wall across a small road where we could find shelter. I looked from behind the wall and saw one of our jeeps which the Panther had run over in its chase.

Theodore Schell and his 11th Airborne Division comrades were under heavy banzai attack on Leyte and about to crack when one soldier made the difference between life and death:

> The Japs surrounding us launched the biggest and most violent of their many banzai charges. I remember saying, "God, now I know how those guys felt on Bataan." Foster left his covered position and charged forward alone, totally exposing

himself to enemy fire, shouting at the . . . paratroopers and rallying them to turn and fight. It was an inspiring sight.

Max Renner also had occasion to come under banzai attack during his combat service with the 27th Infantry Division. He survived an awful night, only to come very close to dying the next morning:

> When morning came and I saw the enemy tight up to our foxholes, piled one on top of another, I was thankful that we held. While walking along the line, counting the dead, I heard a loud yell, turned and saw a Japanese soldier burst from the trees—charging toward me, his sword raised above his head. As the man charged screaming, I fired one round . . . and hit him.

Gordon Rose, of the 36th Infantry Division, and his buddy hunted out a sniper one day at Altavilla in Italy:

> As I jumped the gardens, the sniper would fire shots at me. I told Fuesko to remain in place and cover me with fire on the sniper while I advanced closer to the German. I heard Fuesko yell, "Rose, I'm coming with you!" I yelled back, "Hell no, stay put and cover me!" The sniper shot him just before he got to the wall which was protecting me. I rarely get mad, but I was damned close to it as I determined that the sniper was going to pay for Fuesko's death. I kicked in the door. My finger was on the trigger as I entered the small room. As I swept the room with my tommy gun, I swung it around on him in the corner and continued firing until it was emptied.

John Knutsen, also a T-patcher, was once holed up in a house under German attack near the Moselle River in France:

> At least five men were shooting out of one window as fast as they could fire and reload. A second wave of infantry suddenly appeared, coming straight at our position. Everyone seemed to be firing and reloading, taking turns shooting through the same window. The noise was deafening. The BAR man eventually burned up his weapon from the constant firing.

One evening in the Philippines, Leon Clement, of the 37th Infantry Division, was attacked in the middle of the night by the Japanese:

> They had evidently scouted out our position in the daytime for they didn't hesitate a bit in firing right at our holes from 30 feet distance. We knew our positions were spotted so we waited until they fired again and saw their flash, then pumped our rounds at them. One Nip crawled unseen up to our neighboring hole and tossed in a grenade, killing one and blowing another's foot off.

Even late in the war, combat soldiers faced exceedingly dangerous situations. William Warde, of the 42d Infantry Division, found himself in brutal, urban combat in April 1945 in Germany:

> We faced snipers in buildings, machine-gun fire at every major street intersection, and panzerfausts. At one street corner, we had several men hit by machine-gun fire. As they lay wounded in the street, the Germans continued to fire into them. We literally climbed through smoldering ruins of buildings to force the German machine-gun crew to retreat, so that our wounded could be removed to safety.

Jacob Brown, of the 76th Infantry Division, wrote of a river crossing in Germany late in the war:

> Men were screaming, boats overturned and blew up. Death and fear were all around us. Men fell out of boats and drowned. The whole river was on fire. We were close to the bank of the river and all of the men were in a hurry to get out and on the ground. I walked into rolls of barbed wire and couldn't get out for about two hours.

John Pulliam, a glider infantryman in the 82d Airborne Division, noted an incident in which he did not flinch from killing a German soldier. "There was a German come walking down. The company commander said, 'Somebody better shoot him.' Believe it or not, I didn't hesitate a bit. They told me to quit shooting, you've got him. You think it would really bother you. It didn't. You're psyched up."

Matt Miletich, a replacement in the 84th Infantry Division, was the quarry for a group of Germans who wiped out his squad. He had to rely on wits alone to survive:

> The reflexes I had learned in basic training took over my responses. I dropped into the snow, crawled forward a couple of yards and got the machine-gunner in the sights of my rifle. I fired eight times at the enemy machine-gunner. I saw something move but I didn't know whether I hit him. I quickly shoved a new clip of ammunition in my rifle and fired four more times. The machine gun's bullets were digging huge gaping holes in the snow all around my head and shoulders. How I escaped being hit by them is more than I'll ever know. I dropped my rifle in the snow and played dead, letting my head and body go limp in the snow. The German machine-gunner stopped shooting at me.

Only under the cover of darkness was Miletich able to escape. Lionel Adda, who was at Elsenborn Ridge with the 99th Infantry Division during the Battle of the Bulge, wrote of what it was like to stop a German attack:

> There were two sharp explosions one or two yards to my right—hand grenades, and these were followed by a burst of burp-gun fire. The bullets struck the embanked dirt in front of my hole, and dislodged stones struck me painfully in the face. Gradually the firing decreased in volume. We had stopped the attack. With the increasing light I could see at least a dozen bodies lying in front of us. To my right, just at the edge of the highway, a German lay with his body pointed directly at our gun. I fired two rounds into his body. He was already dead.

Jack Brugh, of the 106th Infantry Division, also bore the brunt of the massive German offensive:

I, along with all the riflemen, began to fire. We killed many Germans. However, many got through and followed on behind the tanks. Spotlights were used as a fright weapon, but it seemed to me that it lit up the area and made their infantry-men targets. In spite of many being killed, they kept coming, and hundreds moved on through our lines.

Bill Oatman, a paratrooper in the 101st Airborne Division, jumped into Normandy on D day and lived to tell about it:

Our plane was hit and the wing was on fire. We were so low that when my chute opened I swung twice and hit the ground. I know that all the men didn't get out. They were too low and their chutes never had time to open. We heard some noise and about eight or ten krauts came running towards our gully. We had pulled pins in our grenades so we just waited till they got pretty well past us. Then, we threw grenades and took off in the other direction. I know we got a few of them because of all the screaming and hollering.

Ray Calandrella also jumped on D day:

Different color tracers were coming up all around us and there just wasn't a thing we could do but float down. Some of my friends never hit the ground alive. I hit the ground very hard and wrenched my right leg but was OK after I rested a few minutes. I had landed in a big field all by myself. I was alone and scared. The Jerries were sending up flares and plenty of them. The rattle of machine guns sounded all night and the next day.

In a letter home, Arthur Kammerer, of the 102d Infantry Division, described combat in the Rhineland campaign in Germany:

As we advanced, not firing now, that nasty p-p-p-p-p-p of a Jerry MG went by us. We hit the ground and laid down every thing we had—which was lots. A BAR when handled properly has more effect than a light 30 caliber MG, and we had five right there. We killed one Jerry right then. We maintained a base of fire while another squad maneuvered to the left of the MG.

Combat correspondent Bill Alcine, who was with the 1st Cavalry Division at Los Negros, described some of the sights he witnessed:

A Jap was sitting up inside [a pillbox], drawing a bead with a rifle. About 20 carbines and tommy guns practically sawed him in half. He folded over like a man in prayer. The GIs heard more noises inside the pillbox but didn't bother to find out who was causing it; they just blew the roof in with TNT and grenades, and the battle for this particular pillbox was over.

Logan Weston, who was with Merrill's Marauders in Burma, recalled a Japanese attack:

Every muscle in our bodies tensed as we peered into the pitch darkness. We could hear the muffled sounds of the Japanese moving in the darkness. Then a sudden burst of machine gun fire would signal the beginning. Japanese soldiers would crawl to within a few feet of our positions, only to be discovered when a shell would burst brightly overhead. We found that grenades were our best defense.

Tanker Jack Brewer, of the 3d Armored Division, recalled his first time under fire. "We had to clean out a pocket of resistance in an apple orchard in the hedgerow country of France. It was quite scary and I realized it was live ammo and we were playing for keeps especially because of the German tank and artillery fire. We did accomplish our mission."

During the Battle of the Bulge, 4th Armored Division tanker W. King Pound had his tank knocked out:

As we worked our way towards the village, Sgt. Caldwell told me to start shooting the co-ax 30 cal. machine gun at some of the thatched roofs of the houses so as to gain illumination. This I was doing when I heard Caldwell hollering at me to get the hell out . . . we've been hit! I jumped out of the turret and started falling back. We could hear Germans coming in their vehicles behind us looking for survivors. We lay down in the snow . . . one of the vehicles passed us. It was a German armored personnel carrier not more than twenty feet away. I could see the Germans looking around. Yes, I was indeed "slightly" scared! Luckily the Germans went on.

Stan Davis, a tank commander in the 10th Armored Division, won a victory during the Battle of the Bulge:

We opened fire at point blank range with both AP [armor piercing] and HE [high explosive] ammo and the German tank returned the fire, putting rounds into the buildings to our right and to our rear, setting the buildings on fire. We continued to fire mostly AP with a few HE as fast as we could reload with the Germans doing the same thing. After several shots were exchanged the German tank stopped firing and we could see shadowy figures bailing out of the tank.

Harry Smith, of the 2d Marine Division, came ashore in the teeth of murderous fire at Tarawa. He wrote candidly to his girlfriend about it:

I was one of the first ten men out, and as these first ten scrambled out many of them were hit. A fellow directly in front of me got shot in the head, the force tore his helmet off and as he fell forward into the water I could see that the top of his head had been blown off and his brains dropped into the water. To this day I don't know how I got to shore in such a shower of machine gun and small arms fire. Men were getting shot all around me.

William Allen, who served in the 4th Marine Division, saw bitter combat as an antitank gunner at Roi-Namur. He said that his crew mainly used their 37mm cannon as an antipersonnel weapon:

A couple of times guys jumped out and kicked the bodies over in front of our gun position so the shells could get over them to hit the guys still charging. They were stacked five high in front of the gun position within about ten or fifteen feet. After daylight came . . . we could walk for two hundred yards and not even touch ground. It was survival. You didn't pay any attention. That was just a matter of eat or be eaten.

Another marine, Leland Belknap, wrote to his father about Japanese snipers:

They were wicked little fellows. They had dug holes in solid rock so they didn't have to show themselves, and we couldn't even see the muzzle of their rifles. They used smokeless powder so that we didn't even see the powder flash. I've seen one of the snipers shoot a man right between the eyes when he was on his knees, and before he hit the ground, he had put another one less than two inches from the first. I saw one sniper shoot six men through the head as good as if he was laying the gun on his head. We never did find the guy.

Arthur Hanssen described what it was like to be a marine tanker on Iwo Jima:

I've never seen so many caves and pillboxes before in my life and most of them have three to four men in them. There are plenty of single-man pillboxes too. The sniper fire is something awful. Yesterday just one sniper got 10 of our men, 8 wounded and 2 killed, in about 1 hour's time. We couldn't find that nip, either. We fired into every cave we saw, with no luck. We got one but not the right one.

Charles Richardson barely survived at Saipan:

I saw several of my friends blown all to pieces. I was scared, but it seems like something told me I would get killed so I just kept going. Bullets and mortar fire were hitting all around me. I was in a small foxhole and the fire was getting close to me. I decided to go back on the beach to rest up and get more ammunition. Somehow I got all turned around and instead of going back, I went forward. If I had gone back to the beach, I would probably have been killed, for the Japs were shelling the beach.

In a letter to his wife, one infantry officer articulated the world of combat:

Just picture a bunch of men—American GIs—but all of them dirty, grimy, about 10 days' growth of beard, haggard look in their eyes. Nothing but men, men, men. Living in foxholes with rain pouring down. Living in mud, eating cold K rations day in and day out. You see your men gradually dwindle away. You make an attack. Something goes wrong. You withdraw, 11 killed and 39 wounded, 7 missing. You move around to flank and make another attack. This time you are successful. You take your objective and lose 17 men.

The fighting, then, was somewhat different for each man involved in combat, even those in the same squads. Each man attempted to find the kind of courage it took to perform effectively. Some succeeded more than others. Most did their jobs well enough to win. At the same time they kept survival at the forefront of their daily goals. They fired their weapons in combat and did whatever else was expected of them. They were not heroes in the classic, Sergeant York sense. Instead they were effective combat soldiers doing a dirty, thankless, but indispensable job. Without their proficiency and courage, the war could not have been won.

Although the United States did not suffer the awful bloodletting experienced by some of the other World War II combatants, it did nonetheless pay heavily in lives to attain victory. The best estimate of U.S. war dead and missing is 405,400. Additionally, 670,800 Americans were wounded in World War II and another 139,700 taken prisoner. This brought U.S. casualties to more than a million in the three and a half years it took to fight the war—an exceedingly heavy cost by American standards.

The vast majority of casualties occurred in ground combat. Of the approximately 400,000 American war dead in World War II, close to 300,000 were listed as killed in action. Approximately 185,400 were from army ground forces or the marine corps as opposed to 91,600 from the army air force and the navy. Of the approximately 670,000 wounded, a whopping 574,300 were from army ground forces and 67,200 more from the marines. In addition, men from army ground forces accounted for 79,800 of the approximately 140,000 U.S. POWs.

Clearly, ground combat was the most dangerous, deadly way for an American to fight in World War II. This was especially true for riflemen in U.S. infantry divisions. There was no more perilous job, as evidenced by the casualty lists of 11 different divisions in northwestern Europe, the scene of the highest American casualties of the war. In every division, at least 15 percent of all riflemen were killed in action, and at least 56 percent were wounded in action. In the 83d Infantry Division alone, 19 percent of the riflemen were killed and 62 percent wounded. In fact for just these 11 divisions sampled, the total number of riflemen killed in approximately 10 months of combat in Europe was 37,215. The total wounded was 136,677. These are staggering numbers in light of the fact that the sampled divisions represented only 11 of the 91 combat divisions that saw action in World War II. For the ground combat soldier, there was little doubt about what the future held. Eventually, if a man spent any significant time in combat, he would be killed or wounded. He could only hope that it would be the latter and not the former. If a man was wounded, he could hope to get out of combat for a time. If he was very lucky, he might get a so-called "million-dollar wound," an injury that was bad enough to keep him permanently out of combat but not bad enough to cripple him for life. Added to the peril of combat was the fact that often wounds and deaths were caused by friendly fire.

For a few men, self-inflicted wounds were the way out of combat. Those who took this route were generally reviled, although they were given proper medical treatment. Others found that they could not mentally handle the intense stress of combat, a condition known as combat fatigue. In general, victims of combat fatigue were not reviled by frontline troops. The prevailing sentiment was that every man had his breaking point and that even good soldiers reached a limit to what they could stand. Usually the best treatment for common combat fatigue was time off the front lines. The more severe cases, though, might never recover.

In Europe, close to 80,000 ground combat soldiers became prisoners. The Germans could be brutal, as at Malmédy when they wantonly massacred American POWs, but they usually treated their American captives with some semblance of decency. Although there were a few sizable U.S. surrenders against the Germans, such as Kasserine Pass in North Africa and Elsenborn Ridge in the Battle of the Bulge, most U.S. POWs in Europe were captured in small encounters.

In the Pacific it was exceedingly rare for American ground combat troops to be captured; the war against Japan was usually a "take no prisoners" conflict. The one exception was in the Philippines in 1942 when thousands of American troops were forced to surrender to the Japanese. Generally, though, the American combat soldier in the Pacific had no intention of surrendering to the Japanese, due mainly to the reputation of Japanese soldiers as being brutal. Psychologically, then, American combat troops in the Pacific did not have the "safety net" of captivity to fall back on in the event that things got too hot in battle. They knew that they must either kill the Japanese or die themselves.

The happy news for wounded American combat soldiers was that U.S. military medicine was outstanding in World War II. From the hospitals far to the rear all the way to the aidmen at the front, the army medical corps generally did an excellent job. Technology, equipment, and expertise were state of the art, and any wounded American could expect to receive the best care possible under the circumstances.

Not surprisingly, the medical corps was held in high esteem by combat soldiers. This was especially true of the frontline aidmen, or "medics," who were always among the combat troops. Every rifle company included a medic, whose job was to administer first aid to the wounded and make sure that they were evacuated back to field hospitals. Almost without exception the medic, inevitably nick-named "Doc," was one of the most popular and highly respected sol-diers in any unit. With the possible exception of submariners, front-line medics have probably been the most unsung American heroes of World War II.

One soldier had such high regard for the medics in his unit that he wrote to *Yank* magazine stating that medics should have their own special combat badge similar to the coveted combat infantryman's badge. "Don't forget that there's an aidman that's with each com-pany in combat. He, too, gets fired upon and sometimes hit or killed. He has no protection for himself because his job under fire is first to save his buddy's life. Just ask any infantryman who has been in combat." Praise for the medics has been nearly unanimous.

Henri Atkins, of the 99th Infantry Division, outlined what life was like at the front for aidmen:

A medic had one of the most dangerous jobs in the infantry. When heavy fighting erupted, the rifleman could dive into a foxhole, but when "Medic!" was screamed out, the medic had to go out into the hail of gunfire or shelling. The medic's hel-met had a large red cross painted on it and, in theory, the combatants were not supposed to shoot him. Try telling that to an impersonal mortar round. The medics were courageous and never did receive the honors they deserved.

Russell Kidder, who was in the 36th Infantry Division, saw firsthand in the Italian campaign how the medics in his unit won the respect of their comrades:

> They . . . fought their way into the hearts of their fellow soldiers—the men with the rifles and machine guns and mortars. Casualties, day and night, exhaustion, pitiful broken men. Day in, day out, the heartbreaking task of caring for broken bodies and shattered nerves, trying to be cheerful, wondering whether or not it was your turn next. The medics didn't let their buddies down. The riflemen knew that their aidman was with them at all times—they knew he had "guts," and skill, and patience. They knew that if they were hit they would get fast treatment. It was a constant source of great comfort and satisfaction.

Milton Landry, an officer in the same division as Kidder, articulated feelings of gratitude for the combat medics. "There aren't enough words in the English language to express my appreciation for what these men did for us. They have never received the recognition that they deserve and I'm sure that every combat man will express this same opinion."

Thomas Yochim was a rifle company commander in the 78th Infantry Division in France. Medics were a great comfort to his men. "Medics . . . repeatedly performed without regard for their own safety. Their exploits were well known by my troops and this had a highly positive effect on morale."

Tankers felt just as positively toward their medics, although at times they would be positioned far ahead of their medical help. This did not prevent 1st Armored Division tank commander Walter Russell from receiving excellent care. Just half an hour after he was hit at Pisa in Italy, he was on his way to a field hospital. Donald Taylor, an armor infantryman in the 1st Armored, credited the medics with saving his life. "I would not be here today had it not been for the excellent medical care I received at the front. I was paralyzed in both legs and my right arm was wholly severed." Glen Alford, a tank crewman in the 3d Armored Division, lauded the medics as "absolutely tops . . . gutsy guys, cool as cucumbers, regardless of what was going on. I choke up whenever I think of the entire medical corps."

Robert Garcia, of the 29th Infantry Division, described his company aidman:

> Dahlen was a darned good medic. Hardworking and always there when you needed him. He was burly and muscular and absolutely tireless. Time after time, when we were fighting . . . I saw him crouching down beside a wounded soldier, doing whatever wonders he could with whatever he had in his medical bag of tricks. All hell could be breaking loose around him, but he calmly went about the business of doing whatever he could for a wounded soldier.

Many combat soldiers would recognize those characteristics in their own medic. J. D. Jones, of the 3d Infantry Division, saw his medic go after a wounded man even after another aidman was already killed trying to save the man:

> He pulled the other medic off and looked at him. Apparently he was dead, but the other man was still alive. And Sammy turned . . . his helmet to get that big old white blob with the red cross on it, and he was just leaning over the man . . . and they [Germans] shot him right between the shoulder blades, killed him instantly. I didn't think the Distinguished Service Cross was enough—he should have gotten the Congressional [Medal of Honor], but he didn't.

Medics were, of course, not unthinking robots. They must have been deathly afraid when confronted with such situations. Mel Cotton, a combat medic in the 91st Infantry Division, remembered what he felt like in just such an instance:

> The sounds for help now arriving through ears that rang in partial deafness, into weary heads that pounded and roared. Your own emotions packed solid with a belly full of tied up guts

just within the human edge of self control; all the time wondering if the next one had your number on it. The combat medic . . . was more often than not just another moving soldier. The only protection he had was a medical or white flag.

John Worthman, a medic in the 4th Infantry Division, recalled how dangerous the job of aidman could be. After starting out as a private, he quickly became a corporal in Normandy. "Our regiment had 80 percent of its aidmen lost in Normandy—wounded, killed in action, or captured. If you remained alive and unhurt and uncaptured, you were almost bound to be promoted. The attrition rate was . . . great." Still, he felt that the job had its rewards. "If you have never felt you were really wanted, be an aidman. Forty men are relying on you to bandage them and keep them alive."

If anything, the job of the medics was even more difficult in the Pacific, where the Japanese had little, if any, respect for wounded men or those who sought to help them. The Japanese actively sought to kill medics. The Germans had a somewhat inconsistent record of shooting at medics. Sometimes they killed those attempting to help the wounded and other times they respected the red cross painted on a medic's helmet. Although some medics were conscientious objectors who refused to fight, most were not. In Europe most of them adhered to the rules of the Geneva Convention and carried no weapons. The Pacific was a far different matter. Aidmen had to carry weapons for self-defense. John Lane, of the 4th Marine Division, claimed that every medic he saw in combat was fully armed. William McLaughlin, of the Americal Division, remembered that "medics carried rifles and were common riflemen."

Respect and admiration for medics was just as high among combat men in the Pacific as it was in Europe. Don Zobel, a member of the 1st Marine Division, felt that on Guadalcanal the "corpsmen," as marines called medics, did an outstanding job:

They were having to deal with the horrible injuries, the pain, the death, and the frustration of not having the necessary supplies or facilities that could many times mean the difference between life and death on a daily basis. There was, for them, no escaping the nightmares of reality. Surely the sights, sounds, and stench of sickness and death would follow these men for the rest of their lives. They performed the best they could and gave it their all.

Tom Rounsaville, of the 11th Airborne Division, had an equally high opinion of his medics. "Aidmen at the front did a great job with limited means. The evacuation time was a problem in getting men to the rear for treatment." Limited supplies and difficult evacuation of the wounded were two frequent problems in the Pacific. It was often difficult to get medical supplies to units deep in the jungle. When a man was hit, getting him out of the jungle could be a major problem for medics. Charles Card, who fought in the 24th Infantry Division, wrote: "Considering the isolation and lack of medical instrumentation and supplies, the aidmen worked remarkably well." Emil Matula, of the 25th Infantry Division, recalled how difficult it was to move casualties at Guadalcanal: "Our company medics were the best. They treated people under fire and our wounded had to be carried on a jungle trail for miles through rough terrain to an evacuation center."

Melvin Coobs, who fought with the 96th Infantry Division at Okinawa, had an equally high opinion of the medics. Like many combat men, he formed a close friendship with his unit's aidman:

> One of my closest friends was a company medic and he certainly exposed himself to danger on many occasions to treat a wounded man. In some areas it was difficult or impossible to tend to wounded men properly but great effort was always expended to get the wounded to the aid station as soon as possible.

John Blount, a medic in the Marshall Islands campaigns, described his job in a letter home: "At the front all the time, quite often in no mans land day and night picking up the wounded whether they be friend or foe. The medic treats them all. To us a wounded man is a wounded man and a life to be saved."

When a man got wounded, a clearly defined process took place. A medic would get to him as quickly as possible and give him first aid. If a medic was not available, then a man's buddy might administer the first aid. However, this was usually not encouraged. Soldiers were trained to keep fighting and let the medics deal with casualties regardless of the circumstances. The reasoning was that if everyone stopped to help the wounded, there would be too few combat troops left to fight the enemy. Generally, the system worked well, but it was not uncommon for one medic to have to deal with several wounded men at once.

After receiving first aid, a wounded man was then moved from the battlefield. This was often a tricky and dangerous process, because at times combat conditions or terrain served to impede litter bearers from moving the wounded. Sometimes in heavy combat it was too dangerous to remove the wounded. Because of mountainous terrain in Italy or jungles in the Pacific, it was not unusual for men to wait a day or two for evacuation.

John Worthman recalled the arduous process of moving the wounded:

> Most wounded had to be carried back to Aid Stations on litters. Carrying litters is cruel work in good terrain and inhuman punishment on wet hillsides under tree bursts. From the Aid Stations to the Collecting Companies, the movement was by ambulances or . . . jeeps. In a rather static campaign as in Normandy or the Huertgen litter bearers were very busy. When the campaign was more fluid as in coming north from Paris . . . litter bearers were seldom used. Everything was on wheels and moving.

Once a man could be moved, he was taken to the battalion aid station, the closest medical facility. Worthman described the way they were treated:

> Upon arriving at the aid station the soldier was triaged. That's a nice French word [that] means to divide the wounded into three groups. One included those who were lightly wounded and in no serious danger. Most of these would return to action. Another group, and easily the largest, included all

serious wounds which required immediate attention and early evacuation. Some of these would return. A third group was for the wounded who could not recover. These wounded were treated for pain relief only.

If a soldier's wounds required further treatment, he was then moved up the chain to regimental, division, and field hospitals in the rear. If a man reached that point, he was often evacuated by ship or plane. In Europe, evacuation was usually to England or North Africa. In the Pacific it was to the closest secure base, whether that be Australia, Pearl Harbor, or, later in the war, Guam.

Donald Greener, a 1st Armored Division soldier who was wounded at Anzio, chronicled his trip through the medical chain:

> I was put on a stretcher . . . then loaded on a jeep with another casualty and taken to our regimental medics then back to division medics, then back to an evacuation hospital at the beachhead, overnight there, then evacuated the next day by LST ship. I arrived in Naples and was taken with the other casualties to a tent city hospital. Everyone always took good care of me.

A few weeks after a soldier was wounded, his family would usually receive a telegram from the adjutant general. John Grove, of the 3d Infantry Division, was wounded several times. The first time his family received a telegram saying, "Deeply regret to inform you that your son Private First Class John A. Grove was slightly wounded in action in France." When he was more severely wounded a few months later, the telegram reflected his state: "Regret to inform you your son was seriously wounded in action in France Six November." As these telegrams indicate, the army did make a serious effort to keep families well informed. Nevertheless, if families wanted any further information about a loved one, they had to depend on letters.

Woundings were a major part of the world of the combat soldier. Most veterans have distinct memories of when they or close comrades were hit. Edward Laughlin, of the 82d Airborne Division, never forgot the carnage of broken bodies. "The vivid picture of bright red blood from a ripped open face, a dangling arm with fingers missing and blood flowing and dripping down on the cobblestone street and other such gruesome sights are still with me after all these years."

John Roche, of the 88th Infantry Division in Italy, recalled helping a desperately wounded comrade who had been blinded by an enemy grenade. "I . . . knelt beside Nash. He told me he couldn't see. I said, 'It's the dirt in your eyes.' 'I can't feel anything in my hands,' he said. 'Tell me I'll see again.' Gently I pressed his shoulder. 'You'll see again. You'll be alright.'"

When Ferdinand Huber, of the 99th Infantry Division, was pinned down under German artillery fire, he saw a man hit in the leg by shrapnel. After no medic came to treat the wounded soldier, Huber tried to help the man:

> I crawled over to help and found that his lower leg was just being held together by a couple of inches of muscle. I pulled his belt and medical kit, tried to put a tourniquet around his leg, dumped the sulfa [disinfecting] powder on the wound, and put the kit bandage as well as I could around the leg. His eyes were glazed, like the look of a wounded rabbit.

Colin McLaurin, an infantry officer in the 29th Infantry Division, remembered being jealous of a wounded soldier. "I recall telling the wounded man to report back to the aid station and at the same time sort of envying him. I envied him because he would be evacuated to a hospital in England where he could rest, sleep, eat, and take it easy for a few weeks at least."

Thomas Rosell, a junior officer in the 34th Infantry Division, helped carry to safety a wounded comrade who had stepped on a mine in Italy. "The sight that I'll never forget is the jagged bone. The mine had just enough charge in it to blow off his foot. The jagged bone sticking out, milk white, pure white. I didn't see a lot of blood, just this jagged bone and red tissue. We put a tourniquet on him."

The experiences of Rex Harrison, a medic in the 36th Infantry Division, illustrate just how difficult it could be for medics to treat and evacuate a wounded soldier from the front:

I examined Smitty and found that he had penetrating wounds of the right arm and leg and that both limbs were broken. I managed to drag him out of the hole, but this effort, together with all the running, completely exhausted me. We were both lying on top of the ground. Small arms fire was splattering us with mud.

Evenutally with the help of another man, Harrison was able to move the wounded soldier to the comparative safety of the platoon command post and then evacuate him to the rear.

Bob Conroy, of the 75th Infantry Division, occupied a forward foxhole during the Battle of the Bulge. It was dangerous to leave the foxhole for fear of German fire. When his foxhole buddy was hit, there was almost nothing Conroy could do for him:

> Gordon got ripped by a machine gun from roughly the left thigh through the right waist. We were cut off. The Germans had overrun our position and we were in the foxhole by ourselves, so basically we both knew he was going to die. We had no morphine . . . so I tried to knock him out. I took off his helmet, held his jaw up and just whacked as hard as I could, because he wanted to be put out. That didn't work. Nothing worked. He slowly . . . bled to death. The next morning . . . it looked as if I'd spent a day in a butcher shop.

Walter Mietus, a medic in the 76th Infantry Division, made the important point that aidmen often had to improvise and that no amount of training could prepare medics for some of the wounds they saw. "There just wasn't enough training for some of the things. For example, a guy was hit with shrapnel and his jawbone was severed. The jawbone was hanging. I was fumbling around and then I looked down on the ground and there was a hangar wire and I took that and it worked very well."

Walter Pippin served with Merrill's Marauders in Burma. The intensity and stress of the war behind Japanese lines, especially the plight of the wounded, affected him deeply:

Even the wounded, choking on their own blood and becoming ill at the sight of their shuddering mass of torn flesh
and muscle, could know no relief except the soul-stealing effect of morphine adminstered in the hopes that they might forget the pain and the fact that there was no way to remove them
from the confusion and death.

Mary Slaughter, an army nurse at Pearl Harbor in 1941, witnessed
the horrible aftermath of the Japanese attack:

The most awful sight my eyes ever beheld. Arms, legs, hands,
faces, insides and outsides gone. Blood, gore—gore and
blood—it was terrible. One lad had his face peppered with
wounds like a pencil had been rammed in three inches. I suppose he had fifteen such marks on his face and his right arm
was blown off at the shoulder. All day long they kept coming
in from surgery—from first aid—from the field—no moans, no
cries, no sound. One of the very first . . . clung to me with the
most pitiful beseeching . . . look in his eyes.

It was disturbing to see others wounded, but nothing was more
frightening than getting hit yourself. Most men remembered clearly
the details of being hit. Getting wounded meant being helpless, a
bitter feeling for young men who sometimes saw themselves as invincible.

Glenn Searles, of the 77th Infantry Division, got hit attacking
Japanese positions on Okinawa:

I got up even with the pit and killed the four Japs with a single burst of my BAR—and then I bought the farm. A Jap with
a Nambu light machine gun popped up . . . not four feet from
me and knocked me down with a burst. A round smashed the
walnut hand grip of my weapon and went through my left hand
and other bullets hit my chest and upper left arm.

Henri Atkins was performing his job of platoon scout ahead of his
buddies when he was suddenly hit by small-arms fire:

What felt like a baseball bat slammed into my left hand. My glove was blown off and a big spurt of blood reddened the white snow. I was in partial shock and felt out of myself. I could not believe that this had happened to me. I was not meant to be shot. Acceptance came slowly as two medics worked on me. My thoughts turned to good thoughts. I was still alive. I should have been killed. I was OK and I was getting out of this frozen hell.

James Simms was hit one cold night during the Battle of the Bulge. A shell landed near his foxhole, killing one of his buddies and wounding him and another man. The other man, one of his best friends, came close to bleeding to death; Simms had a concussion and a major shoulder wound. After struggling to avoid passing out, he managed to pull his buddy out of the hole and find a medic. After an interminable wait, during which Simms was hit again, the medics were able to evacuate the two men in spite of intense shell fire.

Simms described the transition from frozen wasteland to warm hospital:

> I was about to step through a door into an entirely different world, one that has always brought back warm memories. I was about leave a world that was cold and mean, where men had to be brutal to survive. I was about to enter a warm, kind world where a smile was ever ready and the touch gentle.

Alton Pearson, of the 4th Infantry Division, was hit charging a German pillbox during the Normandy campaign:

> I was shot in the left arm breaking my arm at the wrist and through the radial artery in my wrist. I knew I had to do something fast as gushes of blood came out on every heartbeat. I found a foxhole and got in it as 88s were falling in the rear. I put a tourniquet on my arm and put some . . . powder over the wound to form a scab. I held pressure and released it every few minutes until it stopped bleeding.

Vincent Lidholm, a combat soldier in the 6th Infantry Division, was seriously wounded during jungle combat with the Japanese. "A shell exploded in our foxhole killing three of my comrades and leaving me with a . . . debilitating wound. A piece of shell fragment tore through my helmet and skull and destroyed part of my brain. I spent the next year in an army hospital and was finally discharged in June 1945."

Twenty-seventh Infantry Division soldier Gus Mitchell was hit on Saipan. A medic, Mitchell put his training to use in saving his own life:

> I caught three machine gun bullets in my hip from a blast of a hidden Jap sniper. I was able to give myself a shot of morphine, swallow my sulfa tablets and put the gauze dressing to my wounds before I passed out. I went through a medical clearing station and ended up in a field hospital for ship evacuation.

Hershel Horton, a twenty-nine-year-old infantry officer in the 32d Infantry Division, went through an incredible ordeal in New Guinea in 1942. He led a patrol into no-man's-land to retrieve American bodies and was shot by the Japanese. A medic gave him first aid but was unable to move him to safety. Any attempts to rescue him were driven off by the Japanese. Horton lay wounded in a New Guinea swamp for more than a week with no further treatment. He recorded his thoughts in a letter to his family:

> I have tried to make splints and crawl or walk out, but I just can't make it. Today, I managed to stand, but I could go no farther. A Jap shot me in the shoulder and neck. I . . . lay here in this terrible place, wondering not why God has forsaken me but rather why He is making me suffer this terrible end? I know now how Christ felt on the cross. I have had no food of any kind since that morning I was shot. My right hip is broken and my right leg, both compound fractures, else I would have been out of here in those first couple of days. My life has been good, but I am so young and have so many things undone that a man of 29 should do. God bless you My loved ones. I shall see you all again some day. I prepare to meet my Maker.

Horton died alone in the humid swamp not long after writing these last words. When American soldiers were finally able to get to him, they found the letter in his prayer book and sent it on to his family.

Thankfully not many American wounded had to go through the kind of agony that Lieutenant Horton experienced. Clarence Waltemath, of the 87th Infantry Division, was hit by German machine-gun fire and evacuated in a matter of minutes:

> I was just peeking around the corner . . . when something hit me on the side of the head. It felt like a shovel. I said to my runner, "What the dickens is that?" He said, "You were hit with a machine gun." [The bullet] went through my ear and my skull and I got my bandage out and just about that time . . . I fell unconscious. I was practically blind from my wound.

George Karambelas, of the 84th Infantry Division, was hit by machine-gun fire at the Battle of the Bulge. A medic treated him, but before Karambelas could be moved, he was hit again, this time much more seriously:

> I felt an explosion which seemed to be right at my feet and felt a sharp pain on my right foot. I heard the medic groan and he fell over me. I tried to help him but he was already dead. The shrapnel . . . almost cut him in half. Then I heard screams from all around. Several of the men were hit and some were calling for a medic while others were just crying.

None of the other men survived, but, miraculously, Karambelas was able to beg a passing patrol to move him to safety. Had he not reached the aid station, he almost surely would have bled to death.

Earl Schoelles, who fought in Italy with the 91st Infantry Division, was lucky enough to get hit along a highway, which made it easier for him to be evacuated:

> A mortar shell exploded to my right. A piece of shrapnel entered the right side of my neck and traveled a couple of inches

all the way across the left side. Another piece tore the calf of my left leg just below the knee joint. I screamed for a medic. It seemed it took him forever to get to me. I was bleeding badly. The stress of what was happening to me was unbearable. I was hit around 1200 hours and by 1800 they had me on an operating table. I owe my life to the medic. I wish I could recall his name.

Roy Denmon, an armored infantryman in the 6th Armored Division in France, gave a graphic description of what it was like to get hit by shell fragments:

The fragment entered just above my ankle and traveled the full length of my leg and kept going through my left buttock. It stopped a little below my left kidney. A slab of muscle was torn from the left calf almost a foot long and three inches wide. It [the fragment] emerged three inches below the left knee skipping the hollow beneath the knee and entering the thigh five inches above the knee. It tore an 11-inch gash in the thigh and continued on through the buttock. I thought my legs were gone. A couple of soldiers . . . carried me farther into the field, dug a trench for me and went for help. They never returned and no help came for me until the next night. I don't know why I didn't bleed to death.

Harry Joseph was crippled in Belgium when the tank in which he was riding got hit by a *panzerfaust*:

I remember turning in the air, and I was thrown to the left side of the walk. When I sat up, I could see that my left arm and leg had been blown off. I took my [sulfa] tablets and started praying. The medics came up and tagged me. I . . . was sent back to the 51 field hospital and operated on. I never worried about my limbs. I was happy to be alive.

Bill Tosco, an infantry officer, had a close brush with blindness:

Some God-forsaken, low account, no good Nazi threw a grenade at me. It went off right in front of me. Pretty soon I snapped out of my daze and found that I was stone blind. None of the grenade fragments hit me but the flash had blinded me. In a little while some medical corps men found me and I was evacuated back to a field hospital. They took the bandages off my eyes on . . . my birthday and I was able to see again. That was the nicest birthday present I ever had.

Million-dollar wounds, although not common, offered some hope of reprieve for combat soldiers. Whether or not a man returned to duty after his wounding often depended on the tactical situation at the front at the time he was wounded. Typical of how million-dollar wounds occurred was one witnessed by 1st Infantry Division sergeant Harley Reynolds in France. "[The soldier] was actually laughing. He had been shot thru his upper arm. A good flesh wound. He waved goodbye and headed back. That was the last we heard from him." Harry Arnold recalled a comrade who was lucky enough to get out of combat. "Sgt Glisch came walking by me, heading rearward. There was a hole in his helmet and blood running down his face— a face that was covered with a boyish grin. That million dollar wound! I felt left out, and wished I had a bullet through an arm or a leg."

Jack Scott, of the 36th Infantry Division, received his million-dollar wound along the Rhine River near the end of the war. "What a strange feeling when you know you have been lucky and hit hard but no bones broken, no severed limbs, no eyes blown out."

Robert Jackson, a rifle platoon leader in the 96th Infantry Division, was hit at Okinawa and never returned to combat:

My last memory of Okinawa is of lying on a stretcher near the battalion aid station with the smoke swirling about and much feverish activity. The battalion surgeon, a good drinking buddy, came over to my stretcher and congratulated me on "a million dollar wound." With a broken metatarsal, infantry duty was over for me!

Far less pleasant but no less effective in removing a man permanently from combat was the self-inflicted wound. A tiny percentage of combat soldiers chose to wound themselves rather than stay on the front lines. They were treated for their wounds but otherwise reviled and ostracized.

Earl Reitan, of the 3d Infantry Division, saw one such case in France while he recuperated from his battle wounds:

> A young GI was lying there on a cot with a sign over him which said "S.I.W.," i.e., self-inflicted wound. He had shot himself in the foot to escape combat. He received routine medical care, but no one offered him sympathy of any kind or even a friendly smile, whereas everyone was encouraging to me. He was sobbing softly. Possibly he saved his life by his act, but his future was court-martial, a dishonorable discharge, and a return home in disgrace. I decided then and there that I would rather take my chances with combat than end up shunned with an S.I.W. over my cot.

The vast majority of combat soldiers agreed with Reitan's sentiments. The prevailing opinion was that they were well rid of anyone who would shoot himself to avoid combat. If a man was willing to go that far to escape the shooting, then he could not be counted on in combat and thus was worthless or even dangerous to his buddies. Radford Carroll, of the 99th Infantry Division, saw a man who had shot himself:

> This man had placed his hand over the muzzle of his rifle and fired it. He must have jerked with the pain because he had fired it twice. The damage was mainly from the muzzle blast rather than from the bullets; all the flesh was gone from the midsection of his hand and only the bones connected his wrist with his fingers. I felt no pity.

Combat was a place of strenuous physical activity. As such, injuries sometimes occurred. *Wound* was the term used to describe bodily harm caused directly by enemy activity. Sometimes, though, men got hurt participating in combat but not because of anything the enemy did. These injuries, some of them fatalities, were nevertheless counted among U.S. casualties. Glen Cagle, of the 2d Armored Division, was one such case. He tore cartilage in his knee while kicking in a door during village combat. Jeffie Duty was hurt in an automobile accident: "Sometime in the middle of the night . . . I was crossing the road . . . going back to the front and I got run over. From that point on, I never went back to active duty because . . . I was laid up in the hospital for about six or seven months." The war ended before Duty had recovered.

Les Terry, of the 36th Infantry Division, nearly met his death in a motorcycle accident while on recon patrol in Italy:

> I cut one of the corners a little too close and there was a long sounding booooom, and I could feel myself flying through the air. It all sounded like it was happening in slow motion. It seemed forever until I landed on my back in a gully full of bowling ball size rocks. I was hurting so bad I could hardly keep from screaming.

Terry was never able to return to his unit. He recovered from his injuries only after long months of rehabilitation.

There was, of course, an even worse alternative to wounds or injury. Close to 300,000 American combat soldiers were killed in action. Combat fatalities exhibited all the worst aspects of violent death. There was rarely anything clean, dignified, or glorious about dying in a battle zone.

Bart Hagerman, of the 17th Airborne Division, saw many men killed around him:

> People didn't crumple and fall like they did in Hollywood movies. They were tossed in the air. They were whipped around. They were hit to the ground hard and their blood spattered everywhere. And a lot of people were standing close to people and found themselves covered in the blood and flesh of their friends, and that's a pretty tough thing for anybody to handle.

James Simms never forgot a dead soldier he saw during the Battle of the Bulge. He thought of the man's family:

I visualized that allowing for time-zone differences, about this time of day his family would be gathered in a warm bright kitchen at home and more than likely be discussing the last letter they had received from him. In a few days they would receive a telegram that would bear the most bitter news that parents ever have to know.

Usually family or spouses were informed of a soldier's death within two weeks or so after he was killed. A telegram from the adjutant general with two stars at the top would be delivered to the home, such as the one that Mrs. Annie Hogins received on 2 October 1944, informing her that her son had been killed. "The Secretary of War desires me to express his deep regret that your son technical sergeant Marshall A. Hogins was killed in action on Fifteen September in Belgium. Letter follows."

The follow-up letter from the adjutant general arrived the next day and confirmed Marshall's death:

It is with regret that I am writing to confirm the recent telegram informing you of the death of your son, Technical Sergeant Marshall A. Hogins, 20,457,894, Infantry, who was killed in action on 15 September 1944 in Belgium. I know the sorrow this message has brought you and it is my hope that in time the knowledge of his heroic service to his country, even unto death, may be of sustaining comfort to you. I extend to you my deepest sympathy.

Because the government did not encourage families to pursue details about the death of a loved one, the only way to find out the actual circumstances of a soldier's death was to ask his comrades. Due to death and woundings among those comrades as well as the general reluctance to tell families the true circumstances of a man's death, this was a hit-or-miss proposition at best.

However, commanding officers often wrote condolence letters to the families of dead soldiers, which made it possible to find out some information. This was the case with the family of a man nicknamed "Penny" who was killed in North Africa and whose platoon leader wrote a detailed letter about Penny's death:

I . . . was with him at the time of the accident. He had been my runner and orderly. The Jerries started laying it on with everything they had. Penny was right behind me and was hit by a machine gun bullet in the fleshy part of his buttock going up toward the pelvis. It was a very painful wound but he never complained a bit. As soon as we got back to the aid station they gave him blood plasma but I guess it was too late. He died the following morning. I want you to know he died a soldier and a good one. I really have missed him, and so has everyone else.

Most combat soldiers felt that no one outside of the front lines could even imagine what it really looked like to see a man get killed, although some were willing to write on paper about it in later years. Harley Reynolds saw a man trip a mine not more than a few feet away from him. "It blew him in half and splattered me. I was sick every time I thought of it for days." This sort of butchery was the rule rather than the exception.

Glenn Searles saw a man killed in his foxhole by a Japanese grenade:

The grenade exploded between his back and the side of the hole. He was split up the back from his hips to the back of his head as if a meat cleaver had done the job. His spine was divided neatly and his chest cavity was completely empty above the diaphragm. When we dragged him out of the hole his entire brain rolled out onto the ground. I scooped it up with an entrenching tool and placed it in the chest cavity.

Edward Laughlin once went on a detail to pick up dead bodies at an observation post in front of the lines. The sergeant who led the group made a tragic discovery:

The dead GIs were lying grotesquely around, half on each other. Two were face down and the others on their sides. One was a lieutenant—machine gun fire had hit him in the right shoulder and then stitched down his body, through his stomach on the left side. The sergeant started crying. He looked at the rest of us, tears streaming down his face . . . and said, "This was my friend. We have been in a lot of combat together since North Africa."

During an attack, Harry Arnold saw a number of his dead buddies lying in the snow and paused to grieve for them:

> A lump grew in my throat. I forced myself to approach those I knew. All were still frozen in their positions of yesterday—lanky Herman Almond who saved my life one night on an OP [observation post] two months before, little Daniel Anderson with the murky glasses, slight of build, Richard Carey who had been lost and then found, and now lost. I thought of the telegram his family must endure. And there were so many more it was obscene.

One day during a patrol by himself, Don Zobel found a dead marine on Guadalcanal. He had no way to carry the body back all alone. Unfortunately the man was missing his dog tags, making it impossible to identify him:

> There he is . . . a fellow Marine. His face is not recognized; perhaps I have never met him. None of this seems to matter now. He is my brother. How many times had my fellow Marine felt the slicing and piercing of the Japanese bayonet? There must be at least 30 bayonet wounds. His penis is cut off and shoved into his mouth in the Japanese way of the ultimate insult. His once handsome features and dark complexion are now obscured by ants . . . eating away at the flesh. I shed . . . tears for his family whom I will not be able to find. To this day I am bothered by that memory.

There were unfortunately many such instances when men could not be positively identified as having been killed in action. In these cases, a soldier's family would receive a telegram that referred to the soldier as "missing in action." The wife of 1st Infantry Division soldier Julian Brooke received one of these telegrams: "The Secretary of War desires me to express his deep regret that your husband Staff

Sergeant Julian Brooke has been reported missing in action since eighteen December in Belgium." If the soldier's body could be found, the family would receive a telegram definitively informing them that he had been killed in action. Otherwise the man would be perpetually listed as missing in action. This, of course, often led to misplaced hope among family members that the missing soldier was still alive. Usually this was not the case, and family members were left to deal with the ensuing mental anguish of never really knowing what had happened to their loved one.

To avoid these situations, combat soldiers made a concerted effort to remove the bodies of their comrades from the battlefield. Deane Marks, who fought with the 11th Airborne Division in the Battle of Manila, once helped remove the body of a dead buddy from a ruined house:

> Wilson's body had swollen to twice its normal size and the skin had turned black from the afternoon sun of the day before. We laid the litter on the stairway and wrestled the body onto the litter. Rigor mortis was absent, but the swelling of the body had caused his uniform to act as a rigid envelope. His helmet strap had cut through his chin and cheeks. As we moved the body, the skin broke and gas and fluids came out. Someone threw up. When we all lifted the litter and started up the stairs, body fluids ran down the litter onto Porteous and myself. The reality of war cannot even be imagined by anyone who has not been there. Only from a poor sucker infantryman can you learn what it was like.

Jack Clover, of the 36th Infantry Division, helped haul away dead Americans from a mountain near San Pietro after a fierce German counterattack. One particular dead man made a deep impression on Clover:

> He lay with his legs outstretched spread eagle, his arms tucked beneath his chest with helmet askew as he had fallen. In a brief instant I saw him as a kid in grade school. I saw him red-faced playing street football on a crisp, fall afternoon. I saw

him in high school . . . with his girlfriend listening to Glen Miller's "Indian Summer" on the radio. Now I saw him . . . on this bleak, windswept mountainside all alone.

Clinton Riddle, a glider infantryman in the 82d Airborne Division, saw the remnants of a crashed glider a couple of days after D day in Normandy. He paused to look at the bodies of men who had been his best friends only a few days before:

You could almost step on the bodies from one to the other. One of the boys, as he lay there, had his hand extended straight up in the air as though he was reaching for someone or something. I can see that picture in my mind today as plain as I did on that morning. He was wearing a pair of black gloves. I could not bring myself to wear gloves in combat for a long time after that, and even now, I never pull a pair of gloves on without thinking of him.

Charles Lindsay, of the 4th Marine Division, was looking for mines in a field on Okinawa when he found a dead marine:

A perfect specimen of youth, good looking, not a scratch on him except a bullet hole thru his helmet. He must have been killed instantly and there was no blood. I opened his pack to get his poncho to cover him from the flies. Out fell a picture of his mother and a picture of a beautiful girl. I placed the pictures inside his jacket and then I knelt down and prayed. And then just plain cried. To me this was the whole war. No one cared except those that loved him. He would not be rewarded. And think of how many more had died the way he had. These men were the finest fighting men the world had ever known.

Usually men killed in action were tagged and left behind for rear-echelon graves registration teams to find and bury. Chuck Storeby, a paratrooper in the 101st Airborne Division, saw a graves registration team bury badly decomposed bodies in Normandy. "The graves registration team layed them out. They went through their uniforms or pockets . . . or their dog tags and they tried to identify them. If they couldn't they would just bury them as . . . an unknown soldier." Sometimes the graves registration troops, who had a gruesome, thankless job, were somewhat careless in performing their duties. This drew the ire of combat soldiers who did not want to see their dead buddies mishandled or desecrated.

Gene Tippins, a sergeant in the 80th Infantry Division, recalled one such instance and the reaction of his commanding officer, Garland Godby:

> The GRT [graves registration team] made the mistake of trying to throw the bodies of our dead up and over the sides of the truck. Man! Capt. Godby made it to that team leader in about one jump and snatched him real close . . . saying, "You S.O.B., pick those bodies up and lay them into that truck real gentle or I'll kill you." He was so mad there were tears in his eyes. The bodies were laid in that truck gently.

Although the vast majority of combat troops preferred to believe that they would not be killed, some came to terms with the fact that there was a distinct possibility they would never return home. One such soldier sought to prepare his family for that possibility. He wrote a letter that was to be delivered home only in the event of his death. Not long after writing it, he was killed in action in Italy:

> When you begin to face the very basic things in life, you don't mind speaking your heart. I want to thank you for all those thousands and thousands of little things which really make up life—when you, Dad, used to wait for us in the morning to take us to school . . . and wait again after school; and when you, Mom, would sit up at night until all of us were in bed. Though I would never be capable of full payment, I was hoping to do something for you some day. I had hoped to do it at home, but God has other plans. I want you to know that I'll be praying and waiting for you. Please don't have any regrets. God bless you and goodbye for now.

One excruciating aspect of the war was that, far too often, American casualties were caused by so-called friendly fire. Accidents happened. Sometimes American troops fired at other American troops. Sometimes U.S. artillery fell short and ended up killing and wounding Americans. Other times, American pilots mistook their own ground troops for enemy soldiers and strafed or bombed them. There are no reliable records of casualties caused by friendly fire. It happens in every war, but it is not something the military likes to acknowledge. One 96th Infantry Division soldier estimated that 8 percent of his unit's casualties were caused by U.S. fire. Regardless of the specific numbers, it happened with some degree of frequency in frontline units. Harry Arnold wrote with sardonic wit about friendly fire. "In the course of the war we were, at one time or another, subjected to fire from just about every type of weapon in the U.S. arsenal—mortars, artillery, MGs, rifles, bombers. Luckily the navy couldn't make it up the Rhine to bombard us. For that I'm thankful."

Charles Murphy, a combat engineer officer in the 1st Infantry Division, also was subjected to friendly fire. He saw it as unavoidable:

You'd better be prepared to accept it. It's just part of the nasty mess called war. Don't ever kid yourself. It is a nasty mess and if you're in it, you're in it up to your eyebrows. Nothing you can do about it except get prepared to accept it. Now how are you going to prepare civilians for that sort of thing?

James Graff and his 35th Infantry Division buddies found themselves under attack by U.S. bombers on one occasion. He felt that it was not an accident but rather because of selfishness on the part of the airmen:

We knew that the Air Corps doesn't get credit for a mission unless they get rid of their bombs. They unloaded the bombs short of their target and got out so they wouldn't have to face . . . German AA fire. Just another reason for the bad feelings between the infantry and Air Corps. Not that we didn't appreciate the support we received from them, but in this case there was no excuse for it.

Ray Mitchell, of Merrill's Marauders, recalled one hot afternoon in Burma when his outfit was twice subjected to mistaken bombing by American B-25 bombers:

> Bombs were dropped on our lines . . . killing many of our men. We could not understand why, with white markers in place to denote where our lines were. To have this happen the second time after they were aware of the results of the first error has never been explained to us who survived. It is bad to be bombed, but by your own planes twice makes it a double tragedy. I still see those bombs coming down, feel the earth beneath me shudder, see walls of dirt flying over us and the deafening sound of the explosion. Although nearly 50 years have passed, those sounds and feelings will never pass.

More commonly, it was ground fire that caused casualties to friendly troops. One major danger was artillery or mortar rounds falling short. Emil Lindenbusch, of the 6th Infantry Division, lost a good friend who was hit by U.S. mortar fragments. "Shrapnel hit him in the back. I held him until the litter carrier came and took him but he died." Robert Jackson came close to being killed by U.S. artillery. "A short round landed directly at the junction of . . . two companies. Among the many mortally wounded was my runner with whom I lay almost helmet to helmet and whose severed head looked at me. I didn't have a scratch." Rex Harrison treated the survivors of a tank that had been hit by American artillery. Three men were killed and one was seriously wounded. Harrison was still angry about it nearly fifty years later when he wrote to condemn the "stupid son-of-a-*** who couldn't see the big White Star on the side of the tank. I hope he reads this."

Richard Forse, a tanker attached to the 77th Infantry Division, remembered several friendly fire incidents that occurred during the fighting at Guam:

> Many of these happened because of not observing where other men in the same unit were located at night resulting in panicky firing and grenade throwing whenever there was a

noise. A tank driver was killed when he got up and wandered around the perimeter the second night in combat.

Perhaps the most tragic of all friendly fire incidents were those in which only one man was responsible. Time and again, usually at night, a soldier would panic and shoot at a perceived danger without considering the consequences. When this happened the shooter knew that he and he alone was responsible for the death of a comrade. This contrasted sharply with impersonal stray bombs and shells or the collective fire of one unit mistakenly firing at another unit. In those cases, no one knew who had actually done the killing and wounding.

Deane Marks remembered an evening in the Philippines in which one soldier panicked and accidentally shot a comrade:

> GI John Doe's dead body was found about five or six yards to the front of our perimeter. I cannot risk this trooper's real name, even after forty-five years. It was easy to pinpoint the person [shooter], who must have woken up, or was half asleep, and saw a figure in front of him and opened up. GI John Doe was gone now. His family never knew how. The shooter [purposely not named] was pulled out . . . and put in another army division, without prejudice and with nothing on his record. This guy that did the firing is probably still living with it. GI John Doe came . . . all the way from . . . New Guinea . . . to almost the end of Luzon, only to die because some jackass, fresh off the boat, panicked and shot before he looked, or challenged.

Another peril was the threat of captivity. Although the Japanese rarely took prisoners, the Germans did and usually treated them fairly well. The prevailing opinion was that if you could survive the first few minutes of captivity, when emotions were often supercharged from fighting, your chances of staying alive were good. Benjamin Johnson, of the 83d Infantry Division, was captured at Normandy. "After lining us up, our helmets were placed at our feet and all our personal belongings were dropped in them. Rings, watches, lighters, pocket knives, billfolds, etc. Then we were forced to remove our belts, leggings, the top button of our trousers and our shoestrings."

Jack Thacker, who served in the 30th Infantry Division, was also captured at Normandy:

> As I was sleeping . . . in my foxhole, I was roughly awakened by a rifle barrel being jabbed into my side and hearing the word "rouse" . . . over and over. The authoritative tone of voice would have been sufficient for me to obey, but the feel of the rifle barrel left no doubt as to what I should do. I immediately stood up and climbed out of my foxhole. We were rather casually interrogated. There seemed to be little or no belligerence on the part of the captors or the captives. Perhaps because they were field soldiers, their primary interest seemed to be about such things as where we lived, how old we were, and other personal data.

John Roche had a positive experience during his initial captivity in Italy on New Year's Day 1945. After being surprised in his foxhole by a German patrol, he and his buddy were taken to a German head-quarters:

> We . . . claimed not to have eaten so were served a grand meal of boiled beef with horseradish sauce. When I praised it extravagantly, the cook was brought out to hear me laud his efforts. He wished I could be there all the time, he said, to drown out his critics. He knew some English, and was the son of the owner of the Hotel Regina in Vienna. He invited me to stay, gratis, after the war was over. He showed me a picture of his wife of whom he was justly proud.

The experiences of James Mattera, of the 30th Infantry Division, were exactly opposite those of Roche. Mattera was captured by SS troops during the Battle of the Bulge and machine-gunned in the notorious Malmédy Massacre:

> The hail of metal struck like an invisible hurricane-force wind. Those not hit dived to the ground and flattened out. Blood, clothing and bone fragments sprayed in every direction. The pitiful cries and pleas of the wounded for mercy . . . reached a crescendo. Even a robot would have cried. Targeted

by a multitude of guns, I survived, miraculously not even wounded.

Mattera waited until he no longer heard German voices and then made a run for it, dodging bullets until he was finally out of range of the German guns. Somehow he then made it to an American outpost.

Experiences such as those of Roche and Mattera were rare. Most combat soldiers who became POWs were scared when initially captured and did not forge any special bond or adversarial relationship with their captors.

Ben Kimmelman, a junior officer in the 28th Infantry Division, was captured during the Battle of the Bulge:

> After we surrendered, the German corporal took me over and then they put me on the hood of the car. I was sitting with my legs dangling over the grill, and he had a pistol to my head. To my absolute astonishment, I was looking at droves and herds of beautifully uniformed young, healthy-looking, well-fed, well-equipped German troops, and my heart sank. And they came by . . . laughing at me as the trophy.

Clarence Ferguson, a member of the 36th Infantry Division, was captured in Italy when his unit was pinned down by German tanks. He was unceremoniously searched by his captor:

> He jerked me around, unsnapped my cartridge belt, jerked the suspenders off my shoulders and threw them on the ground. In this search he saw my wristwatch, removed it from my arm, and indicated he wanted it. I nodded in assent. Just as he finished, another German soldier rushed up to me and thrust the point of his bayonet into the pit of my stomach. In excited, broken English he muttered angrily, "You kill my buddy?" I asked, "Where?" "There," he said, pointing not far away to where his friend lay dead. I made no admission, and soon he left me to shock someone else in his unorthodox interrogation.

Another T-patcher, Alan Williamson, who was captured at Salerno recalled that when he and his buddies were marched away into captivity he had "the strange feeling that I had died, passed on to the Great Beyond." Since then, other POWs have stated that they had the same eerie feeling.

Jack Brugh was one of the unfortunate 106th Infantry Division soldiers who were taken prisoner during the first few days of the Battle of the Bulge. German tanks drove up to his position and threatened to shoot if he and his comrades did not surrender. As did many Americans, Brugh chose captivity over death:

> As I walked with the other G.I.s toward the tanks and the German soldiers, I was actually shaking with fear. A lot was going through my mind—like what they were going to do to us or with us. They yelled at us in German and lined us up and frisked us to be certain that we were unarmed. One of the guys had inadvertently left a hand grenade in his gun belt. A German sergeant grabbed the grenade and knocked the G.I. to the ground. We walked about four miles and reached the town of Prum. There was an English-speaking German guard with us, and one of the P.O.W.s asked him where we were going. His answer was Siberia, and he said, "You will be there forever, because the German Army has taken Antwerp and is moving through France near Paris." That really frightened me, because after the way they ripped through our division, it was easy to believe.

Ian Morrison was also captured in the initial shock phase of the Bulge. His experiences were typical of many who became prisoners of the Germans:

> We were herded . . . to a barnyard in Schoenfeld where, crowded, cold, hungry and hurting we spent the next 24 hours before beginning the straggling, starving, scared march to a railhead in Germany where a hundred of us were shoved into each awaiting boxcar. A new war of survival as prisoners of the Germans lay ahead.

Sometimes the wounds a man received were not physical but mental. For some the stress of combat became too much and they could no longer function. This condition, called shell shock in World War I and combat fatigue or exhaustion in World War II, was fairly common among U.S. combat soldiers. Although there were those who thought of battle fatigue as cowardice, Gen. George Patton being the most notable of this group, it became obvious during the war that this was patently false. According to one study, it could safely be expected that close to 10 percent of the men in an infantry outfit would eventually become combat fatigue casualties. Additionally, the study found that an average rifle company in combat could expect roughly 75 percent of its men to get wounded. Of those, 18 percent were combat fatigue casualties.

The combat soldiers themselves did not look down on victims of battle exhaustion. Instead they felt pity for those afflicted and merely hoped that it would not happen to them. James Simms explained it this way: "I never saw a combat soldier who was not compassionate and understanding to genuine combat fatigue cases. When he sees a combat fatigue man, he usually counts his blessings because he knows that it could just as easily be him."

At the beginning of the war, the army's policy was to weed out those who were considered unfit for combat or who had experienced mental breakdown. This proved untenable because of high rates of combat fatigue. By 1943, many army psychiatrists began to emphasize the "fatigue" in the phrase combat fatigue, in so doing removing the damaging stigma of mental illness. After treating numerous cases, they realized that combat exhaustion almost always occurred not because a man was psychologically unfit but because he was physically or mentally exhausted. This exhaustion had lowered his resistance to stress the same way it would to disease. Army psychiatrists found that all the average battle fatigue victim needed was time off the line for a few days, decent meals, and sleep. It was then imperative to send him back to his unit. It was found that the farther behind the lines battle fatigue cases were shipped, and the longer they were held out of combat, the less inclined they were to ever function effectively again. For the most part, this system worked, and many combat fatigue cases returned to their units.

Marines of the 2d Marine Division hit the beach at Saipan in June 1944.

Eventually most American combat men had to do what these marines are doing on Saipan—move forward while exposing themselves to enemy fire.

Marine tanks and infantry advance toward Japanese fortifications, Saipan, June 1944.

Marine riflemen advance through the ruins of Garapan. The experiences of these men were actually quite unusual. Most combat troops in the Pacific saw little, if any, urban combat.

Troops of the 2d Marine Division take cover from Japanese snipers in a canefield on Tinian.

Sights and smells of a Pacific battlefield. A decomposing Japanese corpse lies next to a destroyed tank on Okinawa.

Marines carry the body of a dead buddy to a graves registration station. More than 200,000 American combat soldiers met the same fate in World War II.

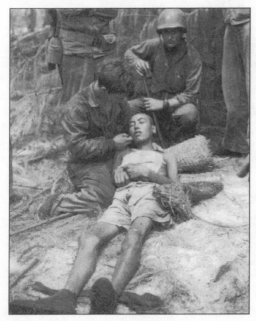

American combat troops tend to a wounded Japanese POW. A surrendering Japanese soldier had about a 50/50 chance of surviving his initial captivity and receiving good treatment.

Marines peek around a corner in search of a sniper at Garapan. Because American combat troops were usually advancing, well concealed snipers were a major peril.

Marines take cover behind a tank on Tinian. The paramount objective for most American combat troops was survival. Very few took unnecessary chances.

A flame tank scorches a Japanese bunker on Saipan.

Sights and smells of a European battlefield. Dead Germans at Normandy.

Combat troops cluster somberly around the coffin of their greatest spokesman, Ernie Pyle, who was killed at Ie Shima in April, 1945.

Combat soldiers of the 29th Infantry Division secure their gear in preparation for an attack in France. Notice the extra bandoliers of ammunition clips perched on the M1 Garand in the foreground.

American tanks roll past German children in 1945. Very few combat men hated German civilians.

A group of combat engineers from the 84th Infantry Division apprehensively prepares to make a river crossing in Germany.

Four lucky 102d Infantry Division combat men pose for a rare photo in front of their shelter for the night. For combat soldiers, shelter was the exception rather than the rule.

Combat troops take cover from mortar fire, Germany 1945. The majority of American casualties were caused by enemy artillery or mortars.

Visibly tense and apprehensive, infantrymen and tankers of the 9th Infantry Division wait for orders to move up a road into enemy territory. Most combat soldiers felt that the anticipation of a battle was usually worse than the battle itself.

Digging in was a central fact of life for combat troops. An American infantryman on the move in Europe might find himself digging as many as two or three holes per day.

A 9th Armored Division tank driver attempts to extract his Sherman from thick and unforgiving French mud. Most European battefields featured copious amounts of thick, glutinous mud.

Two troopers of the 36th Cavalry Regiment prepare to fire a captured German shell at the enemy. Combat men held a special place of fear and hatred in their hearts for German 88mm guns.

Riflemen of the 5th Infantry Division take a short break before resuming their advance up a road in France. Combat troops learned to savor such moments of rest.

A soldier from the 102d Infantry Division searches a group of German prisoners. Along with weapons, helmets were usually the first items removed from German POW's.

A group of engineers from the 30th Infantry Division checks for mines. Combat engineers had the unenviable and dangerous task of finding and disarming enemy mines.

Three 82d Airborne Division paratroopers inspect captured German weapons. Although many combat men admired German weapons, they were usually reluctant to use them for fear of drawing fire from their own side.

During the Battle of the Bulge, two armored infantrymen from the 7th Armored Division take a break and chat. During the severe winter of 1944-45, many combat soldiers camouflaged themselves with white sheets and ponchos.

A BAR man cleans his weapon. Since properly maintained and functioning weapons often meant the difference between life and death, clean weapons were of paramount importance in combat.

Combat soldiers from the 102d Infantry Division march a group of German prisoners to the rear. With a few exceptions, German POWs received excellent treatment at the hands of their American captors.

Medics carry a wounded man to an aid station in Germany. Combat men usually revered medics for their bravery and dedication in saving lives.

Combat soldiers move up a snowy road during the Battle of the Bulge. Judging by the relaxed expressions on their faces and the amount of gear some of them are carrying, these men are probably at least a few miles from the front lines.

Medics enlist the help of German POWs to carry a wounded man to an aid station. The quality of medical care at American aid stations and field hospitals was outstanding and was responsible for saving many lives.

The psychiatrists also realized, however, that every man, no matter how good a fighter, had his breaking point. Just as he would eventually be killed or wounded if he saw enough action, so too would he eventually succumb to combat fatigue. In fact, as the war dragged on, medics found that grizzled veterans were often more susceptible to combat exhaustion than were raw replacements.

Yank combat correspondent Mack Morriss outlined a typical combat fatigue case, whom he referred to as "Corporal Jones," and the way in which such cases were treated by the medics:

> He is not a coward. The last thing in the world he wants hung on him is cowardice. He starts a personal war within himself, his conscience on one side and his instinct for self preservation on the other. His physical fatigue carries a lot of weight in the argument. The tug-of-war in his mind gets worse and worse. He starts trembling so bad he can't hold his rifle. He doesn't want to shake but he does, and that solves his problem. Involuntarily he becomes physically incapable. Properly treated he'll be okay in a few days—when he's had some hot chow, a few good nights of sleep and a chance to get his trouble off his chest.

Henri Atkins saw many cases of combat fatigue in his unit:

> This disabling condition usually strikes after a soldier has been subjected to long and severe shelling or enemy small arms fire. A soldier reaches the point of "I can't take it anymore" and slips into a state of irrational behavior, or refusal to do anything. He just plain "gives up." This condition is just as much a combat wound as a piece of shell piercing a body. Some never reach this point, while others reach it early. The preferred method of treatment was to pull the soldier . . . out of the line and send him back to a warm bed and food and a session or two with a "sympathetic ear." It was important to get him back to the line within a few days. He must be returned to . . . his own friends.

Many times combat fatigue cases were given a concoction called a "Blue 88," which was made up of various calming drugs, mostly barbiturates, to get the soldier to sleep. Before he was captured, Ben Kimmelman helped out in such cases:

> They were given sodium amytal . . . and this would give them a very deep, deep sleep, sort of almost a trance-like sleep for 24, sometimes . . . 48 hours. The assumptions were that this would have some kind of cathartic effect. They would come out of this in . . . 24, 48, 72 hours and they'd be walking around, completely numb. Then they would be given a shower, new clothes and a pep talk and the attempt was made to send them back. I say the attempt because it didn't always succeed.

Glenn Searles spent the night in a foxhole with a man who had cracked. They were under attack on Okinawa and came close to dying when a Japanese soldier threw a grenade into their hole. Searles's buddy panicked, but Searles was able to throw the grenade out of the hole and kill the Japanese soldier. The near miss sent the unfortunate man over the edge:

> The man . . . spent the rest of the night in the bottom of our hole crying. He was evacuated the next day with combat fatigue. Later, on a hospital plane between Guam and Hawaii, I saw him on a stretcher in a straitjacket. When I spoke to him he could not meet my eyes. He was a brave soldier. What a pity!

Steven Sally, of the 1st Infantry Division, saw a good friend lose his mind under artillery fire in North Africa:

> He went crazy and he beat his head against our foxhole till his skin on his forehead was just hanging in strands. He was foaming at the mouth just like a madman. Now these things are something that generals don't write about. They don't know anything about it. These stories are hard to tell. People don't believe it.

Joseph Martin, a platoon leader in the 3d Infantry Division, saw a veteran sergeant who had been through almost a year of combat succumb to battle fatigue at Anzio. "He was . . . going to take off running. They had to tackle him and hold him down and send him back. He was the last person in the world you would have thought that would happen to." Bill Alcine, with the 77th Infantry Division at Ormoc, off the coast of the Philippines, saw a medic suffering from combat fatigue. "His hands were shaking badly. 'I feel okay,' he kept saying. 'I feel okay, but I can't stop trembling. What the hell is the matter with me?' He looked as though he were going to cry. The other medics tried to comfort him, but it didn't do any good."

Walter Russell once had a tank crewman who lost his capacity to withstand combat. It happened near the Arno River in Italy:

> My associate driver asked to leave the tank to relieve himself. About an hour later I realized that he had not returned. I went to look for him and found him and asked him why he had not returned. He was in tears saying he could not continue. I told him to stay where he was and we would pick him up when we left.

Edward Laughlin described what a typical man afflicted with combat fatigue looked like. "Dark eyes that had a haunted look and were sunk way back in his head, skinny and clothes too big, a chain smoker, shaking hands, nervous tics." Charlie Burchett, a member of the 1st Marine Division, said that he and his fellow leathernecks "called combat fatigue 'going Asiatic.' A guy would get that faraway look in his eyes and seem to be just totally withdrawn."

It was one thing to witness mental breakdown in others and quite another thing to experience it yourself. Ferdinand Huber became a combat fatigue casualty in Holland. All he could remember was that "someone took me to the aid station, where I was given a blue bomber [sodium pentathol] . . . and went out like a light."

Although Herchel McFadden, of the Americal Division, was never evacuated, he experienced some of the symptoms of combat fatigue during the fighting at Guadalcanal. "You stay tense and your stomach is churning, your mouth is dry and the adrenaline is flowing until your backbone seems it's going to break."

Frank Miller, a rifleman in the 36th Infantry Division, snapped in southern France after a close call:

I was told that somewhere back through the woods I jumped out on a road and leveled my rifle at a Jeep load of artillerymen, calling them "Germans." Somehow they managed to talk me out of that notion, got my rifle away from me, took me to an aid station nearby, and from there to the hospital. My doctor . . . said I had just reached a point of fatigue that had snapped my normal concentration, and that a lot of rest would put me back in tiptop shape. I was never too happy I "blacked out" up there . . . but slowly accepted it and learned to live with that fact.

When Harold Wells, an infantry officer in the 45th Infantry Division, lost control during a battle in Italy, it was of great concern to more than just himself:

I became so detached from reality I was sent back to the rear area for a week. This experience caused me to have doubts about my ability to function in a combat situation and wonder about the feelings of my troops as far as this ability was concerned. This break in combat allowed me to regain some of my confidence but I never lost the fear of a repetition of this experience. It was such a hopeless feeling when it happened.

Luckily for both Wells and his soldiers, it never happened again. John Snyder was clearly suffering from combat fatigue when he wrote to his wife in 1944 expressing his hopeless depression:

I continue to exist from day to day. At times I seem to be a very old man. Sexually, emotionally, I am dead. My nerves fail to react from any of those causes. I live entirely in memories. Time is of no value to me. There is nothing to look forward to that a specific period of waiting will bring about.

Not long after writing this letter, Snyder was killed in action. Armored infantryman Thomas Isabel, who surivived the war, would have related to Snyder's state of mind. Isabel described his feelings when he was permanently evacuated from the front lines because of combat fatigue: "I was in a pretty bad state of mind when I left the front. I was at a point that I didn't care whether I lived or died. I saw grown men cry like babies."

This state of mind leads one to wonder whether Snyder's mental state had a hand in his eventual death, because a combat soldier who is mentally incapacitated is just as wounded as one who is physically incapacitated. Those who fell victim to combat fatigue would always live with the bitter knowledge that they had a breaking point, and they would know that, under a certain set of circumstances, they could eventually lose control of themselves.

Becoming a casualty was a frightening, dirty, dangerous business. For those affected, it would be the most terrifying experience of their lives. Often survival was due to luck. A shell would explode and one man would be killed and another left without a scratch. Men mastered their horror-filled world and triumphed mainly due to their strong unity and feelings for one another, a deadly brotherhood that grew out of the world of combat and would eventually become the focal point of the soul of the combat soldier.

PART TWO

THE SOUL OF THE COMBAT SOLDIER

To understand the success of the combat soldier, it is important to understand his soul—the way he thought, the values he held, and what motivated him. It is no secret that most American combat men hated the Japanese. Japan had attacked Pearl Harbor by surprise and dared to challenge America. What is more, the Japanese were of a different race and culture, one that most American fighting men could not understand. It is not surprising, in light of these factors and the appalling ruthlessness with which the Japanese went about fighting, that the Pacific war became an incredibly bitter conflict.

Historian John Dower attempted to come to grips with the racial and cultural undertones of the Pacific war in his book *War Without Mercy*. He highlighted the integral role that racism played in the war efforts of both sides. However, he argued that, as soon as the war was over, racial hatred faded rapidly. Although Dower brought to light a sometimes forgotten aspect of World War II, he was primarily interested in American and Japanese culture and not necessarily the behavior of the fighting troops.

For the majority of the American men who did the fighting in the brutal Pacific war, enmity for the Japanese was a way of life from 1941–45 and never really faded for many of them afterward. Their hatred cannot be correctly termed as solely racially motivated. More often, it appeared to grow out of hatred for what the Japanese did or how they thought and operated. There was probably a greater cultural than racial divide. Combat soldiers generally thought of their Japanese enemy as high-quality, motivated soldiers who were often fanatical, ruthless, and dishonorable. In many cases, the Japanese were not thought of as people but as dangerous animals who had to be exterminated in order to ensure one's own survival. Some combat soldiers refused to take Japanese prisoners, but they were in the minority. Those who did take prisoners generally treated them well, although there were exceptions.

To find out how U.S. combat troops felt about the Japanese, army researchers conducted a survey in which men were split into three groups according to combat performance—above average, average, and below average—and were asked how they would feel about killing a Japanese soldier. In the above-average group, 48 percent responded that they would really like to kill a Japanese soldier. That response accounted for 44 percent in the average group and 38 percent in the below-average group. By contrast only 10 percent of the combat soldiers surveyed in Europe "really wanted to kill a German soldier."

In another survey conducted among Pacific war combat veterans, soldiers who had seen Japanese POWs were asked how this made them feel about the Japanese. Forty-two percent said it made them feel like killing them all the more; only 20 percent agreed with the statement that the Japanese were "men like us; it's too bad we have to be fighting them." When asked what should be done with Japan after the war, 42 percent of the combat veterans felt that the whole Japanese nation should be wiped out.

Although the Japanese fighting man was reviled, he was well respected among American combat troops. Although professing not to understand the suicidal fanaticism of Japanese troops, the average GI held grudging admiration for Japanese tenacity and toughness. John Stannard, of the Americal Division, described them as "first class infantry soldiers, brave, tough, strong, patient, dedicated, obedient, loyal. They were the best. I expected them to be first class fighting men and they were." William Ruf, of the 6th Infantry Division, fought the Japanese in the Philippines. He described them as fanatical fighters, well trained, well led, and well armed.

Like most combat men, 11th Airborne Division paratrooper Sy Gottlieb bristled at the stereotypes that some Americans had of the Japanese. In a letter to his family he wrote:

> The Nips are not a bunch of funny looking, helpless nimrods. They are a well-trained army of ruthless men, with good

weapons that they know how to use well. They are smart, have great stamina and determination, and although they do many things which appear foolish too, it is only because we don't understand the workings of the Japanese mind—they do know how to fight.

William Allison, of the 27th Infantry Division, believed that the Japanese were great fighters precisely because of their willingness to die. Forrest Coleman, who fought with the 32d Infantry Division in New Guinea, spoke of his Japanese counterparts as "competent, aggressive, dedicated to their cause and willing to die for their country." Earl Norgard, of the 41st Infantry Division, described them as "dedicated fighters with a mean streak." Richard Forse, a tanker in the 77th Infantry Division, summed up not only his own opinions but also those of his buddies: "We regarded the Japanese as tough, aggressive, agile, fanatical . . . and very good at camouflauge and surprise assault."

The single-minded fierceness of the Japanese fighting soldier led to a state of fearful wariness among American combat troops in the Pacific. Americans who were in combat against the Japanese for any length of time knew that they could never let their guard down if they hoped to survive. Robert Jackson, of the 96th Infantry Division, maintained that this was the case in his outfit:

Each of us developed a wariness, a perpetual crouch and a fear of what lay just ahead. It was quite similar to our childhood fears of what was in the closet. What we knew or had experienced of the Japanese fighting man . . . was that he was suicidally devoted—as an individual—to killing Americans. He was incomprehensible to the American mind. His devotion kept each of us fearful and alert.

It is unsettling to know that your enemy is willing to go further than you are to pursue victory. The major goal of most American combat soldiers was twofold: to do their job and survive the war. The average GI could not conceive of the kind of suicidal dedication that his Japanese enemy demonstrated every day in combat. Justin Gray was one of the rare soldiers who fought in both Europe and the Pacific. "Even though I knew the Germans were fanatical in their attempts to destroy us, I always felt confident they also had a strong desire to live. The Jap doesn't place such a high value on his life. The Japs crawl into our lines even though they know they have no chance of getting out alive."

One combat veteran highlighted this personal aspect of a war that was generally remarkable in its impersonal nature, and the way in which American troops overcame Japanese fanaticism:

Fighting Japs is often an individual affair. A mass battle like the banzai charge is only part of the story. The Jap is willing to move an inch an hour. And he'll go to any lengths to get you. He'll lie crouched in weeds and dust and even muddy malarial water for hours. We're too impatient. The Japs will try to create panic in your line. The only way to survive them is to refuse to be panicked. If you've got guts, you'll hold tight. If they panic you, you're sunk.

This fanaticism that many Americans attributed to the Japanese probably reflects the Japanese belief during World War II that the purity and spiritual strength of the Japanese soldier could overcome Allied material superiority. The Japanese were, of course, dead wrong in this belief but not simply because of overwhelming Allied material superiority. *Yamato damashii,* or fighting power of the Japanese, was overcome by the professionalism and fortitude of American fighting men.

As good as they were, the Japanese were not perfect warriors. Sidney Richess, who fought them in the Philippines with the 40th Infantry Division, leveled a common criticism of Japanese combat troops:

The individual did not seem capable of having a mind of his own. In his blind obedience to orders, he seemed to have a mind-set. Example: after clearing a small barrio with slight resistance, we pushed on with the medics, reserves, headquarters and other support troops. Finally came three tanks, the first of which was fired on by a well-concealed and undetected enemy light machine gun, inflicting no damage whatsoever. The armored vehicle simply turned in its tracks and drove squarely over the position. It was found later . . . that this [MG] crew had been ordered to fire on armor only, which they proceeded to do.

William Allen, of the 4th Marine Division, also felt that the individual Japanese soldier did not think independently. "They were never taught to think for themselves. They were trained to do what they were told, so if their officer got killed . . . they didn't know what to do."

Rifle company commander Charles Henne had downright disdain for the way the Japanese operated during an attack:

The pattern of their attacks against us on New Georgia consisted of (1) movement, noise talking and calling; (2) quiet; (3) exhortation and unison response; (4) movement and noise; (5) banzai, and then they charged. They attacked our . . . position three times not deviating a bit. They were lousy on offense but they were disciplined defenders. They would fight to the death or commit suicide.

American and Japanese culture were so different that there was little, if anything, about Japanese soldiers that Americans could relate to, as Americal Division veteran Herchel McFadden found out:

We were motivated to a high degree of anger and hate toward the Japanese. They had started it [the war] and we knew also what they were doing to our people in the Philippines. They placed no value on life. The soldiers we faced I did not consider as people. They tortured . . . prisoners and mutilated our dead and wounded. We thought of them as the lowest form of life. They were not people.

John Moore, who fought the Japanese on Okinawa, echoed McFadden's sentiments. "I did not consider the enemy as a person. They were our enemy and were to be killed as if they were animals."

Charles Card's attitude toward the Japanese never changed: "I looked upon them as animals and unhuman. Since the war I continue to mistrust, dislike and consider the Japanese as enemies." Bryan Baldwin, of the 25th Infantry Division, referred to them as "sadistic animals. I've never forgiven the Jap soldiers for the atrocities they committed on my friends." Charles Henne still cannot bring himself to forget the behavior of Japanese troops during the war. "By the end of the war my hatred became intense. I want nothing to do with Japs today. Those murderous bastards tied one of our men to a tree and bayoneted and hacked him to death. If space permitted I could make a long list of atrocities I observed." Edward Bailey, of the 81st Infantry Division, claimed that he hated all Japanese and still does today.

Clarence Daniels fought the Japanese in the Philippines during the hopeless early days of 1941–42 and later became their prisoner for four arduous years. He and his buddies had nothing but disdain for their captors. "We thought they were inferior and they thought they were inferior too or they wouldn't have done the things they did." For Charlie Burchett, of the 1st Marine Division, the hatred never faded even after V-J Day. He described his feelings upon hearing that the war was over. "I wished I'd have gotten more of the bastards. I thought they were the most cruel people in the world . . . so that's just the way I felt." In a letter to his mother, Jack Hussey demonstrated a typical attitude of American fighting men toward killing Japanese during the war: "You can tell Dica [his aunt] that I killed those little yellow Japs she was talking about and more besides. I mean myself. I have killed Nips with rifles, grenades, explosives and everything." After killing many Japanese on Saipan, Charles Richardson said that he felt slightly more ambivalent but nevertheless firm that the Japanese deserved their fate. "I hated to do it, but then I think it was for a just cause. They started the thing and we were not going to let them take our freedom, religion and our loved ones away from us. I feel like every Jap I killed—it was God's will. I am putting this in the back of my mind."

Seeing POW camps or evidence of Japanese atrocities did nothing to soften the already bitter attitudes of combat men. Frank Caudillo said that such things motivated his buddies and him to fight harder in New Guinea. "We saw how the natives in New Guinea were treated by the Japanese. Atrocities committed only made for more killing by us." Such atrocities greatly affected the attitude of Roland Lea, who fought with the 7th Infantry Division. "I looked upon them as being inhuman because of atrocities which I saw. I disliked the Japs and always will." Robert Knauss, of the 37th Infantry Division, helped liberate Bilibid prison camp, outside of Manila, where many U.S. POWs were held. He said that this experience served only to increase his hatred for the Japanese. There were, however, some Japanese soldiers who did not behave with brutality, as 77th Infantry Division rifleman Glenn Searles found out during the Philippines campaign:

Not all Jap solders were bloodthirsty and brutal. In the years of occupation, some very decent young soldiers formed attachments with local girls and their families. When the Jap Army was routed, the Filipinos would take these boys in and shelter them, then try to pass them off as family when they came to beg for food. Every time we would take stragglers out of the chow line, there would be loud weeping and wailing from the women, but off to the POW compound they went.

In fact there was a substantial minority of American combat men who bore no particular hatred toward the Japanese. These men looked upon enemy soldiers as human beings who had been misled by bad leaders. Edward Sears, of the Americal Division, recalled finding Japanese bodies on Bougainville and feeling a strange melancholy:

All that was left of them were bones. They were still dressed in their uniforms and some still had their helmets on, just laying there against these big banyan trees. It sure was . . . spooky. No one said a word. As we moved on I was thinking about their mothers. How sad, they gave birth and men take it.

Minoru Hara, of the 6th Infantry Division, a Japanese American himself, referred to enemy soldiers as "poorly led citizens believing in their militaristic government in spite of being fed all kinds of lies."

Perhaps because of his Japanese background, Hara was inclined to have some affinity for enemy soldiers. This was certainly not the background of fellow 6th Division soldier Vincent Lidholm, who "bore them no particular hatred. They were merely human beings like me doing a job as directed by their country." William Ruf said, "All people are the same once you get to know them, good and bad in all races."

After fighting the Japanese from New Guinea to the Philippines, 41st Infantry Division soldier Thaddeus Piewawer realized that "they were as human as I was." For John Sevec, of the 77th Infantry Division, it took the sight of enemy bodies to change his hard attitude toward the enemy: "I realized they were humans just as we were. I began to realize they were ordinary people just like us and had to fight just as we had to."

John Lane, who fought with the 4th Marine Division, also appreciated the humanity of Japanese soldiers on Iwo Jima when he and his buddies searched an abandoned Japanese cave:

> The enemy was human! A lot of gear was strewn about. Along with the debris I spotted sheets of paper with a child's drawing on them, the kind of thing kids all over the world do in kindergarten. The Japanese soldiers had children who loved them and had sent their artwork to them. It had never occurred to me before.

How great a factor was personal feelings when it came to taking prisoners? The answer is mixed. American troops captured approximately 41,000 Japanese soldiers during World War II, the vast majority in mass surrenders at the end of the war. Some American combat soldiers refused to take Japanese soldiers prisoner. They would simply kill every Japanese soldier they saw with no questions asked. Others took prisoners every chance they could. It all depended on the mind-set of the men in any particular unit, their immediate past experiences, and their personal level of hatred and fear of the enemy.

In the case of William McLaughlin, a recon trooper in the Americal Division, his unit took no prisoners because they did not want to "go through the problem of taking care of them on patrol." They would shoot any Japanese they found. It was the same for Melvin Mc Kinney, of the 25th Infantry Division. "We took no prisoners. The rear would have liked one for interrogation but we shot all the Japanese we saw." George Wyatt, who fought with the 1st Marine Division at Guadalcanal, was no different. "There were attempts made to . . . convince us to take prisoners . . . but the majority of us would not . . . even consider the issue, much less actually attempt such a thing."

Another 25th Division man, Emil Matula, explained the most common reason given by Americans who refused to take Japanese prisoners. "We learned not to trust a Jap with any clothes or even a G string on. They were dangerous because they would hide a grenade under their arm or string and as soon as a crowd would get around to see, they would open their arm and blow themselves and others up." Here was a classic cultural difference. Because surrender was disgraceful for Japanese soldiers, in their view they could preserve their honor by pretending to give up while they instead killed themselves and enemy troops. To the American mind, few things were more treacherous, dishonorable, or infuriating. Most American combat men felt that once an enemy had given up, he was to be treated decently as a POW. In exchange for decent treatment, the prisoner was expected not to pose any further threat. By pursuing such "double crosses" as giving up and then detonating a grenade in the faces of one's captors, the Japanese soldier forfeited any right, in the minds of some American combat men, to the normal treatment afforded a captured enemy.

Word of such instances spread like wildfire in combat units. Not only did it foster hatred for the Japanese, it made most men decide that capturing an enemy soldier was not worth the risk of getting double crossed. After witnessing such incidents in his outfit, George Sitzler, of the 37th Infantry Division, recalled that "our motto was 'no prisoners.'" John Drugan, a 41st Infantry Division combat soldier, remembered that he and his comrades were inclined to take prisoners later in the war but not during the first days of combat on New Guinea. "Early in the war we took no prisoners as some would strap grenades to themselves and blow up everyone."

Naturally the attitude of the potential POW also had something to do with whether or not Americans decided to take a man prisoner. Most American combat men were usually in no mood for captives who proved to be difficult or belligerent. This was especially true when combat was fierce and emotions were raw. Glenn Searles recalled one such incident. After an all-night battle on Okinawa, he and his buddies were searching through piles of Japanese bodies when they found a live Japanese officer who lay wounded with his legs blown off. "He was an arrogant bastard and ordered us to take him to our hospital. 'I know the Geneva Convention,' he said. 'You are required to care for all wounded.' One of our men said, 'Piss on you, shithead,' and shot him dead."

Melvin Coobs, of the 96th Infantry Division, took prisoners, the impetus being their intelligence value. Americans who took prisoners usually did so out of common decency. American soldiers were trained to respect the safety of prisoners. Even though it could be dangerous to take Japanese captives, many men reasoned that, in the long run, it would most likely be less dangerous to take POWs, because good treatment would probably reduce the Japanese penchant for fighting to the death. This proved to be true, especially in the final days of the war.

Emil Lindenbusch, of the 6th Infantry Division, did not remember any mistreatment of POWs in his outfit. "All I ever saw were not abused. They were just treated as prisoners."

Merle Miller related an incident at Kwajalein in which 7th Infantry Division soldiers captured a group of Japanese soldiers:

> None had had anything to eat or drink for two or three days. Almost all of them had been told that if any surrendered, their ears would be cut off by their barbaric white enemy. Instead . . . all were given as much K and D rations and candy as they could eat and all the Halizone-treated water they could drink.

Paul Casper, who fought with the 25th Infantry Division, remembered the treatment of POWs in his outfit: "GIs were curious and always were sharing food and cigarettes with captured soldiers." Yashakazu Higashi, a Japanese American who interrogated POWs, said that his subjects were treated "based on the Geneva Convention. Some POWs expressed gratitude regarding their treatment." Higashi was a member of the 32d Infantry Division, an outfit that fought from the early stages of the war until the end. Thus, he was in a position to see many POWs. Another 32d Division man, Whayland Greene, wrote of capturing enemy soldiers at the end of the war on Luzon. "In five minutes we were smoking cigarettes, laughing and trying to talk. They . . . laid their weapons down. After that they were not Japs anymore, they were Japanese soldiers. The hate was gone just that quick."

Milton Pearce, of the 38th Infantry Division, also saw prisoners treated well. "I've seen a Jap prisoner cry when an American gave him a cigarette. His commander had told him he would be shot." Charles Henne described how his men dealt with captured Japanese. "When we took a Jap prisoner he was invariably well treated. We fed them, gave them cigarettes and treated their wounds. I thought they should be shot in combat but never in cold blood. I would not permit that." George Klavand, a member of the 40th Infantry Division, perhaps expressed it best. "They were treated one hell of a lot better than our POWs."

In light of Pearl Harbor, the notorious Bataan death march, the ample evidence of Japanese atrocities against captured Americans on battlefields all over the Pacific, and the general ferocity of most of the fighting in the Pacific war, it is somewhat surprising that American combat troops treated captured Japanese as well as they did. In the infrequent instances when Japanese soldiers were willing or able to surrender, their chances of survival and decent treatment were far better than 50:50. More than 41,000 Japanese soldiers took advantage of these friendly probabilities to survive the war in captivity.

The Pacific war was generally a "war without mercy," as John Dower termed it. But at times the combat men who fought the Japanese found room for mercy. The good treatment of the Japanese who survived capture is evidence of this fact. Still, many combat soldiers who fought the Japanese carry a legacy of bitterness and dislike that will most likely never change.

CHAPTER 8

ATTITUDES TOWARD THE GERMANS

American combat soldiers had ambivalent feelings about their German enemy. On the one hand, combat men loathed Adolf Hitler and nazism and had nothing but contempt for Prussian militarism and German notions of a master race. On the other hand, American combat soldiers respected the Germans as good soldiers and industrious, hardworking people who were not all that different from Americans.

American combat troops who hated the Germans were in the minority. Because Germans were of the same race (most U.S. combat soldiers were white) and a similar culture, it was relatively easy for Americans to relate to them. In addition, the Germans on the Western Front generally fought the war within the confines of the Geneva Convention, which served to mollify feelings of hatred. However, American combat soldiers despised the SS troops as fanatical animals. Also, many American soldiers who witnessed concentration camps found themselves hating the Germans. They literally could not believe their eyes when they saw the camps.

Except for unusual circumstances such as after the Malmédy Massacre at the Battle of the Bulge and in dealing with the brutal SS, American soldiers regularly allowed Germans to surrender. In fact, they were usually glad to take prisoners, reasoning that every German who became a POW was one less German who could shoot at them. In most cases, captured Germans were treated well, especially if they could get past the first few moments of captivity when it was difficult for soldiers to change from killing machines to men of mercy. As in the Pacific, Americans expected a certain etiquette from POWs, and woe to the enemy soldier who did not observe it.

In attempting to gauge the degree of hatred that American soldiers might hold for the Germans, army researchers asked combat veterans how they would feel about killing a German soldier. The respondents were arranged into three groups by combat performance: above average, average, and below average. In the above-average group, only 9 percent "really wanted to kill a German soldier," as compared with 6 percent and 5 percent, respectively, in the average and below-average groups. An overwhelming majority of each group thought that killing a German was simply part of an unpleasant job that had to be done—87, 86, and 86 percent, respectively, by group. Clearly, there was no lust for German blood among a large majority of American combat veterans.

Troops who had seen German prisoners were asked how it made them feel about the Germans. Only 18 percent said that seeing German POWs made them want to kill Germans all the more; 54 percent saw them "as men just like us." When asked what should be done with Germany after the war, only 25 percent wanted to wipe out the whole German nation; 65 percent felt that only German leaders should be punished. Thus, most combat men felt that the German people were simply misled by murderous leaders, a notion that, in many cases, persists to this day.

When it came to the fighting quality of the German combat soldier, there was little disagreement among American combat troops. The prevailing attitude was that the Germans were tough, dedicated, professional, and smart. Alan Williamson, of the 36th Infantry Division, expressed an opinion held by many Americans who fought the Germans. "I could not help but admire the professionalism of the German soldier. He wasn't mad at anybody; in fact, most were friendly. He was just doing a job, and he did it well."

Harry Arnold, a member of the 99th Infantry Division, also respected German fighting soldiers:

> The Germans were . . . adaptable and versatile and, thus . . . dangerous. He was no simpleton who would oblige you by dying today. Tomorrow he would be behind another building or around another curve in the road, behind another MG or Pak 75 [howitzer], and give you another few minutes of terror.

John Piazza, a rifleman in the 45th Infantry Division, was trained to hold the German soldier in high esteem. "We were told in basic training that the enemy was formidable. They were not wrong about the Germans especially at Anzio." John Beeks, of the 78th Infantry Division, was surprised that the Germans were still as dangerous as they were near the end of the war. "Even during the Ruhr [campaign] some units fought very well." Like many Americans, Riland West, a junior officer in the 87th Infantry Division, admired the professionalism of the German soldier. "[He] in general was a good soldier. You could capture him and he'd have a crease in his trousers. I don't know how he stayed that way on the front line. We didn't stay that way." Edgar Piggot, a black soldier who fought with the 92d Infantry Division, felt that the Germans were "well disciplined and well armed. They were fierce and clever fighters right up to the end."

The 1st Armored Division saw more combat than most U.S. divisions in Europe. It fought from the earliest days of North Africa in 1942 until the final days of the war in Italy in 1945. Because of their level of experience, the men of the 1st Armored were in an excellent position to evaluate the quality of the German soldier. For the most part, they came away impressed. Said Donald Greener, an armored infantryman in the 1st: "I respected them as fighters. They didn't give up until they were convinced you were a better man than they were. Sometimes that took a lot of convincing." Tanker James Hagan felt that he had much in common with his German adversaries. "The German soldier was like the American—good, smart, determined, a fighter." James Mahon, a tank commander, treated them "with respect as professional soldiers like ourselves. Nose to nose frontline troops respect each other's abilities. We fought against Germany's best units and they, sir, were tough." Donald Taylor also held them in high esteem. "German soldiers were well trained, well armed and had strong discipline and leadership."

Charles Hogg, a tanker in the 6th Armored Division, was struck by the bravery of the German soldiers he faced. "In the Bulge outside of Bastogne, my respect for them grew as they charged directly into our defensive line of tanks and in some instances, their infantry charge got in among and behind our line of tanks." Al Metcalf, an armored infantryman with the 8th Armored Division, felt that the

"German soldier was a superb soldier. He was well disciplined. He was naturally motivated."

Even though American combat men had a high degree of respect for the quality of German troops, there was a definite opinion that, as the war dragged on, the quality of the German soldier declined. Harold Wells, a combat officer with the 45th Infantry Division, felt that "the Germans were well trained, well led and well armed until late in the war." Gerald VanCleve, of the 75th Infantry Division, recalled that "German replacements . . . were not trained well or dedicated near the end of the war."

This decline, along with the resilience and toughness of the American combat soldier, led most combat men to believe that they were better than the Germans. Harry Arnold, who had a high opinion of the Germans, expressed an attitude shared by many American combat troops:

> I had considerable respect for the abilities of the German soldier, but didn't find him a paragon of virtue. He was often prone to open defensive fire too early and from too great a range for maximum benefit (thank God). Probably the German soldier had no equal in rolling over a surprised and off balance enemy. But when that enemy managed to turn and fight intelligently, effectively and willingly, the perceived superiority of the German diminished.

Roy Denmon, an armored infantryman in the 6th Armored Division, expressed it even more bluntly. "We felt that their abilities as fighters were exaggerated and that we could beat them in most situations." Bartlett Allen, a tank crewman in the 1st Armored Division, summed up the attitude that he and his buddies had toward the Germans as fighters. "German soldiers and equipment were respected but not considered invincible."

Lawrence Nickell, a mortarman in the 5th Infantry Division, expressed the feelings of many of his comrades. "It may come as a surprise to some, in view of German atrocities . . . but most of us felt a good deal of respect and sympathy for the average German soldier. Many of them were there whether they wanted to be or not, and suffered the same hardships we did." James Graff, of the 35th Infantry Division, saw Germans calmly going about their business in the midst of mass destruction, and he was filled with admiration. "With all credit to the Germans as a race, they were industrious and hard-working and it took a lot to continue working while your country was being overrun." Such attributes made GIs feel that they had something in common with the Germans because most Americans admire hard work and determination.

It was not difficult, then, for combat soldiers to see the Germans as ordinary human beings. Radford Carroll, a rifleman in the 99th Infantry Division, was surprised to find that he could not bring himself to shoot a gravely wounded German whom he hoped to put out of his misery. "This was a surprise because I was only wanting to do a good deed, and I would have shot him during the fight a few minutes earlier without hesitation or regret. Human nature is a strange thing."

Nicholas Bozic, an artillery forward observer in the 36th Infantry Division, wrote in his diary of spending a few moments of friendship with a German soldier during a brief truce in which both sides collected their wounded. "The Sgt. and I continued talking about the Italian girls and vino. We had a few good laughs during our conversation. After our little talk, we started to say goodbye when he said, 'Today we laugh and in hours we kill.' So I told him I'd see him in Munich. That was his hometown."

It is important to understand that such feelings of kinship did not extend to SS troops or any German who had obvious ties or sympathies with the Nazis. Charles Hogg felt that "German soldiers were ordinary people fighting for their country. SS troops were political soldiers who fought fanatically. We hated SS troops." Grover Carr, of the 45th Infantry Division, said he and his buddies made a clear delineation between regular German soldiers and Nazis. "With the exception of Nazi troops, they [Germans] were normal, drafted civilians like us. I became more bitter toward the Nazis and more considerate of the regulars."

Most combat soldiers were quick to make the same distinctions. Said Thomas Yochim, of the 78th Infantry Division: "The Wehrmacht reminded us of ourselves, that is, misplaced civilians with a job to do. The SS troops were very well disciplined but were regarded as fanatical."

Jack Hartzog also had nothing against German troops. "They were just like us. They just happened to have the wrong leader who was probably the most wicked man in recorded history." John Beeks, another member of the 78th, found that he "liked the German people. They were clean and pleasant for the most part."

The fact that German civilians were often friendly to Americans also helped contribute to a favorable impression of the Germans as a people. Roy Blair, a combat soldier in the 97th Infantry Division, found this out when his unit entered Germany. "We were taught to hate the enemy; however, most of their civilians treated us very well and, as a result, it was difficult to feel hatred toward the enemy."

Harold Marshall, of the 79th Infantry Division, articulated an opinion commonly held by GIs that somehow the Germans had been fooled by Hitler and the Nazis into making war. "Germans were very intelligent people. Most despised Hitler. I am surprised some were duped to believe in Hitler's cause."

Like many Americans of German ancestry, 87th Infantry Division platoon leader Clarence Waltemath felt some affinity for the Germans. "Most of my family and neighbors were all German, so I knew the German people pretty well. I always said, 'If they had known I was German, they wouldn't have shot me.'"

Ralph Hill, of the 99th Infantry Division, recalled being lost with a group of three other Americans one wintry night during the Battle of the Bulge. They were taken in by a Belgian woman. She fed them and allowed them to get warm next to her fireplace. An hour or so later, five German soldiers came to the door also looking for food and warmth. The woman sternly proclaimed that the Germans and Americans would remain peaceful. "Within an hour, under her guidance . . . comradeship took over to replace the initial terror. She created this by leading Christmas carols, first in English and then in German. Finally, a blending of voices occurred as the same carol was sung in English and German." After a night's sleep, the two groups parted peacefully and headed back to the war in different directions. Said 1st Armored Division tanker Joseph Kocsik: "After we got to talk to them [Germans], we wondered why we were shooting at each other."

Paris Roussos, an armored infantryman in the 1st, also felt little hatred for Germans. "I considered them as human beings caught up in a situation that was not their choice. Since we shared the same agonies, I respected their plight. I had no love or respect for SS troops though. I hated them immensely."

In spite of the fact that American combat soldiers empathized with their German counterparts, the man on the other side of the line was still the enemy. He was out to kill and maim you unless you could do the same to him. This created an ambivalence among American fighting men who held no special hatred for the Germans but who knew that they must fight with ruthlessness if they were to survive.

A letter by a soldier named Harold Etter typified this unique brand of ambivalence that only war can create:

> We get decorations and honors for killing, a German dies the same as an American, he weeps, groans and crys [sic] out in death. While we watch him, someone says, "You Son of a Bitch," and we think that person hard and feel sorry for the poor devil of a Kraut. But this feeling lasts only for a moment, as a glance away is an American with the air sucking in and out of a jagged hole in his chest. What is one to do? Why must this mess go on, why can't I go home and raise my family . . . and that German do the same?

Some combat soldiers felt no ambivalence toward the Germans. They hated them all—Nazi or not—and relished killing them. Combat correspondent Walter Peters came across one such soldier in the hedgerows of Normandy. The Germans had killed his brothers and he felt he had a score to settle. He hoped to exact vengeance by hunting for German snipers:

> Three more to go and I'll have settled a promise I made when they killed by brother Ted. Then I'll kill twenty-five more for my brother Jerry. After that I'm going to kill as many Germans as I can because I hate the whole Nazi system. When I kill a German I like to look right into his eyes. I like to see them drop. When they drop I can almost see a picture of my brothers smiling at me.

John Massey, of the 65th Infantry Division, hated the Germans because he felt they were "a bunch of first class liars. They weren't the supermen they were supposed to be." Sid Rowling, of the 80th Infantry Division, and Morton Semelmaxer, of the 11th Armored Division, both Jewish, found themselves hating the Germans. This was a common attitude among Jewish American combat soldiers. Dewey Blanton, a tanker in the 1st Armored Division, felt that the Germans should have suffered more for their atrocities. "I think they got part of what was coming to them but the bastards deserved a heck of a lot more." For another 1st Armored tanker, Eugene Thibideau, grief over dead buddies led to hatred for the Germans. "I hated the Germans so much for killing some of the best friends I ever had. I still hate them." One soldier wrote home in 1945 that the Germans had no common decency and should be dealt with severely. "From 9 to 90 they've shot at us—still do. From birth to death they hate us and what we stand for, and from dawn to dusk they lie to us, call us 'friend.' We *must* teach these people and they only learn the hard way."

After seeing a death camp, Donald Lembeke found himself hating the Germans. A letter reveals his opinion of what should be done with them:

> Shooting is too good for them. They should be starved, beaten and then shot the same as they had been treating these other people. Maybe I shouldn't have written this but the people over there [in the U.S.] know so little about what goes on over here. They still think the Germans are civilized. They aren't even human.

William Maher, a rifle platoon leader who was eventually killed in action in Normandy, wrote to his parents a few days before his death and voiced his hatred for the Germans. "[They] are a murderous, ferocious gang of cutthroats, and I don't know how they can call upon God for help, as they are prone to do when they get theirs."

Most American combat soldiers did not know about the barbarous German concentration camps until the end of the war. It seems logical that, had they known, they would probably have hated the Germans more than they did. Those who saw the Nazi camps would never forget them. Edward Laughlin, a paratrooper in the 82d Airborne Division who helped liberate a camp in southern Germany, described the prisoners:

> These people were very emaciated and very pathetic. They cried, they laughed, some were numb and wary and some would give senseless screams at intervals and some would sit and stare at the ground. There were a few troopers standing on the outskirts of this crowd and one of them said to me, "They are killing the commandant and his wife!" I walked closer to the center of activity and there on the ground, both on their back, heads hanging back over the street curb and blood flowing from cut throats and multiple stab wounds were the commandant and his wife—dead. Some of the inmates stood there hating and staring, an unnatural light in their eyes. Some walked up and kicked them in various parts of their bodies and some stood there and urinated on them. What was the U.S. soldiers' attitude and reaction toward this? Not our country, not our situations, as these inmates had many terrible things inflicted upon them for over 3 years—they had to do what they had to do. We gave them all the food that we had—K rations, C rations, bread, cheese, coffee. Some of it was too rich for their systems; they overindulged and then vomited.

The attitude of Laughlin and his buddies reflects the attitude of nearly all those who liberated concentration camps. They sympathized greatly with the prisoners and did not frown on quick and dirty justice.

For most liberators, it was not the vengeance that they remembered but rather the incredible depravity and horror of the camps. They literally had nothing to compare it to, and most could not have conceived of such awful scenes. Donald MacDonald, of the 45th Infantry Division, was at Dachau. "My mind refused to accept the testimony of my eyes. I was numbed. I was horrified. I still can't understand." William Meissner, a machine gunner in the 71st Infantry Division, helped liberate a labor camp near Wels. "We were shocked to see the terribly emaciated, starving, filthy victims hobbling down the street, happy to be free at last but terribly ill. Seeing the survivors was enough to shock the sensibilities of even the toughest GI."

Rodney Beaver, an artillery forward observer in the 80th Infantry Division, wrote to his parents about a camp he saw in Austria:

> I can assure you that all the atrocity stories you have been reading so much about lately . . . are absolutely true. It was hard for me to believe until I saw hundreds of men this afternoon who are now only living skeletons. It was absolutely horrible. Men who were once strong and healthy like I, now only a mere shadow of their former self. Most of them were naked, with legs as thin as my wrist . . . skulls for faces, and every rib you could count. And then the crematorium with ashes and human bones, and here and there a pelvis or other bone not completely reduced to ash. It was truly ghastly.

John Pulliam, a glider infantryman in the 82d Airborne Division, also saw victims of Nazi atrocities. "You'd see one fellow laying there dead, the next buddy'd be so weak he couldn't get up. They'd want to hug you and kiss you . . . they were so glad to see you. I could hardly eat for a week." Raymond Buch, a combat engineer in the 11th Armored Division, saw Mauthausen and was "incredulous, horrified and heartsick to see the hundreds of men and women cheated out of their lives and futures."

On a patrol through a nameless town in Germany, 101st Airborne Division paratrooper Bill Oatman found a concentration camp:

> My buddy and I stood there and cried just looking at that pitiful mess of human flesh and thinking what one human can do to another human. There was one family who came over to me and got down on their knees and grabbed me around my legs and started crying. By the time the rest of the outfit got to us, we were ready to start shooting any and all Germans, didn't matter if they were soldiers or not.

The reaction and subsequent attitudes of Walter Richardson, a tank commander in the 3d Armored Division, to the Paderborn and

Nordhausen camps typified those of many combat soldiers who liberated camps. "I got sick and threw up. I had seen rough deals in combat but this was beyond me. I could not imagine treating human beings like this." Thus, even combat soldiers who had seen death and dismemberment for months and years were not prepared for the sort of horror they saw in German concentration camps. In most cases, witnessing such sights led to a hardening of attitudes toward the Germans, but, because the war was over by the time that most men saw the camps, they did not have a chance to act out their newfound animosity in combat.

Even the sight of concentration camps did not prevent American combat soldiers from routinely allowing German soldiers to surrender and from treating them well. In rare cases, prospective POWs were gunned down, but most combat men were all too happy to take prisoners, provided the potential captives followed the proper etiquette. The Germans did not surrender and then blow themselves up as the Japanese did. Instead, they would sometimes kill as many Americans as possible and then, after their ammunition was expended or their situation hopeless, attempt to surrender.

It was understood among American combat soldiers that, in such instances, the German soldier would not be taken alive. Mack Morriss spoke to a squad leader during the bitter fighting at Aachen who summed up the feelings of the GIs: "It's pretty tough to see three or four of your men hit and then see the man who hit 'em try to put up his hands and get a free trip back to the States." In most of these cases, American soldiers had no mercy. As in the Pacific, they believed that the enemy deserved captivity, provided that he agreed to no longer harm Americans. If the enemy abrogated this unwritten agreement, he was to be destroyed. Explained Radford Carroll: "There was a recognized rule: surrender without fighting and all is well, but you don't fight and kill some of our people and then surrender."

As in the Pacific theater, differing concepts of surrender are probably indicative of a cultural divide. German soldiers were sometimes under intense pressure to put up a strong fight before capitulating. Often the SS threatened to carry out reprisals against the families of German soldiers if they surrendered too easily. This was

especially common near the end of the war. The German combat soldier might have felt that he was doing all he could to protect his family. The American saw it much differently.

Ed Laughlin saw the remains of a German soldier who had put
up too strident a fight before attempting surrender. "We noted a German soldier hanging by his neck from a tree limb. This was . . . the
forward artillery observer who had been pinpointing the artillery and
mortar fire at us. He had tried to surrender but instead had been
hung by his own belt for the killing and maiming of our troops."

One soldier participated in gunning down a German who was
seen to have broken the rules:

> I've seen a German soldier in a foxhole fire two panzerfaust
> [bazookas] point-blank at a tank loaded with our infantrymen,
> empty a "burp gun" at the men scrambling off—then throw
> down his empty weapons, raise his arms and step out of his hole
> yelling, "Komerade!" That Kraut died with his gut full of M-1
> ammunition, his hands still half raised. I clenched my teeth so
> hard that little pieces of enamel broke off the edges, and
> wished he could have died slower, more painfully.

Most American combat men felt that taking POWs increased their
chances of personal survival. They also felt that it was the right thing
to do. However, there were exceptions, mainly during the Battle of
the Bulge. James Graff recalled one such instance in early January
1945:

> We had just learned the day before that six [Ameri-
> cans] . . . who were captured had been found shot to death by
> a small arms bullet in the head or heart. As we were watching
> a ridge three Germans appeared. One had on his helmet and
> the other had his arm in a sling. Somebody hollered, "Kill the
> bastards!" Everyone opened fire. Gerstbauer . . . jumped up and
> . . . emptied his rifle in the kraut and all the time the German
> was screaming, 'Kamrad!' . . . which they always hollered when
> surrendering. Bad business, but in such conditions men's feel-
> ings and senses are sometimes dulled.

The notorious Malmédy Massacre was the most frequent motivator for U.S. troops to not take prisoners. Eduardo Peniche, of the 101st Airborne Division, remembered what happened after he and his comrades heard about the massacre:

> Word started around that we were to take no prisoners. Many troopers took advantage of this rumored order and expelled vengeance on any German soldier. Several times . . . I observed a German come out of a bunker or foxhole, hands over head, only to be shot through the head at close range.

Willis Irvin, an armored infantryman in the 2d Armored Division, recalled that, when it came to taking prisoners, "we treated them well until the Battle of the Bulge. Then for a while we had no prisoners."

Killing prospective POWs also went on in the mountains of Italy, where caring for and moving prisoners was sometimes close to impossible in the forbidding terrain. This was true for Thomas Isabel's armored infantry unit in the 1st Armored Division in the winter of 1944:

> When we were on the Gothic line, it took two days or so or more of hard climbing to take prisoners back and then come back. We had a Mexican in the outfit who on occasion took them down the mountain. He would return in about an hour's time. He shot them so he would not have to make the trip.

More common, although not widespread, was for Americans to take Germans prisoner and then mistreat them. Usually when American combat soldiers mistreated prisoners, they were angry about something that the Germans as a whole, or the actual prisoners themselves, had done. James Simms, of the 101st Airborne Division, saw SS captives interrogated in the wake of the Malmédy Massacre. A group of Screamin' Eagles lobbied fiercely to be allowed to take the Germans outside and kill them, but they were overruled by their sergeant, who felt that the prisoners could provide valuable intelligence. There was already enough tension in the air when the German leader insisted that the Americans provide him with his favorite brand of cigarettes:

That is when all hell broke loose. I don't think Sgt. Morris [the main interrogater] really meant to hurt these krauts but the other bearded toughies in there clearly had that in mind. There was a lot of bitter cussing and carrying on, for these men of the 101st were remembering Malmédy and all the other American G.I.s who had died. I was shocked by all this determination to shoot down prisoners but I was to learn that combat does things to good men.

Jack Brewer, a tank crewman in the 3d Armored Division, said that there were also times in his outfit when prisoners were mistreated. "Most prisoners were treated fairly but there were instances of wrongful killing. Some were taken prisoner and later shot, others intentionally murdered."

Dick Peters, an armored infantryman in the 8th Armored Division, remembered an occasion when German soldiers were shot in cold blood:

I learned later that maybe only half of them got back to the prison compound. A lot of times you have to wonder to what extent we were guilty of some of that. War being what it is and people being what they are, a lot of times a fellow gets so angry he just loses control of himself and emotions take over.

Another member of Peters's outfit, Irwin Shapiro, once found himself in no-man's-land with a group of German prisoners. He and his comrades were under attack and had to leave the house they occupied immediately to have any chance of getting to the American lines safely. The sergeant in charge knew that there was no way they could take the Germans with them. At the same time, he did not want the prisoners to get back to German lines safely and then be in a position to kill more Americans one day. As he saw it, there was only one solution. Said Shapiro:

He went up to each of these Germans and put the pistol between their eyes and pulled the trigger. I don't think I could have done that although at that time we didn't know about the concentration camps. I know at that point I could not have done that. I couldn't look a man in the face and just put that gun between his eyes and pull the trigger while the man is pleading for his life.

As opposed to Shapiro's incident, which was militarily motivated, the following tragedy grew out of nothing more than revenge and passion. Said Howard Ruppel, of the 517th Parachute Infantry Regiment, who witnessed the tragedy:

We were spellbound and shocked as these prisoners revealed atrocities to American prisoners. Then by surprise a guy grabbed one of the prisoners, spun him around, shoved him into a closet while drawing his revolver, and before anyone could intervene, bam, bam, bam, three shots rang out. The revelation of a hideous act prompted one to act likewise. I hung my head with shame and compassion. It is sad and pathetic to see a friend break down, worse to witness an act of atrocity.

For the overwhelming majority of German prisoners, the most serious threat they had to worry about in American captivity was assaults on their pride. Usually the most harmful thing combat soldiers would do to prisoners was jeer them if they felt that they were too arrogant, as 36th Infantry Division soldier Frank Miller related:

Someone suggested we parade the SS trooper down the street. The infantryman on the other TD chose their smallest soldier for that chore. They called him "Shorty," and that pint-sized GI walked the Kraut through the throng of people, hollering, "Git along you old Superman, git along." Every few steps, Shorty would reach up and kick the Kraut in the rear, and the crowd would just roar with laughter. You could see the hatred in the Kraut's eyes.

American combat soldiers, who did not react well to arrogance and condescension from their own officers, felt that German officers were often guilty of those two qualities. When they captured German officers, they delighted in cutting them down to size. While guarding a group of prisoners waiting to go to the latrine, James Graff decided to teach one such German a lesson:

> When a high ranking German officer stepped to the head of the line, I moved over and told him to go to the end of the line, but he just ignored me until I prodded him in the belly with my weapon and said, "I told you to get to the end of the line," in no uncertain terms. He moved out of line. It brought a lot of smiles plus some laughs from the other Germans.

Watching a column of captured prisoners, Harry Arnold saw a monocled, Prussian-looking officer riding in a staff car while his men walked beside the car sweating to keep up:

> I motioned to the men around the car to climb aboard. I could as well have ordered them to attack a tank with bare hands. They blanched and tried to ignore my suggestive motions. The old Junker type turned cold eyes on me momentarily, then continued to look stiffly forward. I pointed my rifle threateningly. Now they had to determine which they feared most, the officer in the car or the rifle pointed directly at them. The choice was a hard one for them, the age old traditions of subservience to authority having been ruthlessly ingrained. I determined that the rigid line between master and servant be breached here and now. Fearfully they began climbing in the car.

Radford Carroll saw a black soldier take a German general prisoner. The general was appalled to have been taken captive not only by a black man but an enlisted man:

> There was a short conference between the general and his staff officer, then the staff officer said to the negro soldier that the general refused to surrender to anyone under the rank of major. The negro soldier then gave the general a tremendous kick in the seat of his pants and snorted, "Huh!" You done surrendered to a buck private fifteen minutes ago." Then the negro stole the general's watch.

Some American soldiers in the rear liked to act tough around prisoners. Such rear-echelon troops infuriated combat soldiers. George Kerrigan, of the 36th Infantry Division, summed up the attitudes of most combat men:

> I always figured when a man was . . . taken prisoner he was to be treated fairly (as long as he was acting properly). I met a real hero about 500 miles to rear who was torturing a German prisoner. I made him stop and said, "If you hate these bums as you say, why not volunteer for the front and you can have a hell of a time killing them. We're running short of heroes up there."

Lawrence Nickell outlined the attitude of his unit, one that was shared by most frontline soldiers. "We occasionally, rarely I should say, got the order to take no prisoners. That 'no prisoners' order was routinely ignored, as they would fight to the death if they saw someone shot who was trying to surrender. If the order was followed we would lose more men."

Joseph Kiss, a member of the 2d Infantry Division, knew that he "could never shoot [a prisoner] in cold blood. In fact, I was awfully happy when they quit shooting and surrendered. I noticed a lot of them had wedding rings on."

Many prisoners were taken the way Boyd Miller and his 29th Infantry Division buddies snagged two Germans one night in Normandy. "They nearly jumped out of their skins in fright as we surrounded them, and our sergeant yelled to them to surrender. No problem. They were sent to the rear with a couple of soldiers for questioning and incarceration. The war was over for those Germans."

Thomas Rosell, of the 34th Infantry Division in Italy, saw one German who enjoyed his captivity. "A rather jovial type. This guy spoke some English and a lot of Italian. He asked if he could stay with us. We kept him. He became platoon cook. I think he was very pleased."

Dewey Mann, a rifleman in the 36th Infantry Division, had a pleasant conversation with some Germans whom he and his buddies captured. The conversation revealed that word of good U.S. treatment of POWs spread among the Germans. "The prisoners said that they had heard the Americans would give them clean sheets to sleep on and were anxious to find out if this was true. Cigarettes and candy were shared with the Germans."

Gene Tippins, of the 80th Infantry Division, captured a group of Germans in France in November 1944:

> I heard this voice behind me say, "Comrade." I looked back and there stood a German soldier. He laid down his rifle, put his hands in the air and started moving toward me. Then to my surprise, 5 more Germans emerged . . . giving themselves up to me. I had them lay down their weapons and place their hands on top of their heads.

Tippins then marched his captives back to the rear for processing.

Lionel Adda captured a German during the Battle of the Bulge:

> Directly in front of me, about 15 yards away, a German soldier raised his head and threw away his rifle. I called out instinctively, 'Kamerad, kommen Sie hier.' Sergeant Enlow ordered everyone to hold his fire, and the soldier rose and walked toward me. He was a handsome young man, not more than 18 . . . and with a faint smile of relief on his face.

Frank Iglehart, a member of the 99th Infantry Division, recalled an incident in which he and his buddies captured some SS men from the Viking Division, a unit primarily made up of Scandinavians recruited by the Germans to serve the Reich. One of the SS men was mortally wounded:

> In a low whisper he begged for a drink of water and a debate ensued; give him a bit of surcease or not? Nelson and Sutphen said no—to hell with the son of a bitch. Others said yes, he's had it. The platoon medic won the debate without a word. He held a canteen to the lips of the mortally wounded enemy, and the argument stopped.

Charles Gilmore, of the 1st Armored Division, claimed that all prisoners captured by his unit were treated well even to the point where his sergeant once saved the life a young German who had spit in the face of his American captor. The sergeant shielded the German and removed him from the scene before the soldier could shoot him. Edward Schooner, of the 6th Armored Division, described how he and his fellow armored infantrymen dealt with captured Germans. "In most instances we disarmed, took the helmet, checked for hidden arms, grenades, papers, etc. and then sent them to the rear unescorted."

Guy LeGrand, a sergeant in the 290th Combat Engineer Battalion, saw the face of the enemy one night in France when a weary German soldier surrendered to him:

> He was a young man, not more than 22, standing a little under average height and stockily built. He had removed his light wool cap, revealing a disheveled mass of blond hair. His blue eyes were tired and sunken, he was badly in need of a shave, and his clothing was so mud-covered that it was hardly possible to determine what gear was attached to his belt. He spoke first saying, "I am very hungry and tired."

It was hard not to feel compassion in such cases, and LeGrand fed him, allowed him to bathe himself, and guarded him while he slept soundly. Then he turned him over to the military police.

Even though Howard Ruppel witnessed an unpardonable atrocity by an American soldier on a German prisoner, he summed up the way in which the hundreds of other Germans POWs taken by his unit were treated by him and his buddies. "We treated them with dignity, as dedicated soldiers to their country, and they returned the respect."

CHAPTER 9

THE LEADERSHIP FACTOR

Until only recently, the study of military leadership and the study of military history have been nearly synonymous. By studying those at the top, it was possible to learn and understand the strategy, tactics, and policies of any given war. It was also fascinating to historians to study the personalities of compelling and successful generals in an effort to understand and identify the rudiments of good military leadership. Although this approach is important in the context of military history, it reveals only part of the picture. To truly understand how wars are fought and what they meant to those involved, it is necessary to study the average soldier who actually does the fighting. This sociomilitary approach has the added dividend of lending valuable insight into the realities of military leadership.

That good leadership is important in war is especially true at the junior officer level. In the case of the American combat soldier in World War II, junior officers (platoon leaders, company commanders, and so forth) were far more relevant than those who occupied high command. Generals were otherworldy figures who were often heard (through their directives from on high) but rarely seen. With some exceptions, the average combat soldier probably did not know, or especially care, who commanded his division, his regiment, or probably his battalion, but he certainly knew his platoon leader. In the mind of the combat soldier, the only officers who had any practical relevance were those under whom he served. Anything above a company commander was considered rear echelon. A commanding officer's competence and leadership ability could sometimes make the difference between life and death.

It is outside the focus of this study to determine the overall effectiveness of American junior officers in combat units in World War II. But it is possible to determine what combat soldiers thought about the quality of their leadership. Contemporary opinions are, of course, fairly rare, because officers censored soldiers' letters. No soldier in his right mind would criticize the CO who was going to read and censor his letter. However, half a century after the fact, combat men are rarely shy in expressing opinions of their leaders. Most felt that their officers did a good job. In most cases, combat soldiers have been quick to point out instances of good and bad leadership that they witnessed and give examples of who was a good leader and why and who was a poor leader and why.

Another important factor in studying military leadership is the occasional irrelevance of officers. Because most military history has been written from the top down, it has been taken for granted that officers are always in control of their men and that they are the true leaders to whom all soldiers look in combat. In reality this was not always the case. With surprising frequency combat soldiers looked to their sergeants for leadership day in and day out in combat. A major reason for that was the turnover in officers. Another reason was that NCOs were usually closer to the men.

Junior officers were, of course, the backbone of combat leadership. Their job of leading men in battle was daunting. To do it successfully often required more strength, courage, and character than some of them could muster. They had the most difficult role in the meat grinder of World War II.

At the same time that they shared and experienced the awful realities of war with their men, junior officers were also directly responsible for the welfare of those men. Every platoon leader had to live with the knowledge that his chances of becoming a casualty were even greater than the chances of those he commanded. In addition he had to realize that, if he made any mistakes, men—flesh-and-blood human beings whom he knew and may have befriended—could die.

Radford Carroll, of the 99th Infantry Division, outlined the basic problem for combat soldiers, most of whom were only civilians temporarily in uniform. "One of the hardest things to learn was that the officers were in a separate class. They were the ruling class; we were the servant class. The rules were based on the concept that 'familiarity breeds contempt' and in the case of many of the officers the concept was certainly correct."

Carroll identified the most basic truth about American officers and their men in combat in World War II. "The judgement . . . revolved about whether the leader did his job and so minimized our danger; if so, he was respected and guarded by his men, regardless of personality. If the leader caused needless danger to his men, it was possible that someone might try to remove him in self defence." In other words, if an officer was detrimental to survival, he was hated, and a unit's morale and willingness to fight were diminished. If, on the other hand, an officer abetted his men's chances of survival, he earned the fierce and aggressive loyalty of his men and, in so doing, improved the fighting caliber of his outfit.

This truth transcended all boundaries of background, including race, as one black soldier from the 92d Infantry Division pointed out. "Color means nothing at the front. Everybody has a rough life, and that does a lot to bring the men together. The important thing is not what color an officer is but whether he knows his job. If he does, he'll get the respect of his men. Most of our officers are regular."

Most combat soldiers agreed that, by and large, their officers did a good job. William McLaughlin, of the Americal Division, pointed out the common phenomenon that "the closer we got to the front, the better the caliber of officers." Carlie Berryhill, a combat soldier in the 6th Infantry Division, was effusive in his praise. "I thought our leadership during the war was very good. Officers and noncommissioned officers were the best that the army has ever known." Thaddeus Piewawer, of the 41st Infantry Division, said that the leadership in his outfit was good. Curtis Banker felt that the leadership in his 43d Infantry Division outfit was excellent because they had trained together for a year before going overseas, which gave them a chance to weed out any bad officers.

John Wiegandt, a member of the 45th Infantry Division, said that his leadership was the best possible under the circumstances. Donald MacLeod, also a member of the 45th, had complete faith in his officers, with only a few exceptions. Gerald VanCleve, of the 75th Infantry Division, recalled: "Commanders from the company level and up were very good leaders and had a great deal of compassion for their people." Seventy-seventh Infantry Division soldier Daniel Chomiw related that his "company had a pretty fine bunch of officers that sure did get along with the men" and attributed his unit's combat success to that fact. Jack Hartzog, of the 78th Infantry Division, was hard pressed to remember any bad leaders in his outfit. "I saw very few . . . instances of poor leadership. The examples of good leadership are too numerous to mention." Jack Brewer, a tank crewman in the 3d Armored Division, was impressed with his officers. "I give a great deal of credit for the leadership my division possessed. Most were good under fire and could carry out a mission."

The same was true for 4th Marine Division veteran William Allen. "We respected them even up to the colonel. From the colonel all the way down there was not any officer . . . that we didn't really respect." Another marine, Alto Johns, wrote home from Guam of his high regard for combat officers. "The officers on the line who lead the men are tops with me. Perfectly wonderful and a guy has every confidence in a real fighting officer, which of course means cooperation, and we had it!"

For some men the quality of officers was mixed. There were those who did a fine job and others who did not. Henri Atkins, a lead scout in the 99th Infantry Division, substantiated this observation:

> Our relationship with our officers was very mixed. As combat later showed us, some were above the stress of command, others broke under the stress. Many had their brains locked into the book of regulations! Some were good, and some were bad, some brave and some cowards, some you could look up to and some were despised by all.

Edwin Hanson, of the 37th Infantry Division, pointed out that, where officers were concerned, there was often no middle ground. "Good officers were very good. Bad officers were very bad." Cecil Kemp saw both kinds. "Some were very good, sensitive, able to make correct decisions . . . courageous. Others were too cautious."

A few men felt that their officers were bad. They came away totally unimpressed with the caliber of leadership in the U.S. Army.

John Beeks, a combat engineer in the 78th Infantry Division, expressed his complete disdain for his officers: "We learned who we could depend on. About 9 out of 10 enlisted men. About 1 out of 4 officers." Robert Manning, of the 81st Infantry Division, estimated that "75 percent of platoon leaders were poor and not good in combat." Another 81st Division man, Ross Hadfield, said that his officers were bad because of their chemical dependency. "Too many of the officers were actually alcoholics. The worst case was a CO . . . who was so drunk when we were going into . . . a landing that he couldn't stand." Harold Sletten, of the 96th Infantry Division, voiced a common complaint when it came to bad officers—lack of communication. If a soldier did not understand the purpose behind orders or what was personally required of him, he was not likely to respond well. "The leaders did not let us know what was happening or what we were going to do. This ignorance bothered me very much. The leaders did not make me feel part of the group." William Houser, an officer himself, felt that among his peers only "about five percent were good. Most at all levels were poor, interested in their own welfare first."

Such opinions were generally the exception rather than the rule. The majority of combat soldiers felt that their leadership in combat was of a reasonably high caliber. A survey by army researchers corroborates this assertion. In-line infantry companies, soldiers, and noncommissioned officers were asked how many of their officers were "the kind who are willing to go through anything they ask their men to go through"—something that almost all combat soldiers identified with their best officers. Among the NCOs, 66 percent felt that most or all of their officers met this criterion. Privates were even more complimentary; 71 percent felt that most or all of their officers were willing to do anything they asked their men to do. Even those who were less impressed with their officers still felt that half of them met this crucial criterion. This was true for 20 percent among the NCOs and 17 percent among the privates.

If the perceived quality of officers among combat soldiers was relatively high, what made for a good officer in their eyes? In addition to not asking his men to do anything that he himself would not do, a good officer did not use his rank and privilege to avoid danger, and he did not talk down to his men as underlings. He did all he could to accomplish his mission successfully and at the lowest cost. He gave firm orders and expected them to be followed, but he often took care to make sure that his men understood the reasoning behind the orders.

In addition, good leaders did not pretend that they knew everything, especially if they were new to combat, as William Ruf, of the 6th Infantry Division, pointed out. "A good leader says, 'Sergeant, you let me know when I'm ready for the job.'" Donald MacDonald thought that the best officers were those who were "not too proud to accept the advice of combat-wise enlisted men." Frederick Kielsgard, of the 41st Infantry Division, defined good officers as "those who fought with their men . . . and . . . did not needlessly sacrifice the lives of those under their command." Jack Hartzog, who fought with the 78th Infantry Division, felt that the "good leaders at company level were those who wouldn't expect a soldier to do anything they would not do." Thomas Heck, a tanker in the 1st Armored Division, thought that sensitivity and communication were important. The good officers were "those who looked out for the welfare of their men and explained the purpose of various mission assignments so that there was no misunderstanding as to . . . what was expected."

Other 1st Armored men had similar opinions. Paris Roussos, an armored infantryman, said that "a good officer will explain in detail what needs to be done and then will assume the same risk as the men under him." Thomas Isabel agreed. "A good officer would not ask you to do something he would not do himself. Knowing this the men would do anything for an officer."

Nearly all combat men preferred to be led by officers who had received battlefield commissions. Anyone who had received a commission in battle knew firsthand what it was like to be an enlisted man. What is more, the field commissioned officer was combat tested and courageous. In all likelihood that was how he had been commissioned in the first place.

Richard Kirkman, a tank crewman in the 2d Armored Division, held battlefield commissioned officers in high esteem. "Officers who came up through the ranks were more efficient and practical than those from military college and officers' training school. We felt the boys with field commissions made better officers." Harry Arnold, of the 99th Infantry Division, echoed Kirkman's sentiment. "There is a rapport between the ranks and a leader who has been there that is seldom achieved otherwise. I have never [been] . . . nor will I ever be a supporter of the leadership . . . theory that fails to incorporate a strong apprenticeship method."

When it came to specific examples of good leaders under whom they served, combat men were forthright in their comments. Lawrence Nickell, of the 5th Infantry Division, remembered meeting a new CO who turned out to be a good commander:

> He was a big rough-looking man and when Chaney and I first talked to him we thought he was an enlisted replacement as we could see no insignia on him. Most officers wore no collar insignia but wore a vertical white band on the back of their helmet for identification. Company commanders were prime targets for snipers.

After Henri Atkins's colonel was shot and had walked to an aid station, Atkins was surprised to see him at the front:

> He had a few comforting words to say and then he moved forward under a curtain of shelling. He was a brave and good officer, although he was foolhardy. One does not expect to see a colonel in the front lines. But he was concerned for his men and had come forward to . . . check on his regiment. A good officer!

Jason Byrd, a combat engineer in the 1st Infantry Division, fondly remembered his favorite officer:

> He wasn't like the OCS [officer candidate school] officers we had. He would get us together. He said, "Now men they told me that we've got to go out and secure this area. I want to ask your . . . opinion of how many men I should take . . . and if I could have a volunteer to go with me." I volunteered right off the bat. He was dead honest. He was a man who you knew was a good leader because he would ask for your opinion.

Whayland Greene, a rifleman in the 32d Infantry Division, admired the courage of his platoon leader during patrols on Luzon. "I don't remember him putting an American soldier in front of him. He was one of the best. He took the lead and had me directly behind him." Floyd Todd, of the 37th Infantry Division, looked up to his colonel because "he would not have his men do anything he would not do himself."

William Warde, of the 42d Infantry Division, was forever grateful to an officer who braved German shell fire to go into no-man's-land so that he could tell Warde and his buddies to pull back immediately or risk being cut off:

> I and a number of others most definitely owe our lives to his actions. He stated that if we expected to survive, we would have to make a break for it, now! We could hear and see the approaching German tanks. I will always admire and be grateful to Duffy Stanley for being intelligent and astute to have gotten us out.

Sid Rowling served in the 80th Infantry Division under a company commander named Garland Godby. Thanks to Godby's courage, competence, and common sense, his men were unanimous in their adoration of him. Forty-five years after they had served in combat together, Rowling wrote to Godby and told him of his high opinion of him. "Of all the frontline company commanders you were the most respected. You were a real fighting commander who the men would follow. This I know in my eyes. You were . . . the best." Antonio Renna, of the 81st Infantry Division, related to his CO because he was only a civilian in uniform just like his men. "Our company commander was a jello salesman. He was tall and in excellent . . . shape. He commanded respect and was respectful of those he led."

Donald Dencker, a combat soldier in the 96th Infantry Division, had the highest regard for his company commander, a man of courage. "Our company commander, Captain Fitzpatrick, was a great leader. The men really believed in him, but great company and platoon leaders were always casualties. Captain Fitzpatrick was seriously wounded."

Dencker here identified one of the main drawbacks to good officers. Because they were brave and tended to lead their men instead
of guaranteeing their own safety, they were hit with alarming frequency.

Losing a popular leader could drive morale down. Famous war
correspondent Ernie Pyle saw a unit lose a beloved officer who had
been in command ever since the unit left the States. After the men
carried the body of their dead commander away from the front, Pyle
watched them say good-bye to the man who had meant so much to
them. Pyle was struck by the behavior of one soldier in particular:

> A soldier came and stood beside the officer, and bent over,
> and he . . . spoke to his dead captain, not in a whisper but aw-
> fully tenderly, and he said: "I sure am sorry, sir." The man squat-
> ted down, and . . . took the dead hand, and he sat there for a
> full five minutes, holding the dead hand in his own and look-
> ing intently into the dead face, and he never uttered a sound
> all the time he sat there. And finally he put the hand down, and
> then reached up and straightened the captain's shirt collar, and
> then sort of rearranged the tattered edges of his uniform
> around the wound.

Justin Gray was with some 96th Division men on Okinawa the
night they lost their captain. "The captain had just been killed. A Jap
sniper's bullet caught him in the neck as he was giving us the final
instructions for tomorrow's attack. He died instantly. Many of the
men cried. They didn't try to hide it. They had really loved their CO.
'The company won't be worth a damn now,' one said."

There were times when the death of a good officer had the opposite effect on men. In their grief, they became angry and fought
harder. Mel Cotton, a medic in the 91st Infantry Division in Italy, recalled one such instance:

> Lt. Bruno Rosellini was shot in the heart by a sniper. He died
> in medic Jim Christopher's arms. Many B Company men got
> fighting mad at this time. Considerable individual GI growls,
> profanity, and derogatory [epithets] were leveled at Adolph

Hitler and the enemy on the hill. This chatter was not unusual in combat when a popular leader is killed.

Depending on the caliber of leadership, a unit's fighting acumen could change almost overnight. Charles Rudolph, an armored infantryman in the 1st Armored Division, remembered the positive effect that a good company commander had on his outfit. "Our company commander . . . who was assigned to our unit in November 1944 was a battlewise, competent and understanding soldier who fought for his men just as hard as we fought for him. His men came first, last and always and he really made us into a smoothly operating fighting machine." James McDonald, of the 8th Armored Division, felt that his lieutenant's aggressive attitude helped whip his men into an excellent fighting group. "I guess part of the criteria was just how he treated the people. He was gung-ho and he worked us hard, but you could always feel you got a fair deal from Lieutenant Hammerschmidt." The best officer that George Wyatt, of the 1st Marine Division, saw was a man who would consistently risk his life every day during the Battle of Guadalcanal. "This man risked his life and put himself secondary to the well being of his men. Officers like [Captain] Kirkpatrick were considered one of us and we would automatically make great sacrifices for them and go that extra yard without thinking of ourselves first."

Officers such as the one Wyatt described became part of the "deadly brotherhood." If they demonstrated that they could be counted on in combat and if they made an honest effort to be fair with their troops, they were combat brothers.

One such officer was Walter Gentry, of the 290th Combat Engineer Battalion. Born the son of an educator in Knoxville, Tennessee, by all accounts Gentry was liked and respected wherever he went. He had integrity, character, and natural leadership qualities. He was the ideal leader in a citizen-soldier army, a man who knew how to lead without coercion and a man who had a bright postwar future. In February 1945 during the bitter fighting in Alsace-Lorraine, Gentry insisted on leading a patrol into enemy lines. Something went wrong on the patrol and Gentry was killed, leaving the men in his entire company shocked and depressed.

Gentry's commanding officer wrote to his family:

> Your son was the finest officer and man and the best friend I ever hope to have, his death coming to all of us as a tragic shock. Lt. Gentry led a patrol voluntarily, choosing to do so because he would not entrust the lives of his men to anyone else. He fully knew the risk involved and characteristically would not send his men on any mission he would not undertake himself. There was not a man in the command who did not feel that he had lost a personal friend.

Another man was moved to write to Gentry's mother. "We learned all about his exceptional devotion to duty from his own fellow officers and the men who served with him. They recovered his body immediately as there were many who volunteered to risk their own lives in order to perform this last token of love for Walter."

One of Gentry's enlisted soldiers also wrote to Gentry's mother to express his sympathy:

> I had the privilege and honor of serving under your son Walter, who to me will always be the Finest Officer and Gentleman I . . . will ever meet. We were very friendly and I believe he thought as much of me as I thought of him which was a very great deal. When the going got rough, he not only was a leader but also a mother to the men. I can truthfully say that every man in this company admired and respected him.

Although many families of officers who had been killed received sympathy letters, few received them from enlisted soldiers who had been under their son or husband's command. The outpouring of sincere adoration and love for Gentry marked him as something special. Like Garland Godby, Gentry was probably among the best of all American junior officers in combat.

Of course to be a high-quality, effective leader such as Godby or Gentry, a man had to be competent in his soldierly knowledge, skilled at communication and handling diverse kinds of people, and courageous enough to lead his troops in life-threatening situations.

This took intelligence and common sense, which many officers had. But it also required bravery in great quantities. No matter how qualified to command, not all men could summon that sort of bravery. There were many who simply did not have the strength of character needed to perform the strenuous, challenging job of leading men in combat. The temptation to use rank and privilege to shield themselves from danger was too great for such men. In addition, there were men who were obtuse, condescending, and arrogant as well as men who possessed poor communication skills or simply did not know what they were doing. These were the bad officers; sometimes, through their inferior leadership, they got men killed.

James Simms, a paratrooper in the 101st Airborne Division, was told by another Screamin' Eagle that he had once urinated on the dead body of an officer who was roundly hated by the troopers under his command. This led Simms to express the following opinion:

I don't believe that most combat men would be particularly shocked that it happened. There is a moral here. If you're not a good, tough square shooter, don't be a combat officer, and if you are a stinker and are going to be a combat officer it would be a damned good idea to get yourself unstunk before you get into combat. Combat men do not waste much sympathy on a rat.

Combat soldiers were impatient with bad officers. Such officers were either to be ignored or eliminated, preferably by the enemy. John Roche, of the 88th Infantry Division, outlined the attitude found in most poor leaders:

The officer's attitude was, simply, every good soldier must help us beat the odds against us. Therefore, he must go and do where and what we say without protest . . . performing always up to the top limit of his skill and experience. This way the officers would be safe, and could believe they were proving their effective leadership . . . and even the survival of the fittest.

This notion that an officer's life was more important than the lives of his men was typical of bad officers and was extremely detrimental to morale. Commented Newman Phillips, a combat soldier in the 32d Infantry Division: "Bad leadership was almost always the result of lack of experience or cowardice." The former could be addressed; the latter could not. According to Clyde Upchurch, of the 3d Armored Division, the typical cowardly types were guilty of "not knowing the capabilities of their men, not knowing just what was going on. Some were so scared you could smell them."

Forrest Coleman brought up a point familiar to most combat men. "Staff officers with no combat experience being assigned to line companies to lead troops in battle were more often than not poor leaders." Usually these staff officers were career military men who were given commands not because they were qualified but because they needed command experience to merit promotion. Combat soldiers bitterly resented this sort of "ticket punching" at their expense.

James Graff, a BAR man in the 35th Infantry Division, recalled a brand-new platoon leader who threatened to leave wounded men behind during a patrol. "I wasn't going to leave anybody because I sure wouldn't want to be left. Chris had some very unkind things to say to the lieutenant and he emphasized them with a loaded M1. The lieutenant was finding out things weren't exactly like OCS."

These sorts of threats were no laughing matter. Under the intense stresses of combat, some men were more than willing to harm any officer who posed a threat. John Roche recalled checking out a house one day when he was on a patrol when he saw an officer from headquarters who accused him of hiding to avoid fighting. Not only was Roche outraged, he was wary:

> I had my rifle at port arms already, now I fingered the trigger and flicked off the safety. For it was obvious he wanted to place me under arrest, provided he could arm himself first with his holstered .45 [pistol]. But had he gone for his pistol, I would have had to shoot him, and I would have shot to kill, for dead men tell no tales.

Luckily for Roche, another soldier came along and diverted the officer's attention and Roche was able to resume patrolling with his buddies.

Henri Atkins's first company commander could not deal with the stress of command. He began to shake even before the company got to the front lines. After declining to go on patrols for a number of days, the man, whom Atkins referred to anonymously, finally acceded to lead a patrol into what he thought was a safe area. The patrol was ambushed. Said Atkins:

Captain_____panicked. His borderline stress limit had been reached. In a trembling voice he was heard to cry out, "Men, you crawl back. I'm going to make a run for it." All made it safely back to our lines except the captain, who . . . stepped on a land mine. Word of the captain's wounding soon filtered down to all of the platoons. It was greeted with much hilarity. I hate to say it but his wounding was a blessing for us. Had he remained in command, he could have gotten us all killed.

Radford Carroll despised an officer he referred to as "Lieutenant C," who had all the characterstics of a bad officer—arrogance, insensitivity, poor command knowledge, and, most important, cowardice. Lieutenant C was also a bully. Like many poor leaders, he talked tough when conditions were safe and delighted in abusing his position of authority to torment his soldiers. Word of Lieutenant C's cowardice and incompetence spread quickly once the outfit entered combat. Commented Carroll:

The quality of life for Lt. C began a rapid decline. The men were outraged that they had been bullied by, and were compelled to be subservient to, a man for whom they had only contempt; and it showed. When Lt. C tried to threaten one man, saying that he would put him on outpost duty (a very dangerous . . . job), the man offered to shoot Lt. C and was only stopped by his companions. The men were not rebellious, but they could not be led . . . by a man who huddled in fear in his foxhole. He would not even do his basic duty. If he had not had his good platoon sergeant sleeping with him, he might have had a grenade dropped in his dugout. Lt. C left . . . for hospitalization with a "nervous condition" and we never saw him again. Good riddance!

Bert Morphis, of the 1st Infantry Division, never forgot the tragedy of a green platoon leader who led his soldiers to their deaths:

> Early in the morning, when it was pitch black, he led the platoon on a combat patrol into an area where there were a large number of pillboxes. We passed by one without incident, until the entire platoon passed by. Then a machine gun opened up from behind, killing about half the platoon, including the lieutenant. The poor guy never had a chance to learn, and he took a dozen others with him.

Matt Miletich, a member of the 84th Infantry Division, was a brand-new replacement on his first day of combat, but even he knew that his lieutenant's order was crazy:

> The machine gun was our objective and I expected Lieutenant Burrows to give us some directions as to how we would overpower it. But all I heard was his terse, abrupt order—"Fix bayonets and follow me into the field!" His order hit me like a slap in the face! Surprised and shocked, I told myself, "He's crazy."

Predictably, Miletich's entire platoon was mowed down by the machine gun when it attempted to charge it head-on. Only Miletich survived to tell the story.

In one disgraceful episode, Victor Wade's commanding officer pushed Wade ahead of himself as they left a landing craft during the 3d Infantry Division's invasion of southern France in 1944. "He said it would be better for the landing if I were shot rather than him."

Joe Dine, an officer himself in the 36th Infantry Division, told the story of an extremely incompetent battalion commander who was his CO for a few days in France. This colonel, whom Dine referred to as "Colonel Mann," had no common sense and was given to strange orders and statements:

> God knows how this man ever got any commission—let alone how he reached lieutenant colonel, but he did. For three or four days . . . he commanded our infantry battalion.

If he had lasted any longer, I wouldn't be here to tell this. He had no common sense, just a lot of authority. He relished his role as commander of nearly a thousand battle-tested infantrymen, but it was a dream role, and he resented combat, as it interfered with the joy of command.

One evening Colonel Mann prepared some unrealistic attack plans and summoned his officers to his command post to go over them:

> He probably had four years of West Point instruction in tactics concentrated on that poor little map, with its lines and cross lines and crosses and arrows and gun positions and concentration areas and routes of withdrawal, all prettied up in red and blue grease pencil. We sat there all the time . . . staring at him through eyes bloodshot with exhaustion yet somehow fascinated with the whole foolish, frightening scene. Suddenly, he leaped to his feet, awkwardly drew his pistol and shouted excitedly, "All right, men, on your feet, they're attacking us but we'll defend this command post to the death!" All we could hear was the distant rattle of machine-gun fire. "Colonel," someone said pityingly, "that's a mile or more away."

Although Dine wondered if Colonel Mann suffered from some sort of mental illness, that did not really matter. Most important was that this foolish colonel could endanger the lives of his men.

One of the pet peeves of combat men was arrogance on the part of officers. Glenn Searles, of the 77th Infantry Division, recalled dealing with a condescending air force officer who did not understand combat infantrymen very well. The officer, a liaison pilot in a small scout plane, landed his plane to hunt for souvenirs. When he had finished scavenging, he attempted to take off, only to find that his plane was stuck in the mud:

> The pilot came over to us and ordered us to help get his plane back on the runway. We started laughing and told him that we were infantry grunts—not rear echelon air force. He got mad and threatened to have us court-martialed for dis-

obeying a direct order. He didn't know that officers were polite to the troops under combat conditions.

Thomas Isabel witnessed this sort of arrogance from a new platoon leader. "One green lieutenant . . . would not listen to the advice of battle-wise men. They eventually refused to follow him." James
Luzzi, like Isabel an armored infantryman in the 1st Armored Division, saw an arrogant CO who put no stock in the opinions of his
sergeants. "He was told by noncoms not to go over a ridge and he
was killed by rifle fire." Such men were at least as dangerous as cowards. Charles Rudolph found this out when a self-important captain
took over his company. "Fresh from stateside, he knew all there was
to know about combat, refusing any advice at all from lieutenants
and noncoms. Eventually this attitude put the entire company into
extremely dangerous situations. Only through the skill and know-
how of the platoon leaders did we manage to . . . survive."

Norman Sue, an armored infantryman in the 4th Armored Division, encountered a similar situation. "We had one OCS graduate
come in as our platoon leader. He refused to take noncoms' sugges-
tions. Within ten days he 'accidentally' shot himself in the large toe."

To have any hope of being a good leader to his men, an officer
had to look beyond his own welfare. He could not be self-centered.
In every action he had to consider what was best for his troops. The
concept was simple. In exchange for rank, privilege, and control, an
officer was to look after the needs of his men and had a responsibility to do everything possible to keep them alive. Unfortunately
there were officers who were far too selfish to live up to that sort of
responsibility. Even if they had tried, they could not think of anything
in combat save for their own well-being.

James Simms saw one such leader during the seige at Bastogne.
Because his unit was cut off, it had to be resupplied from the air. This
presented many difficulties. It was not uncommon for airmen to miss
American lines altogether and accidentally drop their loads of food,
ammunition, and medicine on the Germans. Simms saw this happen
and observed the reaction of the selfish officer:

He shook his fist at the sky and said in the most bitter manner I've ever heard, "I hope the Krauts shoot every one of the

goddamned sons of bitches down." To bitterly condemn every man up there . . . was a little more than I could go for. About this time one of our cooks drove up in a jeep. He had one of those big cannisters full of hot soup. This officer rubbed his hands together and with a greedy grin said, "Oh, boy, hot chow." He grabbed a mess kit and piled it just as full as he could. He went off toward the door of the building slurping down food as greedily as a pig at the trough. When he was about halfway to the door he turned his head . . . and as an after-thought said, "Sergeant, see that the men get fed." I never liked that man again, and if he is still living today he is probably still acting the selfish pig.

As important as officers could be to fighting units, at times they were not the real leaders. Sometimes there were so many casualties among officers that enlisted men were compelled to take charge. Other times, the commanding officer was aloof and never seemed to be around his troops when the shooting started. In some cases in the terror-filled confusion of combat, men simply followed the orders of the man in whom they had the most confidence, and sometimes that man was someone other than the commanding officer.

John Stannard, of the Americal Division, saw this happen many times. In his experience, leaders "come in all ranks, shapes and sizes and you cannot identify them until you see them in combat. Especially valuable were those infantrymen who led by example when under fire." Ralph Schmidt, who fought with the 32d Infantry Division, saw "a private assume command of his platoon while his platoon leader was present and without his objections. Leadership comes naturally to many men, others never attain it." There were no formalities in Newman Phillips's outfit. Whoever got the job done successfully was in charge. "In combat the natural leader will assume command when the need arises."

In most cases these natural leaders were NCOs. Many combat soldiers thought of their sergeants as the real leaders of their group. Said William Ruf: "[The sergeants] knew their jobs, had the respect of the troops and were usually go-getters." Roy Yates, of the 7th Infantry Division, agreed. "The real leaders were the platoon sergeants. Officers were always doing some dumb thing and getting killed like waving an arm to direct men. All sergeants would nod their head."

It was the same in Charles Card's rifle platoon within the 24th Infantry Division. "From the perspective of a line company enlisted man, our day to day lives were impacted intensely by NCOs. They were the flesh and blood leaders we knew. Officers . . . were planners, not doers." Gerry Woodrow, of the 40th Infantry Division, stated it simply: "Noncoms were closer to the men, trusted by the men."

It was far more difficult for an officer, a member of the military's ruling class, to earn that trust from enlisted men. A sergeant, even if he was in charge, was still an enlisted man, as was the lowliest buck private. As such a sergeant was not a member of "management" and could thus be trusted. Cecil Kemp found this to be true. "In my unit the real leaders were the noncoms. Through their daily contact with the men, they knew the problems of the men. They were sensitive and caring and could handle tense situations."

This was also often true among tankers. It was not uncommon to see sergeants directing tank platoons and companies. Lawrence Butler, of the 1st Armored Division, was one such soldier. "Being an NCO, I feel we held things together. We knew who to depend on in perilous times. We could maintain discipline."

When Ed Laughlin's unit was in combat, a sergeant who was experienced and possessed natural leadership abilities took command. Laughlin had nothing but respect for him:

> We were not friends or buddies, our backgrounds couldn't have been . . . further apart. I most certainly never had any special favors from him nor were they ever expected and I never felt he was "picking" on me. Perhaps a focusing of our energies and perceptions into a common purpose had something to do with it.

Charles Konkler, an aidman in the 99th Infantry Division, knew that his sergeant was the real leader of his unit. In combat the sergeant acted the part of the commanding officer. "He was caring and wanted to make sure his men had what they needed. He boosted morale. He checked weapons every day, made sure the men had dry socks. He hovered over us like a mother hen."

One such NCO was Curtis Whiteway, also of the 99th Division. His responsibilities as platoon sergeant were the same as those of any officer. "It was my job to teach green men about combat and survival. To lead them in the fight and make all the decisions of combat. You played God. You decided who would live today and who would die."

Often NCOs were compelled to take over not simply because they were better leaders but because there were no officers present. Mac Acosta, a rifleman in the 36th Infantry Division, recalled the turnover that sometimes existed in frontline outfits during combat. "Promotions in a rifle company while in combat come fast to the survivors; one day you're a private, the next you may be a sergeant or a tech; unit leaders change so fast it is difficult to remember who's in charge, and the leaders go out just as fast as they come in." Norman Tiemann, an armored infantryman in the 2d Armored Division, estimated that, due to heavy casualties, "a commissioned officer lasted about a week or so" in combat. Emil Lindenbusch, of the 6th Infantry Division, remembered that "often we were without officers and had to make our own decisions." This was common not only because of high casualties among officers but also because many commanders found excuses to be elsewhere while their men were in combat.

While men were fighting for their lives, there was little time for formalities. Edwin Hanson asserted that "for much of my experience we had no platoon officer." Because the enemy neither knew nor cared if a unit had no proper commander, there was little alternative for combat soldiers but to keep fighting under the tutelage of sergeants or anyone else the men would follow. Donald McNeil, a black soldier in the 93d Infantry Division, saw this happen in his outfit. "Officers were very seldom present. All the leadership was from NCOs."

James McKnight, of the 11th Amored Division, commented: "I never saw an officer in actual combat in four months." Although McKnight's case is the exception rather than the rule, it illustrates the point that, for many combat soldiers, officers were irrelevant at the front. Although headquarters may have pictured an orderly world on the front lines in which duly-assigned commanding officers were always in control and looked to for leadership, the view from the rear did not always correspond with reality.

How did junior officers, who had such a difficult, trying job, view themselves and their roles within combat outfits? Robert Jackson, a rifle platoon leader in the 96th Infantry Division, summed up perfectly the unique status of American officers, particularly the vast majority who were junior officers and citizen-soldiers:

> It was expected that once we were made "officers and gentlemen" . . . we were different from and superior to the enlisted men. Yet . . . we were still civilians in uniform. We were Americans and [it] was a time of strong egalitarianism: there was not the long-term gulf of class, as in other cultures, to separate officers and enlisted men. I had the symbols of rank, I was much better educated than the majority of enlisted men, I had been trained to be an officer/commander, but I didn't feel superior or different.

Most American combat soldiers saw their officers as ordinary men who, like Jackson, might have had the benefit of more education or higher test scores than the other men. Consequently, American officers often had to prove themselves to their men. This democratic atmosphere had a positive effect. Officers who had proven their bravery or skill as commanders were close to their men and could relate to them well because they were not all that different.

The frontline officer had to keep track of more than just his own personal surival. He had the lives of his men to consider. Charles Murphy, a company commander in the 1st Infantry Division, explained what it was like:

> If you make a decision, you're right there, and you're going to catch it with everybody else. You get so little information and so little that you can really depend on that you make your decision usually by the seat of your britches. You make a decision and go with it. Let's hope it's the right one.

It was customary in some armies for enlisted men to dig foxholes for their officers. Any U.S. officer at the front lines who made his troops dig his foxhole was liable to be unpopular. Colin McLaurin, a rifle company commander in the 29th Infantry Division, knew this well. No matter how tired he was, he always dug his own hole. He knew in his heart that "it would not be fair to make a man dig two."

Thomas Rosell, of the 34th Infantry Division, had the misfortune of replacing a popular leader who was moving to a different job. "The men hated to see him go because he had so much experience. They didn't know what to expect from me. I sensed that." Rosell knew that he had to prove himself to his troops.

Martin Tully was a young rifle platoon leader in the 36th Infantry Division in Italy. His outfit was fighting in the mountains and taking casualties, and Tully was not sure what to do. One night a grizzled medic came to take away the bodies of his dead men. Before he left, he said something to the young lieutenant that helped Tully find the strength to be a good leader. "'You ain't too much, but you're all that these men got. Don't do any dumb things, and then maybe they [Tully's troops] won't need *us* to haul them down this goddamn hill.' He gave a 'single finger to the eyebrow' salute, softly said, 'Good luck!' and he was gone."

Combat tended to promote this sort of frank exchanges between officers and enlisted men; there was little time for protocol and sensibilities. Survival and success were paramount. All else was subordinated. Fred Kohl, a platoon leader in the 65th Infantry Division, spent his time in combat "trying to stay alive and do the same for my platoon members and at the same time carry out our mission in combat." This juggling act was the lot of every small unit leader.

Garland Godby recalled the most important aspects of his job as rifle company commander:

You had to have personal contact with the guys in the line because they didn't know what was going on and usually I didn't know what was going on except . . . I knew what we were supposed to be doing. You don't have enough facts and you have to make a lot of decisions based on instincts and it's scary.

William Wood, a tank platoon leader in the 1st Armored Division, underscored the importance of unity between officers and enlisted men in achieving success in battle. "The relationship between officers and men . . . played a big part. Rank was not an obstacle. It was not flaunted. We fought together." Dick Peters, of the 8th Armored Division, received a battlefield commission. His philosophy of leadership was good communication, something that worked very well. "Until I became a platoon leader, I never really fully grasped the importance of getting down to the men what's going on. Once I got to where I had knowledge of . . . what's going on . . . I endeavored to do that for two reasons, to help the guys individually and then also to do the mission for that day."

The responsibility of command never left good junior officers. Those who did the best job were always cognizant of their responsibility for the welfare of their troops. Julian Phillips, a rifle company commander in the 36th Infantry Division, never forgave himself for the death of a supply sergeant whom he had ordered to carry ammunition to the front:

> I could have used any man in the company to carry the ammo chest . . . but no, I had to let Buck, who was not used to artillery shells screaming day in and day out. As I remember those days in the summer of 1944, the death of S/Sgt. Ernest "Buck" West still haunts me. I have always held myself accountable for his death.

Another T-patcher, Milton Landry, also felt responsible for the deaths of those under his command. He recalled a moment in Italy when the realization came to him:

> Then it hit me; all those young healthy brave men dead, some blown to bits never to be identified. What a terrible and dreadful feeling came over me. I know that I did my best to keep them safe and out of harms way the best way I knew how and to get the job done at the same time. I sat down and cried. They were my boys and I loved each and every one of these

splendid American men. The thought came to me of the awesome responsibility of a commander of troops. He is responsible for their feeding, supplying clothing, ammunition, in fact he is responsible for their very lives. He has to do whatever possible to get the job done and at the same time . . . prevent . . . casualties.

Officers had opinions on good and bad leaders even in relation to themselves. Charles Henne, of the 37th Infantry Division, had pride in his success as a rifle company commander:

> I never called for volunteers. I believed if you wanted a [dangerous] job done you led it. I thought a lot about keeping my hide in one piece, completing missions but keeping my men from getting killed if I could. The key to keeping your nerve when everyone else is losing theirs is to keep busy or get mad. My companies were always close knit.

Edgar Wilson, a forward observer in the 80th Infantry Division, once called down artillery fire to help save a group of GIs who had been pinned down by a German counterattack. "When I was finally able to report no further activity, and gave the order to cease firing, one of the remaining nine men stood up, approached me, and said, 'Sir, I've never seen you before, but I'd like to shake your hand.' The other eight joined the huddle, and we all shook hands and congratulated one another."

Garland Godby had an opinion on what usually typified good officers. "They led by example. They didn't talk down. They didn't pull . . . rank. They went on their ability. People would follow them anywhere." Godby's men would hasten to add that this description fit their commander perfectly.

James Mahon, an armored infantry officer in the 1st Armored Division, thought that the best leaders were those "who took personal interest in your well being, who demonstrated competence and compassion and who recognized your capability." Robert Moore, a tank commander in the same division, agreed that character meant more than rank. "Good leaders kept their cool when in combat. Rank had nothing to do with it. I knew whom I could depend on and whom I would follow."

Mark Durley, a platoon leader in the Americal Division, felt that his regimental commander should have been court-martialed due to cowardice and incompetence. In Durley's opinion, only good connections saved the man from his proper fate. Robert Archibald, of the 27th Infantry Division, saw an example of poor leadership on Okinawa. "A Marine major wouldn't believe it when we told him he wasn't going to be able to get his truck convoy . . . forward. The result was 4 out of 6 trucks knocked out and two to three dozen casualties." Colin McLaurin recounted an incident in which a fellow officer demonstrated cowardice in front of McLaurin's soldiers. "I was thoroughly ashamed when I heard a certain captain from battalion headquarters say in a tone that was almost a whine, 'Let's get out of here; I don't want to be a hero. They can have these bars.'" The man was implying that he would rather give up his commission than be exposed to further danger. Officers such as this inspired the scorn of not only enlisted men but also of many of their peers.

Like many civilian soldier officers, Thomas Yochim, of the 78th Infantry Division, had no love for West Point career military men. Yochim, a company commander, was usually down in the mud and filth with his soldiers:

> I developed a genuine dislike of the spit and polish displayed by many senior officers, notably those bearing the aura of West Point. On one occasion I marched a group of wet and muddy GIs into mass on a holy day. Upon arrival we were confronted by a regimental CO, a . . . bird colonel, who emerged from his staff car clean shaven and spotlessly groomed. He inspected my group and gigged us over our unkempt appearance.

It did not matter to the colonel that Yochim's men had been in combat for five straight weeks. This sort of small-minded pettiness (the well-known "chickenshit" detailed by author Paul Fussell) was demoralizing to combat soldiers.

Charles Lindsay, a combat engineer platoon leader in the 4th Marine Division, resented careerist naval academy officers:

> Two Naval Academy colonels joined the outfit. They were . . . assholes. One day, in search of something fresh to eat, a Lt. Timke, my buddy, dynamited the Coral Sea and brought in about twenty fish. The colonels gave him a deck court marshall and he lost rank in grade. That night the colonels ate the fish at the mess.

Some junior officers talked frankly about their own deficiencies as leaders. Robert Teeples, a platoon leader in the 32d Infantry Division, recalled an incident in which his own incompetence nearly cost innocent lives:

> I was leading a patrol in New Guinea and we contacted a number of Japs. After eliminating them we . . . heard a lot of foreign language. I thought they were Japs and I told the artillery officer to call in artillery. The foreign jabbering was made by friendly natives. Thank God the artilleryman was a prudent officer.

J. D. Jones, of the 3d Infantry Division, was excruciatingly honest about his failures of command and his personal cowardice. He felt that this cowardice led to the deaths of more than twenty of his men:

> I'm not proud of my conduct at Anzio. I could have done things a whole lot better than I did. I've discovered that it takes a certain quality to tell a group of men that you go out there and get your ass shot up. I didn't have it. And consequently I didn't do a very good job. I would find excuses to get out of the area and go back down to find this or find that or find an excuse to stay overnight. One night while I was gone they decided to bring the company back. The last platoon that came through got 23 dead. Fired on by their own people. And that broke me. I couldn't do it any longer. I guess you could say I was a coward. For years that haunted me.

Jones did pull himself together and served more than adequately for much of the rest of his time in combat.

In battle, officers' bars did not always make a leader. If an officer did not live up to his responsibilities, his men would eventually refuse to follow him. No directive from headquarters or hindsight portrayal by historians can ever change that fact. In the combat wing of the U.S. Army in World War II, the officer leadership factor was significant, but it was not of crucial importance. Good leaders could help and bad leaders could hurt, but, in either instance, combat men did their jobs.

CHAPTER 10
MOTIVATION, ATTITUDES, AND EFFECTS OF COMBAT

As Elmer D. Jones and his 89th Infantry Division comrades climbed a muddy hillside in Germany one day in the spring of 1945, they saw a Russian woman who had just been freed from years of forced labor at the hands of the Germans. Glad to be rid of her former masters, the woman gratefully greeted the tired American infantrymen. She took special notice of one of Jones's buddies, a weary veteran rifleman:

> As he drew abreast of her with his eyes fixed on his muddy boots . . . she greeted him with, "Cock vas zdrova tovarich?" [How is your health, comrade?]. The . . . rifleman neither broke his plodding stride nor looked up as he replied, "Cocks—k the rubbish yourself lady!" The broad face, framed by a black babushka, erupted into a wide smile. That Russian woman probably had never heard a single word of English before but she believed that this American soldier from the Appalachian Mountains could communicate with her. She did not know that he had absolutely no interest in politics. His sole desire was to remain alive so he could return to his native hills where he could do as he pleased. Hard fighting, sudden death, and heroic acts made up only a small part of an infantryman's war. Most of it consisted of interminably "picking 'em up and putting 'em down," then digging in . . . only to be ordered to move out again. Historians usually neglect this fact.

Incidents such as the one Jones described were probably repeated many times over throughout World War II. There was nothing especially dogmatic about the American combat soldier. He may have been well educated on the issues of the war, but he did not fight primarily for any particular cause or out of any special hatred for his enemies. His great desire was to survive and then go home to his "normal life." To carry out his job, he found it not only desirable but necessary to forge a special bond with his fellow combat soldiers. At the same time, combat took its eventual toll. The most common effects of prolonged combat for veteran soldiers were fatigue and ultimately indifference to one's own fate.

To understand the soul of the combat soldier, it is necessary to find out how he thought, what served to motivate him in carrying out his harrowing duties, and what kind of effect those duties had on him. The single largest motivator for American combat troops in World War II was the deadly brotherhood—a man's immediate comrades. But other factors were important for men in action, the most significant of which was personal prayer.

It is difficult to determine what exactly enables a soldier to suppress his mortal fear and put his own life in danger so that he may carry out his job. Hatred for the enemy played a part in motivating men to fight, but it was not all-encompassing and it did not serve as a primary motivation. The Allied cause also motivated men to fight. In the case of hatred as a motivating factor, the army asked veteran infantrymen in the Pacific the question "When the going was tough, how much were you helped by thoughts of hatred for the enemy?" Thirty percent said not at all. Most of the repondents said that such thoughts helped some or a lot. Because American infantrymen hated Germans less than they hated the Japanese, the percentage of infantrymen relying on hatred was predictably smaller in Europe; close to 40 percent said that thoughts of hatred did not help at all.

John Edwards, a soldier in the Pacific theater, was among those who fought out of hatred. He found courage by imagining what the Japanese would do to his family. "When I think of what they might do, it drives me on and brings out all my hidden courage. It not only puts fight in my hands but also in my heart. Sometimes when I get sad and lonely I think of what could happen and I realize what a lucky guy I am to be able to fight for the things I love." When Stanley Rice, a combat soldier in Europe, received news that his brother-in-law had been killed in action, it only served to increase his hatred and will to fight the Germans. "War seems a cruel useless thing. It is. However after all I've seen and done I can still see why I am fighting. It's to allow your Sherry and my Stan and Nancy a chance to grow up in a world of peace. We are going to destroy these bastards to the last man. I mean it."

The majority of combat men had no such inclination toward intense hatred in combat. Mel Cotton, a combat medic in the 91st Infantry Division, felt that combat soldiers almost never found malice to be a successful motivator when facing bullets:

> The American Soldier, of all soldiers . . . was an individual unto himself. He had an amazing capacity for independence and resourcefulness. He was kind, even to his enemy. While he could, and often did, get fighting mad, he was never a person to hold a grudge. All but a very few would say they did not hate their . . . enemy.

The American combat soldier was remarkably apolitical. Most letters, diaries, and memoirs are devoid of domestic political stances or any sort of commentary on American political leaders or parties. Although most soldiers believed inherently in the Allied cause and felt that the war was just and necessary, such attitudes did not serve to motivate them in combat. In the Pacific theater veteran infantrymen were asked, "When the going was tough, how much did it help you to think of what we are fighting for?" Thirty-seven percent said not at all. In Europe among veteran infantrymen, the Allied cause was an even smaller factor. Nearly 40 percent said that thinking of what they were fighting for did not help at all when things were rough in combat. It was difficult for them in the heat of combat to say to themselves, "I'll charge that machine gun and maybe get killed for our holy crusade against fascism," even though most of them believed that fascism, in theory, needed to be stopped. Some men did find motivation in defending the Allied cause. When asked why he fought, John Piazza, of the 45th Infantry Division, said that he risked his life "to rid the world of the fascist threat."

During the desperate days of the doomed Philippines campaign in early 1942, Henry Lee, a lieutenant in the Philippine Division, clung to the Allied cause to help him face each day. He wrote to his parents:

> I am proud to be a part of the fight that is being made here; and would not, even if it were possible, leave here until it is over. At last I have found what I have searched for all my life—a cause and a job in which I can lose myself completely and to which I can give every ounce of my strength and my mind.

Walter Dillehay, a veteran paratrooper, wrote to his father on the eve of a combat jump:

> If I get it . . . it will be tough, to say the least, on all of you people. Just remember this, Dad, we all have to die sometime but we can't all die for *something*. One can only look at such things in the broad-minded and patriotic sense. There is no room for personal feeling . . . in the military service.

Fifty years after the fact, Charlie Burchett, of the 1st Marine Division, said that he was motivated to fight by patriotism and love of freedom. "I liked what we had in this country and I wanted to protect it and I wanted to get in the heat of the thing so that when it was over I didn't have to bow my head."

James Simms, of the 101st Airborne Division, felt that soldiers from other countries in World War II probably would have died for idealistic notions or for their leaders, but not Americans:

> If an American noncom had told an American soldier, "Charge across that field and die for the president!" the American would have said, "Kiss my arse!" American soldiers do not die for the president, country or flag. The things that the American soldier fights for are very real. I have a friend who said that he had noticed that he and all his friends and relatives never mentioned patriotism in their World War II conversations and letters; it was always about girls or what they were going to do when the war was over. I said, "What the hell do you think they were fighting for?"

Combat soldiers in all theaters were asked, "Do you ever get the feeling that this war is not worth fighting?" Forty-three percent said that they wondered sometimes or very often whether or not the war was worth fighting. The frontline soldier did not see his situation in terms of grand war aims. Instead he cared mostly about his own group and his own situation, a tunnel vision probably caused by the seriousness of his circumstances.

Most men on the line mistrusted and ridiculed those who spoke of the war in platitudes. Writing from the front, Joe Johnson, a black rifle platoon leader in the 92d Infantry Division, underscored the point that grand ideas and causes failed to motivate the men on the line:

> The average "Joe" here has long ceased to fight for some intangible ideology, and flag waving only makes him mad. They mock Roosevelt's "I will not send your sons off to war" and ape Churchill's "on the beaches we will never surrender" speech. They rag the chaplain and laugh at some piece of garrison soldiering that some people adhere to, but they fight and nothing . . . can faze them.

An important motivation within the soul of the combat soldier was prayer. This is not to say that American soldiers were on a religious crusade in World War II. They did not fight for God or to spread any particular religion or creed. Instead many were motivated to cope with their conditions (and perform their duties) by prayer and belief in God. Prayer, and the belief that a benevolent God was listening and cared, helped to comfort combat men in difficult situations and even helped to preserve their collective sanity. Praying gave combat soldiers a crutch to lean on in battle so that they could face the unimaginable terrors of war.

In both major theaters of the war, combat troops were asked how much prayer helped when things were rough in combat. In the Pacific only 17 percent said not at all; 83 percent said that it helped a lot. In Europe prayer was even more widespread. Only 6 percent said that it did not help at all.

Faith in God probably reassured American combat soldiers that there was indeed some sort of order or reason to the madness of war. Most Americans had typically been brought up with religious faith, and it is therefore not surprising that under life-threatening conditions they would turn to God for comfort. William Warde, of the 42d Infantry Division, recalled being stunned when a group of German civilians asked his commander's permission to hold religious services on Easter Sunday. "We Americans were taken aback with the thought that anyone didn't have the freedom to worship as they desired."

It is important to understand that in his oft-made prayers, the American combat soldier mainly appealed to God as a protector. He did not pray to God to destroy the enemy in the assumption that God was naturally on the American side. Instead he prayed most often for personal protection and for the strength to face combat. Lawrence Nickell, of the 5th Infantry Division, summed up what was true for many men in combat: "The belief in a benevolent God was the single greatest sustaining factor in my life."

Max Kocour, of the 90th Infantry Division, underscored that this faith among combat men was usually a general belief in God and was not centered around any particular religion or denomination. "Religions and ethnics were meaningless. We developed *faith*. Regardless of religions, which had been created by man, we felt we were on the right side of faith, under the protection/care of a truly fine Supreme Being."

Radford Carroll, a rifleman in the 99th Infantry Division and a Protestant, recalled being under withering fire one day. Believing that he and his buddies were going to die, Carroll looked around and noticed something:

> I had said my prayers and composed myself for death when I noticed the muttering around me. The fellow just in front was a Roman Catholic, there was a Jew right across the way, a Mormon was nearby, and there were numbers of other religions, all saying their preparations for death as sincerely as I.

As Carroll's incident illustrates, specific religions or denominations became irrelevant in combat as did so many other differences between men of disparate backgrounds.

James McGuinness, an Irish Catholic who fought in the 34th Infantry Division in North Africa, wrote to his parents to express how he had prayed in combat. "I would just stop and pray to the Blessed Virgin and also the Sacred Heart of Jesus to give me the strength and courage to carry on, also to guide and protect me."

For James Revell, of the 99th Infantry Division, "God was my refuge and strength in combat. I found that I could talk to Him as I marched. He became very precious to me in those days." In explaining why he had survived the dangerous night jump into Normandy, 101st Airborne Division paratrooper Arlo Butcher asserted to his mother that prayer had made the difference for him. "No matter what kind of protection you've got, or how deep the hole is, I sure realized the mighty power of God. It was your prayers, Mom, and mine that helped us through this awful mess."

Raymond Jones, of the 1st Marine Division, wrote home after the Battle of Guadalcanal of the pervasiveness of prayer among his buddies and him in combat. "I tell you one thing, no matter how mean you are or if you have never been to church you will pray when you get there [combat]. If you don't know how, you will learn. There wasn't a man there who will say he didn't." It was the same for marine Leland Belknap. "I don't believe there were very many of us who didn't do a lot of praying up there. The only atheist that I know of said he would not pray when he got up front. The first night he came crawling over to the man he had said that to and they prayed together." Charles Parliman recalled that he "prayed that I might live and be able to return home. I wasn't alone either, some of my hard boiled pals also bowed their heads in prayer."

George Smalley's wife was very religious, but he did not share in her faith until he and his comrades entered combat in France:

My darling, at last among the closeness and complete horror of total war, I have found God. It's really a feeling that I shall never forget and never, never lose. When I pray now on bended knees I pour my whole soul out to Him, asking for forgiveness, and asking Him to lead me safely through the battles to come. If you could only see the simple but soul-stirring services so close to battle. Rugged men, with weariness in every step, and with blank stares of battle fatigue, kneeling down with their dirt and grime . . . to ask Him to guide them through safely. . . .

Another soldier told his father how he and his comrades prayed in combat:

Before every battle we all feel like having a little word of prayer. If you could see the faces of the men you would know what and how we feel. We know we are facing death. It is in front of us and we are moving into it. So on all our lips as we move to the front lines you can see the men praying to God to let them live through that battle.

Many American combat soldiers sincerely felt that if they prayed enough, God would hear them and answer their prayers. Said combat medic Robert Arnett, "Never have I prayed so much as I did the first day we were in combat. I will say that is what pulled me through." Bud Graber also felt that prayer was important to survival, not only for himself but his buddies too. "I can rap on wood when I say I came out without a scratch and that was because the Good Lord was with me all the way. I took plenty of time out to pray. I prayed for me and my buddies. I will never neglect my religion when I get home."

William Maher, a rifle platoon leader in Normandy, prayed, but he also gave way to fatalism. "I prayed consistently and still do. No matter how skilled and experienced you are in this game, it all depends on the mercy of God in the final analysis. I said, 'I have witnessed it and I know.'"

In a letter to his parents, Grover Adams summed up the main reasons that most U.S. combat soldiers prayed in World War II:

I've always asked each time . . . that God grant me, first, wisdom to go before and lead my squad; second, courage to stand fast and go on without turning yellow; and thirdly, for divine guidance and protection. As yet I've never been hit. It's all, I claim, due to a trust in the supernatural and faith to believe that God will help those who help themselves.

The recurrent appeals to God for self-preservation among many American combat soldiers sheds light on one of their most commonly held concerns—survival. Not surprisingly, American soldiers had an overpowering desire to survive the war. Most men felt that they were not in the war to die for their country but to serve it and go home. To the combat soldier, the greatest victory was personal survival, not the unconditional surrender of their enemies. American soldiers were not necessarily reluctant to risk their lives, but for them to do so they usually needed some compelling reason. Looking out for a buddy was one good reason. Another was the kind of situation that came up many times in combat—kill or be killed. Combat men quickly understood that, even if they had no particular hatred for their enemy, the reality of war dicated that you either killed the enemy or risked death yourself.

Americal Division veteran William McLaughlin described his behavior in combat as "strictly a case of trying to stay alive. Everything else was secondary." It was the same for Charles Card, of the 24th Infantry Division. "Survival was paramount. It came down to the survival instinct in each and all of us." Frederick Carpenter, of the 27th Infantry Division, recalled spending most of his time in combat worrying primarily about keeping his buddies and himself alive and in one piece. Colin McLaurin, a rifle company commander in the 29th Infantry Division, underscored the parochial view of most combat soldiers while their lives were in danger: "Like everyone else in combat, I did not worry about what went on in someone else's sector. I figured that a man had his hands full taking care of his own area without worrying about other units."

Even for those with the most self-sacrificing attitudes, combat changed their minds. Harry Gunlock, of the 36th Infantry Division, remembered the distinct change in outlook that he and his inexperienced comrades underwent during the invasion of Salerno in September 1943. "I remember when we went ashore we were gung-ho. At last we were in action and our blood was flowing fast. We wanted to get with it, but as the day wore on, and we saw the toll being taken, and the carnage, the idea of survival became our #1 priority." Walter Mietus, a medic in the 76th Infantry Division, usually carried no weapon in combat, but that changed as survival became increasingly important to him. "In the heat of all this bitterness, anger and fear of being done in, it's either you or them."

Indeed, the longer a man was in combat, the more he tended to worry about surviving; being a veteran, he knew better than anyone that it was only a matter of time before he was hit. Said Thomas Isabel, an armored infantryman in the 1st Armored Division, "After about a year on the front I just worried about staying alive. I knew my time was getting short. Infantrymen usually do not live that long." After a short time in combat, Irwin Shapiro, an armored infantryman in the 8th Armored Division, developed the kind of callous attitude necessary to survive in the insane world of combat. "You learn one basic axiom and that is kill or be killed. You learn to think of 'me.' With someone getting killed you say, 'Better him than me' or 'Thank God it wasn't me.' I think that carried me through many situations."

Glen Main, of the 70th Infantry Division, outlined his attitude on survival, which was by no means peculiar to him. "I wasn't fighting for my country at that time. You know who I was fighting for? Me. Of course I wanted to come back in one piece. But I would have been satisfied to come back at all. So I never took any undue chances."

Whayland Greene, a rifleman in the 32d Infantry Division, perhaps explained best the attitude of the American combat soldier on the subject of survival. "Put into the situation that we and thousands of others were, survival for one's self was the first priority by far. The second priority was survival for the man next to you and the man next to him. So, right and wrong, love of country and pride in the unit . . . was a good bit behind."

To most American combat men, victory in the war would have meant nothing if they did not live to see it. Personal survival and the survival of a man's buddies was of paramount importance to the vast majority of combat soldiers. In fact, one of the reasons for the existence of the deadly brotherhood was that a man's buddies in combat—those whom he could depend on—increased his own chance of surviving the war. Thus, combat men entered into an unspoken contract with the men around them to look out for one another; it not only helped get the job done, it enhanced everyone's chance of living to see the end of the war.

The fact that the majority of combat soldiers did not view the war as a great crusade in which they must willingly sacrifice their own lives led to one of their commonly held attitudes. American combat men tended to view their personal war as an ugly job that had to be done so that they could go home and resume their "real" lives. These citizen-soldiers brought a uniquely American businesslike attitude to combat. Everything from cleaning out a stubborn machine-gun nest to going on patrol was a "job" that had to be done. Accordingly, everyone (officers included) was expected to do his share so that the job could get done sooner and with the least amount of sacrifice. Combat soldiers were asked the question, "When the going was tough how much did it help you to think that you had to finish the job in order to get home again?" In both the Pacific and Europe, the majority thought that it helped, to the tune of 72 percent for the Pacific and 63 percent for Europe.

Richard Lovett and his Americal Division comrades worked together in combat to "get the job done so we could all go home." Fred Matter, of the 25th Infantry Division, recalled his unit having the attitude of "let's get it over with and go home." Dewey Hill and his 32d Infantry Division buddies spent their time in action "trying to do our job, not thinking much, only how to stay in one piece and get the job done." It was the same for John Fribis, of the 45th Infantry Division, whose attitude was "let's get this over with and go home." Murphy Simoneaux and Ross Hadfield, of the 81st Infantry Division, collectively felt that combat was "a job to be done . . . so let's get it over with." Herbert Richards, of the 1st Amored Division, remembered thinking constantly in combat that he wanted to get the war over with so he and his friends could go home as soon as possible.

Most American combat men looked upon peace as being normal and war as an unusual circumstance. With no desire to spend their lives in the military and even less desire to be killed in action, combat soldiers saw winning the war as a nasty job that had to be accomplished but at the least possible cost to themselves and in the quickest amount of time possible.

Among those who served in the U.S. military in World War II, only a small minority actually saw combat on the ground. How did this comparatively tiny group, the combat men who actually fought the war, feel about soldiers in the rear and civilians at home?

Combat soldiers had an exclusive attitude about their own immediate group and generally looked down on noncombat outsiders. The constant dangers that the combat troops faced bonded them together. Like any group facing hardship, they looked down on outsiders whose lot was easier, especially rear-echelon soldiers. Bill Mauldin, the famous creator of "Willie and Joe," the two characters who symbolized the combat GIs, explained this condescension toward outsiders:

> While men in combat outfits kid each other . . . they have a sort of family complex about it. No outsiders may join. Anybody who does a dangerous job in this war has his own particular kind of kidding among his friends. If a stranger comes up to a group of them when they are bulling, they ignore him. If he takes it upon himself to laugh at something funny they have said, they freeze their expressions, turn slowly around, and stare at him until his stature has shrunk to about four inches and he slinks away.

The problem was not that combat soldiers did not think rear-echelon troops did their jobs. When asked if they thought that troops in the rear did all they could to help those in combat, 62 percent of combat soldiers in the Pacific and 52 percent in Europe felt that rear echeloners did all they could. Dick Peters, an armored infantryman in the 8th Armored Division, enumerated the views of the majority who felt that support troops did what they could to help. "They had their job. They had their mission. I guess . . . in most cases they fulfilled their jobs of supply and administration and so forth."

European theater combat soldiers were asked, "How resentful do you think soldiers in combat outfits feel about troops who have the rear-area jobs?" Sixty-five percent of infantry noncommissioned officers responded that there was a significant degree of resentment among themselves or their men. Only 6 percent felt that there was no resentment at all. In Italy combat men were asked a similar question. Eighty-five percent said that most men in their unit harbored resentment toward rear-area soldiers. Clearly there was an endemic resentment among combat troops of those whose army jobs kept them out of danger.

These already strong feelings of bitterness could boil over when combat troops felt that they were being treated poorly by rear-echelon types. Glenn Searles, of the 77th Infantry Division, recalled an incident that occurred aboard a troop ship after he and his buddies had been in combat securing small islands near Okinawa:

> While we had been gone . . . some of the crew had slit open our barracks bags stored aboard for us. They were typical "rear echelon commandos," the term we used for any and all service personnel that never actually came under fire. There was hell to pay when we reboarded the ship and found looted bags. The first thing that happened was that a soldier picked up the ship's mascot, a little fox terrier, and threw it overboard. Then the sailors were mad. Fistfights broke out.

Forty years later, Harry Arnold, of the 99th Infantry Division, still had bitter feelings as he related how he and his comrades were once treated on a pass to the rear:

> Walking the sidewalks and crossing the streets were the garrison soldiers, resplendent of uniform, upright certain strides, heroic of countenance. They scarcely noticed our passing. Some regarded us stonily and . . . shook with revulsion. We were accorded a further indignity. We could not use the shower facilities. This rebuke . . . shall always remain in my memory as one of the most callous and unpalatable of my life. Had I been the officer in charge of our group, we would have been in the showers within the hour by employing whatever means necessary. Moreover, the . . . garrison that day would have been left fully cognizant that they existed for one reason—to support the line troops one hundred percent. It takes some time for the infantryman to realize that he is a breed apart and that, as such, he may have more in common with enemy infantry across the way than with the army to his rear. Maybe more would have been achieved had we each reversed directions and attacked to the rear. A feeling of unease pervaded our sense of belonging. We felt somehow denied, shunted aside as if an embar-

rassment to this rear area army. Though we dreaded facing Spandaus, 88s, mortars, and panzers, our gut feeling told us that we belonged up there somewhere . . . going to hell on worn-out feet.

Experiences such as Arnold's were unfortunately all too common. Combat men often felt lost and out of place in rear areas; it was as if they had walked into a different world. They essentially had. As much as they dreaded any return to the lines, many of them felt that up front was where they belonged. It was where a soldier's buddies were, and combat men would generally rather have been in danger with friends than out of danger with hostile strangers.

John Roche, of the 88th Infantry Division, was irritated by the hypocrisy of many rear-echelon soldiers. In a poem he wrote about the lot of the infantry, he included a barb against support troops. "Yours is the job they all work to shun. But when the war's over and the victory is won, they'll tell you how they wish they had shouldered your gun." Charles Fulton, of the 103d Infantry Division, used poetry to describe an infuriating incident in which a noncombat sergeant attempted to intimidate his group of hardened combat men:

"I'm from Division resupply. You, private! Where's your gun?" "I lost it back there," said the guy, "escaping from the Hun." "By Regs, we treat you like a thief," the sarge exclaimed. "You pay!" We stared at him in disbelief. Six rifles rose his way. The snick of safeties could be heard. He gulped, "I'll wait a bit." We shook our heads. It was absurd, the Army's chickenshit. I looked around and said, "I'll bet it's rearward he runs. A Silver Star, he'll claim and get, for seeing loaded guns."

Donald MacDonald, of the 45th Infantry Division, fought at Anzio. He summed up the feelings of all the combat men he knew. "Most after serving in frontline action were willing to exchange with rear echeloners, giving them a chance to experience the realities of war."

In Europe, infantry soldiers were asked, "In your opinion, about how many of the people back home are doing all they should do to help win the war?" Almost 40 percent felt that some people in the United States were not doing all they could. However, most respondents thought that their families were doing everything they could. And almost half of these same troops felt that folks at home did not appreciate the soldiers' sacrifices. Clearly, combat soldiers were unwilling to blame family and friends for any of the deficiencies they saw among civilians at home. It was always other people who were guilty of ingratitude and shirking their duties to the war effort, not a man's mother, father, brother, or sister.

Between the civilians safe at home and the men risking their lives on the front lines, there was a gulf of experience. Those at home could not imagine the kind of life that the combat soldiers were living. As James Simms related, the soldiers understood this clearly, even if civilians did not. "I heard dozens of times: 'There's no way the folks back home can ever understand what we've been through.' After all, you just don't walk into a room full of civilized people that are remote from war and say, 'I have been employed in a human slaughterhouse.'"

Combat troops had a natural antipathy for people who they felt were living the good life back home while they themselves sacrificed and risked their lives. Robert Allen was a young officer in the 1st Marine Division. Allen's father was a successful medical doctor. It is possible that Robert Allen may have been able to avoid combat, but he refused to try. Before he was killed in action on Okinawa, he wrote to his father about "shirkers":

> We are here because our conscience would not allow us to be elsewhere. Yet, there are so many people in this world known as "angle men" who have a different conception of things. Why should they sacrifice when there are so many others that are willing to do the job for them? Why not sit back and profit from this thing? Most of us do not harbor such thoughts yet aren't they the sensible ones? I despise those people. I would kill them with no qualms or questions asked.

George Boocks, of the 5th Engineer Special Brigade, also found himself resenting many of those who were back home safely out of danger. "As the months went by, most of us began to build up a resentment to the people back home. They became those 'damned civilians' and '4F'ers' who were apparently living the 'life of Riley' while we bore the brunt of the war."

Combat men had a special dislike for striking war workers. Whereas draft dodgers and noncontributors could be looked down on as weak cowards, they were not seen as being dangerous to a soldier's chances of survival. Workers who went on strike were seen as directly contributing to the welfare of the enemy, and for that they were loathed.

Leslie Schneider, of the 1st Marine Division, survived the Battle of Guadalcanal only to read about a number of strikes in war-related industries. He wrote to his mother in frustration:

> That just burns me up when I think of those workers getting paid enormous wartime wages, getting all the work they want, plenty of food, clothes and shelter, and still they are not willing to cooperate and keep the production and assembly lines moving. I would like for those discontented workers to be with us for a while on the front lines. Let them do without a decent meal for a month or so, let them wear the same clothes for weeks, let them spend a night or two in pouring rain without shelter. Every time they go on a strike, they are not only slowing up production, but maybe they are actually costing the lives of those who have gone forth to protect them.

After reading of such things, combat men could not help but feel somewhat alienated from the rest of America. Joe Johnson spelled out this difference in perspective in a letter to his wife:

> The headlines say we took a hill; that "hill" was probably a mountain! "Light casualties" probably took the life of your best friend. You can imagine a fella's feeling. But you can't expect people who have never seen these things to understand why men look with disgust on some things that are perfectly sensible to [civilians]. Some of the things folks do in the States really make the guys over here salty; like giving dances and din-

ners for the "poor" Jerry prisoners. I'd like for some of those folk to see what their sons, brothers, cousins and such are facing on all the war fronts.

After fighting his way all the way to Germany, James Fisher had the same sort of gripes:

> When they [civilians] hear about an airstrip being taken or a piece of land taken, they are happy, and they should be, but I often wonder if they stop to think there have been a lot of boys blown all apart and killed and lost arms and legs and eyesight and a lot more I'm not even going to mention. Let them stop and think about just how a group of guys takes a piece of land. Let them think of the machine gun bullets they are ducking, of the 88s and mortars.

As Beauford George fought for his life in the bitter Alsace campaign in early 1945, he also decried the lack of cognizance among civilians of the real cost of war:

> Whereas in the newspapers it merely says, "The casualties in our infantry regiments run high," to us it means our buddies killed, wounded and captured. I've had close friends in all three categories, and it really hits hard. I'd better not hear anyone expound on the "glories of war" or I won't be held responsible for what I do.

The issue of race and attitudes of most combat soldiers is slippery. No surveys were taken to gauge how combat men, who were almost all white, felt about people of different races. It can probably be safely assumed that, especially where blacks were concerned, combat men had the attitudes and mores of the times.

Radford Carroll considered asking for a transfer when his unit began to receive small of groups of black reinforcements:

> I certainly did not regard it as an honor to be in a company with Negro troops. I was raised at a time and place where Ne-

groes were expected to be subservient; they could not vote, eat in the same restaurants as whites or use the same bathrooms. In fact we treated the Negroes the same as officers treated privates in the army. I considered asking for a transfer but . . . I decided to try it out for a little while. After a while you began thinking of the company as your home, and there is a reluctance to change to a strange outfit.

Spencer Moore, a black officer in the 92d Infantry Division, recalled the shabby treatment that he and his men received, even at the front. "Morale was low because the men from the South and poorer districts had no reason to feel great. Everything was still the same, only [we were] in uniform."

Often things were much different once the shooting started. The life-threatening experiences of war changed long-held attitudes and assumptions about race. Many men found that at the front, color simply did not seem to matter. Harry Arnold recalled his feelings and those of his buddies when black soldiers worked with his squad. "Most of us were glad to get them. They proved their worth in subsequent actions." John Symanski, who came ashore on D day at Utah Beach with the 4th Infantry Division, saw black soldiers and came to realize that they were not all that different from the men in his outfit. "It was a black combat engineer outfit that had completed clearing the beaches and waterfront of mines, underwater charges and obstacles. I took a close look at them. They looked awfully frightened and uncomfortable but I guess that we were no different." Garland Godby, of the 80th Infantry Division, had nothing but the highest regard for the black soldiers with whom he came in contact. "I admired the hell out of the black soldiers and truck drivers. They were fearless. They'd go through hell to get you out of there. I did a lot of miles with them and they weren't bitching or feeling sorry for themselves." James Revell lost any racial hatred he might have previously had when his unit received help from a black tank destroyer outfit at a crucial time in combat. "A group of Negro volunteers fresh as daisies accompanied the tank destroyers into town. From that moment those men had a special place in my heart." Ralph Martin, a combat correspondent, spoke with an officer who commanded a group of black volunteers. The officer remembered how many black soldiers came to him begging into his unit so that they could have a chance to prove themselves in combat (most blacks were not allowed to serve on the front lines). After the black soldiers had seen action, the officer, a lieutenant, said that he was proud of his men and wished that outsiders could understand the irrelevance of race on the front lines. "Maybe if people just didn't worry about us being something special. Maybe if somebody could come up here and see how we've been fighting and killing and dying, how it doesn't seem to matter a damn what your color is."

For blacks the hope was that the equality that some had experienced at the front would spill over into civilian life after the war. The views of Joe Johnson were representative of the attitudes of many black frontline soldiers:

> Even as a soldier fighting . . . I'm denied many of the privileges as a Negro, to which the guys who wear the swastika are welcomed. Negroes are doing their bit here, their supreme bit, not for glory, not for honor but for, I think, the generation that will come. If the blood that flows here on Italy's mountains will wash from some folk's mind the stigma that has been bred there for years, then I think that the men who have gone so bravely here will not have given their lives in vain. I'm proud to be one of these few men who are fighters. The American papers call us "Tan Yanks" and other fancy names, but . . . the Italians call us "Americans," just plain Americans. That's all we want to be, and one day I hope we will be just plain Americans.

Tragically, Johnson never lived to see the fruits of what he fought for. He was killed in action in Italy in the spring of 1945.

Although combat soldiers faced grim circumstances every day, they found that humor could be important in preserving sanity. As harrowing and life threatening as the war could be, combat soldiers managed to smile and laugh at times. Howard Ruppel, of the 517th Parachute Infantry Regiment, felt that humor could take a man a long way in battle. In fact it was almost essential to survival:

When circumstances become unbearable, the experienced soldier with some sense of humor [and] the ability to laugh at one's self has a better chance to retain his sanity than the serious minded fellow. The ones who viewed life seriously were the ones who had difficulty accepting hardships, inconveniences, sufferings and privation. They took the war with all the detriments as a very personal thing. These serious minded soldiers were susceptible to go berserk.

Jack Thacker, of the 30th Infantry Division, credited his sense of humor with helping him survive combat and captivity. "One thing that I learned, that I believe to this day, was that a sense of humor supported by one's faith can be the only thing that stands between a sane survival and complete mental chaos." George Wyatt and his buddies in the 1st Marine Division also felt that humor was a big part of making do in combat. "Humor was an important part of our ability to cope with our situation and surroundings. At times the humor was a bit on the wry side but nonetheless important. It was an outlet, a form of venting mixed emotions."

Frontline humor was indeed twisted. Dark circumstances called for dark humor. During the seige at Bastogne, James Simms's buddies kidded him about how his parents would spend his $10,000 GI insurance money, which beneficiaries collected in the event of a soldier's death:

> One fellow would say in a high, feminine voice, "Oh, I've been wanting a fur coat like that." All the time he would go through the motions of leafing through a catalog. Another guy would pretend to leaf through the catalog and he would say in a deep voice, "I've been wanting me a shotgun like that and now I've got the money to get it." They laughed until tears came to their eyes.

This twisted humor served to vent frustrations in a healthy manner. It was not uncommon for men to make one another laugh during combat. Bob Kay, a rifle platoon leader in the 4th Infantry Division, remembered his sergeant cracking a joke as they prepared to charge ashore at Utah Beach. "As I hesitated just a moment, a tantalizing, inviting voice behind me said, 'After you, Lieutenant!' Subtle humor such as this in the face of possible death can only be found in the free-spirited attitude of American troops. I shall forever treasure the 'gibing' remark."

Alto Johns, a marine who fought on Guam, wrote to his sister of something funny that happened while he and his friends were under fire:

> A little humor may be found on the lines when the end looks pretty near. Clements and I were dug in together one night during a heavy bombardment on our lines and a Jap attack in progress at the same time. Clements hollered over to the next foxhole to Sgt. Brunck and asked what time it was. Brunck yelled back that it was twelve-thirty. Clements did not hear the answer, and asked me what Brunck had said. Silly me said, "At the sound of the next bullet, it will be exactly twelve thirty-one." Sure enough, "Sping!" The bullet from a Jap rifle hit the log in front of our foxhole.

Perhaps the best example of combat humor is the following leaflet that marines circulated on the front lines during the fighting on Saipan:

> Tonight! Banzai charge! Thrills! Chills! Suspense! See sake-crazed Japs charge at high port. See everybody shoot everybody. See the cream of the Marine Corps play with live ammo. Sponsored by the Athletic and Morale Office. Come along and bring a friend. Don't miss the thrilling spectacle of the banzai charge, starting at 10 P.M. and lasting all night. Admission free!

This parody of a movie or circus promotion was a common sort of humor among combat men. It was an attempt to normalize their surroundings and find something funny about what was otherwise a dangerous, grim job. Laughter truly was therapeutic for men at the front, for if a man could find anything funny during a time when his

life was constantly threatened and he was tired, scared, and uncomfortable, he could most likely cope with anything.

Simply coping was a big part of enduring combat. No matter how
hardened or experienced a soldier was, he was affected in some way
by his surroundings. No human being could see death, dismemberment, and gore all around him and emerge without any effect.
The vast majority of American combat men lived with the bowel-
gripping, gnawing weight of fear during battle. In previous wars, it
may have been a male ethos to deny one's fear, but World War II
American combat soldiers had no such compunctions. In a variety
of outfits, the vast majority admitted to being scared in action to the
point where they lost control of bowels or were nauseous or experienced violent pounding of the heart. Sixty-nine percent of these
men felt that their fear was nothing unique and was "almost the
same as most of the other men." The prevailing opinion was that
anyone who said he was not scared in combat was either a liar or
an idiot.

While in combat in France in September 1944, Phillip Brown
wrote of the pervasiveness of fear among the men in his outfit:

Fear and the threat of fear still weighs you down enor-
mously. In an existence where courage and bravery are prime
requisites, no one that I have ever talked to has ever admitted
to being unafraid. Whatever requisite a man must possess to be
known as a brave man, the absence of fear is certainly not one
of them.

Another combat soldier in the European theater, Ike Roberts,
agreed:

As for the actual feeling, the day I hit the front line and every
day thereafter I was the same as all the other GIs and our officers—scared as hell and you get more scared at every attack.
But when the word comes, scared or not you climb out and go.
You know damned well it has to be done and it's up to you. If
a man says he's not scared he's one of two things, he's either a
fool or a damn liar.

For most men, fear went with everyday existence. Glenn Searles remembered the feeling of being terrified under shell fire. "No matter how gung-ho you are, after about fifteen minutes of artillery shells screaming in and exploding all around you, you start to quiver not unlike a bowl of gelatin and your teeth chatter. We did a lot of screaming." One of the first things combat men learned about being scared was that it did not mean that you were a coward. In fact most felt that real courage meant being scared and still being able to function. Max Kocour's assessment of the men in his outfit was true of most combat formations. "Most of us, I think, were afraid— but without being cowards. There were few cowards in my American combat universe." Radford Carroll was relieved when he realized the difference between fear and cowardice. "My biggest fear going into combat was that I would turn out to be a coward. My phobias concerning school fights had me refuse many aggressive challenges, and I had a deep fear this might be because of cowardliness. It was a great relief to find that I was not a coward."

Harry Arnold made the point that fear, like many emotions, was not necessarily all inclusive. It came and went in varying degrees. "I remember . . . how fear would seem intolerable, and then would dissipate entirely, then return again with renewed vigor. That taught me that total fear is an extreme that can no more be sustained uninterrupted than can extreme pleasure."

Bill Sabin, of the 1st Infantry Division, was in the invasion of North Africa. He was not prepared for the horrors he witnessed—men with arms, legs, and heads blown off, and his buddies dying all around him. Needless to say he was scared to death:

> It's an empty feeling in which you can't think forward—only of the past—the things you've done when you were a baby, the embraces with your wife or loved one, your mom or dad talking to you, every kind of crazy thing running through your mind. A sickening feeling like you want to vomit but can't. Not pleasant, is it? But it's war.

For Don Mackerer, of the 9th Infantry Division, fear was a constant companion. "I might say that I was a bigtime hero but I was anything but that. I was scared spitless most of the time. Somehow you function." Erwin Pichotte, of the 32d Infantry Division, described the effect of fear on the soldiers in his unit. "Our hearts were beating fast. We were a little hyper and excited, the sort of pressure, excitement and stress that lasted for days." Dan Ray, a member of the 36th Infantry Division, was surprised when he experienced fear symptoms while sighting his weapon to ambush a group of Germans in the Colmar Pocket. "I was shaking so bad from fright I had to brace my knees against the sides of the hole so that I could be ready to function." Salvatore Lamagna, of the 43d Infantry Division, asserted that fear was an integral part of life at the front. It was with a man all the time in everything he did. "A typical day at the front lines is fear. Fear and not knowing if you will live to see another day. Fear of not knowing what you'll run into." The key for each soldier was to stay in control. Many did that by seeing firsthand that the next man was withstanding his fear so maybe he could as well.

Some even felt that fear made them better soldiers. Arlo Butcher wrote to his mother: "Sure I was scared, and every guy in there was, but being scared makes us do a better job, when you see your buddies falling around you."

Combat correspondent Mack Morriss agreed. He felt that fear could be channeled into something positive if a man tried hard enough:

> The man who recognizes fear can often make it work in his favor—because fear is energy. Like anger, fear shifts the body into high. If it is allowed to back up in a man, unspoken and unaired in any way, it can form a clot and create an obstacle to normal action. If the soldier who experiences fear can talk it over with his buddies . . . he can at least get it off his chest. If, in combat, he can concentrate on what he is doing rather than on the emotions, he feels he has come a long way in overcoming fear.

Of course, learning to control fear in this way was easier said than done. In combat a man's first inclination was to panic. Usually, thanks to training and their buddies, men rode out their panic, but it was difficult to forget about fear altogether. Robert Jackson, of the 96th Infantry Division, never forgot being reduced to a blubbering mess while under Japanese shell fire. "I experienced . . . abject and shameful fear . . . when we came under a severe artillery and mortar barrage. It was awesome. That afternoon I tried to dig my way to the center of the earth. I have never forgotten . . . how I screamed in fear and how hard I shoved myself into the dirt of that Okinawa hillside."

Walter Pippin, of Merrill's Marauders in Burma, wrote home to communicate just how paralyzing his fear had been in combat:

> I realized a thousand petty thoughts. Alongside this maze of thoughts hovered a thousand quivering fears, rushing out of the hidden cells of my brain, and around these unfamiliar thoughts and fears was a shield, the overpowering and omnipotent desire to live. I couldn't speak. My vocal cords seemed to have jelled. It was as though my legs had been severed at the knee.

The visceral, animal terror most men felt in combat never really left them even after they had survived the war, for they knew what it was like to face true mortal danger. Les Terry, a recon trooper in the 36th Infantry Division, expressed the feeling of having faced one's mortality: "Even though we were all scared . . . we stayed and faced what we never dreamed we could. After all these years I dream of the bad and scared times and awake in a cold sweat." In that Terry is not alone. Fear was something real to combat soldiers, not just an abstract concept or a dreaded emotion. Fear had a pungent odor, taste, and feeling. It could be used positively or negatively depending on a man's ability to cope with combat. For the vast majority of frontline soldiers, fear was something they experienced every single day of their lives in combat.

One of the effects of combat that caused such acute fear among combat soldiers, even if they happened to emerge unscathed from a firefight, was the knowledge that sooner or later the law of averages would catch up with them and they would be hit. American ground combat soldiers in World War II could look forward to no rotation system or tour of duty. For the vast majority, their fate was limited to a small number of possibilities, most of them undesirable. They could be killed, wounded (physically or mentally), or captured, or the war could end. No matter how wise or experienced a soldier was, if he was in combat long enough, sooner or later one of those things would happen to him. For the infantryman, tanker, or combat engineer, the end of the war seemed an eternity away. Realistically, their only hope of reprieve and survival was the "million-dollar wound."

Like many combat men, Glenn Searles resigned himself to death after seeing most of his buddies killed or wounded. "I came to feel that I wouldn't make it out alive. The odds were too heavily stacked against me."

John Worthman, a medic in the 4th Infantry Division, had the same feeling during the awful Huertgen Forest campaign:

> We were certain that we would soon be wounded or killed. It is not rare to feel this but usually you can shake off the feeling with rest or food or with hard work. After about a week of the Huertgen, I could not shake it off, nor could most of those I knew. This was my personal Valley of the Shadow. I left it with incredible relief and with a sadness I had never so far known.

After fighting for a couple of years with the 7th Infantry Division, Roy Yates found himself wondering how long he would last. "I was thinking about the roll of the dice. Just so long and it's going to come up craps." Mac Acosta, of the 36th Infantry Division, wondered the same thing during the horrible Rapido River crossings in February 1944. "How long can a person gamble continuously and keep winning? Eventually the dice are going to come up 'snake eyes.' It is like Lieutenant Morehead once said. 'We are like a virgin bride, we know we are going to get it and we wonder how bad it's going to be.'"

Another 36th Division man who was also at the Rapido, James Estepp, concurred with Acosta's outlook. "At this stage of the war you knew yours was waiting on you somewhere. Being a dogface you had four things to look forward to: the war being over, being captured, or killed or wounded—and you couldn't have much hope that the war would end at this stage." J. R. McIlroy, of the 99th Infantry Division, chronicled the change that came about among his comrades after they saw enough men killed and wounded. "We never talked about what we were going to do in the future. We really didn't think we had much of a future. We talked about getting a million dollar wound for we realized this was our only way out."

John Stenger saw more than 150 days of combat with the 104th Infantry Division in France and Germany. Toward the end he felt that the odds were catching up with him:

> After a relatively long run of luck you can't help but feel that the next attack or the one after that is going to be your turn. But you don't have a choice; in the infantry you stay on the line until . . . ! Fear and fatigue simply don't matter. You vow that if you survive (in almost one piece) you will never ever complain about anything thereafter.

Such realities could make men feel that they had little control over what happened to them. Howard Ruppel felt the helplessness that came with the seeming randomness of combat:

> There were too many unforeseen factors and circumstances beyond my control. One's life is held in balance by a little piece of metal, smaller than a man's finger . . . being propelled about 1,700 miles per hour. This hurling piece of deadly steel, piercing flesh, rending a vital organ, combined with the wrong time and wrong place, is the difference between life and death.

After being in combat for only a short time with the 1st Armored Division, Paris Roussos "quickly realized that living becomes a matter of destiny or pure luck." Roy Denmon, an armored infantryman in the 6th Armored Division, emphasized this feeling of uncertainty. "The soldier in combat was reduced to the greatest degree of uncertainty. He never knew . . . if he would be dead the next minute or if he would escape this time only to [face death] again."

If a combat soldier was to last for any length of time in action, he had to become acclimated to death. On the front lines, death was everywhere, bombarding all the senses. Harry Arnold described the effect of a pervasive sense of death on combat troops. "Combat infantrymen have a reverence for the dead unequaled . . . for death and the dead are constant companions. This reverance is little akin to the mouthings of solace at formal funerals. It is far deeper, but most of all it is starkly realistic."

Being around so much death took its toll. Edward Laughlin, of the 82d Airborne Division, recalled one of his comrades who, having seen too much of it, subsequently became a shell of a human being. "He just had had too many things happen, had a great excess of miserable combat time, had killed too many people and was, pathetically, turned into a walking piece of wasted human. It is not melodramatic to say that Ray's eyes had death in them."

Garland Godby readily admitted that, as hardened as he became to combat, he often cried when his men were killed. "You can't get over it. I'm not even over it today. You cannot get used to death. It used to hurt me so bad when one of the old-timers got killed."

Matt Miletich, of the 84th Infantry Division, was the only survivor of an ill-fated charge on a German machine-gun position during the Battle of the Bulge. Afterward he stared at his dead buddies who were piled up awaiting burial:

The sight of my friends' bodies lying there and the lifeless face of Harold Moneypenny, with its white eyes fully open and staring up at the tall trees, a black hole open where his mouth was, and his steel helmet still hanging back on his head, exposing his crew-cut hair, is burned indelibly in my memory. I could wind up on a pile like that in a minute, and there isn't a damn thing I can do about it, I thought.

Sometimes the constant presence of death and hopelessness of combat gave men accurate premonitions of their own deaths. Gene Tippins, of the 80th Infantry Division, experienced this with one of his buddies before an attack on the Siegfried line. "Willis looked at me real funny and said, 'Good-bye, Tip, I won't be coming out of this thing.' And as he predicted, in 3 hours he was dead, caught in the back by machine gun fire."

The unfortunate by-product of the grim world of combat on the

souls of the men who fought was often depression. The biggest factor that contributed to this depression was that combat men had
nothing more to look forward to but more of the same even if they
managed to survive. Ferdinand Huber, of the 99th Infantry Division,
described how action affected the temperament of his squad. "The
first pangs of deep depression start to hit. The sinking, sick type of
depression that stays with you and eventually sinks into a permanent
residence in the deep part of your soul." E. A. Struble, a tanker in
the European theater, was quite depressed during combat:

> When you're up there [front lines], life holds very little for
> you. The whole world seems dark, and death is all around you
> following your every footstep. You have nothing to look forward
> to, and you never know what the next moment will bring. You
> look at your dead buddies beside you and think tomorrow it
> will be me.

Frank Barnett, who fought in Germany, underscored the feeling
that men in combat could not look ahead to a better tomorrow. For
them there might not be a tomorrow:

> There is nothing to look forward to . . . tomorrow, or the next
> day or the next week. Except cleaning a rifle, mending a shel-
> ter half to keep out a little bit of the rain, or stealing a pair of
> gloves. Nothing but more damp cold, more sullen wet skies,
> more ugly hills to climb, more cold hash and biscuits to force
> down, more soggy ground to lie on.

Depression and the incredibly strenuous physical exertion that
combat required brought on fatigue. The men on the line knew what
pure exhaustion felt like. Most did not get any more than a few
hours' sleep each night, and much of their time was spent walking
and carrying as much equipment as they could shoulder, not to mention the constant threat of death and dismemberment that further
served to tax the body and mind. Radford Carroll remembered one
particular instance when he "had not slept or rested for more than
72 hours. I had passed the point where my muscles ached; my bones

hurt." Don Hoagland, of the 34th Infantry Division, vividly remembered what he and his buddies looked like when they were finally relieved after weeks on the line near Cassino in Italy. "Where three weeks previously there had been a bunch of rugged, alert men there was now a shuffling, limping group of 'old' men who moved like zombies with drawn faces and staring eyes. They were not beaten, only tired." Curtis Banker, of the 43d Infantry Division, was often so tired in combat that he hoped to get killed so he could rest. Don Zobel, of the 1st Marine Division, had similar feelings at Guadalcanal when he looked at dead marines. He envied them because they were "resting." Walter Mietus witnessed this sort of abject fatigue on the faces of some men whom he and his unit relieved one night. "That's the first time I saw real fatigue in the faces of men. They had that faraway look. I thanked him for the foxhole . . . and he wasn't responsive. He wouldn't smile. He wouldn't . . . acknowledge anything. He just walked away."

For 87th Infantry Division platoon leader Clarence Waltemath, the greatest recollection of combat was total fatigue. "The biggest trouble . . . is that you get so tired. I know I must have been up two or three nights without sleep. You almost would welcome somebody to hit you." William Maher, a rifle platoon leader, wrote home that the fatigue he experienced in combat threatened to drive him crazy. "I rarely sleep at night. I don't dare. At times, from lack of sleep and tension, when you're on the verge of exhaustion, you wonder if you can go on. The other night this happened, and I don't know that I ever made such a direct appeal to God for courage."

The inevitable law of averages, the lack of control, the fatigue, and the sheer horror of combat often combined to produce indifference in many men. Completely worn out both emotionally and physically, they no longer cared about anything. After enough time at the front, Henri Atkins came to terms with the fact that he would eventually be killed, wounded, or captured. "At the time, any one of those possibilities was okay with me. I had been living in such miserable, bitter cold, I didn't really care what happened." James Simms was so tired, cold, and scared at Bastogne that he found himself contemplating suicide. "A click of the safety and tug of the trigger and my suffering would be over." He made sure to put the safety latch of his rifle on. "You see, I didn't want to kill myself. I was afraid that I was going to do it on impulse. Suffering does things to you."

After bitter urban combat in Germany, Conrad Willard, of the 87th Infantry Division, wrote home to relate what he had been through and how it made him indifferent:

> It's the only place in the world where love and hate, pity and revenge, such indescribable passion, yet cold-blooded thought-less terror, seemed part of everything you saw. Men bearing un-believable misery of cold and toil with death as its only reward. I am not ashamed to say I prayed I might get a "lucky" injury, or a quick death. It was inescapable. Everyone "up there" gets it sooner or later.

Frank Barnett expressed best the dullness of thought and mind that often accompanied prolonged combat, when men no longer cared about the outcome, just that their suffering came to an end:

> The infantryman becomes supremely indifferent; his intellect only *records* events, it makes no decisions for him. Drying his feet becomes as unpleasant as getting them wet. Standing in the rain is of no more consequence than sitting in a shelter. Cold food provokes no more excitement than no food at all. Mechanically the body tries to do what instinct tells it is best. But there is no reality; everything is done in a . . . monotonous dream.

John Meier, a rifle platoon leader, wrote of the way in which his men dealt with the insane world of frontline combat:

> My men know the effects of war far more than you or I could ever visualize or even realize. They have suffered a hundred-fold the mental pain that their loved ones are suffering at home now. They have seen the abyss of corruption and hatred and have come to the reality of precious love at the same moment.

After seeing prolonged combat, Arthur Kammerer, of the 102d Infantry Division, wrote of the toll it took on him and others:

In my . . . experiences I've seen it make killers out of some, cowards of some, Christians of most, men of many. All either lose or gain much by it. Most do both. Up until today, I know that I can stand all of it. I'll admit I worry like the devil about patrols and artillery and so on but it has never in any way affected my actions and conduct. There is no telling how long I can control my nerves . . . but so far I have. It is satisfying for me to know these things.

———— CHAPTER 11
THE TRUTH ABOUT REPLACEMENTS

The replacement system that the U.S. Army employed during World War II has found many detractors and few defenders. Instead of replacing ground combat casualties by unit, as the Germans did, the U.S. Army chose to replace its casualties by plugging in new men without regard to unit integrity.

In the German army, units that had been decimated were often withdrawn from the front lines and reconstituted with new men and the remaining survivors of the old unit. In this way, familiarity and cohesiveness could be built up among the new men, who were all in the same boat as replacements. The veterans could then provide leadership when the outfit was sent back to the front.

In the U.S. Army, combat units were fed replacements piece meal, sometimes even while they were still fighting. Thus, most American replacements joined their new units not knowing anyone and feeling alone and disoriented.

This system of filling in replacements individually has attracted much criticism, most of it valid. Not only was this practice somewhat insensitive, it was militarily unsound. Replacements who had a chance to get to know the men around them and who were able to learn the rudiments of combat had a far better chance of survival than those who did not. The lonely individual who joined his foxhole mate with little or no idea of how to survive or what was expected of him in combat was at a distinct disadvantage compared to his German counterpart, who most likely entered combat far more prepared.

The road that an American replacement traveled to get to the front was often depressing and disorienting. After training in the

States, he was shipped overseas, not as part of a combat division in which he could take pride but as part of a disparate group of replacements, none of whom knew his final combat destination. When he arrived overseas, the combat replacement was quickly dispatched to a replacement depot commonly known as a "repple depple."

The repple depples were perhaps the worst aspect of being a replacement. Men were sometimes kept in these veritable halfway houses for up to three months. They were often treated shabbily and were not made to feel part of any military organization. Many of them felt like refugees.

When it finally came time for the men to be assigned to a combat outfit, they were arbitrarily herded to their destination and dumped off with little or no supervision. It was then up to their new units as to what sort of welcome they would receive and how they would be utilized. By most accounts, it was far better for a replacement to arrive when the unit was not in combat. Behind the lines, men had more time to get to know one another in a relatively relaxed setting. Up front, combat soldiers had far more to worry about than taking care of a brand-new man.

In spite of the deficiencies of the American replacement system, and in spite of popular notions to the contrary, American combat replacements were not loathed and mistreated by combat men as dangerous, foolhardy "greenhorns." Nor were replacements useless due to their inexperience. In most cases veterans treated replacements well and did all they could to help them in combat. Replacements were the lifeblood of the U.S. combat army in World War II. They were welcomed with open arms by men on the front lines for the simple reason that, casualties being what they were, new men were always needed to help lighten the load. If a replacement could survive his first firefight or two, he usually became a valuable part of the unit.

Many combat soldiers originally came to their units as replacements. Of four fighting divisions in Italy, only 34 percent of the infantrymen in line companies came overseas with their units. The rest joined the units as replacements. Thus, combat men could not afford to ostracize and avoid replacements. Indoctrinating them was a way of life on the front. It was a constant cyclical process, because the composition of a combat unit changed almost daily in frontline outfits. A new group of replacements would come in and become veterans in a matter of days in combat. Casualties would thin their ranks and the next group would join the outfit and so on. Intact through the entire bewildering process was the brotherhood, which formed quickly between replacements and veterans in action. Men sharing hardship under fire solidified trust at a rapid rate.

In the European theater, former replacements were asked whether or not the veterans had made an effort to be helpful to new men. Eighty-two percent stated that the experienced men had "done as much as they could." Of the veterans, 88 percent agreed with the statement that "when a replacement comes to an outfit during combat, the veterans usually try to help him out all they can." Typically veterans would do all they could to help replacements not only out of common decency, but because it was in their own self-interest. The faster a replacement learned his way around in combat, the faster he could become a dependable contributor to the oufit, something that benefited everyone and took heat off the veterans.

In some cases replacements were resented; after all, they were there because someone's buddy had been hit. John Stenger felt this kind of resentment from the survivors of the 104th Infantry Division rifle company that he joined in Holland. "It was an uncomfortable feeling replacing someone who had been killed or wounded a few days earlier. The survivors looked tired and haggard, almost in shock."

Some combat men looked down on replacements and were loath to associate with them. Others were reluctant to get to know new men because they had lost too many good friends in combat and did not want to put themselves through those painful feelings of loss again. These cases were the exception.

The results of one army survey illustrate how quickly most replacements became valued members of their units. Former replacements were asked, "How long was it after you arrived in your present outfit before you felt you really belonged in the outfit and were an important part of it?" Sixty-five percent answered anywhere from one day to one week. Commented Robert Klenk, who joined the 6th Infantry Division as a baby-faced eighteen year old: "I was received well. Some told me to listen to the old-timers and I would learn well. A couple kidded me and asked me if I brought my mother." Said Marvin Reickman, who joined the 24th Infantry Division in the Philippines as a young man: "The older men were helpful in teaching us how to stay alive and be effective. They treated us with kindness." Charles Stewart was an infantry replacement in the 27th Infantry Division on Saipan. The men in his unit treated him so well that he made lifelong friendships with them. Each year he hosts a reunion for them out of gratitude for the way they welcomed him. Whayland Greene, a rifleman replacement in the 32d Infantry Division, had similar experiences. He was "pleasantly surprised at how concerned older personnel were for the younger guys. They could not have been any better to us."

Evan Voss expected to be gruffly treated when he made it to the 36th Infantry Division in Italy. Instead everyone from the top sergeant on down was polite and helpful. "We were . . . greeted by the first sergeant. He was sure different than I expected. This guy . . . greeted us politely and graciously and answered all the stupid questions we asked. Everyone came over, introduced themselves and made us feel quite 'at home.'" William Eberhart joined the 75th Infantry Division during the bitter Colmar Pocket campaign. Even though the unit was in combat, the veterans treated him well. "It was no problem for me and the others. We just relied on their help and friendship during combat." It was the same for Jacob Westra, of the 78th Infantry Division. "They were glad to see us and made us welcome to their unit." Robert Russell entered combat with the 84th Infantry Division during the height of the Battle of the Bulge. "I didn't know anybody. They were good to me, tried to be helpful. You just gradually fit into your unit. It didn't take long."

Sometimes, even if a newcomer felt anonymous or alone within the group, one veteran soldier would befriend him and integrate him into the brotherhood. Such was the case for Glenn Perry, who joined the 96th Infantry Division as a raw replacement during the fighting on Okinawa. "I was made very welcome . . . by a fellow . . . from my hometown who was killed the same day I was wounded. I think I was one of the last to talk to him at the aid station."

Armored divisions were no different when it came to welcoming replacements. The experiences of Lewis Bryant, in the 1st Armored Division, were typical of many. "[The veterans] immediately started to tell me the right and wrong way to do things. All were most helpful to get me started . . . to keep me alive and to do my duty."

It was common to look out for new men by buddying them up with a veteran. When Charles Rudolph joined the 1st Armored, he said, "They introduced me all around, assigned me to a squad and teamed me up with an old-timer for indoctrination. It was a very friendly team atmosphere." Roy Denmon, of the 6th Armored Division, was paired with a veteran and was "received well enough. I would guess they were happy to get any help available, even green ones like me." Charles Hogg, also of the 6th Armored, received a warm welcome when he joined a veteran tank crew. "My tank commander welcomed me and tried to tell me what was important and how best to survive. I will always cherish their memory. They made me feel wanted even though I was combat green."

The attitudes of most veterans mirrored those of 99th Infantry Division rifleman Harry Arnold. "We older men always felt sorry for the new replacements coming in, and did what we could to point them in the right direction to improve their survival chances." Commented James Simms, of the 101st Airborne Division: "The veteran has more compassion for the novice than the green man ever realizes." Ray Poynter, who served with the Americal Division in the Pacific, was always happy to see replacements. "I felt lucky to have new men coming in to be with us. New men were treated special and given help." Paul Dixon, of the 6th Infantry Division, recalled that he and his buddies "welcomed them and tried to make them feel at ease and ease their anxiety." Emil Matula, of the 25th Infantry Division, could not remember any problems where replacements were concerned. "They were all great people and were blended in with the veterans with no problem." Joe Carey, who served with the 43d Infantry Division, claimed to have "welcomed them with open arms."

Harold Wells, a junior officer in the 45th Infantry Division, explained the process by which replacements were welcomed, incorporated, and indoctrinated. "We welcomed them and tried to make their experience as painless as possible. We tried to buddy them up with a veteran and tried to make the assignment after dark if possible during combat. We felt like they were as lonesome and lost as anyone could be."

Communication with the new men made them feel part of the team and gave them something to think about rather than dwelling on their natural fear and apprehension. The worst thing to do with a new replacement was ignore him. Donald Vanhooser, of the 65th Infantry Division, was mindful of this. "I tried to make them feel part of the squad and let them know what we were doing, our purpose and to keep their head down." Gerald VanCleve, of the 75th Infantry Division, emphasized that he and his veteran buddies went out of their way to befriend new men because it made everyone more comfortable and made for better soldiers. "We became friends right away and trust became natural. We would joke with them about being rookies but we respected them." Donald Dencker remembered how badly replacements were needed in the 96th Infantry Division during the Okinawa campaign. This led the survivors to treat new men well. "We welcomed them. We needed all we could get. When you're fighting 70 percent understrength, there are plenty of positions to fill."

Armored engineer Mitchel Chafon gave new men lots of concerned attention. "I was glad to see them. We lost no time in checking out a new man and bringing him up to date on what we were doing. We had so many replacements [that] everyone was glad to help them all they could."

Such attitudes were widespread in the veteran 1st Armored Division. Tanker Paul Jani and his buddies "treated our replacements with words of encouragement and tried to make them feel at home. We tried our best to get them through their first combat." Donald Taylor, who received a battlefield commission, echoed the sentiments of many combat men. "We received replacements with open arms because we needed them so badly." Said Eugene Thibideau, "Replacements were very common in a combat unit. We always treated them well and tried to put them at ease and answer their questions about combat." John Margreiter, an armored infantryman in the 7th Armored Division, recalled that in his unit "we were always happy to see them for they were always needed. After all, there was a big meat grinder up there [at the front]."

The inexperienced men made mistakes, sometimes out of fear, sometimes out of bravado, and sometimes out of just plain ignorance. In the European theater two groups of combat veterans were asked what, in their opinions, were the most common mistakes made by new replacements. In the first group—those who had come overseas with their outfit—48 percent mentioned bunching up as a mistake made often by replacements. Talking loud or making noise at night netted another 35 percent. Shooting before they are able to see their target was next at 27 percent, followed by not taking advantage of available cover (26 percent) and freezing up (15 percent). Among the second group—men who had joined their outfits as replacements—bunching up was deemed the most common mistake by 59 percent of those queried. Making noise was next at 37 percent, followed by shooting before seeing a target (25 percent), not taking advantage of available cover (24 percent), and freezing up (14 percent).

"The first mistake recruits make under fire," related one combat veteran, "is that they freeze and bunch up. They drop to the ground and just lie there." Bunching up under fire, though, was by no means a mistake made only by new men. Both groups of combat veterans indicated that as many as one-fifth of veteran soldiers tended to do the same thing even though they knew it was dangerous. The tendency of combat soldiers to bunch up under fire is yet another sign of the deadly brotherhood. The only good reason to bunch up was for mutual moral support. Even though it was irrational, men did it, often indicating that their need for comradeship was sometimes greater even than their need for survival.

The other major errors—making unnecessary noise, shooting blindly, not taking cover properly, and freezing up—were almost always made by replacements. Edward Laughlin joined the 82d Airborne Division as a replacement during the Battle of the Bulge. Late one afternoon he and some other new men were inspecting abandoned German weapons at positions that their unit had recently overrun. Curious about the workings of a German light machine gun, Laughlin decided to fire it:

All hell broke loose at the sound of the machine gun. Running at us came several combat-scarred sergeants and officers, pale faced and wild looks in their eyes, pointing loaded weapons at us—ready to kill! Soon as they got a good look at us they pulled up short and then they may as well have shot us considering the chewing out we got for firing that gun. We were repeatedly and quite harshly told how stupid and dumb we were.

Charles Miller, of the 75th Infantry Division, recalled being on patrol with a new man leading and hearing a shot fired. "Everyone stopped and looked around, and when nothing happened, I asked him what he had fired at. He replied, 'Nothing, I caught the trigger on a button on my overcoat.' I told him to lock his weapon until he saw something to shoot." The mistake of that one new man could have gotten Miller's entire patrol killed. Such errors became serious business not just to the new men but to everyone.

Charles Fulton, of the 103d Infantry Division, witnessed a case in which the errors of replacements hurt only the new men who committed them. Two brand-new men on their first night in combat attempted to heat up their food by lighting a fire. Fulton related what happened in a poem he wrote:

"Put out that fire!" the sergeant screamed, "before the Germans zero in." A whistling sound through the air there reamed. It spent its fury on two guys who never learned to play war games. Replacements, now, were dead GIs. I wondered what had been their names.

Then there were those new men who fired blindly without making any attempt to ascertain a target, sometimes with disastrous consequences, as 5th Infantry Division soldier Lawrence Nickell related:

A replacement soldier with only a few days of combat experience was on the outpost line. The group checking the outpost missed him in the dark . . . and then approached the outpost. The replacement thought they were an enemy patrol, did not halt them or call for the password, and killed the company commander.

Edward Sears, of the Americal Division, was wounded at Cebu when his foxhole buddy, a replacement, mistakenly fired:

> He thought he heard or saw something and started shooting. I yelled at him to stop but he kept on shooting. His rifle was about 10 inches from my face. When he was shooting, the flash from the muzzle of the rifle burned my eyes. He put me out of action. I swore at him a few times and I suppose it made me feel better at the time. I knew he felt bad about it.

Sears never returned to combat. He wondered fifty years later if perhaps the replacement saved his life by wounding him.

Albert Kudzia, a veteran infantryman in the 36th Infantry Division, knew of one replacement who was apparently killed by a sniper when he could not find proper cover. The incident happened in France while Kudzia's rifle company was attacking a small town:

> A replacement joined my unit and I instructed him to be sure to keep up with his squad once we hit the town. Unfortunately, he trailed too far behind, and when he got into the city, he turned left instead of right and we located his body in one of the doorways. I don't wish to mention his name as . . . relatives might hear of this article and would be quite depressed over how he met his death.

Far more commonly, the errors made by new men were not deadly. They were part of learning how to act up front and how to blend in with the other men. Sometimes it came down to saying the wrong thing at the wrong time. Robert Benz, who joined the 1st Infantry Division as a raw replacement, quickly came under artillery fire with one of the outfit's veterans. Being completely inexperienced, Benz did not know that veterans were just as scared in combat as new men. "He had combat experience, so I wrongly assumed this [shell fire] no longer bothered him. I made a feeble attempt at humor and he returned a disgusted look. He was shook up!"

Although most American replacements were valued additions to their units, some combat veterans felt that replacements were of poor quality, especially those who came from other branches of the service later in the war when the army realized that it needed more combat infantrymen. James Graff, of the 35th Infantry Division, buddied up with one such man named Sokolowski:

> He had been a truck mechanic in an antiaircraft outfit in the States. An infantryman was a highly specialized and trained individual. We had many weapons to master, plus the training to make you a combat soldier. Men like Sokolowski were next to worthless as an infantryman and many of these retrainees were to become casualties . . . because of it.

Arthur Bolton, an armored infantryman in the 3d Armored Division, echoed Graff's contempt for the so-called "retrained riflemen." "The worst were replacements who had been trained for the air force or for ground troop service and then assigned to the infantry."

Being trained as an infantryman did not guarantee that a replacement would do well in combat, however. Mark Durley, a junior officer in the Americal Division, felt that the replacements in his outfit "were not effective until several months of campaigning, mainly because their stateside training did not prepare them for jungle fighting." Some replacements were simply cowards, such as the man described by 4th Infantry Division rifle platoon sergeant Alton Pearson:

> We regrouped our men and I was three short. One was Blake and I don't remember the names of the other two. I asked a soldier at my right flank if he saw a man of Blake's description. He said, "I saw a cloud of dust going to the rear." I never saw Blake any more and was glad of it.

Although Del Kendall, of the 36th Infantry Division, generally thought that his unit's replacements were all right, he said there were always some who were poor. "They always left for sick call, sounding like a guard-house lawyer, with their aches and 'bad back.' They talked their way into KP [kitchen patrol] duty or digging six by six [trenches] . . . for the kitchen."

Garland Godby, of the 80th Infantry Division, felt that replacements who came to his unit while it was in combat usually did not turn out well. With the tremendous casualties in line companies, though, it was an unsolvable problem:

> We were always short of men in an infantry company. I got down to a hundred and thirty and that's about what I wound up with because you get new men in and you cannot absorb new men in a combat situation. They don't know how to fight and you don't know them so usually they get killed or wounded. It's not their fault. I used to cry if I lost good men but I never cried over most replacements.

Henri Atkins, a rifleman in the 99th Infantry Division, was not enamored of the replacements in his unit. "There were three problems: (1) they were usually not well trained; (2) they would arrive in a unit in which they would know no one; and (3) they had not yet been 'bloodied.' They needed the TLC [tender loving care] of a veteran or a kick in the rear to bring them out of their fear."

Others felt that the quality of their replacements was inconsistent. Edwin Hanson, who was once himself a replacement in the 37th Infantry Division, voiced an ambivalent opinion. To him, replacements were "very mixed. Some fit right in and did what was expected. Some never did fit. Eventually they were sort of ignored or transferred."

Deane Marks, of the 11th Airborne Division, gave a tangible example of the mixed quality of replacements in his outfit:

> Laddie and Sennart came in as replacements after Leyte. Sennart thought he was a one-man army. He wouldn't listen to anyone. He also kept his fanny down and was always well to the rear. On the other hand, Laddie paid attention, came along well, did what he was told and in general proved to be a very good infantryman.

Victor Wade was an eighteen-year-old replacement with the 3d Infantry Division. When he joined his outfit at Anzio, his platoon sergeant "thought that I would either be killed or wounded in our first action in combat. I am glad to say that I fooled him." The sergeant later told Wade that he looked so young that he could not imagine him surviving combat. He was pleasantly surprised.

In the Pacific, Lynn Moerke, of the 6th Infantry Division, found that of the many replacements his unit received, "most of them were reliable and conducted themselves well." Another man in Moerke's outfit echoed his sentiment. Replacements "did a swell job after the mental adjustment." Carlie Berryhill agreed: "After a little experience they were the same as any other soldier."

Most veterans agreed that in the fast-moving world of combat, it did not take long for a new man to get acclimated. Gilbert Hilkemeyer, of the 24th Infantry Division, felt that "after the first day they were okay." Roland Acheson, of the 32d Infantry Division, felt that in his unit it took new men two days to become part of the group. "If they made it [through] the first three days, they usually made it." One of Acheson's 32d Division comrades, Dewey Hill, felt that in most cases replacements "did a fine job." Byron Brown, of the 37th Infantry Division, downplayed any differences between the fighting quality of veterans and replacements. "After their initial baptism of fire, replacements generally were as effective as veterans." Thaddeus Piewawer, a rifleman in the 41st Infantry Division, recalled that replacements "learned real fast how to handle themselves in combat."

Men in European theater divisions were no different in their assessments of new men. Harold Wells remembered that at Anzio, "If we could get them [replacements] past the initial shock period, they soon became one of the unit and were as effective as anyone else." Thomas Yochim, of the 78th Infantry Division, remembered his replacements acclimating well to combat. "Once they had their baptism of fire, most adapted admirably well to their environment." Donald Trachta, who fought with the 97th Infantry Division, found new men to be "very effective. I made many good friends and had lasting friendships with them."

The high quality of American replacements also held true in armored divisions, where men were added to tank crews or armored infantry formations one at a time. In the 1st Armored Division, combat men overwhelmingly felt that their replacements did a good job and blended in well. Lewis Bryant, an armor infantryman, felt that "after a short period of time with some help from the veterans, they [replacements] became as good as a veteran." Charles Rudolph asserted that "in one or two weeks they were just as effective as the vets." Donald Taylor thought that replacements did as well as they did because they knew they were needed. It gave them a sense of importance and helped them fit into the group quickly. Hartson Sexton, a tank commander, said that when a new man was added to his crew he was "usually quite good. If they lasted more than a few days, they were veterans."

Tanker Jack Brewer, in the 3d Armored Division, said that when replacements came to his crew they did a good job, caught on quickly, and soon became part of the close-knit family that made up small-unit combat teams at the front. "Most of them were good. They soon caught on as to how to survive."

Replacements were the lifeblood of the frontline army. It usually took only a short time before the replacements were accepted into the brotherhood of men at the front, the brotherhood that forged the unique bond that enabled American combat men to fight and endure.

As he sat at his kitchen table one hot summer day fifty years after World War II, Garland Godby, a former rifle company commander in the 80th Infantry Division, expressed amazement at how well his men, most of whom were just ordinary Americans, held up under the stress of combat. Somehow his soldiers had restrained their fears and performed their duties in an outstanding fashion. When asked what he thought was the most significant single factor in bringing this about, Godby did not hesitate. "Brotherhood. Everybody sharing the same dangers, the same joy and the same sorrow. I had the entire scope of humanity in those men."

In a few sentences, Godby identified the main reason why American combat soldiers fought effectively in World War II. It was the bond, which can only be termed a "brotherhood," that developed among those at the front lines, who did the bulk of the fighting. This brotherhood motivated American soldiers to fight and at the same time provided them with a small, tight-knit "family" in which they could feel secure and needed. Along the way, soldiers became as close as brothers, forging a unique friendship that in many cases exists to the present day.

Elmer Jones, a rifleman in the 89th Infantry Division, described the deadly brotherhood that he experienced:

> The dog soldier feared separation from his squad more than he feared the enemy. He felt secure among men whose individual characters and capabilities he knew as well as he knew his own. They had been welded together by combat, and

rightly or wrongly the infantryman was convinced that his chances of surviving the next firefight were much better with his own squad than they would be in any other. His first sergeant and platoon sergeant were like fathers (sometimes cruel stepfathers), and the other members of his squad were his brothers.

So it was for most American ground combat soldiers in World War II. Men of different backgrounds and personalities were drawn together during combat. With their lives on the line, they learned that they could depend on one another. Indeed, most found that they had no choice but to depend on one another. At the front there was no time for differences of race, region, religion, or class. Combat stripped away the barriers of everyday life. The result was that combat men often bared their souls to one another. Those who fought together experienced a trust and friendship with their fellow combat men that they would find rare in civilian life. Many combat soldiers felt that even family and close friends could not know or understand them the way their buddies had.

Two surveys conducted by the army examined the deadly brotherhood and highlighted its crucial importance for combat motivation. Combat soldiers from five veteran infantry divisions were asked the simple question, "Do you feel proud of your company?" Only 9 percent were not proud. Seventy-eight percent were either fairly proud or very proud.

Pride in one's unit was by no means unique to combat outfits, but the kind of overwhelming pride indicated by the responses to this survey pointed to more than just a simple pride at belonging to a specific military organization. To combat men, unit pride did not primarily mean the actual military organization but rather the men who made up that organization. Men did not risk their lives for the "Big Red One" or the "Screamin' Eagles," even though they may have taken pride in their membership in those units. Instead they risked their lives for the men who made up the unit. A man's outfit was not just another number on an order-of-battle sheet. It was his home, his family. When the average combat soldier thought of his unit, he thought of the men who served in that unit. So when asked whether he was proud of his unit, the combat man was essentially being asked if he was proud of the men in his group. The vast majority held a fierce pride in their own tight-knit team of men with whom they fought, which is reflected in the results of the survey.

In another survey, American combat soldiers in both Europe and the Pacific were asked, "When the going got tough . . . how much did it help to think that you couldn't let the other men down?" In the Pacific only 13 percent replied not at all; 87 percent said that it helped some or a lot (26 and 61 percent, respectively). In Europe the responses were nearly identical. There was a core of 13 percent who felt that such thoughts did not help them at all in tough combat; 87 percent said that these thoughts helped some or a lot (31 and 56 percent, respectively). In other words, nearly nine out of ten American combat soldiers in World War II found the strength to endure even the worst combat and continue fighting because they could not bear the thought of letting their buddies down. For most, the threat of death was preferable to betraying one's combat brothers. This complicated blend of peer pressure, teamwork, and fellowship was the main reason why American combat soldiers fought successfully in World War II.

There is no shortage of evidence to support the latter contention. In fact, when studying the soldiers themselves, one cannot help but be impressed by the pervasiveness of the brotherhood in motivating men to fight.

Lawrence Nickell, a mortarman in the 5th Infantry Division, wrote that comradeship was the main reason why he and the other men in his outfit fought:

> The thing that keeps a soldier going in the face of horrendous violence and unbelievable living conditions is simply self-respect and the psychological need for the respect of your fellow soldiers. You want them to support you when you are pinned down or in a bad spot and they need to feel that they can count on you. We had a lot of propaganda thrown at us about the cause for which we fought, and it was a good cause, but it was not as important as . . . the respect that men had for one another.

Henri Atkins, a point man in the 99th Infantry Division, agreed:

> What kept me or anyone sane despite the constant nearness of death was . . . the nearness of our . . . buddies, of others watching what we did or how we acted and our ability to function while in a state of disassociation in which we were numb and simply did not care what happened to us. But we also wanted to show up well, to appear fearless while inside we were scared to death. As a soldier, you do not wish to let your buddies down.

Tankers were no different. Paul Jani, of the 1st Armored Division, fought in the bloody campaigns of Italy and survived three knocked-out tanks. In his experience, "Men showed that . . . their love and respect for their comrades gave them the capacity to endure and accomplish the unthinkable."

In fact, this propensity to draw motivation from one another was universal in combat outfits regardless of theater or combat conditions. Half a world away from Jani's tank, Richard Cohen, of the Americal Division, found that he fought "initially for my country, but later in combat the unit and fellow soldiers became a more important motivator." Another Americal man, John Stannard, realized that in combat "the feeling of camaraderie and unity increased. I felt more responsible and determined not to let the unit or my comrades down. Somehow danger itself seemed a little less important."

After experiencing combat, 4th Infantry Division medic Clinton MacLeod wrote to the parents of one of his comrades that their son had given MacLeod "that extra something that so many of us lack when the going is tough." Minoru Hara, of the 6th Infantry Division, felt that "the camaraderie brought out individual courage to enable us to fight and do our utmost." Newman Phillips, who was in the 32d Infantry Division, stated that he "fought in combat because I did not want to appear as a coward to my buddies."

An entire unit of men such as Phillips, sublimating their acute fear so as not to let the other men down, made for a formidable fighting machine. Said Ellis Blake, a rifle platoon leader in the 33d Infantry Division, "When a soldier sees he can trust and depend on his platoon and squad members, the morale and efficiency go up."

In pondering why he and his comrades shouldered their weapons and carried out hopeless, deadly patrols across the Rapido River in Italy during 1944's freezing winter, 36th Infantry Division soldier John Goode could come up with only one reason. "Why did we do it? We did it for our squads, platoons, or company. Even battalion and regiment were too abstract." John Beeks, a combat engineer in the 78th Infantry Division, said that not carrying out one's responsibilities was unthinkable among the tight-knit groups of buddies that existed in each unit at the front. "I knew my squad, platoon and company. I would never let them down and most of them never let me down. We trusted each other."

Joe Johnson, a black infantry officer in the predominantly black 92d Infantry Division, wrote home that in his outfit "men generally realize their responsibilities to the group or team and shoulder them." Henry Emerson, of the 97th Infantry Division, knew that carrying on in combat was usually a matter of sticking together. "I think everybody was scared of getting killed and the thing that kept us going was the cohesion of being buddies." Clyde Upchurch, an armored infantryman in the 3d Armored Division, summed up what most combat men found to be true. "I wanted to prove I was brave and not be yellow in front of others. We became very dependent on each other for protection. I never felt that I was fighting so much for my country. We really fought for each other's survival."

Harry Arnold, of the 99th Infantry Division, recalled finding unknown strength during combat as a direct result of one of his buddies. "We had taken a liking to each other immediately. A big man, craggy of feature, Loesch had that rare quality among men of radiating confidence and assurance. It was impossible to be around him and not feel that, somehow, everything would turn out all right."

As intense as the cold was during the Battle of the Bulge for 101st Airborne Division trooper James Simms, he was able to endure it by leaning on his buddy and vice versa:

> Some nights the cold got to you worse, then guard was real bad. Other nights you had more strength and toughness and on those nights you would try to give your partner extra good measure. If you sensed a weakening in your partner, you

seemed to gather extra strength to compensate. One thing you didn't want to do . . . was cheat your buddy. There is a . . . very strong loyalty that grows between combat men.

In the suffocating heat of the Leyte landing in the Philippines, Charles Card, of the 24th Infantry Division, felt immobilized by fear until he saw his buddies moving around fighting the Japanese. He recalled being "really scared, quite emotional and insecure. I needed to see my comrades' response to gain self-control and then go forward." Immediately following his captivity at the hands of the Germans, 106th Infantry Division soldier Jack Brugh took heart from the words of one of his comrades:

> He said, "Jack, we have seen our buddies killed right in front of our eyes, endured an awesome German attack, been cold and hungry, lived in fear for days, and still, we survived. And we will take whatever the Germans throw at us and continue to survive." I can remember Buddy's remarks as though they were yesterday. It challenged me to face whatever came next.

Sometime after combat, Paul Jani and his tank commander shared a story that illustrated how Americans in combat drew strength to fight and endure from one another. "Albert Dunn said he looked into the turret. I wasn't scared so he thought why should he be afraid? I looked up at him and his head looked out of the open turret [a very dangerous, vulnerable position for a tank commander] so I thought why should I be scared?"

A combat man's fear usually did not abate with increased exposure to combat. In many cases it became more intense as men felt the odds catching up with them. Through it all, most combat soldiers were able to control their fear and perform their duties well due to the brotherhood. They found that in moments of fear or weakness there was usually someone close by who seemed to be functioning. This would serve to motivate the fearful man. Few men were lion-hearted heroes each day in action. One buddy would shoulder the burden one day, and the next man would do it another day. Today's coward was often tomorrow's hero and vice versa.

This strong reliance and dependence on one another made men fight harder, last longer in combat, and forge close friendships that provided worth and substance to the usually hellish existence of the combat soldier. However, there were times when the closeness that combat brothers shared was not necessarily good. When a buddy was killed, the effect on the other men could be devastating. Although combat soldiers knew intellectually that any one of them could be killed or wounded, it did not make it any easier when it actually happened. If a buddy was killed, it was truly like losing your brother. Said Julian Phillips, of the 36th Infantry Division: "It was always okay to push a rifle company into a bad position and never worry about casualties at Headquarters. To them, a death was just a number. But to us, losing a man on the line was like losing someone in our family."

Bill Sabin, of the 1st Infantry Division, witnessed the death of one of his best buddies in North Africa. "Just as I was about to call him, he got it—right through the helmet. I knew if I'd moved just an inch I would have gotten it too. So I had to lay there and see my buddy go to his death. With LePre gone, I felt lost. I cried like a baby. I loved him like a brother." Sabin said that one of LePre's other buddies, a man named Luke, had an even worse reaction to the death. "I never saw a man lose his head as fast as Luke did. He scooped up three hand grenades from the ammunition box and ran across the field. Luke must have gone pretty far, as he silenced two machine gun nests. We just hoped and prayed." Luckily, Luke returned a few hours later unhurt.

Victor Wade, of the 3d Infantry Division, was wounded in late 1944. During his convalescence, he learned of the death of one of his comrades and became severely depressed. "I spent Christmas of 1944 in that hospital in deep despair thinking about Schlitz. The doctors were concerned about my depression."

After his two closest friends went down in action, Alton Pearson, of the 4th Infantry Division, found it difficult to stomach any further combat. "At that time I was ready to get out of the war. All the men were good soldiers, but I knew without Herlyn and Johnson I was worthless." Another 4th Division man, John Symanski, lost a buddy to a mine and was glad he did not see it actually happen. "His shovel struck a hidden land mine, and blew him sky high. I am glad I was not one of the salvage crew. Whenever we lost a man like this, it was similar to losing a member of your personal family."

In combat it did not take long for men to become close. There was no arbitrary amount of time required to forge trust. It could happen in a few days or a few minutes. On the front lines it happened quickly. William Eberle, of the 36th Infantry Division, recalled meeting a soldier one night prior to an attack in Alsace. It did not take long for the brotherhood to develop:

> I struck up a friendly acquaintance with a young man from Syracuse. He was a likable fellow. It was his first time in combat and he told me of the thoughts racing through his mind. He . . . asked me to locate him after the attack and I promised him that I would. However, the news of his death a few hours later struck me with a terrific shock. His limbs were torn away from a German 88mm shell. [He was] an acquaintance for only a few moments but it seemed that I had known him . . . longer. I bowed my head in silent prayer. You get that way in the infantry. One's mind and soul are bound very close together.

Another 36th Division soldier, David Arvizu, remembered the grief that he experienced when two of his buddies were killed in the Vosges Mountains in November 1944. After feeling as though he could no longer go on, he had to take a day or so to recover before he could face combat again:

> I sat down on a tree stump. I was still in a state of mental shock. I thought about what had happened to Bob and Joe, then started crying. I felt a sense of guilt thinking that maybe if I had done something differently Joe would still be alive. Quite a while later I caught up with the tail end of the company and then joined my platoon. I was glad that the men sensed what I had been going through and did not ask where I had been or what I had been doing. Bob Cassidy . . . and Joe Brocato . . . represented in every way the combat infantryman in World War II—loyal to country, comrades, and devotion to duty.

Max Kocour, a mortar forward observer in the 90th Infantry Division, explained how losing buddies affected him in combat. "A number of my closest buddies from Normandy on were killed or seriously wounded. For several hours I went through what could be called confidence shock; many of the people who were inspirations to me were gone."

Amid the cold and snow at Elsenborn Ridge, Nelson Ottis and his 99th Infantry Division brothers went on patrol one day. It was a patrol that Ottis would never forget:

> Wadsworth took first scout position and I took second as we were very close buddies. We were ambushed by a machine gun and Wadsworth took several bullets in the chest. I took several in my helmet as I dived and several through my clothes. My watch was shot off. I finally found Wadsworth in the deep snow. He was dead. I sat and held him in my arms and cried.

Too often there was little or nothing that combat soldiers could do to prevent such tragedies. Death and destruction were often random and impersonal. The survivors were left with a feeling of powerlessness and subdued rage. The rage they felt could be directed at the enemy, but it usually came about because of the hopelessness of their circumstances. Slowly but surely, each member of a man's combat family would disappear either from death or wounds. When asked how his morale held up in combat, 1st Armored Division tanker Marion Earley replied balefully: "How would you cope if you lost your tank crew one by one and many friends which were closer than brothers?"

If a man was in combat long enough, and saw enough buddies die, he paid a high price. Most would never be the same after losing buddies. After seeing enough of his marine friends die around him on Guadalcanal, Don Zobel actually came to believe that they were dying because he had eaten with them:

> They are all dead, I thought. They are gone and I am here by myself with no one that I know. I did not want to eat with anyone ever again for it seemed that each time I ate with or be-

came close to someone they were to die. I would stay to myself, I decided in my delirium, to protect others from dying because they had associated with me. I had to get away. Too many friends were gone.

Zobel's apparently irrational thoughts probably stemmed from the hopelessness, powerlessness, and frustration that he felt at losing so many men close to him without being able to do anything about it. By withdrawing and refusing to eat with anyone, Zobel was attempting to reassert some measure of control over his circumstances.

The reaction of C. Russ Martin, a sergeant in the 1st Infantry Division, when his twin brother was killed in North Africa is even more intriguing. After the death of his brother, Martin experienced something that can only be termed as supernatural:

Twins, we feel for one another, and the minute he got killed I knew it, a sensation and a kind of a relief, you know, from worrying about him. I didn't have to worry about him anymore. A boy walked up to me and said, "You know your brother got killed?" And I said, "Yes, I do." Now this wasn't an ordinary soldier. This boy was clean-shaved, he was clean . . . and I've often thought, and I know, that it was an angel. He didn't look like the rest of us. He was an angel, come and telling me.

The loss of a close buddy could cause paralyzing grief that took years to ease. Such was the case with Kenneth Cole, of the 3d Marine Division, when he learned of the death of his best friend on Iwo Jima. Cole had been severely wounded in an earlier campaign and was back in the United States, permanently out of combat. Still he felt guilty that he had not been there with his buddy, and he had trouble accepting that his friend was gone. He wrote to his mother:

I just can't make myself understand that I won't see Boone anymore. Even though you have seen men die in the same outfit with you it is impossible to make yourself believe that anybody can get killed that is as close to you as Boone was to me.

He taught me practically everything I know about being a Marine. If it hadn't been for Boone I would have been a white cross on Bougainville instead of coming back to the States. Now that the time has come and gone when I might have done something for Him I failed Him by being one of the USO Stateside Marines [a derogatory term meaning rear echelon]. Mom, I could sit here and write all day and would never be able to do Him justice or tell you the real way I feel about the tragedy.

Cole's acute grief pours from his sentences, and his capitalized pronoun reference to Boone as "Him" is striking. As was true of many combat men, to this marine there was nothing that could ever compensate for the loss of his friend. To make matters worse, the deaths of these loved ones came in the most violent, sinister fashion.

Living with this kind of personal tragedy was something that set combat veterans apart from other Americans. Because of what they experienced, most combat men felt that only other combat veterans could truly understand them or their experiences. This "only we undertand" sort of sentiment still exists fifty years later and is widespread among those who saw combat. Rex Harrison, who fought with the 36th Infantry Division, summed up the feelings of many combat veterans. "An individual who hasn't experienced the trauma of witnessing sudden death, fatal wounds, extreme heat/cold or smelled gas gangrene is never initiated into that select group of warriors who . . . still 'flash back' and bring these memories back in all their ugliness."

The gulf of experience between those who fought in World War II and the vast majority who did not experience war firsthand never really faded. In explaining why he does not talk about the war with anyone but his buddies, Americal Division veteran Herchel McFadden said, "Others don't know a damn thing about what you're talking about and don't care." Another Americal man, John Stannard, agreed. "Infantry combat is a unique experience. You must have participated in it to understand it." Minoru Hara felt that "others can't seem to understand the psychological trauma we had to go through." Marvin Reickman, of the 24th Infantry Division, maintained that fellow combat veterans are "the only ones who understand the feelings, fear and emotions that I went through." By contrast, those who have never had to experience that sort of mortal danger will forever be outside the circle. Robert LaChausee, a lead scout in the 38th Infantry Division, stated simply that those who had not seen combat simply don't understand and never will.

How does a man who has truly faced his own mortality at an early age communicate what that was like to someone who has never had to do so? The answer of most combat veterans is that they do not. The outsider can listen to the words, but he or she can never really feel the emotions, and it is the emotions generated by combat experiences that stay with most combat soldiers forever.

It is deeply satisfying to those in the brotherhood to encounter another combat man, someone who understands. Harry Arnold described the satisfaction of sharing experiences with another veteran:

> Some of my most pleasurable moments over the years have been at those rare times when I was able to trade combat experiences with other combat men. All that is required is that the other fellow know what the hell you are talking about and what he is talking about, and that there is enough beer to keep the voice box reasonably damp and the stories flowing.

George Boocks, of the 5th Engineer Special Brigade, which came ashore at Normandy, was moved to write:

> Our outfit was made up of boys from all over the states. From New England to California, from Michigan to Florida. I found that outside of regional accents, for the most part they were much the same, with the same hopes, fears, and longings. Sharing the same problems day after day, some of us became very close, like family.

Near the end of the war when a trickle of blacks was allowed to join combat outfits, combat correspondent Ralph Martin was surprised to see black and white soldiers sharing fellowship. One soldier told Martin: "The front is a great leveling force. There's a great deal more actual democracy up there than in garrisons back in the States, where people have time to get into arguments about things like seating arrangements on buses." A black soldier with whom Martin spoke had become close with white soldiers, which affected his outlook on race relations:

> When I was being treated for my wounds . . . there was no such thing as white and colored. Everybody was alike. Fighting together and suffering together brings people closer. The white American soldier has learned what artificial barriers of any sort mean and will be just as determined as the colored soldier to do away with them later.

George Wyatt, of the 1st Marine Division, wrote of his fellow marines and the irrelevance of prewar differences:

> We were an ordinary group of men. Our backgrounds were wide ranging and our dispositions varying. Together as a team we formed a common unity. Our differences were set aside and seemed insignificant. All of us did things for each other and made sacrifices without thinking. It was automatic. We banded together and knew our fellow Marine would give the same generous consideration to us.

The result of such teamwork and selflessness was the kind of feeling that John Symanski described. "These men with whom I served . . . are still my best and most important friends. Time and time again, these men put their lives 'on the line' for each other."

James Simms, an Alabamian, recalled being teamed with a man from the Northeast. They became the best of friends:

> Cappaletti was of Italian extraction . . . from a northern city. I was Anglo-Saxon Scotch-Irish from the rural South. I didn't know whether he would be careless, reckless, or any other thing that might not add to our well-being. As it turned out I need not have worried because we went through our combat together without one cross word.

In discussing the brotherhood between combat men, James Simms recounted an excellent example:

One night during a snowstorm a lieutenant came down to our hole shortly after dark. He had a bottle of brandy with him and he said, "I've figured that if each man takes only one good swallow, there will be enough to go around." I think every man would have choked before he would have taken any more than his share. There wasn't enough to do much good . . . but it was the thought that did the most good. The lieutenant could have kept it all for himself and we wouldn't have known the difference.

Jack Thacker, of the 30th Infantry Division, was captured at Normandy. One of his closest buddies was moved to write a letter to Thacker's wife expressing his feelings. "To me Jack was more than a soldier friend. There were few times when either of us made any plans that the other wasn't included in them. He was as close to me as a brother could have been. You have truly a wonderful husband."

Del Kendall, of the 36th Infantry Division, remembered an instance in France when his unit was getting ready to move up to the front again. As he listened to the banter among his buddies, he realized what a tight bond they all had and it warmed his heart. "This was the bond, the glue, that held the combat infantry together. It was young men, new men, and the old men that made it truly a band of brothers."

Conrad Willard, of the 87th Infantry Division, had a similar realization after days of bitter urban combat in which he and his buddies had been worn to a frazzle. He wrote about what the bond of the deadly brotherhood meant to him:

Men, hungry, days without enough food to meet the expenditures their duty demanded of the body, carefully dividing a small piece of bread equally, among four or five buddies, and each man, though the room was ink dark, knowing he'd get his share. To me it was the kind of brotherly love Christ intended for all of us to have at all times.

During the harrowing early days of the Battle of the Bulge, 99th Infantry Division soldier James Revell found himself bound closer to his lieutenant than he ever believed possible. "The lieutenant and

I were no longer lieutenant and sergeant, but just buddies digging like moles. Under those conditions the very depths of a man's heart are opened to you and you keep the trust."

If the sorrow at losing a comrade was deep, so was the joy at discovering that a buddy presumed dead was actually alive. Elturino Loiacono, an armored infantryman in the 10th Armored Division, was separated from his unit during the confusion of the Bulge. He played dead in a foxhole while German soldiers searched his body for souvenirs. Somehow they did not discover that he was alive, and he made it back to his unit, where he received a warm reception. "My sergeant, who was sick with a terrible cold, began to cry, telling me that he thought I had been killed."

The sense of dedication that men had for one another was another aspect of the bond. Richard Trant, of the 5th Marine Division, was slightly wounded during the Battle of Iwo Jima. While aboard a hospital ship, he and two of his fellow marines decided to jump ship to get back to their unit on the front lines:

> Don't think that I am any brave hero who wants to get into combat by jumping ship because I am not one of them and never expect to be. Somehow, though, I couldn't stay aboard ship wondering how Ted, Jerry, and the rest of my buddies were. We finally got to our companies and I really felt good at the reception I got. They all rushed out of their foxholes and hugged me and clasped my hands.

It was not unusual for this to happen. Combat men wanted to be where their frontline family was even if it put them in danger. The bond between fighting soldiers was so deep that most were willing to risk their lives to be with their buddies. As Trant indicated, this attitude did not stem from a desire to be a hero but from a desire to be with your own group and do your part.

It is important to understand that incidents such as Trant's usually occurred when a man was not wounded seriously. Men who were seriously wounded were more than willing to leave the front and recover. It was only when combat troopers' wounds were not serious enough to require evacuation that they felt guilty about being safe while their buddies were fighting. Radford Carroll, of the 99th Infantry Division, witnessed this many times. "Many of the wounded soldiers felt guilty because their buddies were still in danger while they were in the hospital. They would 'escape' from the hospital . . . and make their way back to their 'home.'"

The bond existed in all combat units in all theaters of war. William Ruf, of the 6th Infantry Division, asserted that it had nothing to do with how long a man had been in the unit. "We trained together for two years and were extremely close. This feeling seemed to pass on to the replacements." Emil Matula, of the 25th Infantry Division, had fond memories not of the war but of the brotherhood, which he said was marked by "togetherness and being together as a unit . . . like living with brothers." Newman Phillips said that in combat "there is a bond closer than family or friends. We remain in close contact to this day."

In recalling the deep bonds of comradeship that he felt with his fellow 35th Infantry Division buddies, James Graff wrote that he would never forget the unique feeling of the brotherhood:

> I will always cherish my association with the men in the 3d Platoon. I have made some very lasting friendships. You become close to men whose lives depend on you and yours depends on them. The comradeship of combat overshadows the friendships of a civilian. I am proud to be a member of an elite fraternity, that of the combat infantryman.

The kind of pride and brotherhood that Graff felt was what led 36th Infantry Division soldier Michael Stubinski to sign a letter to one of his buddies "Your combat brother" nearly fifty years after they had been in combat together. In recalling how he felt about the men with whom he fought, 36th Infantry Division combat engineer Jack Scott wrote: "I loved them, tried to fight for them and had unlimited respect for their calm and resolute determination to get the job done." The same bond existed for Richard Fedderson and his buddies in the 41st Infantry Division in the Pacific. "We were a band of brothers, like a family."

Glen Main, of the 70th Infantry Division, explained why this family-like bond developed among men at the front. "When you're . . . on the front line, you know your buddies. You know the other men in your company better than their wives even know them. You know how they're going to act because your life depends upon their actions."

When men found out that they could depend on one another when their very lives were at stake, the trust forged between them was boundless. Chuck Storeby, of the 101st Airborne Division, attempted to explain the depth of this trust for his comrades. "The men I served with I'd trust today . . . with my life. I would give them any amount of money they asked for."

The searing experiences of combat revealed the true measure of a soldier's character. At the front you could not fool anyone. There was no time for phoniness or for anyone who did not do his share. Those who did not have what it took to live up to their responsibilities to the group were quickly weeded out. The majority, who did have what it took, went on existing each day doing their share and looking out for their buddies.

After training and fighting for years with the 6th Cavalry Regiment, Robert Seabrook summed up the bond and the brotherhood that he experienced:

> When a young man has spent five years with the same regiment it becomes like a second family. Soldiering with the other men, eating, sleeping, training with them in all kinds of weather, sharing bad and good times together, and then finally going through combat with them, they become like brothers and a deep bond develops.

Al Metcalf expressed what the deadly brotherhood was all about in speaking of his 8th Armored Division comrades. "The quality of men that we had were as good as you could get. We were a cross section of a nation. We had college men, farmers, would-be doctors, mechanics, everything. We had men from every walk of life. And we had a very definite purpose. It was like a family."

The brotherhood's crucial importance was described by Clarence Stoeckley, of the 27th Infantry Division:

> It would be difficult for any outsider to understand that the experiences we shared borders almost on a sacred bond. We

understand and feel this bond between us to be as strong or possibly even stronger than that amongst siblings. We know we are here not only by "the Grace of God," but also because we depended on and trusted each other, and no one let us down.

So it was for most American combat soldiers in World War II. They came from every conceivable background and region, but in combat none of that really mattered. They learned to depend on their comrades and they were motivated to fight by the love, respect, and regard they had for those soldiers around them.

There were two things that were unthinkable to combat men— letting your buddies down and appearing cowardly in front of others. Along the way, many combat soldiers were able to perform feats that they probably never thought possible.

As often as not there was little choice for the American fighting men in World War II. Doomed to fight until they were killed, wounded, or captured or until they broke down mentally, they had little other option than to lean on one another to endure and win the most destructive, bloody war in history. Sharing misery and danger brought men together and was a major reason for the existence of the brotherhood. But in a larger sense, the brotherhood grew out of the shared experience of war, not just the bad but also the good. Combat men shared mutual fear and tension in difficult times, but they also shared laughter in times of joy and fellowship in times of boredom. Like it or not, they were all in it together. This promoted trust, equality, and the kind of fierce loyalty and pride that led to excellent fighting soldiers.

Although they hated the war and would never wish to repeat it, most World War II combat veterans cherish the unique feeling of the deadly brotherhood they once shared with other Americans. Clearly this brotherhood was the centerpiece of their soul. In all probability, even today the memory of the brotherhood reminds combat veterans that amid the hatred and depravity of total war, they found in themselves the capacity for selflessness, trust, and love. Ironically enough, it may have been just such a capacity for these peaceful qualities that was the greatest reason they won the war and survived to tell about it.

A few days before he was killed in action in Normandy, Lt. William Maher wrote home to his parents to communicate what he thought would be the unforgettable legacy of combat for all those Americans who experienced it. "This experience will leave its stamp on every one of our men who survive it." Even though Maher himself did not live to find out the truth of his statement, the vast majority of combat veterans did. For those combat men who survived, the war left an indelible impression on them. In assessing their wartime service, some swell with pride. Others attribute to it personal growth that would not have happened otherwise. Although some wish to forget the war altogether, most cannot. It is buried too deep in their memories and was far too significant an experience in their lives to be forgotten.

The young, vigorous men who fought the ground war on behalf of the United States in World War II have left their youth far behind. The World War II generation has gone from young adulthood to middle age to old age. William Manchester, who fought with the marines on Okinawa, wrote that, decades after the war, he frequently had dreams that included his two selves—the old man of the present and the young, lean, hard-bitten marine of the past. In his dream he would see the two figures trudging up a hill:

> One, wearing muddy battle dungarees and the camouflage helmet cover that we wore to distinguish us from army infantrymen, was the scrawny Atabrine yellow, cocky young Sergeant of Marines who had borne my name in 1945. The

other was the portly, balding, Brooks-Brothered man who bears it today.

The inevitable passage of time has taken its toll on the ranks of those who fought the war. Third Infantry Division veteran Victor Wade wrote in the conclusion of his war memoir: "We who were the laughing youths of yesterday no longer feel the blood singing in our veins. The newsprint is smaller than it used to be; the hills and steps are steeper now. The aches and pains are more frequent. The easy chair is more inviting." Many veterans have died; some are in such frail health that the troubled physical existence that Wade described would be welcomed as an improvement.

For some, such as 11th Airborne Division paratrooper George Lorio, there will always be pride at having been a combat infantryman. "While there were many times of exhaustion, fear and heartache at the loss of comrades in combat, I am, in the end, so very proud 'to have been there.'" Richard Talley, of the 36th Infantry Division, also is proud at having done his part in combat. "Anybody who put his life on the line in combat did a hell of a lot. It doesn't matter whether he gets hit or whether he gets a medal. A combat soldier is symbolic of all that's great about the USA."

For most combat veterans the pride exists but is unspoken. They wonder why they survived the war while so many of their buddies died. Ray Wells, who like Talley served in the 36th Division, posed a question asked by many survivors. "Why were we the living allowed to come back; how were we chosen to continue with our lives when so many others made the extreme sacrifice and lie in those cemeteries row upon row of crosses, so far away?"

There is never a definitive answer. David Laing, of the 84th Infantry Division, told himself that there must be a purpose for being spared. "The thing I will not be able to understand is why I was allowed to live . . . and others died. I like to think my God has a purpose and duty that is not carried out." Said John Stenger, of the 104th Infantry Division, "Like most combat infantry veterans I have a vague sense of 'survivor's guilt.' I feel that I should have been braver and that I should be ashamed for those moments when I felt cowardly." Like many emotions generated by their combat experiences, the guilt comes and goes for most men. Perhaps what they are really playing out in their minds is not guilt but grief and sorrow that their dead buddies could not have lived and enjoyed long, productive lives as well.

Combat often left psychological damage. James Simms, who fought at Bastogne with the 101st Airborne Division, experienced a nervous tic for a time after the war. "I developed a tic that would cause my eye to wink. Then a place somewhere else on my body would quiver, then another place, and so on." In time the tic went away, never to return. Years after the war, George Wheeler, of the 8th Armored Division, still could not stand the sound of a jackhammer. "When I'd walk down the street and heard a jackhammer start up, I'd duck into a doorway. A jackhammer does sound very much like a fifty caliber [machine gun]." For Ferdinand Huber, of the 99th Infantry Division, the psychological damage was far more serious. It was more than a decade before he could return to any semblance of normality. "Nothing seemed to work out well for me. In retrospect it was my own fault, as I should have had full control over it, but I did not realize it at the time. It took a good 15 years to become levelheaded again. Any discussion about my war years caused me to shake all over."

Some survivors kept their psyches intact by forcefully repressing any memories of the war, as 8th Armored Division veteran Dick Peters found out one day after the war when he attempted to visit a buddy. The man refused to see Peters, not out of personal animosity but because he did not want to dredge up unpleasant memories. "He said, 'Dick . . . I have no pleasant memories of the war and when the war was over it was over. I wanted to completely disassociate myself with the war and the people.'"

Howard Ruppel, a paratrooper in the 517th Parachute Infantry Regiment, wanted nothing to do with anyone or anything about the war. He refused to join veteran organizations in an effort to forget the war:

> I didn't want to rehash, refight, relive, recreate images, or relive memories in a social atmosphere. I sought no recognition or special attention. I didn't want to be thought of as a

hero. I didn't want my past life to interfere with my future life. I wanted to get on with living, in the manner I chose.

Most survivors have no desire to leave their experiences behind them in such fashion. Indeed, even if they did, most could not forget combat completely. Bart Hagerman, who served with the 17th Airborne Division in the Battle of the Bulge, articulated the sense that in some ways the war never really ended:

> Every time it snows . . . I'll think about those days during the Bulge. It brings back memories of the friends that I lost and the desperate feeling that we had in those days, and it kind of irks me that, after 50 years, I still think that way. I should forget it and go on about my life, but I guess it made such an impression. It'll always be with me I guess.

Most veterans, such as 90th Infantry Division veteran Willie Green, are powerless to expunge the memories from their minds. "It was a horrid experience branded in my memory never to be erased."

Eldon Jacobsen, of the 97th Infantry Division, cited these reasons for that:

> The life and death aspect of combat has made a lifelong impression on me. It did make other situations in life seem insignificant. The initial instance of combat was an experience that will be remembered for a lifetime. The relationship built up with members of our unit will be meaningful for a lifetime.

As Jacobsen hinted, combat was unforgettable partly because surviving it gave a man the sense that the rest of his life was somewhat anticlimactic. No matter how difficult life may have gotten since World War II for some combat men, they know that they have probably survived the worst.

Harry Arnold, of the 99th Infantry Division, explained it this way:

> We have a certain affliction which ordains that each day, for the rest of our lives, we remember some part of these experi-

ences. Why? I suppose it's awfully complex but the fact remains, we can't 'not remember.' Even those who decline to discuss such things, I know that they remember each day too! All young men who experience significant combat . . . face a future of constant anticlimax, for all else pales by contrast. We spend the rest of our lives in our assumed roles, quite normally, but the Real Play has ended.

Ed Stewart, who served with the 84th Infantry Division in Europe, also experienced this sense of anticlimax in the postwar years. For him the war is always present. "It doesn't go away. It sleeps sometimes, but then it awakens again. Things are happening, people are doing things that you never dreamed you'd ever see or hear about. It's an enormity of an experience, and everything after that has been a footnote."

W. E. Brewer, who fought with the 41st Infantry Division, talked about how combat fostered personal growth. Because of the war he "grew up real fast. I had a lot more understanding and greater respect for freedom." Harold Wells, of the 45th Infantry Division, claimed that his frontline experience "was probably the most important happening of my life. It changed my concept of the limits I placed on my life. I aspired for better things for me and my family." Glenn Searles, of the 77th Infantry Division, felt that because he functioned and survived in combat, he developed an inner strength that has lasted his entire life and served him well in many situations.

Debs Myers, a combat correspondent, described the arduous journey taken by the American combat soldier in World War II:

> He learned how to sleep in the mud, tie a knot, kill a man. He learned the ache of loneliness, the ache of exhaustion, the kinship of misery. From the beginning he wanted to go home. He learned . . . that every man is alike and that each man is different. Maybe he was white or black or yellow or red . . . on the line it didn't make much difference. He was often bored; he wasn't always brave; most times he was scared. Maybe he's just a memory in a photo album now, or a dog tag stuck on a cross of wood near a tiny town whose name you can't pronounce.

George Wyatt, of the 1st Marine Division, articulated the legacy of combat for the survivors, the lucky ones who did not end up as a "dog tag stuck on a cross of wood." To them the war will always be viewed in light of the rest of their lives:

> We were sent in as killing machines but unlike the weapons we used, we could think and feel. We laughed and cried and felt pain and hunger. We knew fear as no man should ever have to. The things we saw and the things we did were to give us a lifetime of nightmares and guilt. Each of us, the survivors, will have to deal with our experiences in our own way.

Sometime after the bloody Okinawa campaign, a young marine named Riddick Kelley sat down to write a letter home. He sought to make his mother understand something of what he had just been through and the way he felt about the men with whom he had fought. "Never was there a finer group of men anywhere in the whole world. The hardships, suffering and heroic acts these men committed are much too numerous and unbelievable to ever be recorded, but as long as I live, their names and valorous deeds will be imbedded in a memory that's not soon forgotten."

Such is the legacy of the American combat soldier in World War II. Tens of thousands of ordinary Americans, children of a democracy, put aside their individual hopes and dreams and fought and died for one another and, by extension, their country. Underestimated by their enemies, they proved in the end to be superior fighting men.

For those American combat soldiers who survived, the war would never really end. Everywhere they went and in everything they did, it shaped them and influenced their perspective. The deadly brotherhood they forged in the life-and-death world of combat made them good soldiers; but in a larger sense, it was their gift to one another, their reward for enduring an experience that was both horrifying and defining.

The American combat soldier was truly brave but not in the classic definition of the word. He did not abound with courage and fling himself recklessly into combat for the romance of a great cause. Instead he performed as only a modern warrior can. He endured. In view of the enormity of the destruction and bloodshed as well as the efficiency and ruthlessness of the enemies he faced, combat in World War II was probably more deadly and frightening than in any other American war up to that time. The fact that the American soldier daily shouldered his weapon, carried out a deadly job, and won a monumental victory makes him not only indisputably brave but also a classic example of an industrial-age warrior. For in the modern age of mass war, being brave did not have much to do with individual courage and skill—there was little that a single motivated soldier could accomplish. Rather in the modern age, being brave meant having collective courage as a team, a deadly brotherhood. Drawing from one another's determination and courage, American combat soldiers daily demonstrated this modern form of bravery, a "team heroism" that harvested enormous success. This is the legacy of the American combat soldier in World War II.

NOTES

Introduction

As I wrote, Howard Ruppel, unpublished memoir, p.1, World War II Veterans Project, Special Collections, University of Tennessee, Knoxville, MS1892, Box 8, Folder 4 (hereafter referred to as SCUTK).

Out of all the men, Richard Roush, *Bulge Bugle* (August 1990), p. 20.

confusion is still the god of war, Frank Barnett to parents, 8 July 1945, Collection Number 68, University of Missouri-Columbia (hereafter referred to as WHMC).

They were not, James Simms, unpublished memoir, dedication page, MS1881, Box 26, Folder 1, SCUTK.

My Son, Excerpted from *The Story of the 310th Infantry Regiment, 78th Infantry Division in the War Against Germany, 1942–1945,* pp. 8–9, self-published.

Chapter 1

This was not true, For an excellent breakdown on the makeup of American combat divisions, see Shelby Stanton's *World War II Order of Battle* (New York: Galahad Books, 1984).

One study found, Samuel A. Stouffer, *The American Soldier: Studies in Social Psychology in World War II, Combat and its Aftermath,* No. 2 (New York: John Wiley and Sons, 1949), p. 102.

Troops from these outfits, Robert Palmer, Bell I. Wiley, and William R. Keast, *The United States Army in World War II: Procurement and Training of Ground Combat Troops,* No. 2 (Washington, D.C.: Historical Division, Department of the Army, 1948), p. 49.

They were a clear minority, Kent Roberts Greenfield, Robert Palmer, and Bell I. Wiley, *United States Army in World War II: The Organization of Ground Combat Troops,* No. 2 (Washington, D.C., Historical Division, Department of the Army, 1947), p. 170.

This is because, For an excellent breakdown of the number of fighting troops within each American combat division, see I. C. B. Dear and M. R. D. Foot, ed., *The Oxford Companion to World War II* (Oxford: Oxford University Press, 1995), pp. 388–89.

Historian Lee Kennett, Lee Kennett, *GI: The American Soldier in World War II* (New York: Warner Books, 1987), p. 95.

I would venture to say, Frank Nisi to father, 23 June 1945, WHMC.

The front lines soldier, Roland Lea, World War II Questionnaire #3360, United States Army Military History Institute, Carlisle Barracks, Pennsylvania. (Hereafter referred to as USAMHI.)

parasites from the quartermaster battalions, Brendan Phibbs, *The Other Side of Time: A Combat Surgeon in World War II* (Boston: Little, Brown and Company, 1987), p. 16.

A typical American, Stanton, *Order of Battle,* p. 52.

Also, it was common, Dear, *Oxford Companion,* p. 1101.

Armored infantry units, James McDonald interview with Dr. Charles W. Johnson, 8 August 1987, SCUTK.

The airborne and cavalry, Stanton, *Order of Battle.*

The Infantry walks, Radford Carroll, unpublished memoir, p. 6, SCUTK.

At full strength, David Williams, unpublished memoir, p. 18, SCUTK, MS1892, Box 12, Folder 9. Also see Dear, *Oxford Companion,* for the official numbers on the makeup of a U.S. infantry company. The numbers are virtually identical to Williams's figures.

The 517th Combat Team, Ruppel, unpublished memoir, p. 20.

had a rotation system, Lloyd Pye, *Ex-CBI Roundup* (October 1992), p. 16.

The army did make, Leonard Kjelstrom, World War II Questionnaire #2502, USAMHI.

In the Army Air Force, Carroll, unpublished memoir, p. 76, SCUTK.

The test consisted of, Kennett, *GI,* p. 35.

Class I had a score, Palmer, *Procurement and Training,* pp. 15–17.

It was also common knowledge, Kennett, *GI,* p. 35.

The consensus among army leadership, J. Acheson Duncan, "Some Comments on the AGCT." *Journal of Applied Psychology* 31 (April 1947), pp. 143–49.

Thus, blacks were, Kennett, *GI,* p. 35.

and a whopping, Palmer, *Procurement and Training,* p. 17.

This meant simply, Palmer, *Procurement and Training,* pp. 23–39.

I think we resented it, Irwin Shapiro, interview with Dr. Charles W. Johnson, 23 September 1995, SCUTK.

the ASTP was, Henri Atkins, unpublished memoir, p. 4, SCUTK.

In addition, Geoffrey Perret, *There's a War to Be Won: The United States Army in World War II* (New York: Random House, 1991), pp. 373–74.

Instead they received, Francis Steckel, *Morale and Men: A Study of the American Soldier in World War II,* unpublished dissertation, p. 70. Steckel shows that close to 90 percent of U.S. Army officers received their commissions in one of the following ways: officer candidate school, Aviation Cadets, ROTC, and directly from the enlisted ranks.

Even those who, "The People of the U.S.A.—a self portrait." *Fortune* 21 (February 1940), pp. 14, 20, 28, 133, 136, 138.

In our entire, Curtis Whiteway, Answers to "Questions for Veterans," p. 3, MS1892, Box 12, Folder 7, SCUTK.

It's a shame, Garland Godby, interview with the author, 22 August 1995, SCUTK.

Chapter 2

Our cooks really keep, Beauford George to Ms. Kleeman, 15 January 1945, WHMC.

Our cooks were great, Bert Morphis, *Bulge Bugle* (August 1990), p. 21.

Headquarters would try, Henri Atkins, unpublished memoir, pp. 44–45, SCUTK.

Some time after dark, Charles Miller, *Bulge Bugle,* (February 1991), p. 20.

If conditions were favorable, Lawrence Nickell, unpublished memoir, p. 37, SCUTK.

In the middle of the night, Ferdinand Huber, unpublished memoir, p. 17, SCUTK.

We didn't carry, David Williams, unpublished memoir, p. 24, SCUTK.

Just as we were getting famished, Earl Reitan, unpublished memoir, p. 16, MS1764, Box 17, Folder 16, SCUTK.

In the evening, John Roche, unpublished memoir, p. 73, MS1881, Box 20, Folder 11, SCUTK.

At Company C, Frank Miller, *Fighting 36th Historical Quarterly* (Spring 1989), p. 42.

Mess Sgt's are noted, Harry Arnold, *Easy Memories,* unpublished memoir, p. 57, MS1764, Box 4, Folder 2, SCUTK.

C rations were two cans, Williams Meissner, unpublished memoir, p. 19, MS1881, Box 18, Folder 18, SCUTK.

We would break open, John Lane, unpublished memoir, p. 66, MS1298, Box 3, Folder 29, SCUTK.

A case of C rations, Paul Swenson, unpublished memoir, p. 1, MS1608, Box 15, Folder 44, SCUTK.

Most of our rations, Carlie Berryhill, World War II Questionnaire #4014, USAMHI.

On New Guinea, Frank Caudillo, World War II Questionnaire #7423, USAMHI.

C rations were terrible, Salvatore Lamagna and Francis Stone, World War II Questionnaires #2234 and 7390, USAMHI.

Tanker Tom Wood, World War II Questionnaire #550, USAMHI.

You'd eat a can, Evan Voss, *Fighting 36th Historical Quarterly* (Fall 1987), p. 12.

We hated them, Charles Henne, World War II Questionnaire, USAMHI.

After continual griping, The Railsplitter (8 May 1945), p. 4.

It was a little frightening, Harry F. Martin, *The Purple Heart Magazine* (July–August 1992), p. 20.

These K rations, Lathrop Mitchell, diary, p. 29, MS1881, Box 18, Folder 24, SCUTK.

The K rations, Denis Huston, unpublished memoir, pp. 3–4, SCUTK.

The American GI, Max Kocour, unpublished memoir, p. 26, SCUTK.

By burning the containers, Easy Memories, p. 54, SCUTK.

There were two advantages, Carroll, unpublished memoir, p. 20, SCUTK.

Food isn't nearly, Yank (11 February 1944).

the K ration in combat, Murphy Simoneaux and Phillip Jewett, World War II Questionnaires #592 and 7559, USAMHI.

I broke open, James Simms, unpublished memoir, p. 44, SCUTK.

It was quiet, Boyd Miller, *The Twenty-Niner Newsletter* (July 1995), p. 42.

Most GIs did not like, Edward Laughlin, unpublished memoir, p. 19, MS1892, Box 6, Folders 11, 12, SCUTK.

usually the K variety, Easy Memories, p. 54, SCUTK.

There was an even bulkier, Carroll, unpublished memoir, p. 20, SCUTK.

Unfortunately it was bulky, Nickell, unpublished memoir, p. 37, SCUTK.

We received the rations, Colin McLaurin, *The Twenty-Niner Newsletter* (November 1995), p. 12.

We envied the tankers, Howard Gaertner, unpublished memoir, p. 6, USAMHI.

a very hard chocolate, Nickell, unpublished memoir, p. 37, SCUTK.

On a long patrol, Ray Poynter, World War II Questionnaire #7223, USAMHI.

It was powerful stuff, Swenson, unpublished memoir, p. 1, SCUTK.

Like the present day, Jack Thacker, unpublished memoir, p. 12, MS1764, Box 18, Folder 10, SCUTK.

Donald Dencker, World War II Questionnaire #2876, USAMHI.

You should keep from, Yank (11 February 1944), p. 1.

drinking water, Colin McLaurin, *The Twenty-Niner Newsletter* (November 1995), p. 12.

water discipline, Yank (26 May 1944).

Of course, Easy Memories, p. 26, SCUTK.

I think they tried, Thomas Rosell, interview with Dr. Charles W. Johnson, 17 August 1993, SCUTK.

As we went through, William Meissner, unpublished memoir, pp. 19–20, SCUTK.

We outran our rations, Joseph Martin, interview with Dr. Charles W. Johnson, 11 March 1986, SCUTK.

If we went, Riland West, interview with Mrs. Lin Folk, 6 April 1992, SCUTK.

We had to eat, Raymond Jones to mother and father, 6 January 1943, SCUTK.

We'd eat the same, Clarence Daniels, interview with Dr. Charles W. Johnson, 29 August 1984, SCUTK.

rice twice a day, E. L. "Jim" Horton, interview with Dr. Charles W. Johnson, 16 August 1993, SCUTK.

The men grabbed, Harry Martin, *The Purple Heart Magazine* (July–August 1992), p. 19.

The warehouse was full, Earl Reitan, unpublished memoir, pp. 31–32, SCUTK.

We found a half, James Graff, *Reflections of a Combat Infantryman,* unpublished memoir, p. 8, MS1608, Box 11, Folder18, SCUTK.

A couple of cows, Easy Memories, p. 128, SCUTK.

A cow was killed, Dewey Mann, *Fighting 36th Historical Quarterly* (Spring 1991), p. 28.

Getting tired of canned rations, Robert Seabrook, unpublished memoir, p. 25, MS1608, Box 15, Folder 12, SCUTK.

We observed, Easy Memories, p. 62, SCUTK.

Once on Luzon, Frank Caudillo, World War II Questionnaire #7423, USAMHI.

In the beginning, Herman Steenstra, World War II Questionnaire #231, USAMHI.

D bars, K rations, J. R. McIlroy, *The Checkerboard* (September 1992), p. 5.

of course rations, William Eberhart, World War II Questionnaire #2271, USAMHI.

I had an initial, Laughlin, unpublished memoir, p. 31, SCUTK.

would have been pleased, Eugene Schermerhorn and Donald Vanhooser, World War II Questionnaires #2149 and 2166, USAMHI.

Combat boots, Seabrook, unpublished memoir, p. 32, SCUTK.

ootwear was very poor, Cecil Roberts, David Harrison, Charles Harbold, and Walter Richardson, World War II Questionnaires, USAMHI.

The men want boots, Pete Kelley, *Yank* (18 February 1945).

the bootpacks froze, James McKnight, World War II Questionnaire #2888, USAMHI.

I think they dropped, Simms, unpublished memoir, p. 83, SCUTK.

The boots were canvas, Herchel McFadden, John Drugan, and Salvatore Lamagna Questionnaires, USAMHI.

We wouldn't wear, Lester Clear, World War II Questionnaire #271, USAMHI.

Only the replacements, J. R. McIlroy, *The Checkerboard* (September 1992), p. 5.

Always too tight, Laughlin, unpublished memoir, p. 28, SCUTK.

We would ditch them, Easy Memories, p. 41, SCUTK.

The helmet, Nickell, unpublished memoir, p. 35, SCUTK.

The helmet was not really, Huber, unpublished memoir, p. 9, SCUTK.

If you ever wore, Henne Questionnaire, USAMHI.

In Europe, Rosell interview, SCUTK.

We were issued, Charles Murphy, interview with Dr. Charles W. Johnson, 13 April 1993, SCUTK.

That winter I wore, John McAuliffe, *Bulge Bugle* (February 1993), p. 19.

Our clothing, Lawrence Butler, World War II Questionnaire #588, USAMHI.

Most of the infantrymen, Pete Kelley, *Yank* (18 February 1945).

I don't believe, Leonard Stein, Robert LaChausee, Daniel Chomiw, and Robert Teeples, World War II Questionnaires, USAMHI.

It was powered, Dear, *Oxford Companion,* p. 1101. Also see Peter Young, ed., *The World Almanac of World War II* (New York: Bison Books, 1981), p. 397.

75mm on the M4, Butler Questionnaire, USAMHI.

They were very, Raymond Janus, Henry Brown, Glen Alford, and Eugene Thibideau, World War II Questionnaires, USAMHI.

The machine guns, Oxford Companion, p. 1101, and *World Almanac,* pp. 399–400.

In Luxembourg, Godby, interview with the author, SCUTK.

It was an impressive, Easy Memories, p. 208, SCUTK.

It consisted of a short, Nickell, unpublished memoir, p. 87, SCUTK.

the 60mm mortar shell, Henne and Robert Manning, World War II Questionnaires, USAMHI.

The 81mm, World Almanac, p. 377.

Sometimes an 81mm shell, Henne and Donald MacLeod, World War II Questionnaires, USAMHI.

The 81s break, Rex Whitehead, *The Checkerboard* (December 1991), p. 8.

It probably was not as good, Oxford Companion, p. 953.

blow a hole, Gene Curry, unpublished memoir, p. 31, MS1608, Box 1, Folder 17, SCUTK.

One had to wear, Donald Greener, World War II Questionnaire #426, USAMHI.

Snipers really looked, Charlie Burchett, interview with the author, 6 March 1995, SCUTK.

The flamethrower consisted, Laughlin, unpublished memoir, pp. 39–41, SCUTK.

The most commonly used, Oxford Companion, p. 1016, and *World Almanac,* p. 369.

the most valuable thing, Yank (26 May 1944).

I captured a German, Michael Stubinski, unpublished memoir, p. 3, MS1881, Box 28, Folder 19, SCUTK.

The grenades were launched, Carroll, unpublished memoir, p. 23, SCUTK.

At 31 pounds, Oxford Companion, p. 1016, and *World Almanac,* p. 366.

I was a machine gunner, Thomas Yochim and James McKnight, World War II Questionnaires #4745 and 2888, USAMHI.

A machine gun, Colin McLaurin, *The Twenty-Niner Newsletter* (July 1995), p. 9.

I can remember, Rosell interview, SCUTK.

It was a little heavy, Oxford Companion, p. 1016.

no good in the field, Robert Peck, Ivan Sheperd, William Wheeler, and Ralph Schmidt, World War II Questionnaires, USAMHI.

It only let me down, Richard Talley, *Fighting 36th Historical Quarterly* (Winter 1987), pp. 42–44.

The M3, Carroll, unpublished memoir, p. 48, SCUTK.

It had such a low, Godby interview, SCUTK.

At about 20 feet, Horace Leach, *Ex-CBI Roundup* (December 1992), p. 25.

My M3 jammed, Walter Powell, World War II Questionnaire # 2325, USAMHI.

I didn't like, Richard Lovett, World War II Questionnaire #1293, USAMHI.

I was very happy, Herb Miller, interview with Dr. Charles W. Johnson, 8 August 1987, SCUTK.

I carried a carbine, Melvin Coobs, World War II Questionnaire #2403, USAMHI.

It took, World Almanac, p. 362, and *Oxford Companion,* p. 1016.

We've never yet, Yank (26 May 1944).

The BAR, William Allen, interview with the author, 16 February 1994, SCUTK.

You used it, Godby interview, SCUTK.

it wouldn't fire, Jack Hartzog and Richard Durkee, World War II Questionnaires #2581 and 6278, USAMHI.

We had a BAR, Pete Opengari, *Fighting 36th Historical Quarterly* (Spring 1992), p. 30.

We thawed them out, Yank (18 February 1945).

It was loaded, Carroll, unpublished memoir, p. 9, SCUTK.

The German rifleman, Curry, unpublished memoir, p. 41, SCUTK.

During an encounter, Sidney Richess, unpublished memoir, p. 10, USAMHI.

It would fire, Robert Russell, interview with Dr. Charles W. Johnson, 19 January 1990, SCUTK.

The greatest fault, Thomas Yochim, Charles Brennan, John Margreiter, and Newman Phillips, World War II Questionnaires, USAMHI.

Chapter 3

The weather over here, Don Mackerer to Mrs. Blair, 17 November 1944, MS1881, Box 16, Folder 1, SCUTK.

The severity of the winter, H. McKinley Conway and Linda Liston, ed., *The Weather Handbook: A Summary of Weather Statistics* (Atlanta: Conway Research, Inc., 1974), pp. 190–91.

What gets you, Godby interview, SCUTK.

in a war, Ken Weaver to mother, April 1945, WHMC.

The rain pinged, Sydney Kessler, *That Which Was Once a War: Fragments of Three Seasons,* "The Epoch," Cornell University, 1963, pp. 16–17.

A night of misery, Easy Memories, pp. 92, 105, SCUTK.

The water was so cold, Huber, unpublished memoir, p. 10, SCUTK.

I often wonder, Jason Byrd, interview with the author, SCUTK.

I wonder sometimes, Brice Jordan to wife, 26 May 1945, MS1881, Box 13, Folder 20, SCUTK.

I made the mistake, Victor Wade, unpublished memoir, p. 6, MS1881, Box 31, Folder 17, SCUTK.

I think everyone's, Bert Morphis, *Bulge Bugle* (August 1990), p. 21.

Simple walking, Ruppel, unpublished memoir, p. 36, SCUTK.

We made heaters, Henri Atkins, unpublished memoir, p. 48, SCUTK.

One of the things, Ed Stewart, quoted in the documentary "The American Experience: The Battle of the Bulge." Public Broadcasting System, 9 November 1994.

No matter how, J. R. McIlroy, *The Checkerboard* (September 1992), p. 5.

Snow sifted, Carroll, unpublished memoir, p. 51, SCUTK.

If the deep snow, Easy Memories, p. 52, SCUTK.

About the most, Simms, unpublished memoir, pp. 112–13, SCUTK.

only two battle casualties, Walter Gentry to family, 25 January 1945, MS1259, Box 4, Folder 3, SCUTK.

If you didn't get, Bart Hagerman and Jim Foster, "The American Experience."

Trench foot is NOT, Kenny Dallas to parents, 23 June 1945, WHMC.

My feet had been, Laughlin, unpublished memoir, p. 64, SCUTK.

My feet were frozen, Dan Ray, *Fighting 36th Historical Quarterly* (Winter 1987), p. 20.

Many of our, Evan Voss, *Fighting 36th Historical Quarterly* (Fall 1987), p. 10.

We had been warned, Seabrook, unpublished memoir, p. 23, SCUTK.

All of us, Atkins, unpublished memoir, pp. 45–46, SCUTK.

A Boston guy, Bob Conroy, "The American Experience."

We ran out, Murphy interview, SCUTK.

Pitcock complained, Graff, unpublished memoir, p. 57, SCUTK.

Then misery took over, Francis Lambert, *The Ivy Leaves: Official Publication of the National 4th Infantry Division Association* (June 1994), p. 38.

I hadn't washed, Bob Wandesforde, *Bulge Bugle* (June 1990), p. 18.

mud was in everything, Dallas to parents, WHMC.

You ate in mud, Gene Tippins, unpublished memoir, p. 18, SCUTK.

Our feet, Thibideau Questionnaire, USAMHI.

The going, Nickell, unpublished memoir, p. 68, SCUTK.

On through the dark, Easy Memories, p. 41, SCUTK.

It was pitch black, Justin Gray, *Yank* (29 December 1944), p. 11.

On the war front, Meissner, unpublished memoir, p. 19, SCUTK.

They were stone walls, Nickell, unpublished memoir, p. 25, SCUTK.

You have a hillock, Murphy interview, SCUTK.

most of them, Colin McLaurin, *The Twenty-Niner Newsletter* (November 1995), p. 14.

I vividly recall, Jack Brugh, unpublished memoir, p. 2, MS1881, Box 2, Folder 10, SCUTK.

under combat conditions, Douglas Smith to family, 30 October 1944, WHMC.

Fresh snow, Ruppel, unpublished memoir, p. 36, SCUTK.

Our two-man hole, Evan Voss, *Fighting 36th Historical Quarterly* (Fall 1987), p. 11.

Weary and worn, Zane Schlemmer, *Belgian-American Association Newsletter* (December 1994), p. 4.

Everyone began to dig, Carroll, unpublished memoir, p. 33, SCUTK.

It was bitterly cold, Bert Morphis, *Bulge Bugle* (August 1990), p. 21.

Our foxhole, Franklin O. Bland to family, 29 January 1945, WHMC.

These damn holes, William N. Maher to mother and father, 1 July 1944, WHMC.

In one break, Mack Morriss, *Yank* (24 December 1944), p. 1.

The nerve racking, Byrd interview, SCUTK.

I worked with cleaning, J. D. Jones, interview with Dr. Charles W. Johnson, 27 October 1989, SCUTK.

wooden boxes, Graff, unpublished memoir, p. 31, SCUTK.

It had three prongs, Byrd interview, SCUTK. For more on German mines, see *Oxford Companion,* p. 752, and U.S. War Department, *Handbook on German Military Forces* (Baton Rouge: Louisiana State University Press, 1990), pp. 486–88.

All of a sudden, Wade, unpublished memoir, p. 6, SCUTK.

The Germans, Atkins, unpublished memoir, p. 52, SCUTK.

Anything that had any, Byrd interview, SCUTK.

Enter a house, Stubinski, unpublished memoir, p. 7, SCUTK.

I felt mother nature, Milton Landry, *Fighting 36th Historical Quarterly* (Spring 1992), p. 8.

Just after dark, Carroll, unpublished memoir, p. 42, SCUTK.

even when nature called, Evan Voss, *Fighting 36th Historical Quarterly* (Fall 1987), p. 12.

We learned to tend, Jones interview, SCUTK.

If caught short, Donald MacDonald, World War II Questionnaire #5926, USAMHI.

God bless the USA, Max Kocour, unpublished memoir, p. 26, SCUTK.

We lined them up, Steven Sally, interview with Dr. Charles W. Johnson, 28 November 1989, SCUTK.

We were baffled, Nickell, unpublished memoir, p. 58, SCUTK.

One day I saw, Curry, unpublished memoir, p. 10, SCUTK.

At that time, Don Mackerer, interview with Dr. Charles W. Johnson, 1 February 1991, SCUTK.

We knew, Byrd interview, SCUTK.

They were in formal, Harley Reynolds, unpublished memoir, pp. 21–22, SCUTK.

She said she, Edgar Wilson, speech to the Scottish Rite Speakers Club, 15 May 1985, Files of the Center for the Study of War and Society, University of Tennessee (hereafter referred to as CSWS).

That's war, Curry, unpublished memoir, p. 24, SCUTK.

I suspect, Nickell, unpublished memoir, p. 104, SCUTK.

The way we did it, Murphy interview, SCUTK.

When we entered, Carroll, unpublished memoir, p. 65, SCUTK.

Here we were, Kocour, unpublished memoir, p. 7, SCUTK.

the French liked, Meissner, unpublished memoir, p. 16, SCUTK.

The people cheered, John Worthman, unpublished memoir, p. 13, MS1764, Box 20, Folder 3, SCUTK.

If these girls, Alton Pearson, unpublished memoir, p. 11, CSWS.

There was a platter, Robert Garcia, *The Twenty-Niner Newsletter* (November 1995), p. 28.

the townspeople, Roger Garland to wife, 20 September 1944, MS1314, Box 2, Folder 1, SCUTK.

the Belgians were, Easy Memories, p. 13, SCUTK.

She showed me, Walter Mietus, *Belgian-American Newsletter* (December 1994), p. 3.

This old fellow, Jeffie Duty, interview with Mrs. Lin Folk, 25 February 1992, SCUTK.

Some old lady, Mack Morriss, *Yank* (29 October 1944), p. 5.

people were glad, Warren Taney, *Fighting 36th Historical Quarterly* (Spring 1989), p. 78.

it would be difficult, R. K. Doughty, *Fighting 36th Historical Quarterly* (Fall 1989), p. 50.

girls swarmed, Dan Ray, *Fighting 36th Historical Quarterly* (Spring 1991), p. 50.

They are a rough, Mitchell diary, p. 30, SCUTK.

nothing could ever, Mel Cotton, *Powder River Journal* (December 1993), p. 11.

We were in high, Nickell, unpublished memoir, p. 26, SCUTK.

Sad to say it, Tippins, unpublished memoir, p. 1, SCUTK.

Bodies of both, Thacker, unpublished memoir, p. 11, SCUTK.

I am sure, Bob Kay, *The Ivy Leaves* (June 1994), p. 45.

As the snow melted, Laughlin, unpublished memoir, p. 21, SCUTK.

For most of a day, William Warde, unpublished memoir, p. 17, MS1764, Box 19, Folder 1, SCUTK.

The dead, George Boocks, unpublished memoir, p. 19, MS1892, Box 2, Folder 13, SCUTK.

The dead and dying, Worthman, unpublished memoir, pp. 2–3, SCUTK.

I have seen, John Meier to parents, 14 November 1944, WHMC.

a dead German, Stubinski, unpublished memoir, p. 6, SCUTK.

Most were frozen, Bert Morphis, *Bulge Bugle* (August 1990), p. 21.

I knew better, Carroll, unpublished memoir, p. 57, SCUTK.

Now that touches you, Byrd interview, SCUTK.

First thing, Russell interview, SCUTK.

On a rafter, Vic Ciffichiello, interview with Dr. Charles W. Johnson, 8 August 1987, SCUTK.

He finally said, Frank Miller, *Fighting 36th Historical Quarterly* (Spring 1989), p. 45.

They said, Simms, unpublished memoir, p. 62, SCUTK.

our division helped, Don Loth, unpublished memoir, p. 1, MS1881, Box 15, Folder 9, SCUTK.

I didn't have a lot, Curry, unpublished memoir, p. 38, SCUTK.

Emerson and I, Easy Memories, p. 104, SCUTK.

with so many towns, Atkins, unpublished memoir, p. 92, SCUTK.

we would find things, Martin interview, SCUTK.

Quickly canteen cups, Del Kendall, *Fighting 36th Historical Quarterly* (Fall 1982), p. 60.

It tasted good, Harvey Reves, *Fighting 36th Historical Quarterly* (Winter 1989), p. 44.

I soon found, Warde, unpublished memoir, pp. 20–21, SCUTK.

They offered me, Laughlin, unpublished memoir, p. 47, SCUTK.

drinking's just not part, Godby interview, SCUTK.

after crossing, George Polakiewicz, *Battleground Newsletter* (22 February 1994), p. 15.

Carrying a pack board, Nickell, unpublished memoir, p. 91, SCUTK.

Chapter 4

During the exceedingly, The Weather Handbook, pp.198, 208, 213.

the jungle was, William Hoelzel, World War II Questionnaire #5109, USAMHI.

I could compare, George Wyatt, unpublished memoir, p. 6, MS1764, Box 20, Folder 7, SCUTK.

The sun bore down, E. B. Sledge, *With the Old Breed at Peleliu and Okinawa* (Toronto: Bantam Books, 1981), p. 143.

We stopped, John O'Brien, *The Orion Gallivanter* (June 1991), p. 5.

With not a breath, Harry Wiens, unpublished memoir, pp. 137, 150, CSWS.

You would get steamy, Wyatt, unpublished memoir, p. 35, SCUTK.

It was miserable, Harry Swan, *Winds Aloft* (January 1990), p. 21.

the rains became, With the Old Breed, p. 267.

We were constantly, Robert Jackson, unpublished memoir, pp. 23–24, USAMHI.

You couldn't see, Richard Lovett, World War II Questionnaire #1293, USAMHI.

Patrolling in the jungle, Edward Sears, unpublished memoir, p. 2, MS1881, Box 24, Folder 4, SCUTK.

We had lost, Lewis Goodman to parents, September 1945, WHMC.

The mosquitoes, Justin Gray, *Yank* (27 May 1945), p. 4.

the flies grow, Byron Peterson to "people," 25 August 1943, WHMC.

You'd have to take, Burchett interview, SCUTK.

In this garbage, With the Old Breed, pp. 145–46.

As the men, Jackson, unpublished memoir, p. 25, USAMHI.

I heard the damndest, Wiens, unpublished memoir, p. 104, CSWS.

Mud was another, Wyatt, unpublished memoir, p. 10, SCUTK.

The mud was, With the Old Breed, pp. 257–58.

Kunai grass grows, Wyatt, unpublished memoir, p. 6, SCUTK.

The sand on the beach, Ira Hayes, unpublished memoir, p. 4, MS1259, Box 1, Folder 11, SCUTK.

The sand got into, Bill Reed, *Yank* (1 April 1945), p. 1.

It was found, Samuel Milner, *U.S. Army in World War II: Victory in Papua* (Washington, D.C.: Office of the Chief of Military History, Department of the Army, 1957), pp. 223, 323.

Of the 8,580 cases, Frank Hough, Verle Ludwig, and Henry Shaw, *History of U.S. Marine Corps Operations in World War II: Pearl Harbor to Guadalcanal* (Washington, D.C.: Historical Branch, U.S. Marine Corps, 1960), pp. 323, 359.

I guess malaria, Lewis Brown, interview with Dr. Charles W. Johnson, 18 August 1993, SCUTK.

I had malaria, Raymond Jones to mother and father, SCUTK.

Malaria, which had, Wiens, unpublished memoir, p. 142, CSWS.

They would look like, McFadden Questionnaire, USAMHI.

We all contracted, Sears, unpublished memoir, p. 2, SCUTK.

living in the same, Antonio Renna, World War II Questionnaire #5291, USAMHI.

Our feet, Jackson, unpublished memoir, p. 23, USAMHI.

My feet were hurting, Whayland Greene, unpublished memoir, p. 3, MS1881, Box 11, Folder 16, SCUTK.

Keeping feet healthy, Wiens, unpublished memoir, p. 116, CSWS.

If under fire, Leonard Lazarick, World War II Questionnaire #2219, USAMHI.

Wyatt, not daring, Justin Gray, *Yank* (27 May 1945), p. 4.

Anything that moved, Wiens, unpublished memoir, p. 106, CSWS.

This led to, For more on the mass suicides of Japanese civilians, see Haruko Taya Cook's article in *Military History Quarterly* (Summer 1995), pp. 12–19.

It was a bad, Charles Stewart, World War II Questionnaire #5006, USAMHI.

What we found, Charles Lindsay, unpublished memoir, p. 19, MS1881, Box 15, Folder 18, SCUTK.

They must have thought, Glenn Searles, unpublished memoir, pp. 13–16, SCUTK.

As they passed, Lindsay, unpublished memoir, p. 28, SCUTK.

Out of nowhere, Dick Hanley, *Yank* (11 March 1945), p. 8.

There were civilians, Searles, unpublished memoir, p. 10, SCUTK.

They were stacked, Burchett interview, SCUTK.

I saw one, Searles, unpublished memoir, p. 19, SCUTK.

It is difficult, With the Old Breed, pp. 143–45.

The air was always, Wiens, unpublished memoir, p. 136, CSWS.

You did not, John Lane, unpublished memoir, pp. 50, 51, 63, MS1298, Box 3, Folder 29, SCUTK.

A Japanese soldier, Horace Leach, *Ex-CBI Roundup* (December 1992), p. 24.

The sight and smell, Merle Miller, *Yank* (31 March 1944), p. 10.

A Jap laying, Searles, unpublished memoir, p. 23, SCUTK.

The stench, Sears, unpublished memoir, p. 4, SCUTK.

This seems so, Wiens, unpublished memoir, p. 101, CSWS.

The way you extracted, Studs Terkel, *The Good War: An Oral History of World War II* (New York: Pantheon Books, 1984), pp. 62–63.

We benefitted, Wyatt, unpublished memoir, p. 20, SCUTK.

making illicit, Horace Fader, World War II Questionnaire #200, US-AMHI.

They would steal, Burchett interview, SCUTK.

It was great, Jackson, unpublished memoir, p. 27, USAMHI.

The men could see, Dick Hanley, *Yank* (11 March 1945), p. 8.

Everybody wanted, Lane, unpublished memoir, p. 69, SCUTK.

On one occasion, Deane Marks, *Winds Aloft* (January 1990), p. 14.

Chapter 5

He cited, S. L. A. Marshall, *Men Against Fire: The Problem of Command in Future War* (Washington, D.C.: The Infantry Journal Press, 1947), p. 56.

By the most, Roger Spiller, "S. L. A. Marshall and the Ratio of Fire." *Royal United Services Institute* (Winter 1988), p. 68.

In exploring, Marshall claimed to have been in combat in World War I. Saying that he was commissioned directly from the ranks, he also claimed to be the youngest officer (eighteen years old) in the U.S. Army during World War I. On different occasions he said that he commanded anything from a squad to a company in combat in an infantry unit. However, his service record does not substantiate any of his claims. His unit, an engineering outfit, never saw combat. Also, army records show that he was not commissioned until after the war and then only in a port battalion. For more on this, see Harold Leinbaugh, "In Defense of the Infantry," *Checkerboard* (May 1990), and Frederick Smoler, "The Secret of the Soldiers Who Didn't Shoot," *American Heritage* (March 1989). Smoler, a historian, followed in Spiller's footsteps and verified that Marshall's ratio of fire theory was indeed fraudulent.

They say, Dick Peters, interview with the author, 23 September 1995, SCUTK.

scared at first, Robert Knauss, World War II Questionnaire #4127, USAMHI.

I strongly suspect, Laughlin, unpublished memoir, p. 59, SCUTK.

Did the SOB, Quoted in Frederick Smoler, "The Secret of the Soldiers Who Didn't Shoot," *American Heritage,* p. 42.

Weigley, a traditional, Russell F. Weigley, *Eisenhower's Lieutenants: The Campaigns of France and Germany, 1944–45* (Bloomington: University of Indiana Press, 1981), p. 26.

One German criticism, Easy Memories, p. 208, SCUTK.

Although we were, Marvin Reickman, World War II Questionnaire #3493, USAMHI.

if we have to, Newman Phillips, World War II Questionnaire #216, USAMHI.

I think the, Donald Trachta, World War II Questionnaire #352, US-AMHI.

When the order, Melvin Bush to family, c. 1944, WHMC.

Looking back, Jackson, unpublished memoir, p. 26, USAMHI.

After I fired, Laughlin, unpublished memoir, p. 48, SCUTK.

Fire and movement, Michael Doubler, *Closing With the Enemy: How GIs Fought the War in Europe, 1944–45* (Lawrence: The University Press of Kansas, 1994), pp. 266, 304–05. Doubler's book employs many U.S. Army field training manuals and is an excellent study of the way in which American field commanders employed their soldiers against the enemy in Europe.

A point man, Atkins, unpublished memoir, p. 55, SCUTK.

Normally the riflemen, Nickell, unpublished memoir, p. 90, SCUTK.

First heavy, Worthman, unpublished memoir, p. 14, SCUTK.

If we were, Harold Wells, World War II Questionnaire #3832, US-AMHI.

We advanced on foot, West interview, SCUTK.

We were trained, Kocour, unpublished memoir, p. 8, SCUTK.

We'd have a, Edward Piggot, World War II Questionnaire #7178, USAMHI.

you normally, Bartlett Allen, World War II Questionnaire #459, US-AMHI.

We would take up, Clarence Hitchcock and John Jones, World War II Questionnaires #549, 534, USAMHI.

The armored point, Hartson Sexton and Charles Hogg, World War II Questionnaires #2332, 3463, USAMHI.

Men threw ropes, Mack Morriss, *Yank* (24 December 1944), p. 2.

We would follow, Raymond Buch and Robert Gravlin, World War II Questionnaires #7205, 4125, USAMHI.

He wasn't afraid, Byrd interview, SCUTK.

You don't fight, Bill Mauldin, *Up Front* (Toronto: Bantam Books, 1945), pp. 11–13.

Hollywood movies, Wyatt, unpublished memoir, p. 3, SCUTK.

A perimeter, Searles, unpublished memoir, p. 9, SCUTK.

We started out, Frank Caudillo and Emil Lindenbusch, World War II Questionnaires #7423 and 3736, USAMHI.

We were on the move, Leonard Kjellstrom and Bryan Baldwin, World War II Questionnaires #2502 and 7607, USAMHI.

Never take anyone's, Yank (11 February 1944), p. 1.

We would be, Phillips, LaChausee, and McLaughlin Questionnaires, USAMHI.

Most of the time, Melvin Coobs, World War II Questionnaire #2403, USAMHI.

We were an engineer unit, Charles Brennan, World War II Questionnaire #1776, USAMHI.

Sometimes we'd go, Richard Forse, World War II Questionnaire #3173, USAMHI.

tanks were useless, Carlie Berryhill, Robert Klenk, Leonard Stein, and Bryan Baldwin, World War II Questionnaires #4014, 4490, 7551, 7607, USAMHI.

All of a sudden, Edwin Hanson, unpublished memoir, p. 2, US-AMHI.

Air support, Lyle McCann and Donald Dencker, World War II Questionnaires #5333 and 2876, USAMHI.

The supporting air, Bill Reed, *Yank* (1 April 1945), p. 2.

Our only, William Hoelzel, World War II Questionnaire #5109, US-AMHI.

We didn't have, Cecil Forinash, interview with Stan Tinsley, 17 August 1991, SCUTK.

We had good, Roy Yates, World War II Questionnaire #5991, US-AMHI.

The most serious, Jones to parents, SCUTK.

While we were, Pearson, unpublished memoir, p. 5, SCUTK.

As he floated, Harry Gunlock, *Fighting 36th Historical Quarterly* (Spring 1992), p. 55.

They called in, Russell interview, SCUTK.

Sometimes our tanks, Curry, unpublished memoir, p. 32, SCUTK.

Our favorites, Laughlin, unpublished memoir, p. 23, SCUTK.

Absolutely useless, Roche, unpublished memoir, pp. 220–21, SCUTK.

I managed, Graff, unpublished memoir, p. 51, SCUTK.

The 7th Armored, Nickell, unpublished memoir, p. 51, SCUTK.

All of a sudden, Bud Berkelbach to father, 23 April 1945, WHMC.

We got to, Murphy interview, SCUTK.

From the trail, Easy Memories, p. 24, SCUTK.

I began to fire, Nicholas Bozic, *Fighting 36th Historical Quarterly* (Summer 1985), p. 25.

High praise, Yochim Questionnaire, USAMHI.

It is always, Mel Cotton, *Powder River Journal* (December 1993), p. 15.

Artillery was terrific, Jesse Brewer and Spencer Moore, World War II Questionnaires #5035 and 2929, USAMHI.

A destroyer, Murphy interview, SCUTK.

We could not, Donald Greener, John Piazza, and Harold Wells, World War II Questionnaires #426, 6814, and 3832, USAMHI.

We went on, Atkins, unpublished memoir, p. 43, SCUTK.

I disliked, Easy Memories, p. 141, SCUTK.

Jungle patrol, Wyatt, unpublished memoir, p. 27, SCUTK.

The mission, David Arvizu, *Fighting 36th Historical Quarterly* (Spring 1989), pp. 58–59.

high powered, Simms, unpublished memoir, p. 33, SCUTK.

I don't know, Richess, unpublished memoir, p. 43, USAMHI.

When bullets, Joseph Kiss, *Bulge Bugle* (February 1993), p. 17.

He pulled the string, Reynolds, unpublished memoir, p. 16, SCUTK.

I was really, Pearson, unpublished memoir, p. 8, SCUTK.

Every time, Searles, unpublished memoir, p. 26, SCUTK.

I heard the crunch, Laughlin, unpublished memoir, pp. 48, 80, SCUTK.

I took a group, McLaughlin Questionnaire, USAMHI.

I was first, David Snoke to parents, 6 June 1945, WHMC.

Our first shot, Harold Hoffen, *Bulge Bugle* (May 1992), pp. 16–17.

The Japs, Theodore Schell, *Winds Aloft* (January 1990), p. 7.

When morning came, Max Renner, *The Orion Gallivanter* (March 1990), p. 9.

As I jumped, Gordon Rose, *Fighting 36th Historical Quarterly* (Winter 1992), pp. 16–17.

At least five, John Knutsen, *Fighting 36th Historical Quarterly* (Fall 1991), pp. 49–50.

They had evidently, Leon Clement to mother, 12 September 1945, WHMC.

We faced snipers, Warde, unpublished memoirs, p. 18, SCUTK.

Men were screaming, Jacob Brown, *76th Division Association Newsletter.*

There was a German, John Pulliam, interview with the author, 11 September 1995, SCUTK.

The reflexes, Matt Miletich, *Bulge Bugle* (November 1989), p. 18.

There were two, Lionel Adda, *The Checkerboard* (February 1991), p. 4.

I, along with, Brugh, unpublished memoir, p. 8, SCUTK.

Our plane was hit, Bill Oatman, oral history, SCUTK.

Different color, Ray Calandrella to parents, 2 September 1944, WHMC.

As we advanced, Arthur Kammerer to family, 13 March 1945, WHMC.

A Jap was sitting, Bill Alcine, *Yank* (14 April 1944), p. 3.
Every muscle, Logan Weston, *Ex-CBI Roundup* (June 1993), p. 29.
We had to clean, Brewer Questionnaire, USAMHI.
As we worked, W. King Pound, *Bulge Bugle* (June 1990), p. 21.
We opened, Stan Davis, *Bulge Bugle* (November 1989), p. 14.
I was one, Harry Smith to "Darling," c. 1943, WHMC.
A couple of times, Allen interview, SCUTK.
They were wicked, Leland Belknap to father, 13 March 1945, WHMC.
I've never seen, Arthur Hanssen to family, 19 March 1945, WHMC.
I saw several, Charles Richardson to sister, n.d., WHMC.
Just picture, "Captain Adkisson" to wife, July 1945, WHMC.

Chapter 6

In addition, John Ellis, *World War II: A Statistical Survey* (New York: Facts on File Publishers, 1993), p. 254. Ellis uses every known statistical source from official histories to encyclopedias in compiling his numbers and provides information on all major and minor combatants.

There was no more, American casualties killed, wounded, and captured in northwestern Europe in 1944–45 were double the casualties suffered by all army units for the entire Pacific war. Factoring in North Africa and Italy, and even taking into account marine casualties, the ratio would grow to almost two and a half casualties in the ETO for every one in the Pacific.

These are staggering, The units sampled by the army researchers were the 4th, 29th, 30th, 79th, 83d, 90th, 5th, 8th, 35th, 28th, and 80th Infantry Divisions. Thus, the list did not even include the two infantry divisions that suffered the highest casualties of all, the 1st and 3d.

Technology, For an excellent study on the high quality of American medical care in World War II, see Albert Cowdrey, *Fighting for Life: American Military Medicine in World War II* (New York: The Free Press, 1994).

Don't forget, Peter Sobkowiak, *Yank* (5 January 1945).

A medic had, Atkins, unpublished memoir, p. 71, SCUTK.

They fought, Russell Kidder, *Fighting 36th Historical Quarterly* (Fall 1989), pp. 54–55.

There aren't enough, Milton Landry, *Fighting 36th Historical Quarterly* (Spring 1992), p. 45.

Medics repeatedly, Yochim Questionnaire, USAMHI.

absolutely tops, Donald Taylor and Glen Alford, World War II Questionnaires #413 and 7860, USAMHI.

Dahlen was, Robert Garcia, *The Twenty-Niner Newsletter* (November 1995), p. 26.

He pulled, Jones interview, SCUTK.

The sounds, Mel Cotton, *The Powder River Journal* (December 1993), pp. 10–11.

Our regiment had, Worthman, unpublished memoir, pp. 3–5, SCUTK.

They were having, Wyatt, unpublished memoir, p. 40, SCUTK.

One of my closest, Tom Rounsaville, Charles Card, Emil Matula, and Melvin Coobs, World War II Questionnaires #4928, 2274, 1443, and 2403, USAMHI.

At the front, John Blount to mother and father, 21 February 1944, WHMC.

Upon arriving, Worthman, unpublished memoir, pp. 17, 20–22, SCUTK.

I was put, Greener Questionnaire, USAMHI.

deeply regret, John Grove, MS1608, Box 2, Folder 10, SCUTK.

The vivid picture, Laughlin, unpublished memoir, p. 7, SCUTK.

I knelt, Roche, unpublished memoir, p. 119, SCUTK.

I crawled over, Huber, unpublished memoir, p. 11, SCUTK.

I recall, Colin McLaurin, *The Twenty-Niner Newsletter* (November 1995), p. 14.

The sight, Rosell interview, SCUTK.

I examined Smitty, Fighting 36th Historical Quarterly (Summer 1988), p. 37.

Gordon got ripped, Bob Conroy, "The American Experience."

There just wasn't, Mietus interview, SCUTK.

Even the wounded, Walter Pippin to family, 16 February 1945, WHMC.

The most awful sight, Mary Slaughter to family, n.d., CSWS.

I got up, Searles, unpublished memoir, p. 27, SCUTK.

What felt like, Atkins, unpublished memoir, pp. 66–67, SCUTK.

I was about to, Simms, unpublished memoir, pp. 123–37, SCUTK.

I was shot, Pearson, unpublished memoir, pp. 18–19, SCUTK.

A shell exploded, Vincent Lidholm, World War II Questionnaire #3296, USAMHI.

I caught three, Gus Mitchell, *The Orion Gallivanter* (March 1987), p. 3.

I have tried, Herschel Horton to family, 11 December 1942, WHMC.

I was just peeking, Clarence Waltemath, interview with the author, 28 August 1995, SCUTK.

I felt an explosion, George Karembelas, *Bulge Bugle* (November 1990), p. 20.

A mortar shell, Earl Schoelles, *Powder River Journal* (Summer 1985), p. 10.

The fragment, Roy Denmon, World War II Questionnaire #2328, USAMHI.

I remember turning, Harry Joseph to Bob Wear, 1945, WHMC.

Some God-forsaken, Bill Tosco to Judy Swihart, 1944, WHMC.

He was actually, Reynolds, unpublished memoir, p. 17, SCUTK.

Sgt Glisch, Easy Memories, p. 81, SCUTK.

What a strange feeling, Jack Scott, *Fighting 36th Historical Quarterly* (Summer 1987), p. 46.

My last memory, Jackson, unpublished memoir, p. 35, USAMHI.

A young GI, Reitan, unpublished memoir, p. 21, SCUTK.

This man, Carroll, unpublished memoir, p. 50, SCUTK.

Sometime in the middle, Duty interview, SCUTK.

I cut one, Les Terry, *Fighting 36th Historical Quarterly* (Spring 1988), p. 53.

People didn't crumple, Bart Hagerman, "The American Experience."

I visualized, Simms, unpublished memoir, p. 54, SCUTK.

The Secretary of War, Marshall Hogins, MS1230, Box 1, Folder 27, SCUTK.

I was with him, Lt. Langland to Mr. Penniston, 13 June 1943, WHMC.

It blew him, Reynolds, unpublished memoir, p. 18, SCUTK.

The grenade, Searles, unpublished memoir, pp. 25–26, SCUTK.

The dead GIs, Laughlin, unpublished memoir, pp. 55–56, SCUTK.

A lump grew, Easy Memories, p. 91, SCUTK.

There he is, Wyatt, unpublished memoir, pp. 32, 34, SCUTK.

The Secretary of War, Julian Brooke, SCUTK.

Wilson's body, Deane Marks, *Winds Aloft* (January 1992), p. 12.

He lay with his legs, Jack Clover, *Fighting 36th Historical Quarterly* (Fall 1981), pp. 15–16.

You could almost, Clinton Riddle, unpublished memoir, p. 10, CSWS.

A perfect specimen, Lindsay, unpublished memoir, p. 17, SCUTK.

The graves registration, Chuck Storeby, oral history, SCUTK.

The GRT, Tippins, unpublished memoir, p. 3, SCUTK.

When you begin, Edward McCrystal to parents, n.d., WHMC.

One 96th, Donald Dencker, World War II Questionnaire #2876, USAMHI.

In the course, Easy Memories, p. 107, SCUTK.

You'd better, Murphy interview, SCUTK.

We knew that, Graff, unpublished memoir, p. 26, SCUTK.

Bombs were dropped, Ray Mitchell, *Ex-CBI Roundup* (January 1994), p. 4.

Shrapnel hit him, Lindenbusch Questionnaire, USAMHI.

A short round, Jackson, unpublished memoir, p. 26, USAMHI.

Stupid son-of-a, Rex Harrison, *Fighting 36th Historical Quarterly* (Spring 1990), p. 53.

Many of these, Forse Questionnaire, USAMHI.

GI John Doe's, Deane Marks, *Winds Aloft* (January 1990), p. 15.

After lining us up, Benjamin Johnson, unpublished memoir, p. 27, MS1881, Box 13, Folder 4, SCUTK.

As I was sleeping, Thacker, unpublished memoir, pp. 15–16, SCUTK.

We claimed, Roche, unpublished memoir, pp. 132–33, SCUTK.

The hail of metal, James Mattera, *Bulge Bugle* (May 1994), p. 29.

After we surrendered, Ben Kimmelman, "The American Experience."

He jerked, Clarence Ferguson, *Fighting 36th Historical Quarterly* (Spring 1990), p. 36.

the strange feeling, Alan Williamson, *Fighting 36th Historical Quarterly* (Spring 1986), p. 8.

As I walked, Brugh, unpublished memoir, pp. 10, 12, SCUTK.

We were herded, Ian Morrison, *Bulge Bugle* (February 1990), pp. 13–14.

Of those, Stouffer, *Combat and Its Aftermath,* pp. 48–58.

I never saw, Simms, unpublished memoir, p. 156, SCUTK.

In fact, Cowdrey, *Fighting for Life,* pp. 136–52.

He is not, Mack Morriss, *Yank* (31 March 1944), p. 8.

This disabling, Atkins, unpublished memoir, p. 39, SCUTK.

They were given, Ben Kimmelman, "The American Experience."

The man spent, Searles, unpublished memoir, p. 27, SCUTK.

He went crazy, Sally interview, SCUTK.

He was going, Martin interview, SCUTK.

His hands, Bill Alcine, *Yank* (4 February 1945), p. 11.

My associate driver, Walter Russell, World War II Questionnaire, US-AMHI.

Dark eyes, Laughlin, unpublished memoir, p. 65, SCUTK.

called it 'going Asiatic,' Burchett interview, SCUTK.

someone took me, Huber, unpublished memoir, pp. 13–14, SCUTK.

You stay tense, McFadden Questionnaire, USAMHI.

I was told, Frank Miller, *Fighting 36th Historical Quarterly* (Spring 1989), p. 49.

I became so detached, Wells Questionnaire, USAMHI.

I continue, John Snyder to wife, 25 June 1944, WHMC.

I was in a, Thomas Isabel, World War II Questionnaire #3748, US-AMHI.

Chapter 7

Although Dower, Please see John W. Dower, *War Without Mercy: Race & Power in the Pacific War* (New York: Pantheon Books, 1986).

In the above, Stouffer, *Combat and Its Aftermath,* p. 34.

first class infantry, John Stannard and William Ruf, World War II Questionnaires #4330 and 3915, USAMHI.

The Nips are, Sy Gottlieb to family, 3 July 1945, WHMC.

We regarded, Forrest Coleman, Earl Norgard, and Richard Forse, World War II Questionnaires #1406, 5429, and 3173, USAMHI.

Each of us, Jackson, unpublished memoir, p. 24, USAMHI.

Even though, Justin Gray, *Yank* (27 May 1945), p. 5.

Fighting Japs, Yank (13 October 1944), p. 4.

The individual, Sidney Richess, World War II Questionnaire, p. 29, USAMHI.

They were never, Allen interview, SCUTK.

The pattern, Henne Questionnaire, USAMHI.

We were motivated, McFadden Questionnaire, USAMHI.

sadistic animals, John Moore, Charles Card, and Bryan Baldwin, World War II Questionnaires #4648, 2274, and 7607, USAMHI.

By the end, Henne Questionnaire, USAMHI.

We thought, Clarence Daniels, interview with Dr. Charles W. Johnson, 29 August 1984, SCUTK.

I wished I'd have, Burchett interview, SCUTK.

You can tell, Jack Hussey to mother, 12 July 1945, WHMC.

I hated to do it, Charles Richardson to sister, n.d., WHMC.

I looked upon them, Frank Caudillo, Roland Lea, and Robert Knauss, World War II Questionnaires #7423, 3360, and 4127, USAMHI.

Not all Jap, Searles, unpublished memoir, p. 11, SCUTK.

All that was left, Sears, unpublished memoir, p. 2, SCUTK.

all people are, Minoru Hara, Vincent Lidholm, and William Ruf, World War II Questionnaires #6782, 3296, and 3915, USAMHI.

I realized, Thaddeus Piewawer and John Sevec, World War II Questionnaires #4536 and 2438, USAMHI.

The enemy was, Lane, unpublished memoir, p. 69, SCUTK.

The vast majority, Ellis, *Statistical Survey,* p. 254.

We took no, McLaughlin and McKinney Questionnaires, USAMHI.

There were attempts, Wyatt, unpublished memoir, p. 21, SCUTK.

our motto was, Emil Matula and George Sitzler, World War II Questionnaires #1443 and 4551, USAMHI.

Early in the war, John Drugan, World War II Questionnaire #7819, USAMHI.

He was an arrogant, Searles, unpublished memoir, p. 24, SCUTK.

All I ever, Lindenbusch Questionnaire, USAMHI.

None had, Merle Miller, *Yank* (31 March 1944), p. 10.

based on the Geneva, Paul Casper and Yashakazu Higashi, World War II Questionnaires #2402 and 7500, USAMHI.

In five minutes, Greene, unpublished memoir, p. 6, SCUTK.

They were treated, Milton Pearce, Charles Henne, and George Klavand, World War II Questionnaires #5161 and 2856, USAMHI.

Chapter 8

An overwhelming, Stouffer, *Combat and Its Aftermath,* p. 34.

I could not help, Alan Williamson, *Fighting 36th Historical Quarterly* (Spring 1986), p. 8.

The Germans were, Easy Memories, pp. 92–93, SCUTK.

We were told, Piazza Questionnaire, USAMHI.

Even during, John Beeks, World War II Questionnaire #4410, US-AMHI.

The German soldier, West interview, SCUTK.

I respected them, Piggot and Greener Questionnaires, USAMHI.

In the Bulge, James Hagan, James Mahon, Donald Taylor, and Charles Hogg, World War II Questionnaires #632, 521, 413, and 3463, USAMHI.

German soldier, Al Metcalf, interview with Dr. Charles W. Johnson, 7 August 1987, SCUTK.

the Germans were, Wells Questionnaire, USAMHI.

German replacements, Gerald VanCleve, World War II Questionnaire #2454, USAMHI.

I had considerable, Easy Memories, p. 202, SCUTK.

German soldiers and, Denmon and Allen Questionnaires, USAMHI.

It may come, Nickell, unpublished memoir, p. 110, SCUTK.

With all credit, Graff, unpublished memoir, p. 56, SCUTK.

This was a surprise, Carroll, unpublished memoir, p. 69, SCUTK.

The Sergeant and I, Nicholas Bozic, *Fighting 36th Historical Quarterly* (Summer 1985), p. 27.

With the exception, Charles Hogg and Grover Carr, World War II Questionnaires #2137, USAMHI.

liked the German, Yochim, Hartzog, and Beeks Questionnaires, US-AMHI.

Germans were very, Roy Blair and Harold Marshall, World War II Questionnaires, USAMHI.

Most of my, Waltemath interview, SCUTK.

Within an hour, Ralph Hill, *The Checkerboard* (February 1993), p. 11.

I considered them, Joseph Kocsik and Paris Roussos, World War II Questionnaires #502 and 594, USAMHI.

We get decorations, Harold Etter to mother, 2 January 1945, WHMC.

Three more to go, Walter Peters, *Yank* (23 July 1944), p. 5.

a bunch of, John Massey, World War II Questionnaire #2276, US-AMHI.

Because of their, Sid Rowling letter to Garland Godby, 29 June 1989, CSWS, and Morton Semelmaxer, World War II Questionnaire #7298, USAMHI.

I hated, Blanton and Thibideau Questionnaires, USAMHI.

From 9 to 90, "Josef" to aunt and uncle, 22 May 1945, WHMC.

Shooting is too good, Donald Lembeke to Betty Faris, n.d., WHMC.

The Germans are, William Maher to mother and father, 1 July 1944, WHMC.

These people, Laughlin, unpublished memoir, pp. 42–44, SCUTK.

My mind, Donald MacDonald, World War II Questionnaire #5926, USAMHI.

We were shocked, Meissner, unpublished memoir, p. 25, SCUTK.

I can assure, Rodney Beaver to parents, 18 May 1945, WHMC.

You'd see one, Pulliam interview, SCUTK.

incredulous, horrified, Buch Questionnaire, USAMHI.

My buddy and I, Oatman oral history, SCUTK.

I got sick, Walter Richardson, World War II Questionnaire #1239, USAMHI.

It's pretty tough, Yank (29 October 1944), p. 5.

There was a, Carroll, unpublished memoir, p. 56, SCUTK.

We noted, Laughlin, unpublished memoir, p. 11, SCUTK.

I've seen a, "Josef" to aunt and uncle, WHMC.

We had just, Graff, unpublished memoir, pp. 18–19, SCUTK.

Word started around, Eduardo Peniche, *Bulge Bugle* (December 1992), p. 20.

we treated them, Willis Irvin, World War II Questionnaire #4830, US-AMHI.

When we were, Isabel Questionnaire, USAMHI.

That is when, Simms, unpublished memoir, pp. 30–31, SCUTK.

Most prisoners, Brewer Questionnaire, USAMHI.

I learned later, Peters interview, SCUTK.

He went up, Shapiro interview, SCUTK.

We were spellbound, Ruppel, unpublished memoir, p. 33, SCUTK.

Someone suggested, Frank Miller, *Fighting 36th Historical Quarterly* (Spring 1989), p. 47.

When a high, Graff, unpublished memoir, pp. 72–73, SCUTK.

I motioned, Easy Memories, pp. 181–82, SCUTK.

There was a short, Carroll, unpublished memoir, p. 72, SCUTK.

I always figured, George Kerrigan, *Fighting 36th Historical Quarterly* (Spring 1991), p. 39.

We occasionally, Nickell, unpublished memoir, p. 111, SCUTK.

could never, Joseph Kiss, *Bulge Bugle* (February 1993), p. 17.

They nearly jumped, Boyd Miller, *The Twenty-Niner Newsletter* (July 1995), p. 42.

A rather jovial, Rosell interview, SCUTK.

The prisoners said, Dewey Mann, *Fighting 36th Historical Quarterly* (Spring 1986), p. 20.

I heard this voice, Tippins, unpublished memoir, pp. 8–9, SCUTK.

Directly in front, Lionel Adda, *The Checkerboard* (February 1991), p. 4.

In a low, Frank Iglehart, *The Checkerboard* (December 1992), p. 14.

In most instances, Charles Gilmore and Edward Schooner, World War II Questionnaires #619 and 1674, USAMHI.

He was a young, Guy LeGrand, unpublished memoir, p. 5, SCUTK.

We treated them, Ruppel, unpublished memoir, p. 26, SCUTK.

Chapter 9

The judgement revolved, Carroll, unpublished memoir, pp. 10, 29, SCUTK.

Color means nothing, Yank (4 March 1945), p. 3.

chance to weed out, McLaughlin, Berryhill, Piewawer, and Banker Questionnaires, USAMHI.

Most were good, VanCleve, Chomiw, Hartzog, and Brewer Questionnaires, USAMHI.

We respected, Allen interview, SCUTK.

The officers, Alto Johns to sister, 30 July 1944, WHMC.

Our relationship, Atkins, unpublished memoir, pp. 35–36, SCUTK.

Too many of the, Hanson, Kemp, Beeks, Manning, and Hadfield Questionnaires, USAMHI.

about five percent, Harold Sletten and William Houser, World War II Questionnaires #2111 and 563, USAMHI.

This was true, Stouffer, *Combat and Its Aftermath,* p. 120.

those who fought, William Ruf, Donald MacDonald, and Frederick Kielsgard, World War II Questionnaires #3915, 5926, and 2419, US-AMHI.

good leaders, Hartzog Questionnaire, USAMHI.

Officers who came up, Heck, Roussos, Isabel, and Kirkman Questionnaires, USAMHI.

There is a rapport, Easy Memories, p. 71, SCUTK.

He was a big, Nickell, unpublished memoir, p. 54, SCUTK.

He had a few, Atkins, unpublished memoir, pp. 68–69, SCUTK.

He wasn't like, Byrd interview, SCUTK.

I don't remember, Greene, unpublished memoir, p. 5, SCUTK.

he would not, Floyd Todd, World War II Questionnaire #6490, US-AMHI.

I and a number, Warde, unpublished memoir, p. 13, SCUTK.

Of all the, Sid Rowling to Garland Godby, 29 June 1989, CSWS.

Our company commander, Renna and Dencker Questionnaires, US-AMHI.

A soldier came, David Nichols, ed., *Ernie's War: The Best of Ernie Pyle's World War II Dispatches* (New York: Random House, 1986), p. 197.

The captain, Justin Gray, *Yank* (27 May 1945), p. 1.

Lt. Bruno Roselli, Mel Cotton, *Powder River Journal* (December 1993), p. 15.

Our company commander, Charles Rudolph, World War II Questionnaire #519, USAMHI.

I guess, McDonald interview, SCUTK.

This man risked, Wyatt, unpublished memoir, pp. 22–23, SCUTK.

Your son, Edward Telling to Mrs. Gentry, March 1945, MS1259, Box 4, Folder 3, SCUTK.

We learned, Pliney Elliot to Mrs. Gentry, 14 April 1945, SCUTK.

I had the privilege, Emanuel V. DeRubba to Mrs. Gentry, 28 February 1945, SCUTK.

I don't believe, Simms, unpublished memoir, p. 31, SCUTK.

The officer's, Roche, unpublished memoir, pp. 93–94, SCUTK.

not knowing, Phillips and Upchurch Questionnaires, USAMHI.

Staff officers, Coleman Questionnaire, USAMHI.

I wasn't going, Graff, unpublished memoir, p. 32, SCUTK.

I had my rifle, Roche, unpublished memoir, p. 76, SCUTK.

Captain—panicked, Atkins, unpublished memoir, pp. 40–41, SCUTK.

The quality of life, Carroll, unpublished memoir, pp. 26, 28, SCUTK.

Early in the morning, Bert Morphis, *Bulge Bugle* (August 1990), p. 21.

The machine-gun, Matt Miletich, *Bulge Bugle* (November 1989), pp. 17–18.

He said, Wade, unpublished memoir, p. 4, SCUTK.

God knows, Joe Dine, *Fighting 36th Historical Quarterly* (Winter 1984), pp. 39–40.

The pilot, Searles, unpublished memoir, p. 20, SCUTK.

We had one, Isabel, Luzzi, Rudolph, and Sue Questionnaires, US-AMHI.

He shook, Simms, unpublished memoir, pp. 76–77, SCUTK.

The real leaders, Stannard, Schmidt, Phillips, Ruf, and Yates Questionnaires, USAMHI.

Being an NCO, Card, Woodrow, Kemp, and Butler Questionnaires, USAMHI.

We were not, Laughlin, unpublished memoir, p. 25, SCUTK.

He was caring, Charles Konkler, *The Checkerboard* (August 1991), p. 12.

It was my job, Whiteway, responses to "Questions for Veterans," SCUTK.

Promotions in a rifle, Mac Acosta, *Fighting 36th Historical Quarterly* (Summer 1984), p. 15.

a commissioned, Norman Tiemann, World War II Questionnaire #3755, USAMHI.

Officers were very, Lindenbusch, Hanson, and McNeil Questionnaires, USAMHI.

I never saw, James McKnight, World War II Questionnaire #2888, USAMHI.

It was expected, Jackson, unpublished memoir, p. 32, USAMHI.

If you make, Murphy interview, SCUTK.

it would not, Colin McLaurin, *The Twenty-Niner Newsletter* (July 1995), p. 11.

The men hated, Rosell interview, SCUTK.

You ain't, Martin Tully, *Fighting 36th Historical Quarterly* (Fall 1992), p. 52.

trying to stay, Fred Kohl, World War II Questionnaire #2175, US-AMHI.

You had to, Godby interview, SCUTK.

The relationship, Wood Questionnaire, SCUTK.

Until I became, Peters interview, SCUTK.

I could have, Julian Phillips, *Fighting 36th Historical Quarterly* (Spring 1985), p. 39.

Then it hit me, Milton Landry, *Fighting 36th Historical Quarterly* (Spring 1992), pp. 9, 10, 47.

I never called, Henne Questionnaire, USAMHI.

When I was, Edgar Wilson to John Leake, 20 October 1988, CSWS.

They led, Godby interview, SCUTK.

Good leaders, Mahon and Moore Questionnaires, USAMHI.

A Marine major, Robert Archibald, World War II Questionnaire #6368, USAMHI.

I was thoroughly, Colin McLaurin, *The Twenty-Niner Newsletter* (November 1995), p. 18.

I developed, Yochim Questionnaire, USAMHI.

Two Naval Academy, Lindsay, unpublished memoir, p. 4, SCUTK.

I was leading, Robert Teeples, World War II Questionnaire #5039, USAMHI.

I'm not proud, Jones interview, SCUTK.

Chapter 10

As he drew, Elmer D. Jones, unpublished memoir, pp. 1–2, MS1881, Box 6, Folder 3, SCUTK.

Thirty-eight percent, Stouffer, *Combat and Its Aftermath,* p. 174.

When I think, John Edwards to mother, 14 May 1944, WHMC.

War seems, Stanley Rice to sister, 10 January 1945, WHMC.

The American Soldier, Mel Cotton, *Powder River Journal* (December 1993), p. 13.

Nearly 40 percent, Stouffer, *Combat and Its Aftermath,* p. 174.

to rid the world, Piazza Questionnaire, USAMHI.

I am proud, Henry Lee to parents, 12 February 1942, WHMC.

If I get it, Walter Dillehay to dad, 5 February 1945, WHMC.

I liked, Burchett interview, SCUTK.

If an American, Simms, unpublished memoir, pp. 199–200, SCUTK.

The average, Joe Johnson to wife, 1945, WHMC.

In the Pacific, Stouffer, *Combat and Its Aftermath,* p. 174.

We Americans, Warde, unpublished memoir, p. 17, SCUTK.

The belief, Nickell, unpublished memoir, p. 61, SCUTK.

Religions and ethnics, Kocour, unpublished memoir, p. 7, SCUTK.

I had said, Carroll, unpublished memoir, pp. 71–72, SCUTK.

I would just, James McGuinness to parents, 23 May 1943, WHMC.

God was my, James Revell, *Fighting 36th Historical Quarterly* (September 1992), p. 10.

No matter, Arlo Butcher to mother, n.d., WHMC.

I tell you, Jones letter to parents, SCUTK.

I don't believe, Leland Belknap to father, 13 March 1945, WHMC.

prayed that I might, Charles Parliman to family, 17 April 1945, WHMC.

My darling, George Smalley to wife, 11 September 1944, WHMC.

Before every battle, "Herbert" to father, n.d., WHMC.

Never have I, Robert Arnett to mother and father, 7 January 1945, WHMC.

I can rap, Bud Graber to parents, 11 August 1944, WHMC.

I prayed consistently, Maher to mother and father, 1 July 1944, WHMC.

I've always, Grover Adams to mother and father, December 1944, WHMC.

Survival was paramount, McLaughlin and Card Questionnaires, USAMHI.

Like everyone else, Colin McLaurin, *The Twenty-Niner Newsletter* (November 1995), p. 14.

I remember, Henry Gunlock, *Fighting 36th Historical Quarterly* (Spring 1992), p. 55.

In the heat, Mietus interview, SCUTK.

After about, Isabel Questionnaire, USAMHI.

You learn one, Shapiro interview, SCUTK.

I wasn't fighting, Glen Main, interview with Dr. Charles W. Johnson, 30 October 1995, SCUTK.

Put into the situation, Green, unpublished memoir, p. 8, SCUTK.

In both, Stouffer, *Combat and Its Aftermath,* p. 174.

a job to be done, Lovett, Matter, Hill, Fribis, Simoneaux, Hadfield, and Richards Questionnaires, USAMHI.

While men, Mauldin, *Up Front,* p. 51.

When asked, Stouffer, *Combat and Its Aftermath,* p. 296.

They had their, Peters interview, SCUTK.

While we had, Searles, unpublished memoir, pp. 16–17, SCUTK.

Walking the sidewalks, Easy Memories, pp. 106–7, 110, SCUTK.

Yours is the job, Roche, unpublished memoir, p. 3, SCUTK.

I'm from Division, Charles Fulton poem, MS1881, Box 11, Folder 6-7, SCUTK.

Most after serving, MacDonald Questionnaire, USAMHI.

A sizeable minority, Stouffer, *Combat and Its Aftermath,* pp. 321–22.

I heard dozens, Simms, unpublished memoir, p. 249, SCUTK.

We are here, Robert Allen to father, 10 February 1945, WHMC.

As the months, George Boocks to Dr. Charles W. Johnson, 8 April 1992, CSWS.

That just burns, Leslie Schneider to mother, 10 February 1943, MS1881, Box 20, Folder 29, SCUTK.

The Headlines say, Johnson to wife, 1945, WHMC.

When they hear, James Fisher to mother, n.d., WHMC.

Whereas in the, Beauford George to Ms. Kleeman, 15 January 1945, WHMC.

I certainly, Carroll, unpublished memoir, p. 58, SCUTK.

Morale was low, Spencer Moore, World War II Questionnaire #2929, USAMHI.

Most of us, Easy Memories, p. 126, SCUTK.

It was a black, John Symanksi, *The Ivy Leaves* (June 1994), p. 32.

I admired, Godby interview, SCUTK.

A group of Negro, James Revell, *The Checkerboard* (September 1992), p. 11.

Maybe if people, Ralph Martin, *Yank* (4 March 1945), p. 2.

Even as a soldier, Johnson to wife, 1945, WHMC.

When circumstances, Ruppel, unpublished memoir, pp. 32–33, SCUTK.

One thing, Thacker, unpublished memoir, p. 16, SCUTK.

Humor was an important, Wyatt, unpublished memoir, p. 13, SCUTK.

One fellow, Simms, unpublished memoir, p. 102, SCUTK.

As I hesitated, Bob Kay, *The Ivy Leaves* (June 1994), p. 44.

A little humor, Johns to sister, 30 July 1944, WHMC.

Tonight! Banzai charge! Yank (13 October 1944), p. 3.

In addition, Stouffer, *Combat and Its Aftermath,* pp. 201–02.

Fear and the threat, Phillip Brown to aunt and uncle, 16 September 1944, WHMC.

As for the, Ike Roberts to sister, 26 January 1945, WHMC.

No matter how, Searles, unpublished memoir, p. 23, SCUTK.

Most of us, Kocour, unpublished memoir, pp. 4, 6, SCUTK.

My biggest fear, Carroll, unpublished memoir, p. 22, SCUTK.

I remember how, Easy Memories, p. 207, SCUTK.

It's an empty, Bill Sabin, unpublished memoir, pp. 10–11, MS1881, Box 20, Folder 13, SCUTK.

I might say, Mackerer interview, SCUTK.

Our hearts, Erwin Pichotte, World War II Questionnaire #247, US-AMHI.

I was shaking, Dan Ray, *Fighting 36th Historical Quarterly* (Winter 1987), p. 20.

A typical day, Salvatore Lamagna, World War II Questionnaire #2234, USAMHI.

Sure I was scared, Arlo Butcher to mother, n.d., WHMC.

The man who, Mack Morriss, *Yank* (31 March 1944), p. 10.

I experienced, Jackson, unpublished memoir, p. 30, USAMHI.

I realized, Pippin to family, 16 February 1945, WHMC.

Even though, Les Terry, *Fighting 36th Historical Quarterly* (Summer 1990), p. 73.

I came to feel, Searles, unpublished memoir, p. 25, SCUTK.

We were certain, Worthman, unpublished memoir, pp. 17–18, SCUTK.

how long, Yates Questionnaire, USAMHI.

How long can, Mac Acosta, *Fighting 36th Historical Quarterly* (Summer 1984), p. 11.

At this stage, James Estepp, *Fighting 36th Historical Quarterly* (Winter 1990), p. 69.

We never talked, J. R. McIlroy, *The Checkerboard* (September 1992), p. 5.

After a relatively, John Stenger, unpublished memoir, p. 4, CSWS.

There were too many, Ruppel, unpublished memoir, pp. 21, 32, SCUTK.

The soldier in combat, Roussos and Denmon Questionnaires, US-AMHI.

Combat infantrymen, Easy Memories, pp. 119–20, SCUTK.

He just had, Laughlin, unpublished memoir, pp. 66–67, SCUTK.

You can't, Godby interview, SCUTK.

The sight, Matt Miletich, *Bulge Bugle* (November 1989), p. 19.

Willis looked at me, Tippins, unpublished memoir, p. 5, SCUTK.

The first pangs, Huber, unpublished memoir, p. 8, SCUTK.

When you're, E. A. Struble to sister, 7 June 1945, WHMC.

There is nothing, Frank Barnett to mother and father, 8 July 1945, WHMC.

had not slept, Carroll, unpublished memoir, p. 52, SCUTK.

Where three weeks, Don Hoagland, *Battleground Newsletter* (22 February 1994), p. 13.

That's the first, Mietus interview, SCUTK.

The biggest trouble, Waltemath interview, SCUTK.

I rarely sleep, Maher to mother and father, WHMC.

At the time, Atkins, unpublished memoir, p. 56, SCUTK.

A click of the safety, Simms, unpublished memoir, p. 68, SCUTK.

It's the only place, Conrad Willard to parents, 13 May 1945, WHMC.

The infantryman becomes, Barnett to mother and father, 8 July 1945, WHMC.

My men know, Meier to parents, 14 November 1944, WHMC.

In my experiences, Kammerer to family, 13 March 1945, WHMC.

Chapter 11

Many of them, Stouffer, *Combat and Its Aftermath,* pp. 272–76. Stouffer provides an excellent description of life as a combat replacement and chronicles many common complaints.

They were welcomed, See Stanton, *Order of Battle,* for a breakdown on casualties in combat divisions. In most cases, combat outfits suffered anywhere from 100 to 200 percent casualties.

The rest had, Stouffer, *Combat and Its Aftermath,* p. 242.

It was an uncomfortable feeling, Stenger, unpublished memoir, p. 3, CSWS.

Sixty-five percent, Stouffer, *Combat and Its Aftermath,* p. 280.

pleasantly surprised, Robert Klenk, Marvin Reickman, Charles Stewart, and Whayland Greene, World War II Questionnaires #4490, 3493, 5006, and 2934, USAMHI.

We were greeted, Evan Voss, *Fighting 36th Historical Quarterly* (Fall 1987), pp. 7–8.

They were glad, William Eberhart and Jacob Westra, World War II Questionnaires #2271 and 4790, USAMHI.

I didn't know anybody, Russell interview, SCUTK.

I was made, Glen Perry, World War II Questionnaire #2465, USAMHI.

My tank commander, Bryant, Rudolph, Denmon, and Hogg Questionnaires, USAMHI.

We older men, Easy Memories, p. 204, SCUTK.

The veteran has, Simms, unpublished memoir, p. 94, SCUTK.

We welcomed them, Ray Poynter, Paul Dixon, Emil Matula, Joe Carey, and Wells, World War II Questionnaires #7223, 2738, 1443, and 2047, USAMHI.

I was glad, Vanhooser, VanCleve, Dencker, and Chafon Questionnaires, USAMHI.

we were always, Jani, Taylor, Thibideau, and Margreiter Questionnaires, USAMHI.

Freezing up (14 percent), Stouffer, *Combat and Its Aftermath,* p. 283.

The first mistake, Fighting 36th Historical Quarterly (Summer 1981), p. 32.

All hell broke loose, Laughlin, unpublished memoir, p. 26, SCUTK.

Everyone stopped, Charles Miller, *Bulge Bugle* (February 1991), p. 20.

PUT OUT THAT FIRE! Fulton poem, p. 5, SCUTK.

A replacement soldier, Nickell, unpublished memoir, p. 88, SCUTK.

He thought, Sears, unpublished memoir, pp. 4–5, SCUTK.

A replacement joined, Albert Kudzia, *Fighting 36th Historical Quarterly* (Summer 1987), p. 19.

He had combat, Robert Benz, *Bulge Bugle* (August 1990), p. 22.

He had been, Graff, unpublished memoir, p. 16, SCUTK.

were not effective, Arthur Bolton and Mark Durley, World War II Questionnaires #2443 and 218, USAMHI.

We regrouped, Pearson, unpublished memoir, p. 7, SCUTK.

They always left, Del Kendall, *Fighting 36th Historical Quarterly* (Winter 1985), p. 18.

We were always, Godby interview, SCUTK.

There were three, Atkins, unpublished memoir, p. 64, SCUTK.

very mixed, Hanson Questionnaire, USAMHI.

Laddie and Sennart, Deane Marks, *Winds Aloft* (January 1990), p. 14.

thought that I would, Wade, unpublished memoir, p. 2, SCUTK.

after the first, Moerke, Ruf, Berryhill, and Hilkemeyer Questionnaires, USAMHI.

Once they had, Acheson, Hill, Brown, Piewawer, Wells, and Yochim Questionnaires, USAMHI.

Most of them, Trachta, Bryant, Rudolph, Taylor, Sexton, and Brewer Questionnaires, USAMHI.

Chapter 12

Brotherhood. Everybody sharing, Godby interview, SCUTK.

He felt secure, Jones, unpublished memoir, p. 2, SCUTK.

Seventy-eight percent, Stouffer, *Combat and Its Aftermath,* p. 138.

The thing that keeps, Nickell, unpublished memoir, p. 73, SCUTK.

What kept me, Atkins, unpublished memoir, p. 43, SCUTK.

men showed, Jani Questionnaire, USAMHI.

the feeling, Cohen and Stannard Questionnaires, USAMHI.

that extra something, Clinton MacLeod to Mr. and Mrs. Boice, n.d., MS1764, Box 5, Folder 5, SCUTK.

fought in combat, Hara and Phillips Questionnaires, USAMHI.

When a soldier, Ellis Blake, World War II Questionnaire, USAMHI.

Why did we do it? John Goode to Henry L. Ford, 11 February 1992, CSWS.

I knew my squad, Beeks Questionnaire, USAMHI.

men generally realize, Johnson to wife, 1945, WHMC.

I think everybody, Emerson Questionnaire, USAMHI.

I wanted to prove, Upchurch Questionnaire, USAMHI.

We had taken, Easy Memories, p. 120, SCUTK.

Some nights, Simms, unpublished memoir, p. 114, SCUTK.

really scared, Card Questionnaire, USAMHI.

He said, Brugh, unpublished memoir, p. 11, SCUTK.

Albert Dunn said, Jani Questionnaire, USAMHI.

It was always OK, Julian Phillips, *Fighting 36th Historical Quarterly* (Spring 1985), p. 33.

Just as I was, Sabin, unpublished memoir, pp. 11–12, SCUTK.

I spent that, Wade, unpublished memoir, p. 7, SCUTK.

At that time, Pearson, unpublished memoir, p. 19, SCUTK.

His shovel struck, John Symanski to Wanda & Friends, 6 June 1994, CSWS.

I struck up, William Eberle, *Fighting 36th Historical Quarterly* (Summer 1981), p. 43.

I sat down, David Arvizu, *Fighting 36th Historical Quarterly* (Spring 1990), pp. 61–62.

A number of my, Kocour, unpublished memoir, p. 15, SCUTK.

Wadsworth took, Nelson Ottis, *The Checkerboard* (February 1991), p. 7.

How would you, Marion Earley, World War II Questionnaire #453, USAMHI.

They are all dead, Wyatt, unpublished memoir, p. 43, SCUTK.

Twins, we feel, C. Russ Martin, interview with Stan Tinsley, 28 August 1991, CSWS.

I just can't, Kenneth Cole to mother, 18 March 1945, WHMC.

An individual, Rex Harrison, *Fighting 36th Historical Quarterly* (Fall 1988), p. 37.

the only ones, McFadden, Stannard, Hara, Reickman, and LaChausee Questionnaires, USAMHI.

Some of my most, Easy Memories, p. 210, SCUTK.

Our outfit, George Boocks to Dr. Charles W. Johnson, 8 April 1992, CSWS.

The front, Ralph Martin, *Yank* (4 March 1945), pp. 2–3.

We were an ordinary, Wyatt, unpublished memoir, pp. 1, 12–13, SCUTK.

These men, Symanski to Wanda & Friends, CSWS.

Cappaletti was of Italian, Simms, unpublished memoir, pp. 22, 113, SCUTK.

To me, "Roy" to Helen Thacker, 29 October 1944, MS1764, Box 18, Folder 7, SCUTK.

This was the bond, Del Kendall, *Fighting 36th Historical Quarterly* (Winter 1985), p. 19.

Men, hungry, Willard to parents, WHMC.

The lieutenant and I, James Revell, *The Checkerboard* (September 1992), pp. 10–11.

My sergeant, Elturino Loiacono, unpublished memoir, p. 4, US-AMHI.

Don't think that I am, Richard Trant to parents, 10 April 1945, WHMC.

Many of the wounded, Carroll, unpublished memoir, p. 43, SCUTK.

there is a bond, Ruf, Matula, and Phillips Questionnaires, USAMHI.

I will always, Graff, unpublished memoir, p. 93, SCUTK.

Your combat brother, Michael Stubinski to "Bob," 5 November 1992, MS1881, Box 28, Folder 19, SCUTK.

I loved them, Jack Scott, *Fighting 36th Historical Quarterly* (Summer 1987), p. 46.

We were a band, Richard Fedderson, World War II Questionnaire #5001, USAMHI.

When you're on the front line, Main interview, SCUTK.

The men I served with, Storeby oral history, SCUTK.

When a young man, Seabrook, unpublished memoir, p. 1, SCUTK.

The quality of men, Metcalf interview, SCUTK.

It would be difficult, Clarence Stoeckley, *The Orion Gallivanter* (June 1992), p. 5.

Epilogue

This experience, Maher to parents, WHMC.

One, wearing muddy, William Manchester, *Goodbye Darkness: A Memoir of the Pacific War* (New York: Dell Publishing Co., Inc., 1979), p. 20.

We who were, Wade, unpublished memoir, p. 9, SCUTK.

While there were, George Lorio, *Winds Aloft* (January 1990), p. 10.

Anybody that put, Richard Talley, *Fighting 36th Historical Quarterly* (Winter 1987), p. 44.

Why were we, Ray Wells, *Fighting 36th Historical Quarterly* (Winter 1992), p. 55.

The thing I will, David Laing, unpublished memoir, p. 4, MS1608, Box 12, Folder 1, SCUTK.

Like most, Stenger, unpublished memoir, p. 6, CSWS.

I developed a tic, Simms, unpublished memoir, p. 264, SCUTK.

When I'd walk, George Wheeler, conversation with Dr. Charles W. Johnson and the author, 31 October 1995, SCUTK.

Nothing seemed to work, Huber, unpublished memoir, p. 25, SCUTK.

He said, Peters interview, SCUTK.

I didn't want to, Ruppel, unpublished memoir, p. 45, SCUTK.

Every time it snows, Hagerman, "The American Experience."

It was a horrid experience, Willie Green, *Bulge Bugle* (May 1993), p. 18.

The life and death, Eldon Jacobsen, World War II Questionnaire #288, USAMHI.

We have a certain, Harry Arnold to Dr. Charles W. Johnson, 30 May 1990, CSWS.

It doesn't go away, Stewart, "The American Experience."

grew up real fast, W. E. Brewer, interview with Stan Tinsley, 16 May 1990, SCUTK.

it was probably, Wells Questionnaire, USAMHI.

He learned how, Debs Myers article, CSWS.

We were sent, Wyatt, unpublished memoir, p. 1, SCUTK.

Never was there a finer, Riddick Kelley to mother, 24 June 1945, WHMC.

SELECTED BIBLIOGRAPHY

Abzug, Robert H. *Inside the Vicious Heart: Americans and the Liberation of Nazi Concentration Camps*. New York: Oxford University Press, 1985.

Adams, C. C. *The Best War Ever: America and World War II*. Baltimore: Johns Hopkins University Press, 1994.

Ambrose, Stephen. *Band of Brothers: E Company, 506th Regiment, 101st Airborne: From Normandy to Hitler's Eagle's Nest*. New York: Simon & Schuster, 1992.

———. *D-Day June 6, 1944: The Climactic Battle of World War II*. New York: Simon & Schuster, 1994.

Arbuckle, J. W. *A Front Seat in Hell*. Johnson City: The Overmountain Press, 1991.

Astor, Gerald. *A Blood Dimmed Tide*. New York: Donald I. Fine Inc., 1992.

———. *June 6, 1944: Voices of D-Day*. New York: St. Martin's Press, 1994.

Balkoski, Joseph. *Beyond the Beachhead: The 29th Infantry Division in Normandy*. Harrisburg: Stackpole Books, 1989.

Bartov, Omer. *Hitler's Army: Soldiers, Nazis and War in the Third Reich*. New York: Oxford University Press, 1991.

Bassett, John T. *War Journal of an Innocent Soldier*. New York: Avon Books, 1989.

Blum, John M. *V Was for Victory: Politics and American Culture During World War II*. New York: Harcourt Brace Jovanovich, 1976.

Blumenson, Martin, ed. *The Patton Papers*. 2 vols. Boston: Houghton Mifflin, 1974.

Bonn, Keith. *When the Odds Were Even: The Vosges Mountain Campaign, October 1944–January 1945*. Novato, Calif.: Presidio Press, 1994.

Bourke-White, Margaret. *They Called It Purple Heart Valley*. New York: Simon & Schuster, 1944.

Brookhouser, Frank. *This Was Your War: An Anthology of Good Writings from World War II*. Garden City: Doubleday, 1960.

Brown, John S. *Draftee Division: The 88th Infantry Division in World War II*. Lexington: The University Press of Kentucky, 1986.

Burgett, Donald. *As Eagles Screamed*. Boston: Houghton Mifflin, 1967.

Calvocaresi, Peter, and Guy Wint. *Total War: The Causes and Courses of World War II*. London: Penguin Press, 1972.

Capa, Robert. *Slightly Out of Focus*. New York: H. Holt, 1947.

Cawthon, Charles R. *Other Clay: A Remembrance of the World War II Infantry*. Boulder: University Press of Colorado, 1990.

Chandler, Alfred, ed. *The Papers of Dwight D. Eisenhower*. 9 vols. Baltimore: Johns Hopkins University Press, 1970–78.

Clarke, George H., ed. *New Treasury of War Poetry: Poems of the Second World War*. Freeport: Books for the Libraries Press, 1968.

Coleman, John S. *Bataan and Beyond: Memories of an American POW*. College Station: Texas A&M University Press, 1978.

Conway, McKinley H., and Linda L. Liston, ed. *The Weather Handbook: A Summary of Weather Statistics for Selected Cities Throughout the United States and Around the World*. Atlanta: Conway Research, Inc., 1974.

Cooke, E. D. *All but Me and Thee: Psychiatry at the Foxhole Level*. Washington, D.C.: Infantry Journal Press, 1946.

Costello, John. *The Pacific War*. New York: Quill, 1981.

Cowdrey, Albert. *Fighting for Life: American Military Medicine in World War II*. New York: The Free Press, 1994.

Davis, Kenneth. *Experience of War: The United States in World War II*. Garden City: Doubleday, 1965.

Dear, I. C. B., and M. R. D. Foot, ed. *The Oxford Companion to World War II*. Oxford: Oxford University Press, 1995.

Doubler, Michael. *Closing with the Enemy: How G.I.s Fought the War in Europe, 1944– 45*. Lawrence: The University Press of Kansas, 1994.

Dower, John. *War Without Mercy*. New York: Pantheon Books, 1986.

Drez, Ronald. *Voices of D-Day*. Baton Rouge: Louisiana State University Press, 1994.

Dupuy, Trevor N. *A Genius for War: The German Army, 1807–1945*. Englewood Cliffs, N.J.: Prentice-Hall, 1977.

Egger, Bruce, and Lee Otts. *G Company's War: Two Personal Accounts of the Campaigns in Europe*. Tuscaloosa: University of Alabama Press, 1992.

Eisenhower Foundation. *D-Day: The Normandy Invasion in Retrospect*. Lawrence: The University Press of Kansas, 1971.

Ellis, John. *On the Front Lines: The Experience of War Through the Eyes of the Allied Soldiers in World War II*. New York: John Wiley & Sons, Inc., 1990.

————. *World War II: A Statistical Survey*. New York: Facts on File Publishers, 1993.

Frank, Richard. *Guadalcanal*. New York: Random House, 1990.

Fritz, Steven G. *Frontsoldaten: The German Soldier in World War II*. Lexington: The University Press of Kentucky, 1995.

Fry, James C. *Combat Soldier*. Washington, D.C.: National Press, 1968.

Fussell, Paul. *Wartime: Understanding and Behavior in the Second World War*. New York: Oxford University Press, 1989.

Gobel, Kurt. *The Making of a Paratrooper*. Lawrence: University Press of Kansas, 1990.

Gray, J. Glenn. *The Warriors: Reflections on Men in Battle*. New York: Harcourt, Brace, 1959.

Greenfield, Kent R. *The United States Army in World War II: Organization of Ground Combat Troops*. Washington, D.C.: Historical Division, Department of the Army, 1947.

Hanson, Frederick. *Combat Psychiatry: Experiences in the North African and Mediterranean Theaters of Operations, Army Ground Forces, World War II*. Washington, D.C.: U.S. Government Printing Office, 1949.

Hastings, Max. *Overlord*. New York: Simon & Schuster, 1984.

Henderson, William D. *Cohesion: The Human Element in Combat*. Washington, D.C.: National Defense University Press, 1985.

Holmes, Richard. *Acts of War: The Behavior of Men in Battle*. New York: The Free Press, 1985.

Hough, Frank O., Verle E. Ludwig, and Henry I. Shaw. *History of the United States Marine Corps Operations in World War II: Pearl Harbor to Guadalcanal*. Washington, D.C.: Historical Branch, U.S. Marine Corps, 1960.

Hoyt, Edwin P. *The G.I.'s War: The Story of American Soldiers in Europe in World War II*. New York: McGraw-Hill Book Company, 1988.

Infantry Journal, Inc. *Infantry in Battle*. Washington, D.C.: The Infantry Journal, Inc., 1939.

Johnson, Franklyn A. *One More Hill*. Toronto: Bantam Books, 1949.

Jones, James. *The Thin Red Line*. New York: Dell Publishing Co., Inc., 1962.

————. *WWII*. New York: Grosset & Dunlap, 1975.

Kahn, Sy M. *Between Tedium and Terror: A Soldier's World War II Diary, 1943–45*. Urbana: University of Illinois Press, 1993.

Keefer, Louis. *Scholars in Foxholes: The Story of the Army Specialized Training Program in World War II*. Jefferson: McFarland & Co., Inc. Publishers, 1988.

Keegan, John. *The Face of Battle*. New York: Penguin Books, 1976.

————. *Six Armies in Normandy: From D-Day to the Liberation of Paris*. New York: Penguin Books, 1982.

————. *The Second World War*. London: Hutchinson Publishers, 1989.

Kellett, Anthony. *Combat Motivation: The Behavior of Men in Battle*. Boston: Bluver- Nijhoff Publishers, 1982.

Kennett, Lee. *G.I.: The American Soldier in World War II*. New York: Warner Books, 1987.

Kluger, Steve. *Yank, the Army Weekly*. New York: St. Martin's Press, 1991.

Leinbaugh, Harold P., and John D. Campbell. *The Men of Company K: The Autobiography of a Rifle Company*. Toronto: Bantam Books, 1985.

MacDonald, Charles B. *Company Commander*. New York: Bantam Books, 1947.

————. *A Time for Trumpets: The Untold Story of the Battle of the Bulge*. New York: William Morrow & Company, Inc., 1985.

McCormick, John. *The Right Kind of War*. New York: Onyx Books, 1992.

McGivern, William P. *Soldiers of '44*. New York: Ballantine Books, 1979.

Manchester, William. *Goodbye Darkness: A Memoir of the Pacific War*. New York: Dell Publishing Company, 1979.

Marshall, S. L. A. *Men Against Fire*. New York: The Infantry Journal and William Morrow & Company, 1947.

————. *Night Drop*. Boston: Little, Brown & Co., 1962.

Martin, Ralph G. *The G.I. War, 1941–45*. Boston: Little, Brown & Co., 1967.

Mauldin, Bill. *Up Front*. New York: H. Holt & Co., 1945.

Meyer, Robert, ed. *The Stars & Stripes Story of World War II*. New York: D. McKay Company, 1960.

Milner, Samuel. *The United States Army in World War II: Victory in Papua*. Washington, D.C.: Office of the Chief of Military History, Department of the Army, 1957.

Murphy, Audie. *To Hell and Back*. Toronto: Bantam Books, 1949.

Nicholls, David, ed. *Ernie's War: The Best of Ernie Pyle's World War II Dispatches*. New York: Random House, 1986.

Palmer, Robert R. *The United States Army in World War II: Procurement and Training of Ground Combat Troops*. Washington, D.C.: Historical Division, Department of the Army, 1948.

Perret, Geoffrey. *There's a War to Be Won: The United States Army in World War II*. New York: Random House, 1991.

Phibbs, Brendan. *The Other Side of Time: A Combat Surgeon in World War II*. Boston: Little, Brown & Co., 1987.

Polenberg, Richard. *War & Society*. New York: J. B. Lippincott Co., 1972.

Potter, Lou. *Liberators: Fighting on Two Fronts in World War II*. New York: Harcourt Brace Jovanovich, 1992.

Pyle, Ernie. *Here Is Your War*. New York. H. Holt & Co., 1943.

———. *Brave Men*. New York: H. Holt & Co., 1944.

Reep, Edward. *A Combat Artist in World War II*. Lexington: University Press of Kentucky, 1987.

Richardson, F. M. *Fighting Spirit: A Study of Psychological Factors in War*. New York: Crane, Russak & Company, Inc., 1978.

Ross, Bill. *Iwo Jima*. New York: Vanguard Press, 1985.

———. *A Special Piece of Hell*. New York: St. Martin's Press, 1991.

Ryan, Cornelius. *The Longest Day*. New York: Simon & Schuster, 1959.

———. *The Last Battle*. New York: Simon & Schuster, 1966.

———. *A Bridge Too Far*. New York: Simon & Schuster, 1974.

St. John Arnold, Thomas. *Buffalo Soldiers: The 92nd Infantry Division and Reinforcements in World War II*. Manhattan: Sunflower University Press, 1990.

Sherrod, Robert. *Tarawa: The Story of a Battle*. New York: Duell, Sloan and Pierce, 1944.

Sledge, E. B. *With the Old Breed at Peleliu and Okinawa*. Toronto: Bantam Books, 1981.

Spector, Ronald. *Eagle Against the Sun*. New York: Vintage Books, 1985.

Standifer, Leon. *Not in Vain: A Rifleman Remembers World War II*. Baton Rouge: Louisiana State University Press, 1992.

Stanton, Shelby. *World War II Order of Battle*. New York: Galahad Books, 1984.

Stouffer, Samuel A. *The American Soldier, Studies in Social Psychology in World War II: Adjustment During Army Life*. Vol. 1. New York: John Wiley & Sons, 1949.

———. *The American Soldier, Studies in Social Psychology in World War II: Combat and Its Aftermath*. Vol. 2. New York: John Wiley & Sons, 1949.

Swank, Roy, and Walter E. Machand. *Psychology for the Fighting Man*. Washington, D.C.: The Infantry Journal, 1943.

Swineford, Edwin. *Wits of War: Unofficial G.I. Humor-History of World War II*. Fresno: Kilroy Was There Press, 1989.

Terkel, Studs. *The Good War: An Oral History of World War II*. New York: Pantheon Books, 1984.

Uris, Leon. *Battle Cry*. New York: G. P. Putnam's Sons, 1953.

U.S. War Department. *Handbook on German Military Forces*. Baton Rouge: Louisiana State University Press, 1990.

vanCreveld, Martin. *Fighting Power: German and U.S. Army Performance, 1939–1945*. Westport: Greenwood Press, 1982.

Webster, David Kenyon. *Parachute Infantry: An American Paratrooper's Memoir of D-Day and the Fall of the Third Reich*. Baton Rouge: Louisiana State University Press, 1994.

Weigley, Russell F. *The American Way of War: A History of United States Military Strategy and Policy*. New York: MacMillan Publishing Co., Inc., 1973.

Weinberg, Gerhard. *A World at Arms*. New York: Cambridge University Press, 1994.

Wharton, William. *A Midnight Clear*. New York: Knopf, 1982.

Wilson, George. *If You Survive*. New York: Ivy Books, 1987.

Manuscript Collections

Carlisle, Pa. United States Army Military History Institute, World War II Archives.

Columbia, Mo. Western Historical Mansucript Collection, University of Missouri-Columbia. Collection Number 68, World War II Letters. Files 1-3466.

Knoxville, Tenn. University of Tennessee Special Collections Library, Collections Number 1230-1892, World War II Collection.

Knoxville, Tenn. Center for the Study of War and Society, University of Tennessee, World War II Files.

Index